Politics

Politics

An Introduction to the
Modern Democratic State

Fourth Edition

LARRY JOHNSTON

UNIVERSITY OF TORONTO PRESS

Library and Archives Canada Cataloguing in Publication

Johnston, Lawrence Walker, 1955–
          Politics : an introduction to the modern democratic state / Larry Johnston.—4th ed.

Includes bibliographical references and index.
Issued also in electronic formats.
ISBN 978-1-4426-0533-6

          1. Democracy—Textbooks. 2. Political science—Textbooks. I. Title.

JA66.J63 2012   321.8   C2012-905265-5

We welcome comments and suggestions regarding any aspect of our publications—please feel free to contact us at news@utphighereducation.com or visit our Internet site at www.utppublishing.com.

NORTH AMERICA
5201 Dufferin Street
North York, Ontario, Canada, M3H 5T8

2250 Military Road
Tonawanda, New York, USA, 14150

ORDERS PHONE: 1-800-565-9523
ORDERS FAX: 1-800-221-9985
ORDERS E-MAIL: utpbooks@utpress.utoronto.ca

UK, IRELAND, AND CONTINENTAL EUROPE
NBN International
Estover Road, Plymouth, PL6 7PY, UK
ORDERS PHONE: 44 (0) 1752 202301
ORDERS FAX: 44 (0) 1752 202333
ORDERS E-MAIL: enquiries@nbninternational.com

This book is printed on paper containing 100% post-consumer fibre.

The University of Toronto Press acknowledges the financial support for its publishing activities of the Government of Canada through the Canada Book Fund.

Cover and text design: Michel Vrana
Cover photos: DenisNata, Shutterstock; caracterdesign, iStockphoto; piovesempre, iStockphoto.

Printed in Canada

Contents

TEXT BOXES

The Dimensions of Politics and an Approach to Its Study

...WHICH PROVIDES THE READER WITH

· an overview of characteristics that identify "politics" or "the political"
· an important distinction between institutions, processes, and outcomes
· reasons for studying the modern democratic state from a comparative perspective

WHAT POLITICS IS ...

The material in this book is intended to provide some answers to the question:

What is the study of politics about?

This is a deceptively simple question that can, or rather *must*, be answered in a number of ways. Each obvious answer raises more questions. For example:

"Politics is about the government."
(a) Is the government the same as the state?
(b) Is politics about what government does or doesn't do?
(c) Is politics about who is in the government and how they got there?
(d) Which (level of) government?

"Politics is about elections."
(e) What is an election?
(f) Election to what?
(g) Who are the electors and who gets elected?
(h) How are elections organized?
(i) Why have elections?
(j) What about states without elections?

"Politics is about who has power and who doesn't."
(k) What is power?

(k1) Is power the same as authority?

(k2) Are there different types of power (political, economic, military)?

(k3) How is power exercised (and who does it affect)?

(l) Is power national or global?

(m) How do the powerful become so?

A popular definition offered by Harold Lasswell in the 1930s contains its own set of additional questions: "*Politics is who gets what, when, and how.*"

Some definitions of politics may be too general to get us started—politics is "*any mixture of conflict and cooperation*" (Laver 1983: 1)—or, even worse, only make sense to those who have already been studying politics:

> *Politics concerns the formulation and execution of decisions that are binding upon the population of a community or society and the relationships between those who make or implement such decisions and those who are affected by them.* (Johnston, 2)

Nonetheless, considering all of these questions and answers, a few patterns become clear.

POLITICS IS "RELATIONAL"

It's been said that "wherever you find people, you find politics." Several of the lettered statements made above (such as c, g, k3, and m) reflect the relational aspect of politics: relationships between officials in government and ordinary citizens, between those who seek elected office and those who vote for them, between the powerful and the marginalized, among those with common interests, and between those whose interests are in conflict.

POLITICS IS "BEHAVIOURAL"

Relationships between people are expressed in what they do with or to each other, either directly (having a discussion, giving instructions) or indirectly (making a rule that applies to others, disobeying a law). Much of the study of politics involves examining human behaviour: What are people doing? What did they do in the past? What can we expect them to do under a different set of circumstances?

POLITICS INVOLVES "INSTITUTIONS"

Much of the behaviour we examine is structured by the rather elusive entities known as **institution**s. Readers may associate "institution" with a building: a school, a hospital, a courthouse, a bank, an office building, a place of worship, or even a parliament. However, this physical place matters only to the degree that it is necessary for the activities that go on inside. What makes a school is not its bricks, steel, and glass, but how the teachers and students within are organized in order to achieve the set of purposes known as "education." Certain routines that are central to this institution (dividing pupils into classes, assigning and grading homework) would seem inappropriate in another institution (such as a hospital or a library). The same building might be used by a school board, a college, or a university; the difference would be what people did within that space. Similarly, a place of worship is what it is because of the activities that are intrinsic to it (prayer, praise, preaching) regardless of whether it is an edifice built for that purpose or a rented space in a strip mall. Intense debate can arise about whether the activities that take place in some spaces (such as places of worship) should be permitted in other institutional spaces (such as schools, courtrooms, parliaments).

Institutions may be understood as consisting of recognized patterns of behaviour (practices or routines) that are organized to accomplish identifiable purposes. The institution is found in the *roles* played by people according to the *rules* necessary to achieve the purpose for which the institution exists. The building that houses the institution is usually designed and equipped to facilitate the activities and roles that *are* the institution, and that's how we recognize that a school is not a bank, and a library is not a hospital.

Just as a study of education is incomplete without a mention of schools, the study of politics requires attention to political institutions, such as legislatures, executive offices, the courts, and government bureaucracies, and to their relationships with each other, to society at large, and to people like you and me.

POLITICS IS "DYNAMIC"

It is easy (for some people) to see institutions, however necessary they might be, as dull, static, and ultimately uninteresting objects of studies (not recognizing the remarkable ability of institutions to accommodate or resist change). They may be more interested in the dynamic aspects of politics—what's going on? Human behaviour is not only structured by institutions, it is channelled by **process**. In the study of politics there is no shortage of process to examine.

"Process" signifies a transformation, a change or exchange, a "flow" of something from somewhere to somewhere else. In the most general sense, "the political process" refers to a flow of information from the public to the government and a return of public policies in return. Within this framework, more specific dynamic relationships are worth examining: How is public opinion formed? How does the electoral system work? What role do interest groups have in shaping outcomes? What is the relationship of the legislative process to public policy?

In politics, processes are often *internal* to institutions, such as the way laws are made within parliaments or adjudicated in the courts. Process may also take place *outside* political institutions, such as the formation of public opinion (e.g., support for or against military intervention abroad; belief in the reality of climate change) or the rise of a social movement (e.g., anti-globalizationism). Process may be something that happens between or *among* institutions, such as the formation and administration of public policy, or *between* political institutions and society at large, as happens with elections, or the administration and enforcement of laws.

Finally, some processes become institutionalized. Elections, held under formal rules embodied in law, are a prime example. Election rules may apply to the organization, financing, and operation of political parties and even regulate the activities of private companies such as the broadcast media. Even the most unfettered market economies exist within a framework of supportive laws that recognize and protect private property, control the supply of money, and enforce contracts. So, while it is common to regard institutions as *static* and processes as *dynamic*, it is clear that institutions structure *activity* and that processes often benefit from an established *framework*.

POLITICS IS ABOUT "OUTCOMES"

A process delivers an **outcome**. It may not be the expected, desired, or most popular result, but whether the result is a minority government, a law limiting the use of hand-held communication devices, or the wrongful conviction of a criminal suspect, it is an outcome that we can associate with an identifiable process. In some situations, nothing (i.e., maintenance of the status quo) may be the intended outcome. Some people seek power in order to control or influence outcomes, some participate in political activity because they believe it makes a difference to do so, and some *stop* participating because they've come to believe their voice is never heard. Words such as "legitimacy" and "accountability" are used when evaluating outcomes and assigning responsibility for them. When political parties and candidates seek our vote, they often promise to deliver a better set of outcomes than their rivals.

POLITICS IS "SOCIAL"

Along with related disciplines such as anthropology, economics, human geography, and sociology, politics is concerned with human behaviour within the context of a **social whole** such as a community, a nation, a society, a tribe, and so on. The societal aspect of politics is part of what constitutes the context (or environment) within which political institutions are situated and political processes take place.

The social sciences are each concerned with a specific aspect of the life of humans on this planet, each occupied with what it believes is the most interesting (if not most important) features of that life. Each discipline offers its own explanation of a societal event, whether it's a world war, a global recession, or the digital revolution. Ideally, these various viewpoints complement rather than contradict each other. An insight that becomes part of the common understanding of those studying one subject is found to shed light in another area. The broader study of politics includes those studying political anthropology, political economy, political geography, and so on.

POLITICS IS "HISTORICAL"

The political reality we study today is the product of larger forces such as history and culture. Canada, the United States, Australia, and New Zealand are four countries that share the experience of being former British colonies, and yet each country's colonial experience and subsequent emergence from colony to **nation-state** took a unique path. Within each geographical pairing—Canada and the United States, Australia and New Zealand—there is a special bond, but also a rivalry, and sometimes a friction. Australia, Canada, and New Zealand remain parliamentary democracies with a common head of state, while the War of Independence left the United States with a mixed model of republican government. On some dimensions, such as federalism and the make-up of the national legislature, New Zealand is the odd country out. Each country has a different record with respect to treatment of its indigenous peoples. Each has a different electoral system. Many of the similarities between these four countries (and Great Britain) can be explained on the basis of a common culture. An explanation of their differences often has a historical basis.

POLITICS IS "CULTURAL"

Politics is also (fundamentally, some might say), about ideas. Concepts, principles, values, beliefs, goals, objectives, norms, understanding, and reasons are all parts of the whole that is culture. A culture is necessarily shared, through time and across generations, and shapes the politics of any people. In addition, it is possible to identify the ideas that make up a **political culture**. Prior to the last century, those who studied and thought about political matters were almost always historians and/or philosophers.

Politically interesting ideas vary in their level of abstraction and in their purpose. Two giants of classical political thought, Plato and Aristotle, continue to be of interest today because they asked two fundamental questions that apply in any age:

"What is the good life for humans?"

"What kind of political society is conducive to providing the good life?"

These questions continue to apply because a final answer to either has never been obvious to everyone. They also hold our interest because the way our political life is organized says something about how we *have* answered them, *so far*.

Certain principles help organize our political life—ideas such as the "rule of law," "constitutionalism," and "democracy"; or norms of justice such as "rights" and "due process." And everyone, of course, has an idea of what it means, or should mean, to be "free."

On a more everyday level, most of us have ideas about what is right and wrong; applied to politics, these ideas help us judge which policies we support or oppose. When organized in a systematic manner, they provide an ideology; when measured by a random sample survey, they constitute public opinion.

A COMPARATIVE APPROACH

This book follows Aristotle by taking a comparative approach to the study of politics. This means that it focuses on:

- · the differences between political entities (or polities) that have a lot in common; and
- · the commonalities linking polities that are otherwise quite different.

This approach means a greater emphasis on institutions, processes, and types of outcomes than on the particular political personalities (and their failures and successes) and the watershed type of events that are more typically prominent when studying the politics of a particular country.

The study of Canadian politics, for example, requires coming to understand the character and history of the relationship between the national government and the provinces (i.e., federalism), and how that relationship has been complicated by the uniqueness of Quebec among the provinces. A comparative study approaches Canada's federal/provincial experience as one example of a federal system, to be contrasted with the national/sub-national state relationships in other federal systems, such as those found in Australia, Germany, Switzerland, and the United States.

In the aftermath of the 2010 UK election and the formation of a coalition government in that country, the Institute for Government noted as follows: "There are many lessons that the current UK coalition government can learn from other countries, and already there is evidence of it having taken on board the experience of the devolved UK administrations in Scotland and Wales." These comments confirm a belief in the utility of comparative knowledge for contemporary policy makers—and suggest that policy makers are capable of recognizing it, too.

As a general introduction, the comparative approach taken here seeks to acquaint students with elements of the politics of the modern democratic nation-state. In the best of all possible worlds, this might

- · provide a framework that allows students to interpret and make better sense of the political facts and commentary they access through the modern media;
- · enable citizens to bring a broader perspective and more informed background to their political participation and decision making; and
- · encourage individuals to consider further political studies as an option in their academic program.

REFERENCES

Institute for Government. *Rough Guide to Coalition Government*. The Institute, n.d. Web.

Johnston, Larry W. *Politics: An Introduction to the Modern State*. 3rd ed. Toronto: University of Toronto Press, 2007.

Laver, Michael. *Invitation to Politics*. Oxford: Basil Blackwell, 1983.

CHAPTER 1

Co-operation, Coercion, and Consent —Opening Ideas

...WHICH PROVIDES THE READER WITH

· a vocabulary of basic concepts identifying the necessary role of the state in ordering modern societies

· a discussion about the legitimate exercise of power and the enduring idea that good government is centred on the welfare of the governed

· an introduction to public norms such as popular sovereignty and the rule of law

· an explanation of why and how the democratic state is a limited state

· an account of civil society, its institutions, and their role in the democratic state

We live in a political world. Politics is as fundamental to human society as weather is to our natural environment (and just as difficult to predict). In the same way that the rain falls regardless of whether we understand why it falls, so too, our lives are shaped by political circumstances and changed by political decisions, whether we take an interest in them, or understand them, or not.

When Aristotle, the Greek philosopher from antiquity, began his *Politics* by observing that humans are "political animals," he was suggesting that being active in the politics of our community is an essential part of our nature. Such an idea provides a strong basis for valuing **democracy** (originally a Greek word for "rule by the people"). Today, most democracy is indirect—others usually make the political decisions, and our experience is at the receiving end. Understanding how and why that happens and what it means may better prepare us for the opportunities to participate that do come our way, even when this is limited to providing feedback to those holding political office.

OUR SOCIAL NATURE

Our world is political because we share space with others. Our lives are necessarily and not accidentally social: we live in neighbourhoods and communities; we work and play and communicate with others. Collective activity requires a degree of predictability, regularity, or order; if not, there is waste, miscommunication, or even chaos. The ways and degrees of maintaining order are at the heart of the political dimension of our social existence.

As a species, humans have always survived by working and living together, which requires either co-operation or coordination. Such cohesion can be the product of personal or political relationships.

Consider the fact that in today's cities (where most of us live), the people we encounter and share public space or engage in any transaction with are mostly strangers. By contrast, a forty-year-old adult in the North American or African forest several hundred years ago, spending his or her entire life in a social grouping resembling an extended family more than a society, may have never met a stranger. Living in a world where most people are strangers puts limits on co-operation as a means of organizing human activity.

Co-operation requires people to have knowledge of each other, an awareness of capacities and weaknesses, and a degree of trust. It is not something we expect to arise spontaneously among strangers, and when on occasion it happens (mostly in emergencies or crises), we usually comment on the fact.

Michael Laver's definition of politics as "any mixture of cooperation and conflict" (see Introduction) suggests that where there is no conflict, there is no need for politics. Since conflicts can always be solved by force, where "might makes right," a very short definition of politics might be "solving conflicts without

force." On the world stage, finding a "political solution" to a crisis is the opposite of calling out the troops.

In a world of scarce resources, conflict is always possible, and its likelihood increases when we have to compete with strangers for necessities of life such as arable land, sources of energy, transportation routes that provide access to supplies—a list that has grown in size and complexity over the centuries. This competition becomes intense whenever population growth puts people with different languages, cultures, religions, and traditions in contact with each other. This is reflected in another of Laver's formulations: "We need government when communities fail." Where co-operation is not possible or consistently reliable, we need coordination, which implies direction by someone with authority or command by someone or some agency with the ability to enforce that command.

Anthropologists who have studied hunter-gatherer **bands** report that they have no politics, no government, no permanent leadership. Conflict within the band is not really an option because survival requires the concerted effort of all band members. One either conforms to the decisions of the group or is left aside, perhaps to perish. In marginal environments, "ostracism" (being ignored by everyone) can be a very harsh penalty.

Co-operation, based on personal relationships, contrasts with coordination, based on a political relationship, such as that between a leader and followers. The degree to which either is possible or necessary depends on the nature of the social whole in which we live. There are many ways in which our social environments can differ. **Community** and **society** are terms used to describe the social wholes in which individual life is experienced. All human life occurs within such wholes, which is why stories about castaways (from

ORANGES AND CONSTITUTIONS

Beginning with "co-operation" and "coordination," this text uses a number of "this or that" distinctions, which put matters into one category (blue) or another (green). Such an identification or classification is a useful first step in coming to understand things; as a stage in the comparative process, it highlights *differences*.

Many of these distinctions are also somewhat artificial—the reality to which they are applied may not be so clear cut. Blue and green are easy to identify in the abstract, but what about teal or aquamarine or other shades of blue-green? Which of the "black" clothes in my closet are really black?

We distinguish between A (co-operation) and B (coordination) in the first place so that we can become clearer about what is unique to each. Co-operation seems to be about persons who are equals, trusting each other and agreeing how to work together; coordination seems to be about one person giving instructions to another person or persons in order to achieve a particular result. In real life, though, once more than a few people are involved in a project, some direction is required, and a project of any complexity under the direction of a coordinator will, in turn, require considerable co-operation among those who are being directed.

An analytic distinction highlighting the difference between A and B is possible because A and B have something in common. Co-operation and coordination are *both* about how people act collectively rather than simply as individuals. A proper comparison involves clarifying differences *and* recognizing *similarities*. If the intersection of common features is too small, perhaps we're comparing incomparables. The old saying about not comparing "apples and oranges" is rather odd, given how much apples and oranges have in common, as fruit. Unlike, say, apples and pretzels, or oranges and constitutions.

We make *analytic* distinctions to highlight differences between items that have something in common. *Categorical* distinctions, on the other hand, recognize differences of a more fundamental nature. "Animal, vegetable, or mineral" is a useful set of categories for the objects found in nature; "natural or artificial" divides the objects that would exist if there were no humans from those that humans have made. The distinctions between these categories have very little ambiguity. "Legislative, executive, or judicial" is a set of categories that political scientists use to identify governmental bodies and/or their functions—whether it is as categorical as "animal, vegetable, or mineral" remains to be seen.

One is unlikely to confuse an animal with a mineral. Similarly, there is nothing much to be learned by comparing any particular animal with any particular mineral (e.g., one is alive, the other dead, etc.) that would not be learned by comparing any other animal with any other mineral. Comparing two animal species, or two mineral formations, is more likely to produce something interesting. In this sense, categorical distinctions have much more of an either/or character. An important part of knowledge is recognizing when to treat distinctions as analytical and when to regard them as categorical.

Dafoe's novel *Robinson Crusoe* to the film *Cast Away* to television series as different as *Gilligan's Island* and *Lost*), in which the social whole is missing or has been drastically shrunk, are always compelling.

COMMUNITIES ARE COHESIVE

A community is marked by homogeneity and cohesion: its members share language, culture, and beliefs of a moral and religious nature; their behaviour is governed by common norms and customs; and a particular way of living, such as farming or fishing, may be shared. Membership is total (one belongs or not) and often requires a commitment, participation, or performance of duty. Communities are conservative in the sense that they attempt to maintain the integrity of what is held in common; they are organic in the sense that the welfare of each member is of interest to others. These characteristics suggest that community is like family, only on a larger scale. Like families, the best communities are nurturing and supportive, although communities, like families, can also be dysfunctional. Membership in a community, as in a family, is involuntary. One is born into a community, and although one may leave it, the community's influence is not so easily left behind.

Evidence suggests that humans have almost always lived in communities. As a population expands and covers more territory, it either divides into separate communities or becomes less homogeneous, more differentiated. The more the members of a society vary in their experiences, values, and beliefs, the weaker their sense of a common life in which all participate. Societies in which community is weak are more like collections of individuals; it is much easier to choose to live in a society than to become a member of a community (the community may reject me, but the society may simply not recognize me). One may hide in a crowd but not in a group. If belonging to a community is analogous to membership in a family, then living in a society is like participating in a campus club or joining an online social network.

SOCIETIES ARE IMPERSONAL

The distinction here between community and society lines up with the earlier contrasts between co-operation and coordination and between personal and political relations. However, as illustrated in *Figure 1.1*, it may be more useful to talk about varying degrees of community within and between societies.

family .... community .... society
co-operation .... coordination
personal .... political
Figure 1.1a

Because most contemporary societies no longer have the characteristics of community (or have them in a weak sense), it is sometimes difficult to appreciate fully the distinction between community and society—few of us have lived in a community so strong that it has no concept of the individual. Community is more likely or possible in societies that are small (both in population and extent) and in societies of lesser rather than greater complexity. Modern societies generally are extensive, populous, pluralistic, and complex in their organization or structure. If we reflect on our experiences in families, or of living in a village, or as members of a religious congregation, we recognize that our relationships to other people are fundamentally different in those settings than when we are riding the bus or subway, attending a rock concert, or sitting in a lecture hall.

One important difference is that community is personal and familiar, while society is impersonal and, in a curious way, invisible. Members of a community, for example, can usually describe their community and why it is important to them; on the other hand, individuals (including students!) often fail to recognize the ways that they reflect the society in which they have grown up.

Just as community (or the degree of community) dissolves as societies grow and change, sometimes societies incorporate or have been put together from distinct (even hostile) communities. For reasons that include military conquest and colonization/

decolonization, two or more communities may come to share the same territory. At the risk of generalizing too much, human history has been a movement from simple communities to complex, pluralistic societies.

Consider again the first line of *Figure 1.1*:

family ... community ... society
Figure 1.1b

These three terms are not mutually exclusive. Early human life was probably lived in groups that were basically very extended families. As population size grew and recognition of (and rules about) *kinship* (who is related to whom) became established, it was possible to distinguish between the community and its families. Similarly, "society" is different from "community" or "family," but it also may contain communities and families (see *Figure 1.2*).

In this sense, the contrasts between co-operation and coordination and between personal and political relationships are important but obviously of an analytical and not categorical nature. A community or society of sufficient size will be organized in some of its activities through co-operation and in others by coordination; *personal* relationships will bind those who are friends or relations, and *political* relationships will govern the interactions of strangers.

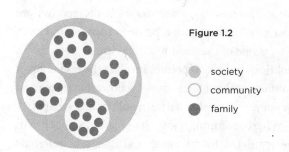

Figure 1.2

● society
○ community
● family

AUTHORITY AND LEADERSHIP

Co-operation, it was suggested, is based on trust, knowledge of each other's capabilities, and a degree of equality. These are conditions most likely to exist between family members, friends, and/or neighbours. By contrast, coordination involves giving directions, which requires recognizing leadership and, thereby, an inevitable inequality or hierarchy.

All social wholes have leaders, but the nature of leadership changes as the social whole expands. In the hunter-gather society, leadership is situational: one person leads the hunt, another recognizes the signs of approaching storms, another one settles disputes that arise within the band, while yet another performs the symbolic rituals that arise when there is a birth or death—no one is always the leader, and there is no fixed hierarchy.

Examining the various ways humans have lived in social wholes, political anthropologists distinguish between bands and **tribes**, on the one hand, and chiefdoms and states, on the other. In bands and tribes—a tribe being an integrated group of bands in a region—leadership is fluid and shared in the community. In **chiefdoms** and **states**, leadership is centralized and accompanied by a social hierarchy—a ranking of everyone from top to bottom, which may involve classes or castes—that assigns to each level its own duties, responsibilities, and perhaps privileges. Leadership rests, ultimately, with one individual, however that individual happens to be chosen or designated. (A more complete description of these differences is provided in Chapter 2.)

Political anthropologists also note that leadership in a state[A] possesses the means to coerce individuals (force them to comply with an order or command), and one definition of government—that is, the state[G]—emphasizes its monopoly on the legitimate means of **coercion** within society.

"THE STATE"—KEEPING IT STRAIGHT

Many political terms are confusing because they are used in several different ways—"the state" is one of them. The only solution is to identify the different meanings and the context in which each is likely to be used:

The state[A]—the anthropological (**A**) designation for the form of "early civilization" in which the political system has centralized leadership with the ability to coerce, as opposed to bands, tribes, and chiefdoms (see Chapter 2).

The state[G]—the permanent structure of authority/power by which the people of a specific territory (area of land) are governed (**G**). Although the state[G] is often called "the government," some political scientists prefer to use "government" for the people in charge of the state[G] at a particular point of time (see also The Government—Keeping it Straight, p. 18).

The state[C]—used to distinguish those areas of public life that are governed (the state) from those that are not (civil society) (**C**), discussed later in this chapter.

A state[F]—in **federal** (**F**) countries such as Australia, Canada, Germany, and the United States, sub-national units are sometimes called states (formally so in Australia and the United States). This is particularly appropriate because the sub-national units in a truly federal system cannot be dissolved or reconstituted by the national state[G] (see Chapter 8).

To state the obvious, the context for political studies is people living in a state[A], and an important focus of study is the kind of leadership in the state[G]. It is also appropriate, given the nature of the modern state, to shift from talking about "leadership" (which, in normal use, is a *personal* attribute) to discussing the **authority** of the state in relation to command, coercion, and consent. ("Leadership" can then be reserved for discussing the ability of individuals—whether in government or at the head of a political party, for example—to inspire or motivate others to follow them.)

COMMAND, COERCION, AND CONSENT

A command is something everyone understands: it is a direction that must be followed, which often requires doing something we'd rather not, or not doing what we're inclined to do. Commands and the forms they take—proclamations, edicts, laws, regulations, requirements, bans, decrees, injunctions, rules,

directives, advisories, etc.—are a significant dimension of politics. So, too, are related questions such as "Why do we recognize (obey) the authority of the state?"; "Is there a basis for refusing to recognize the authority of the state?"; and "What are the ways by which we challenge the authority of the state?" These are not merely theoretical questions. If we obey only because we are forced to, if significant numbers of citizens don't recognize the authority of the state, and if refusal to obey involves violent or destructive actions, the consequences can be quite costly.

To make another distinction, we obey willingly (we *consent*), or we obey because we are forced (we are *coerced*). The distinction between **consent** and **coercion** is one of the most basic and important ideas in political thought. If politics involves the resolution of conflicts without force, then it follows that there must be some relationship between politics and consent.

Where community is strongest, conduct will be regulated by customs, tradition, and religious

Figure 1.3

beliefs, all part of what the people hold in common. Correspondingly, in societies where community is strongest, *politics* will be very much bound up with religion, moral beliefs, customs, taboos, and so forth. In pre-industrial societies, both warrior and pastoral, the position of the chief is typically very much a matter of tradition and religion. The ability of the chief to command relies largely on the ability to secure consent. Respect, mythology, personal attributes such as physical prowess or wisdom, and/or the ability to reward allies may inform this consent.

In societies without a state[A], authority rests on consent and consent alone. As a consequence, authority in such societies is limited. A state[A] differs from a chiefdom or tribe because it can coerce (force obedience from) those who do not consent. Here, authority is supplemented by **power**, defined narrowly as "the means of coercion." In theory, the authority of a state[G] is limited only by the means it has to enforce its commands upon those who do not consent. However, many believe that political society functions best with a maximum of consent and a minimum of coercion.

Coercion imposes decisions by the use or threat of force, and history teaches that force includes a broad array of options, from the loss of liberty or property, to involuntary labour or service, to physical punishment, to torture, and ultimately to the loss of life (which secures the obedience of others). In practice, the exercise of power means being willing to enforce decisions

by making it known that penalties will be applied to those who fail to obey or conform *and* by carrying out the application of the penalties when the situation arises. Idle threats are not coercive.

Just as those who are strong may be tempted to believe that "might makes right," coercion can be attractive to those who control its means and are determined to get their own way. Convincing or persuading others in order to gain their consent may seem bothersome if we can simply impose our will upon them. The state requires power in order to protect innocent citizens (the majority) from those who would injure them (the criminal minority). History also records many cases in which a criminal few have used the power of the state to oppress the many. Power can be essential in times of emergency or situations requiring prompt action.

On the other hand, force is costly. It requires the expenditure of resources to maintain the police or military, jails and courts, and prisons or penal colonies, and it requires people to guard the prisoners, collect the fines, or carry out the executions—financial and

IDLE THREATS

In 2008 Canada instituted a "do not call" registry that was supposed to allow consumers to place their telephone number on a list that telemarketers would be prohibited from dialing. Fines for telemarketers calling a prohibited number were $1,500 for an individual caller and $15,000 for a company. In July 2010 it was widely reported that although there had been 300,000 complaints filed about violations, only 11 fines totalling $73,000 had been levied, and of this amount only $250 had been collected. Some have suggested that such feeble enforcement makes the registry all but useless.

REGIME

Regime is interchangeable with *country* or *nation-state* in everyday usage, but it is used here because of its emphasis on the political rather than the territorial or social aspects of the *polity* (a good synonym for regime). Lawrence describes regimes as "institutional systems that may span multiple governments." Whenever there is a "significant change in the constitutional system of the state," a new regime is begun. More precisely, we might specify a constitutional change in the fundamental relationships between the executive, the legislature, and the electorate (see Chapter 5) as the basis for identifying a regime change.

human resources that might be used more productively elsewhere. To continually require the use of power is a costly proposition; any state which must do so is an obviously unpleasant and inherently unstable regime.

Just as force comes in many shapes, so too does the nature of consent vary considerably. The discussion so far has implied that consent is a matter of rational calculation or thoughtful judgment; consent can also—perhaps more commonly—be a matter of habit, something reflexive, even a disposition that we internalize as we are socialized (see also *Persuasion or Manipulation?* below). Underlying our consent, even in the cases where our actions were not preceded by a conscious "do I or don't I?" calculation, is a belief in the **legitimacy** of the state.

LEGITIMACY AND OBLIGATION

Legitimacy is a central concept of political thought; it is even reflected in our everyday discussion of political events or in news reports about regimes and their rulers. It also has a considerable history. The flip side of legitimacy is **obligation**. To acknowledge the legitimacy of the state (or of "the government," or of "the law," etc.) is to recognize our responsibility to consent to its pronouncements. The basic question underlying any

PERSUASION OR MANIPULATION?

The useful analytic distinction between consent and coercion is perhaps too simplistic. As noted in this chapter, obedience to the state may be a matter of habit, something unthinking that reflects a general **deference** to authority. It matters, though, *how* that deference comes about: is it because the government has generally implemented policies to which public opposition was minimal? or because the government has routinely used violence to stifle dissent to its actions?

Similarly, habitual obedience is problematic if the government sees it as an opportunity to enact policies that might not be supported if more widely debated. A related concern is the extent of government advertising, which has the legitimate purpose of presenting information to the public about government programs but can also be abused for partisan purposes (e.g., to increase support for the party in power at the expense of the opposition parties). Securing consent by the presentation of information, it may be argued, is the legitimate activity of persuasion. On the other hand, the selective presentation of information and the use of misinformation are examples of manipulation, not persuasion. Some legislatures empower an official with the task of reviewing government-paid advertising and reporting on whether it constitutes legitimate public information or questionable **propaganda**.

discussion of legitimacy/obligation is "Why?" or "On what basis does the legitimacy of the state rest?"

There are several ways to approach this topic. Is the existence of the state legitimate? In other words, is it *inevitable* that there will be a state? Is it *necessary* that there will be a state? Arguably, in a world of finite resources and with human population projected to continue to grow to at least 9 billion, it is difficult to conceive how humans could live peaceably without states.

Is the state properly constituted? This question goes back to the time of Plato and Aristotle (see *Good States and Bad States*, p. 16). What are the proper tasks of the state? Is there anything the state should not do? Medieval monarchs claimed absolute authority, but revolutions in the seventeenth, eighteenth, and nineteenth centuries led to the creation of the **limited state**. The limited state has become so established that the modern version of absolutism—the totalitarian state—is regarded by almost all as entirely lacking in legitimacy. A primary means of limiting the state is the **constitution**, the special body of law and principles that defines the institutions of the state, their powers, and any restrictions on their exercise. A complete constitution also contains rules for its own amendment and identifies who is to settle any disputes about its application.

If a constitution is established and effectively defines the architecture of the state, the question of legitimacy may turn to the adequacy of the government: are those in power, those controlling the state, properly there?

A key difference between regimes is the means by which individuals come to occupy their office. In a hereditary **monarchy**, the office of king or queen is occupied according to local rules of succession (who is "next in line"). In an absolute monarchy or dictatorship, many of those holding subordinate offices are selected

The victory of George W. Bush over Al Gore in 2004 on the basis of disputed Florida election results was one of the few times since the American Civil War (1861–1865) that the legitimacy of the Presidency had been called into question. This is different from questioning the fitness of incumbent presidents, elected fairly, to continue in office after criminal activities (Richard Nixon) or personal improprieties (William Clinton).

personally by the monarch or dictator according to his or her own whims and purposes. In a legal-rational system, individuals are usually elected to the most important offices, and their ability to appoint individuals to positions may be subject to a public process of scrutiny and approval. Most public servants will be hired on the basis of open competitions, often involving an examination to determine fitness (**merit**) for the position(s).

Although the rulers of states in the past frequently claimed authority on **traditional** or **charismatic** grounds, **legal-rational** authority characterizes most contemporary states. Weber's categories (See box on p. 20) tend to emphasize *who* has power (as in charismatic and traditional authority), or *how* they have acquired it (as in traditional and legal-rational authority), rather than *what they do with it*. In most established regimes, the legitimacy of the state is no longer in question, and apart from election irregularities or constitutional violations, the legitimacy of the government (as opposed to its popularity) is rarely questioned. Instead, attention is usually focused on the uses that government makes of the power of the state—the laws it passes, the policies it implements, the taxes it imposes, and the rules, regulations, and penalties it prescribes to enforce its decisions—whether its actions

GOOD STATES AND BAD STATES

The question "What makes the state legitimate?" may seem odd—except, perhaps, in the United States—but a distinction between good (legitimate) and bad (corrupt) regimes goes back millennia, and it is constructive to consider some of the contexts in which these distinctions and their application were debated.

Both Plato and Aristotle—two of the foundational political philosophers—considered these questions in the fifth century B.C.E. As the first comparativist, Aristotle studied over 100 constitutions before classifying states on the basis of who exercises authority: namely, rule by one person, rule by a few people, or rule by many. Second, he noted that regimes may be "just" or "corrupt," depending on the ends served by the exercise of authority. In a **just regime**, the purpose of government is the common good; in a **corrupt regime**, government is used for the advantage of those in power. For Aristotle, then, rule by one could take a good form (kingship) or a corrupt form (tyranny), with the same holding for rule by a few or rule by the many.

Plato's *Republic* presents five types of regimes, each dominated by a particular type of individual. The ideal regime is characterized by the good and just man; the worst, by the lover of power. Plato implies that a descent from the best to the worst, moving successively through each type of regime, may be inevitable.

Two contextual details are worth noting. First, Plato and Aristotle were writing at a time when the typical polity in their part of the world (ancient Greece) was the city-state, a relatively small regime, in terms both of population and territory. Second, the principal criterion used to determine good regimes from bad was an ethical one—in Aristotle's case, whether a regime permitted its citizens to fulfill their end (**telos**) as humans (see Chapter 3). More immediately transparent to us today is the idea that authority should be exercised for the good of the polity (the people), not for the benefit of the ruler(s).

Legitimacy also received much scrutiny in feudal Europe (the Middle Ages), in the ongoing struggle between monarchs and popes (the leaders of the Roman Church). Did monarchs require the blessing of the Church to be the legitimate rulers of their kingdoms? If a monarch fell out of favour with the Pope to the degree that he or she was excommunicated (see **excommunication**), did this remove the obligation of his or her subjects to be obedient? These issues became particularly contentious during the periods of history shaped by the Reformation and the Enlightenment.

So closely intertwined were political and church authority (as any viewer of *The Tudors* knows), that when King Henry VIII of England was excommunicated by Pope Clement in 1533 (because of actions Henry had taken to have his marriage to Catherine of Aragon annulled so that he might marry Anne Boleyn), Henry's response was to establish, by law, the independence of the English (Anglican) Church and his own place as head of the Church. The significance of these events for later English history and politics cannot be overstated.

The Western European journey from a time when emperors were made legitimate in their rule by a papal blessing (and could fight long wars over such matters) to the modern separation of church from state was a long and often very bloody one. It involved a number of historical episodes that still inform much of who we are and what we do today (see Chapter 3).

	PLATO		ARISTOTLE	
best	Aristocracy		"Just" Regimes	"Corrupt" Regimes
	(rule of the noble)		(for the common good)	(benefitting the rulers)
	Timocracy		Kingship	Tyranny
	(rule of warriors)		(rule of one)	(rule of one for one)
	Oligarchy		Aristocracy	Oligarchy
	(rule of the wealthy)		(rule of the few)	(rule of the rich)
	Democracy		Polity	Democracy
	(rule of the poor)		(rule of the many)	(rule of the poor)
	Tyranny/Dictatorship			
worst	(rule of the tyrant)		(best)	(worst)

are legitimate and whether we are always obliged to adhere to them.

"May I Do It?" Vs. "Can I Get Away With It?"

There is an important distinction in modern democratic regimes between constitutionality and political soundness. Any action or policy decision a government makes can be considered from two perspectives: first, is it "constitutional," and second, is it "politically acceptable" or "politic"? (See meaning 3 in *Politic*, below.)

POLITIC

politic *adj*
1. artful or shrewd; ingenious *a politic manager*
2. crafty or unscrupulous; cunning *a politic old scoundrel*
3. sagacious, wise, or prudent, esp. in statesmanship *a politic choice*
4. (Government, Politics & Diplomacy) an archaic word for political
Collins English Dictionary—Complete and Unabridged (www.thefreedictionary.com/politic)

To ask whether a decision is constitutional is pointless unless there is a process by which this can be authoritatively answered *and*, where the answer is no, the decision can be effectively rescinded and/or reversed. Some regimes have had a constitution but no effective process for identifying and correcting constitutional breaches. In these cases, the constitution was largely for show, or perhaps to satisfy the expectations of other regimes.

A constitution is merely an empty body of law without constitutionalism, a commitment to abide by the rulings of whatever body is entrusted with determining questions of constitutional law. Ideally, the body that makes constitutional rulings is politically independent or autonomous from the government. Arguably, the process of changing the constitution should also be sufficiently difficult to prevent a government from simply changing the rules whenever its action is ruled to be unconstitutional.

On the other hand, a course of action that is constitutional may be very unpopular, therefore *im*politic, just as a course of action that has widespread support might be ruled unconstitutional.

THE GOVERNMENT—KEEPING IT STRAIGHT

Many people, including most North Americans, are more likely to talk about **government** than "the state." While the distinction is made here between "state" and "government," it is also true that we are familiar with the state only through our encounters with government. Put most simply, government is the people who exercise the authority of the state, but that, too, can mean different things:

The government[P]—in a **parliamentary** [P] system of state (as in Canada, other Commonwealth countries, and most of Europe), that portion of the elected representatives which is "in power." Strictly speaking, this is the prime minister and cabinet, who collectively bring legislation to the legislature, are responsible for the state's budget, and oversee the non-elected officials who carry out the administration of laws and **policy**. When the prime minister and cabinet belong to the same political party, it is common (in Canada, at least) to refer to other elected members of that party as government members, or simply as the government, whether they sit in cabinet or not.

The government[B]—commonly refers to the offices and agencies that enforce laws, administer regulations, and deliver programs. This involves everything from the court system, to health inspection, to student loans, to building roads and operating public transit. Collectively, these government departments are also described as the **bureaucracy**[B], even though "bureaucracy" is, strictly speaking, a way of managing people in large organizations, governmental or otherwise.

If we think of government as the "who" and "how"—the people and activities—of the state, we can appreciate the contrast between the transience of governments and the (relative) permanence of the state. Impermanence is particularly true of government[P], the body that controls the decision-making process. Italy has become infamous for the number of governments it has had since 1946 (at last count 61), a statistic continually emphasized by critics of its electoral system. One of the reasons Italy didn't descend into chaos was the permanence of the Italian state, represented in part by the government[B]—the government employees who carry out the day-to-day business of administering laws and implementing policies.

Once upon a time, when the extent of government was much smaller, it was the case that almost everyone who had a position in the bureaucracy (government[B]) lost their jobs when the government[P] changed. That practice ended in the late nineteenth and early twentieth centuries in many countries, including Canada and the United States, with the development of a full-time, professional civil service. With that change, customs officers, tax collectors, roads superintendents, municipal clerks, bridge inspectors, and other officials held a job, not an appointment.

Today, government employees are known collectively as the public service and individually as public servants. These terms—public and service/servant—underline the fact that government employees are not employed by those in power (government[P]) but by the public, for whose benefit government[B] exists. The latter idea is as old as politics itself, but at times and under certain types of state/government, it slips into the background.

LIMITING THE STATE

The idea that the state could be limited did not begin to make sense until the fifteenth or sixteenth centuries, at the end of the feudal period in Europe, which was characterized by the rule of absolute monarchs. One such monarch was France's Louis XIV, whom history records as having said in 1655: "L'État c'est moi" ("I am the State"). While many regimes today continue to be monarchies (Australia, Belgium, Canada, Denmark, Luxembourg, the Netherlands, New Zealand, Norway, Spain, Sweden, and the United Kingdom among them), each is now a constitutional monarchy. While the monarch remains the head of state in these places, the powers of the monarch are severely limited under the constitution, and this is understood by everyone.

The authority of the state may be *limited* in several ways, each of which is discussed at greater length elsewhere in this book:

INSTITUTIONALLY. The constitution identifies certain institutions (see Introduction) within the state and defines their powers and their relationships to each other. For example, the **legislature** makes laws, the **executive** administers them, and the **judiciary** settles disputes about and under the law (see Chapter 5).

FEDERALLY. The constitution divides authority between the national state and sub-national states (e.g., provinces or states), and it assigns or distributes specific powers (e.g., subjects of law such as education or national defense, or the ability to impose taxes) between them (see Chapter 8).

JUDICIALLY. The constitution explicitly protects the **rights** of citizens by defining protections (legal rights, equality rights, the right to vote) or enshrining freedoms (free speech, freedom of religion) and allows individuals to apply to the courts for a remedy when their rights have been infringed (see Chapter 13).

MONARCHIES AND REPUBLICS

A republic is a regime in which the head of state (usually a president) is simply a citizen, and *any* citizen (theoretically) could become the head of state.

Most monarchies have a hereditary succession, that is to say, the *next* monarch will come from the same family as the current monarch, from the "royal" family. This means that the number of people who can become head of state in such a regime is very small, and there is nothing that most people can do to become one of them. In constitutional monarchies, the powers of the **head of state**—the monarch—are largely formal; the greater share of the executive power rests with the **head of government**. In theory, anyone could become the head of government.

The historical pattern has been for regimes to move from monarchy to republic, a possibility that Australian citizens, for example, rejected in a 1999 referendum. The reverse move, the restoration of monarchy in a republic, is less common, with Spain being one of the more notable exceptions. One of history's more interesting footnotes is Simeon II, the last monarch (tsar) of Bulgaria, who was deposed from the throne in 1946 when he was nine years old and returned from exile following the fall of communism to be elected prime minister in 2001 and lead Bulgaria's government until 2005. Although he apparently never renounced his claim to the Bulgarian throne, upon taking office as prime minister, Simeon Sakskoburggotski swore an oath to uphold the country's republican constitution.

MAX WEBER ON LEGITIMACY

The German sociologist Max Weber (1864–1920) is responsible for defining the state in terms of its monopoly on the legitimate use of force, for first identifying many of the key characteristics of bureaucracy, and for a theory tracing the origin of capitalism to what he called the "Protestant work ethic." He also argued that three types of legitimacy, often in combination, are at the basis of all authority.

Charismatic—the leader is believed to possess extraordinary personal qualities that justify his or her rule. This is not simply a matter of being talented, but of being *uniquely gifted*. Such an embodiment in one person (e.g., the Dalai Lama) is often explained by reference to the supernatural, the leader being chosen by God, the Fates, or History—some force external to the society itself.

Traditional—this type of authority derives its legitimacy from its long history and what Weber called a "habitual orientation to conform" (79). Following customs or adhering to past practice is presented as a basis for identifying the right course. While it is easy to see this as unthinking devotion to the past, it may also be recognition of the lessons learned by experience.

Hereditary monarchy is often cited as a political example of traditional authority, but even within modern democracies, attachment to specific institutions or symbols (e.g., the constitution, the flag, a particular electoral system) may be as much about preserving tradition as anything else.

Legal-rational—here legitimacy derives from "belief in the validity of legal statute and functional 'competence' based on rationally created rules" (79). Consistent with this view are several ideas referred to in this chapter: the emergence of the *rule of law*, the *depersonalization of authority* and power, and the distinction between the institution (or *office*) and the *office holder*. For example, whether president or prime minister, that individual exercises only the powers associated with that office, having come to that position through a rule-governed process such as an election, and exercises that authority for a fixed or limited period of time. A special body of law may limit how the individual who is prime minister or president uses the authority of their office, and even provide a process by which a president or prime minister who exercises powers improperly may be stripped of them.

The following graphic is meant to suggest some general associations, to be approached on the basis that all of the distinctions, including Weber's categories of legitimacy, are analytic:

LEGITIMACY	CENTRAL ?s	CHARACTER	SOCIAL WHOLE
Charismatic	Who?	Personal	Band
Traditional	How? Who?		Community
Legal-Rational	What? How? Who?	Impersonal	Society

LEGISLATIVELY. Most constitutions are special laws, unique because of their subject matter and rules about how they can be changed. The authority of the state may also be limited by ordinary legislation passed by a parliament or legislative assembly. The laws that govern elections, for example, are often contained in ordinary **statutes**.

Laws requiring governments to balance their budgets demonstrate how limits on the state can be self-imposed; in this case, a law passed by one government puts limits on the use of the powers of the state by future governments. Of course, a future government could change the law and remove that limit, but it would risk paying a political price for doing so. As a general rule, it is difficult to re-assume a power that has been surrendered.

DEMOCRATICALLY. Because governments are able to expand or contract the activity of the state, it matters how long any particular government is in office and how difficult it is to replace that government. Whatever else democracy may or may not be, competitive elections in a free environment provide a regular, peaceful process by which one government may be replaced with another.

CULTURALLY. Over time, in any stable regime, norms become established and expectations are created concerning the state, government, and the constitution. Some become embedded in the institutions and culture of the regime. In regimes such as the United Kingdom and New Zealand, the constitution places few restrictions on the authority of the state, but its powers are rarely exercised to the fullest, in large part because of the strength of the norm of limited government. One reason constitutions work is that people believe they matter: a constitution is part of what is required by the *rule of law*, one of the most basic principles of contemporary political life. Public norms (see below) such as *fairness*, *justice*, and even *equality* can also act as brakes on the policy making of governments.

As citizens, we are obliged to obey the government when it acts within the constitution, makes decisions consistent with existing law, and when the decision makers have gained office fairly through the prevailing legal and cultural practices. This does not mean that we will be content with every action or decision made by governments—inevitably, we will disagree with public policy decisions in the course of our lives. But so long as they are made by those we have authorized to make them, according to legitimate processes and under accepted rules, we have, in effect, already given our consent. This is the point of all collective decision making: by agreeing to follow a particular way of making the decisions that affect all of us, we also commit to the outcome, not knowing in advance what it might be.

AN ALTERNATIVE TO DOMINATION

Writing in *Harper's* in 2008, discussing the failure of the Bush regime to halt nuclear proliferation and specifically questioning the so-called Bush doctrine of an imperial United States as the sole remaining superpower to police the world, Jonathan Schell observed as follows:

In the early modern age, an alternative to dominance was proffered at the national level. It was the conception of the state based on law and the will of the people embodied in the long tradition of democratic consent. It took root in England, in the Glorious Revolution of 1689, and was developed further in the hands of the American revolutionaries of 1776 and the Constitution builders of 1787. In responding to the universal danger posed by nuclear proliferation, the United States therefore had two suitably universalist traditions that it might have drawn on, one based on consent and law, the other based on force. Bush chose force. It was the wrong choice. (12)

POLITIC(S)

Unless we require all decisions to have unanimous consent, it is to be expected that whatever process is used, we will be disappointed some of the time. And of course, if we don't like the way the group makes its decisions, we have two choices: to leave the group, or to persuade it to change its decision or its decision-making processes. This is where the second consideration—"Is it politic? (Can I get away with it?)"—comes into play.

The set of decisions or actions that governments can make constitutionally is much larger than the set of actions that are politic, that the public will support. The constitution, for example, provides the government with the ability to levy taxes, but it offers no advice on when taxes should go up, when they should go down, or how they are to be applied. When the government decides to decrease the sales-tax rate, or increase a tuition tax credit, it is making political decisions. The constitution establishes which level of state may make laws concerning education, but deciding whether to permit charter schools or require standardized grade-level testing are political acts. The decisions that policy makers take are generally political decisions, reflecting the beliefs of the policy makers and their supporters, made with an eye to the degree of public support or criticism they are likely to generate. In some cases, a political judgment lies behind a decision *not* to act in a way that is constitutionally permitted. The resistance of Canadians to privatized health care and the American resistance to public health care is a contrast that has nothing to do, in either case, with the constitutions of those regimes, and everything to do with the history of their politics and political cultures.

In situations where the government is acting constitutionally, citizens who believe it is acting inappropriately may seek a remedy through the **political process** (see Chapters 9–11). In such cases, individuals or groups attempt to persuade the government to take a different course of action. An important element in this process is the communication of information, but ultimately, the principal means of persuasion is the withdrawal or redirection of support. Citizens who are unable to change the government's policies will attempt to change the government. It is not the state that is under suspicion but those who are exercising its authority. As noted, one of the most important functions of the electoral system is to provide citizens with a regular, peaceful opportunity to replace the government of the day. The political process generally, and elections specifically, are means by which citizens express their political will.

Popular Sovereignty

Implicit in the discussion of constitutional and political limits on the exercise of authority is the idea of **popular sovereignty**—the doctrine that the authority of the state flows from the people who are members (citizens) of the regime. If this seems obvious today, it was not always so. A phrase from the late feudal period, "the divine right of kings," reflected the belief that the origin of authority is supernatural, emanating from God or the gods. The role of the Reformation and the Enlightenment in undermining this idea in Europe is discussed in Chapter 3, but grounding political authority in the divine is possible only in a regime where most people agree on the identity of the divine being and on who (e.g., a pope, an ayatollah, a prophet, a lama) speaks for the divinity. Most developed countries today have a population that is religiously heterogeneous and/or have a **secular** constitution (one that separates the state from religion).

Another view at odds with popular sovereignty is the idea that some people are especially suited, by their nature, to lead others. Plato was an early proponent of this view, but it characterizes all perspectives that believe there is a natural **aristocracy**, or ruling class, or political caste, which should govern the other classes or castes. All feudal societies are justified in large part by such a world view. So, too, are slavery, apartheid, and **patriarchy**—any practice of domination that is justified on a view of inherently unequal human natures.

The idea of popular sovereignty has become so ingrained that even dictators who have little or no regard for the wishes of their subjects make every effort to suggest that their actions are in harmony with the popular will. Recognition that legitimate authority flows upward from the people also explains why dictators hold "elections" (usually rigged, never free or competitive) to confirm their popular base.

Public Norms

Popular sovereignty is an example of a public norm, an expectation about the state (or the activities of state actors) in the same way that an ethical norm (e.g., truth-telling) is an expectation about our behaviour as private individuals. To the degree that there is agreement about public norms, they provide a means for citizens to judge their governments on a basis *other than* "what's in it for me?"

Justice is another public norm, or, more precisely, has evolved into a set of public norms concerned with how the state serves its citizens. The "rule of law" is one of these norms, discussed at greater length in

PUBLIC NORMS AND INSTITUTIONS

The relationship between public norms and institutions is a complicated one. Sometimes institutions are created in order to bring about or realize what were once only ideals. The Constitution of the United States and the Canadian *Charter of Rights and Freedoms* provide obvious examples. It would be accurate to say that each of these embodies an idea "whose time had come" and that there was broad public support for such developments.

At the same time, when ideas become imbedded in institutions, they are carried forward to subsequent generations. This is not a bad thing—who wants to continue reinventing the wheel?—especially if there is flexibility to adapt to and incorporate the changing values of the society. Sometimes, though, there is a disconnect between the public norms that have gelled in the institution and the expectations that are fed by values that have become dominant in society.

Three examples will be explored more thoroughly later in this book:

1. the clash of public sovereignty with the ideas of parliamentary sovereignty embedded in Westminster-style parliaments in countries such as Canada, New Zealand, Australia, and, of course, the United Kingdom;
2. the clash of plurality election rules (still used to elect the legislature in Canada, the United States, and the United Kingdom) with ideas of fairness and transparency in a multi-party system; and
3. the contrast between the confrontational, one-dimensional, and often simplistic quality of much public political debate, whether in the media or in legislative chambers, and the rational, critical models of information gathering and discovery that underpin our science and technology.

Chapter 13, along with two other concepts: rights and equality. Some of these norms are so imbedded in our political culture and institutions that we may take them for granted, have trouble explaining them, or even fail to recognize when they have been violated. It is difficult to call a particular government to account when it acts contrary to a public norm that is imperfectly understood or the significance of which is insufficiently appreciated.

Some public norms are more immediate and familiar, such as the presumption of innocence, protection from discrimination, or the principle of habeas corpus (that one may not be detained indefinitely without being charged with a crime or offence). Some apply specifically to government actors—bribery (a public official accepts or solicits a payment from someone seeking preferential treatment); embezzlement (stealing public money or assets for one's own private purposes); and nepotism (using the power of one's position or office to reward family or friends) are all examples of **political corruption** (sometimes referred to in law as "graft").

Growth in the complexity and size of the state and the machinery of government has been accompanied by increasing emphasis on norms of *transparency* (allowing access to government information) and *accountability* (requiring government executives—political and administrative—to answer for the state of government operations). This has led, in turn, to the creation of positions within the state (but autonomous from government) with functions related to transparency, accountability, and *integrity*—positions such as public auditor, information commissioner, ombudsman, and budget officer.

AUTHORITARIAN REGIMES

While a majority of the world's regimes call themselves democratic, a significant portion are **authoritarian** regimes (including some of those claiming to be democratic). In an authoritarian state, the executive is led by an individual or group (e.g., a military **junta**) that has no intention of surrendering control of the state. In some cases no process exists for the peaceful transfer of control to another individual or group; in others a process is in place that superficially resembles an election, but either the result is rigged through systematic electoral fraud or voter intimidation, or the ballot contains no alternatives to the existing leadership.

The term dictatorship is often used in conjunction with authoritarian regimes, and it is possible to distinguish personal dictatorships (like Daniel Moi in Kenya, 1978–2002, or Augusto Pinochet in Chile, 1973–1990) from party dictatorships (such as the former Soviet Union and the People's Republic of China). The former, which may be sustained by a cult of personality, often end, not surprisingly, with the death of the dictator, and often end violently. The degree of repression and violence that dictatorship uses to control opposition can vary significantly. While supporters of democracy view dictatorship as a wholly illegitimate form of government, some dictators have enjoyed a considerable measure of popular support.

Totalitarian regimes seek to exert control over all areas of life, to the degree that this is possible. Totalitarian regimes are usually informed by an ideology of total government but manage to achieve much less than total control. It may be a weak generalization, but personal dictators seem less inclined towards totalitarianism (North Korea's Kims excepted), being preoccupied with suppressing any potential opposition to their rule.

In short, all totalitarian regimes are authoritarian, but not all authoritarian regimes are totalitarian.

Ring Road 3: Beijing, China.

CIVIL SOCIETY

In all political systems, considerable areas of our life remain outside the active administration of the state; this is the realm of **civil society**. It is tempting to define civil society as areas of our social activity where the state is absent, but this requires two qualifications. First, civil society should not be confused with regimes where the government has little control over significant portions of its territory. The inability of a state to establish its authority in all parts of its jurisdiction is generally regarded as weakness, not strength. Second, civil society includes areas of behaviour that the state may not be regulating now, but could be, if it were necessary. For example, family life is an important component of civil society, but the state intervenes when family life threatens the well-being of its members—situations of child abuse or domestic violence, failure to ensure that children are schooled, for example—and the state defines the rules of marriage and divorce.

Any line between state and civil society is artificial (i.e., an analytic distinction) and a constantly shifting boundary. Consider the antithesis of civil society, the *totalitarian* state, which, in theory, recognizes no limits to the reach of its power ("in theory" because no government has the will, let alone the means, to direct everything its citizens do, all the time). In totalitarian states (see *Authoritiarian Regimes*, p. 24) there are often elements of unregulated activity, such as black markets or underground religious congregations, but the boundaries are uncertain and insecure. What matters is not the mere existence of areas of life where the state is absent, which is inevitable, but the official withdrawal or abstention of the state from specific arenas of social interaction.

In states with effective constitutions the boundaries of civil society may be more clearly drawn, but where civil society is most firmly established, it may not even be recognized as such. In these countries an expectation of civil society is implicit in the political culture, even though few people use the term "civil society." Social science has accumulated much evidence that a strong civil society is an essential component of a free and democratic society.

THE CONTENT OF CIVIL SOCIETY

Comparing states reveals that what falls within civil society varies widely. In many countries, a separation of church and state places religious institutions and practices within civil society. In such cases the state neither enforces nor do its policies reflect the precepts of any particular religion—although this may be truer in theory than in practice.

By contrast, when the Taliban came to power in Afghanistan, the boundaries of civil society contracted significantly, especially for women and girls, but even for men to be clean-shaven or bearded ceased to be a personal decision.

In some of the most pluralistic regimes of the world, such as Canada, the official (legal) treatment of days of the week or year that have religious significance tends to favour some religions over others. Of course, these religiously **pluralist** societies exist only because their governments enforced laws of tolerance and protected the religious rights of minorities, often creating a secular state in the process.

The well-known opposition of a substantial number of US citizens to any form of gun control reflects their view that gun ownership should remain within civil society. This contrasts with an anti-gun culture in the United Kingdom, where even police have routinely not been armed. Obscenity provisions, anti-sodomy laws, prohibitions against child pornography, protection from sexual exploitation, and legalized prostitution reveal different possible shapes of civil society.

INSTITUTIONS OF CIVIL SOCIETY

The state has the ability to define and refine the boundaries of civil society, the constitution and ordinary laws being instruments that map its terrain. Arguably, the state needs to reconsider its relationship to civil society only when the institutions of civil society fail or when its own occupations of civil society prove to be counterproductive. Earlier it was suggested that the ideal state exercises its authority with the consent of the citizens but reserves the ability to coerce those who withhold consent, particularly when this refusal threatens the security of those who do consent. In a similar way, in a world of scarce resources, it may be in everyone's interest to leave much control of social life to the institutions of civil society, until or unless these institutions fail to function, or function in a way that threatens the well-being of the regime (with how this is defined and by whom being an important consideration).

Margaret Thatcher (British prime minister, 1979–1990) famously said that "there is no such thing as society: there are individual men and women, and there are families." Most social scientists would disagree and note her qualification—"and there are families"—which is less often quoted than the rest of the statement. The family is not the only institution of civil society, although it is arguably the first. The church is another, with a smaller role in some regimes, a larger role in others, and in most a weaker role today than it once had. It is difficult for most people raised in the modern, developed world to appreciate just how large the role of the church once was in regulating the life of every person.

Like other institutions of civil society, the family and the church are each characterized by their own structure of authority and by their own forms of power. Parents may discipline their children in ways prohibited to other adults (teachers, counsellors, or even the police). Religious bodies may deny certain rites or withhold blessings or pardons, a punishment that may be more severe (to the believer) than any means of coercion that the state possesses. In many people's lives, the sources of private power and authority to which they are subject (their employer, their landlord) may be much more immediate and therefore real than political power, which remains abstract and remote. It is their own authority and power that enables institutions of civil society to perform their functions, and it is often the use (or abuse) that they make of that power that prompts the state to intervene in civil society.

By the same token, some institutions of civil society—such as the family, the church, the charitable organization, and the trade union—are able to nurture and support their members in ways that the state cannot or will not. This, too, is part of the strength of such private institutions, and in some cases the very reason for which they exist. When their ability to provide relief falls short of the society's need, the state has often replaced private benevolence or philanthropy with programs of social welfare.

The Market Economy

Several examples of the give and take between the state and civil society are provided by the **market economy** that underpins developed-world democracies and is regarded by many as a central institution of civil society. As is explained in greater detail in Chapter 14, the market economy has two primary features: the private ownership of property, and reliance on private transactions between buyers and sellers ("the market") as the mechanism for distributing goods and labour. A careful look at human experience shows that neither private property nor a market economy "just happens." Each requires a particular framework of laws, protections, supports, and sanctions that governments must be willing to provide and maintain. There is a strong argument to be made for regarding the market economy as a joint product of civil society *and* the state.

Consider, for example, the difference between *possession*, which is what I occupy or hold (perhaps by might), and *property*, which indicates my *entitlement* to what I possess (by right). Establishing a system of such entitlements involves two developments: recognition by others of the legitimacy of each person's possession(s) and a power that is able to protect each person against anyone who would usurp (take) their property. Historically, protection of property has been one of the primary functions of the state. Conversely, in societies lacking a state, the idea that property (in either land or goods) could be "owned" ("be *mine*") might be incomprehensible.

In much of the so-called developed world, the economy is the source of considerable, even formidable, forces of private power, and for this reason, the banking system, financial markets, and other elements of a market economy are viewed as institutions of civil society. However, the market economy rests on a foundation of supportive public policies *as well as* a considerable degree of autonomy from the exercise of public power by the government/state.

DOES CIVIL SOCIETY PRECEDE POLITICS?

In any human community one can expect to find a kinship structure, a process for sharing or allocating scarce resources, and a central belief system—that is, family, economy, religion. Chapter 2 discusses pre-political societies without formal governments or anything resembling "the state." In such settings, the maintenance of well-being depends entirely on the systems of distribution and redistribution, the family, and religion. It is tempting to say that in pre-political communities there is only civil society, even though it is anachronistic to speak of civil society before the emergence of a political regime (i.e., state and government) with which civil society can be contrasted.

CIVIL SOCIETY AND FREEDOM

Just as it is unwise to ignore the significant sources of private authority and power that structure civil society, it is misleading to distinguish civil society and the state as where or when we are free and where or when we are not. Our existence as social beings is always constrained, even if only by the values and customs of our culture. Within the family, as members of a religious community, or by occupying a place within a particular economic system, we are subject to rules, remain limited in our choices, and must accommodate the interests and desires of others. Such is life. What distinguishes the institutions of civil society is that they do not have at their disposal the same range of coercive sanctions that the state can ultimately draw upon to enforce its laws. Logically, if not historically, the state emerges at that point in a society's development when its non-political means of control are no longer adequate.

CIVIL SOCIETY AND MODERNIZATION

Recall Laver's observation that "we need government when community fails." In part, the tremendous growth of the state in the twentieth century was a response to the inadequacy or decline of the institutions of civil society, or to changes in their character. Consider the effects of modernization on just one institution of civil society—the family. Over time the trend has been towards fragmentation (or "desegmentation") of the family. When elderly family members can no longer rely on children or grandchildren to care for them in their declining years, the existence and level of pensions or income supplements become significant, as does the availability of retirement homes and/or long-term care facilities. When parents cannot afford to withdraw from the labour force and have neither parents nor siblings who can look after their children, the availability and quality of child care are critical.

Into the late nineteenth century, churches and benevolent organizations provided the bulk of assistance to the economically unfortunate or to those persons disabled in one way or another. With a decline in the strength of the church and a growing egalitarian belief that *all* have a right to a minimum standard of well-being, the inability of private charity to meet these needs is not surprising, particularly during

Fall Fair: Jocelyn Township, Ontario.

periods of prolonged economic stagnation. In many ways the state took up the slack with policies to be identified later under the heading of the welfare state. Setting aside the large military budgets of some states during the Cold War era, the major expenditures of governments since 1950 have been on health care, education, and social assistance.

CIVIL SOCIETY AND DEMOCRACY

The relationship between the state and civil society is an important theme in this text, and one to which certain events in the last two decades have brought

more attention. Political scientist Robert Putnam received considerable attention for suggesting that a sustainable democracy requires a healthy civil society. Put generally, people bring to the political realm the habits, behaviours, values, and skills that they have acquired and use elsewhere in public life. Democracy, for example, is not simply about the existence of free, competitive elections; it is about working with others, being able to compromise, having realistic expectations of efficacy (what one can expect to accomplish by participating), being able to accept defeat, seeing beyond one's own interests most narrowly defined, and developing a sense of obligation to participate or take responsibility even when it is inconvenient or fails to be "fun." These life skills are often imparted through the activities and institutions of civil society—in schools and church groups, clubs and associations, the workplace, labour organizations, boardrooms, and, of course, in the family. Acquiring these facilities and transferring them to the political realm are what make us **citizens** (those who rule themselves) and not simply **subjects** (those who are ruled).

On one level, Putman's idea seems obvious: why would we expect someone who has never participated in decision making to be a citizen rather than a subject? Few of us would expect to step on the golf course for the first time and shoot par, or throw "turkeys" on our first visit to the bowling alley. On the other hand, seemingly rational people have also believed that it is possible to overthrow a long-running dictatorship and within months put an effective democratic government in its place.

The experience since 1990 of republics that were once part of the Soviet Union has been illustrative. The absence of adequately developed institutions of civil society has contributed in several cases to environments in which organized crime has flourished, personal dictatorships have arisen, or stagnation and civil unrest have persisted. The collapse of the existing state, with its centralized provision of education, health care, and employment, occurred without alternative bodies in place to whom or to which these functions could be transferred. The result, in some places, has been a serious decline in public health and in life expectancy.

More generally, theories such as Putnam's recognize that the political realm cannot be treated in isolation from the larger social context. It is generally believed today, for example, that a democratic society cannot be sustained without a competitive mass media that is free from political pressure and whose ownership is not concentrated within a narrowly drawn elite. In the twentieth century, the conventional mass media (newspapers, radio, and television) came to be regarded as an essential institution of civil society. The role of newer electronic media and devices is quickly becoming established in the first decades of this century.

BEYOND THE STATE

This book concentrates mostly on what generally transpires within the regime, its state and its civil society. The reason is simple: politics is about the regulation of our interactions with others, and for most of us, most of our relationships are with our fellow citizens. In other words, most politics is *intra*-national. As there are now about 200 regimes in the world, many of which are federal states with autonomous subnational governments, there is a great deal of data available for comparative analysis.

This contrasts with the study of international relations, concerned with world politics, or what some call "geopolitics," in which the primary actors are countries. International relations (IR) focuses on the conflicts between regimes, the alliances they form, and their diplomatic and military manoeuvres—what is commonly described as "foreign policy." The study of international relations is no less important in today's world, with almost 200 countries, than it was 100 years ago when there were fewer than 80.

Phenomena such as the globalization of trade, culture, and communications, and the economic consequences of climate change, are examples of *trans-national* forces. In today's world, citizens increasingly expect their governments to tackle problems that do not recognize borders, including the economy, the environment, public health, regulation of the Internet, and the preservation of human rights. This means that the modern state is often concerned not just with what happens within its territory but also about how its own policies affect the well-being and activities of citizens in the wider world. Similarly, globalization means that the citizens of any given country are increasingly affected by decisions made somewhere else, outside the direct control of their own state. Do tougher environmental protection laws increase the costs of goods and services for consumers, or make it difficult for domestic firms to compete in the global marketplace? Do higher taxation rates cause companies to relocate to less restrictive regimes, or provide the state with the means to deliver good social programs and sound infrastructure, which in turn might attract investment from abroad?

MULTINATIONAL BODIES

In a world of freer trade, international finance, and transnational corporations, many problems invite a response from multinational bodies, international organizations, or countries acting in concert. Internal conflicts that threaten to disrupt the global economy or send streams of refugees abroad cannot be regarded simply as civil wars. The state does *not* become less relevant in the era of globalization, but its challenges change, as must its ways of responding to them.

The globalization of trade and communications has, arguably, exerted pressure on all countries to adopt what are at least formally democratic political systems. This poses the greatest challenge in states where authoritarian rulers have shown little inclination to surrender power. In newly democratized countries, where political practice and political culture were previously not democratic, the immediate task is to consolidate popular sovereignty by developing the institutions and habits that make democracy work. In all democracies, even the most "advanced," the challenge is to ensure that citizens have the knowledge, the tools, and the interest in keeping government representative and accountable. In the age of globalization, democracy is threatened by the fact that our lives are increasingly shaped by forces, institutions, and actors over which or whom we have, at best, a very indirect measure of control.

CONCLUSION

This chapter has introduced *some* of the concepts and ideas most basic to the study of politics. What they share is an interest in the development and exercise of authority and power within the various kinds of community and society that humans inhabit. The foundational character of these ideas means that they will be referred to repeatedly in the chapters that follow. Although the purpose of Chapter 2 is to discuss different approaches within political science, a significant portion of that chapter expands on the relationship between the changing nature of human community and the emergence of the modern state as a product of that evolution. In Chapters 3 and 4, the particular character of liberal representative democracy, or the politics of the so-called developed world, will be situated within a historical context.

REFERENCES

Laver, Michael. *Invitation to Politics*. Oxford: Basil Blackwell, 1983.

Lawrence, Christopher N. "Regime Stability and Presidential Government: The Legacy of Authoritarian Rule, 1951–90." Web. October 22, 2011.

Putnam, Robert. *Bowling Alone: The Collapse and Revival of American Community*. New York: Simon & Schuster, 2000

Schell, Jonathan. "The Moral Equivalent of Empire." *Harper's Magazine*, Notebook: (February 2008): 9–13.

Weber, Max. "Politics as a Vocation." *From Max Weber: Essays in Sociology*. Ed. H.W. Gerth and C. Wright Mills. New York: Oxford University Press, 1958. 77–128.

FURTHER READING

Benn, Stanley I., and Richard Stanley Peters. *Social Principles and the Democratic State*. London: Allen & Unwin, 1959.

Blondel, Jean. "A Plea for a Genuine 'Micro-Political' Analysis in Political Science." *Government and Opposition* 45.4 (October 2010): 553–593.

Crick, Bernard. *In Defence of Politics*. New York: Penguin, 1964.

Flinders, Matthew. "In Defence of Politics." *The Political Quarterly* 81.3 (July–September 2010): 309–326.

Kisby, Ben. "The Big Society: Power to the People?" *The Political Quarterly* 81.4 (October–December 2010): 484–491.

Moe, Terry M. "Power and Political Institutions." *Perspectives on Politics* 3.2 (June 2005): 215–233.

Öberg, PerOla, and Torsten Svensson. "Does Power Drive Out Trust? Relations between Labour Market Actors in Sweden." *Political Studies* 58.1 (February 2010): 143–166.

CHAPTER 2

The Many Ways of Studying Politics

"Politics is not a science ... but an art."
—OTTO VON BISMARCK (GERMAN CHANCELLOR), 1884

...WHICH PROVIDES THE READER WITH

- the distinction between the normative and empirical dimensions of politics
- an outline of the social scientific research process
- the presentation of atomism, class analysis, and pluralism as alternative orientations to the study of politics
- a political-anthropology explanation of the emergence of the pre-industrial state
- a caution about the difference between studying politics and doing politics

In an age that encourages specialization, it sometimes seems there are as many ways of doing political science as there are political scientists. A book for readers who have yet to specialize must remain more general. This chapter introduces some principal variations in studying political matters.

It is also the case that while many political scientists are engaged in primary research of one kind or another (see *Survey Experiments*, p. 42), students are more likely to be *reading about* primary research. To understand and critically assess the work of political scientists, we need to know something about their methods and approaches.

We can meet Bismarck (who, to be fair, was talking about the practice of politics) halfway and say that the study of politics is *both* a science *and* an art, because it has two dimensions: the **normative** and the **empirical**. This is one basis on which political study has diverged in its methods, political philosophy taking primary ownership of the normative dimensions of the subject matter, other political sub-disciplines being more focused on the empirical study of political life.

POLITICS AS PHILOSOPHY

The study of politics has its roots in moral or ethical philosophy, at a time when such philosophy was about providing a rational basis (rather than, but not necessarily opposed to, a religious basis) for identifying right from wrong. Examples of such thinking applied to politics are the distinctions encountered in the previous chapter between good and bad states, and public norms such as legitimacy and justice. Many of the authors studied by students of politics are philosophers (for examples, see Chapter 3) who came to political questions in their investigations of moral theory, which is, of course, a form of normative discourse.

Normative discourse involves critical, rational debate about the ends of human life, viewed as goals or states of being to which humans (ought to) aspire, and about the means of achieving such goals. (Should I always seek pleasure? Should I care about what others think of me? Should I set aside my career to care for my family? Should I be free to engage in behaviours that might harm others? To whatever answer is provided, the next question is "why?") Propositions about the end(s) of human life often appeal to our understanding of what human nature is, should be, or could become. In this way, claims about the good life seek a foundation in our experience of human life or in expectations of what experience suggests is possible in human life. Our beliefs about the lives humans ought to lead and about human nature (or even if there is *a* human nature) carry implications for the politics of the societies in which we live.

Aristotle famously claimed that humans are specifically political animals. The word "political" derives from the Greek word *polis*, which refers to the community in which one is a citizen. In saying that we are political animals, Aristotle could be saying simply that all humans live and take part in the life of a community. He might also mean that the human is an animal governed not by instinct but by politics—our actions are not simply ingrained responses to biological imperatives but are consciously regulated. Human behaviour is intentional. This means not only that our actions are

---

EMPIRICAL AND NORMATIVE

Empirical refers to the data of experience (phenomena), anything that is subject to observation and (ideally) to measurement. The operation of institutions, the behaviour of political actors, laws and their enforcement, the content and development of public policies, and the influence of ideas, attitudes, and values are among the phenomena that the empirical dimension of political inquiry seeks to explain more clearly.

Normative refers to beliefs we use to make judgments about what the political world should be or to assess its current shape. What is the good life for humans? What is the best kind of state or government? How do we balance equality and liberty on the scales of justice? These are examples of normative questions, and normative discourse seeks to justify a particular state of affairs, or present a case for its reform.

The term "empirical" is sometimes described as dealing with just "the facts." Whatever that may mean, it is the case that empirical inquiry, no less than any other activity of the mind, is informed by sound theory. To describe, record, or identify facts (phenomena? experience?), we need concepts, and theory is simply a more or less organized body of concepts. All knowledge has an essentially theoretical component, such as the names we put to things in order to be able to talk about them in the first place.

deliberate but also that the regulation or prohibition of actions is deliberate, achieved by means of rules or laws rather than automatic and instinctive (biological) checks. Rules or laws are specifically human inventions that require language and culture—the life in community that humans share.

Rules also represent decisions made by someone about what is (or is not) to be done. When we discuss, debate, or deliberate about such decisions, we engage in normative discourse. Since politics is concerned with decisions to regulate human behaviour, it is inescapably normative in character.

When governments make decisions and enforce them upon populations, they address ends. Certain views about the good life for humankind, or about

what it means to be human, are logically tied to certain kinds of government or to specific government policies. For example, the belief that all individuals are basically rational, self-interested actors more readily disposes us to democratic government than the belief that there is a natural hierarchy of those with the capacity to govern and those without. Likewise, the priority we attach to certain views of liberty or security, respectively, may lead us to oppose or support policies on more specific issues such as gun control or mandatory criminal sentences. The reverse is also true: certain actions or decisions by governments reflect common beliefs about the good life (compulsory childhood education) or about what is proper for humans (anti-discrimination legislation).

Admittedly, not everyone finds it awesome to study the body of normative discourse that comprises political philosophy from Plato to Charles Taylor (or Jürgen Habermas or Alasdair MacIntyre). It *is* important, though, that all students of political science understand the normative character of their discipline *and* have a basic familiarity with the normative problems and issues that underlie the institutions and structures of government today. Terms like "liberty," "equality," "rights," "sovereignty," "justice," "democracy," "the common good," "opportunity," "fairness," "welfare," "authority," and "power" are so imbedded in our understanding of political life that the use of at least some of them is all but inescapable. Each has a normative component that involves beliefs about what is right or proper, and each of these terms also has several possible meanings.

For example, you may believe that liberty means the *absence* of a law or restraint on your behaviour. One of your friends thinks that freedom *requires* the presence of laws and restraints that protect the weak from the strong, and I remain convinced that my freedom requires participating in making the laws to which I am subject. We each value freedom, but find there are times when we can't agree on whether a policy preserves, enhances, or infringes upon our liberty. We may also discover that, considered more closely, our beliefs about liberty conflict with our understanding of equality, or that justice as we have defined it doesn't always lead to the outcome we think is best. Rules of good reasoning and clear communication—and the matter of just getting along with each other—motivate us to try to resolve contradictions and iron out inconsistencies.

Not just as political scientists but as educated citizens, we use the critical faculties of our reason and the analytic skills we develop in order to increase our understanding of each other. We want coherence and consistency in the use of normative terms like "freedom" or "justice" so that we will understand the practical outcomes entailed by their use, particularly when this means a political position, a policy decision, or legislation that binds each of us.

POLITICS AS SOCIAL SCIENCE

As a science, political inquiry is concerned with explaining the objects of political experience. This empirical dimension increasingly displaced political philosophy in political science departments in the twentieth century for two reasons, one negative and one positive. The negative impetus was dissatisfaction with the ability of a purely philosophical approach to investigate adequately an increasingly complex political world, especially with the development of democratic politics and the growth of the modern, bureaucratic state. The positive incentive was the development of methods patterned after the natural sciences and incorporating insights from other social science disciplines such as psychology, sociology, anthropology, and economics (none of which existed as recognizably separate disciplines prior to the nineteenth century).

Controversy has often accompanied the adaptation of scientific methodology to political inquiry, particularly because natural science is not only experimental but conducts its experiments in controlled situations. There are limits, practical and ethical, to experimenting with human subjects, and obtaining a controlled setting is easier said than done. (Nonetheless, just google the term "Stanley Milgram" and see what comes up.)

Nonetheless, there are non-experimental scientific traditions, such as the field work conducted by botanists and zoologists, observing individuals and species, devising classifications, analyzing similarities and differences, and noting associations with other variables such as climate, or soil, or the presence of other species such as predators or parasites. Much of the work done in political science is observational and analytic (and may also involve identifying predators and parasites). While the political scientist comparing political institutions and processes cannot conduct experiments with a nation and its political institutions, he or she is able to treat how different regimes make laws, hold electors, or deliver health care and education as if they are (or were) experiments. The comparative political scientist studies the data created by the real world of nation-states rather than what might be produced by experiments in the laboratory or through mathematical simulations.

Whatever the methods, students of political science should be concerned with acquiring accurate representations and reliable explanations of political reality.

One measure of whether an explanation is scientific is whether it can be generalized. If the explanation is valid *here*, it should allow us to predict an outcome *elsewhere*. This happens frequently in the physical sciences. The social sciences have also sought to provide **law-like generalizations**, with mostly modest success. There are few, if any, examples of political science producing a law-like generalization—a statement of relationship between *a* and *b* such that whenever *a* is observed, *b* will invariably follow—that is not a truism (such as, the sun will rise tomorrow) or trivial (such as, if the Pirate Party wins x per cent of the vote, the share for the other parties is 100 minus x).

Another hallmark of science is that its propositions should be falsifiable—capable of *not* being true. If, for example, I wish to investigate whether the growth of the Internet has negatively impacted political participation, I need to be able to distinguish the evidence that would confirm this **hypothesis** (a proposition about the relationship between variables) from the evidence that would refute it. If *every* sort of evidence can be explained as confirming the hypothesis, something other than science is happening. This is why science can neither prove nor disprove the existence of, say, God—there is no empirical test that can measure something that is either everywhere, nowhere, or entirely beyond our comprehension, depending on one's perspective. There are many theological and philosophical propositions upon which the scientific method is unable to shed any light, from the profound questions about the ultimate nature of reality to the simple existence of good or evil. Some critics say that Marx's theory of historical materialism and Freud's theory of psychoanalysis are ways of looking at experience that are also **dogmatic** (incapable of being proven or disproven).

The less ambitious example of exploring a connection between Internet use and political engagement is helpful in demonstrating other challenges that all social sciences face. In any proposition about a relationship where *x* leads to *y*, we are talking about two variables—"variables" because something like the following is being tested: if I increase *x* by so much, what change will I observe in the amount of *y*? If your exposure to the Internet (*x*) increases, will you be more likely or less likely to vote in the next election or attend a campaign rally (*y*)? In this question, political activity is the **dependent variable**; Internet exposure is the **independent variable**.

But, what if we're wrong about which variable is independent and which is dependent? In this case, instincts may suggest that putting it the other way around won't make as much sense—will increasing the frequency with which we vote or attend political realities change the frequency with which we access the Internet? An example such as this may illustrate that matters are rarely as simple as a relationship between x and y, even in the natural sciences.

The scientist wishing to verify the boiling point of water will conduct his or her experiment with distilled water, eliminating factors that are extraneous to *x* and *y*—ocean water, because of its salinity, boils at a higher temperature and freezes at a lower temperature than filtered water. In the social sciences we rarely have that opportunity—the water, so to speak, always has impurities. Another scientist may be interested in measuring the effect of other variables (like salt or the level of oxygen in the water) on the relationship between x and y. These other factors—z and q—may be viewed as **intervening variable**s.

We know, for example, that people use electronic media for different purposes, such as video gaming,

THE RESEARCH PROCESS

Insofar as empirical research attempts to uncover relationships between variables, the research process involves several components and stages. We begin with **theory**, which states our beliefs and current knowledge about the phenomena in which we are interested by means of a concise, logical organization of concepts.

On the basis of our theory, we generate **propositions**, conditional statements predicting relationships between our concepts (or variables); for example, political participation should be higher in countries where non-voting is penalized.

Propositions, in turn, lead to hypotheses, which are propositions more concretely stated as guesses about the correlations we will find between variables; for example, as income and level of education increase, the rate of political participation will rise.

The next challenge is to *operationalize* the hypothesis; how will we measure income and define political participation? These are practical questions of utmost importance if we are to generate reliable findings.

Research design indicates the process of deciding what operations will best test our hypotheses and deliver observations for analysis; this may involve a survey of opinions, a search of databases, a content analysis of newspapers, and so on. Performing these operations enables us to record *observations* or *data*. Further *analysis* is required in order to identify any relationships between variables that are revealed by the data.

To the degree that our hypotheses have been confirmed or refuted, we may reconsider our propositions and theory. Our research is successful if it allows us to refine our theory (improve our current knowledge about phenomena), which should allow us to generate new propositions and hypotheses for further research.

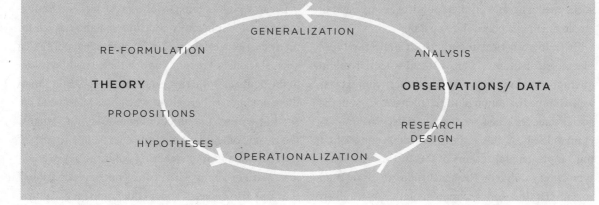

GENERALIZATION

RE-FORMULATION

ANALYSIS

THEORY

OBSERVATIONS/ DATA

PROPOSITIONS

RESEARCH DESIGN

HYPOTHESES

OPERATIONALIZATION

accessing news, downloading music and movies, and for social networking. Perhaps the associations between Internet use and political engagement depend on what people are using the Internet for. If we measure these relationships and find differences, we can further employ mathematical tools that have been developed to determine whether these differences are statistically significant or merely coincidental. Even if we find that there is an association between Internet use and political engagement, we still cannot be confident that the former is responsible for the latter, for at least two reasons.

First, it might be that Internet use and political engagement are both dependent variables related to a third, independent variable, such as socio-economic status or age cohort. Second, it could be that, contrary to our instincts, political engagement does affect Internet use, rather than vice-versa. This might be something clarified by collecting data over time—did increasing or decreasing use of electronic media have any relationship to increasing or decreasing political engagement? In some circumstances, perhaps, those who became politically engaged discovered that social networking tools could be put to good use in this area of activity, or they were even required to use social media because of their political engagement or employment in a political occupation.

These hypothetical situations illustrate the types of empirical inquiry that a social scientist might attempt—in this case in a behavioural context—as well as some indication of the challenges posed in the social sciences when so many variables are in play. Human life is, in this respect, **overdetermined**; finding simple generalizations of the "if this, then that" type is very unlikely. The conclusions we draw from social scientific work are more tentative, more likely to express tendencies and probabilities than certainties or proofs.

The overdetermined character of so much of what social scientists want to study has led to the creation of statistical techniques that make **multivariate analysis** possible. A basic knowledge of statistics and probability theory is an asset for any social scientist, even if it is only to understand the work produced by others.

The element of control that is essential to screening out extraneous factors when conducting many scientific experiments is all but impossible when dealing with the behaviour of humans—or else that control becomes an extraneous factor influencing their behaviour. Accordingly, some areas of political science have moved from the observational to the mathematical and to computer modeling that draws on the power of data-processing technology. What these types of inquiry tell us about the real world is sometimes a matter of debate.

The failure of the discipline to generate law-like generalizations such as those produced by the natural sciences should not distract political science from more modest goals such as explaining political phenomena through the identification of causal tendencies, or from recognizing that empirical accuracy remains central to good political study.

Because politics often involves a clash of competing interests, it is inherently controversial and has led to many passionate debates. To the degree that politics is a social science, it reminds us that there is a dimension to the political world that is not merely "opinion," that there *are* matters here about which it is possible to be right or wrong. The functioning of electoral systems, the review of legislation by the courts, or the role of civil servants in implementing public policy are not just matters about which one can have opinions; they are also subjects about which one may acquire

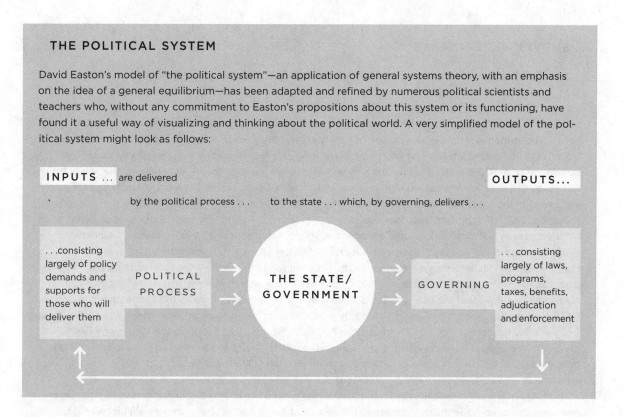

THE POLITICAL SYSTEM

David Easton's model of "the political system"—an application of general systems theory, with an emphasis on the idea of a general equilibrium—has been adapted and refined by numerous political scientists and teachers who, without any commitment to Easton's propositions about this system or its functioning, have found it a useful way of visualizing and thinking about the political world. A very simplified model of the political system might look as follows:

INPUTS ... are delivered

by the political process ...   to the state ... which, by governing, delivers ...

OUTPUTS...

...consisting largely of policy demands and supports for those who will deliver them

POLITICAL PROCESS

THE STATE/ GOVERNMENT

GOVERNING

... consisting largely of laws, programs, taxes, benefits, adjudication and enforcement

knowledge. It may be a harsh judgment, but many citizens are as ignorant about areas of the political world as they are about the activity of enzymes or the relationships between subatomic particles. Nonetheless, experience demonstrates that a lack of knowledge is no impediment to holding strong opinions.

A push for a more rigorously scientific approach to politics culminated in the 1960s in behaviourism or **behaviouralism**. This was in part the quest to create a *value-free* political inquiry patterned on the natural sciences and focused on the observation and measurement of political behaviour of individuals. Behaviouralism hoped to generate law-like generalizations that would lead to successful predictions about future behaviour. It was criticized for being too abstract and for being

empirically conservative. Over time, many practitioners concluded that a "value-free" political science is not possible given the ineradicably normative character of the subject matter and of its investigators.

In the strictest sense, behaviouralism focused attention on individuals and their behaviours at the expense of institutions or social processes and perhaps for this reason flourished in sub-disciplines such as political psychology and political sociology. Nonetheless, the behavioural approach made political scientists self-conscious about scientific methodology, developed a considerable body of empirical theory (including the enduring notion of the **political system**—see above), and encouraged interdisciplinary linkages with other social sciences.

The empirical approach taken in this book is that of comparative analysis. In politics the possible objects of comparison—from the political systems of nation-states, to specific institutions like legislatures, to political actors like prime ministers or presidents, to ideologies or popular values—are countless. The importance of comparing matters that are comparable was discussed in the Introduction. For example, we usually compare the political systems of countries in the developed world with the systems of other countries in the developed world rather than with systems in the developing world, or compare democracies with each other rather than with totalitarian or authoritarian regimes.

(Having said that, there may be some dimensions on which we find it useful to compare all regimes, as do many international bodies such as UN agencies or private organizations such as Freedom House. The latter, discussed in Chapter 4, measures the degree to which key freedoms are present in all regimes. This provides one way of evaluating all the regimes that hold elections; in the absence of certain liberties, elections cannot possibly be fair or democratic.)

Which similarities matter? What are the differences that make a difference? In asking these questions we begin to move beyond *description* towards *explanation*. Why do coalition governments survive longer in Germany and Sweden than in Italy and the Netherlands? Does the experience of other countries tell Canada anything about the wisdom of reforming versus abolishing the Senate? After the 2010 general election in the United Kingdom produced the first "hung parliament" (i.e., no party held a majority of seats) in almost 40 years, some scholars looked to the experience of non-majority governance in Canada, New Zealand, and elsewhere for lessons that might be applied to the situation (see Paun and Hazell).

Most comparative political analysis rests on three assumptions:

- · that a political system performs specific functions within a society or community;
- · that this is generally true of the political systems of all societies; and
- · that the more societies are alike, the more similar will be their political systems and the functions these systems perform.

It is also clear, though, that every political system, every society, is unique in significant respects that are connected with its history, culture, traditions, and customs. For this reason, the politics of each society will resist explanation solely in terms of functions or institutions common to other societies and will require an account of the mix of factors unique to that society.

UNITS OF ANALYSIS: INDIVIDUAL, GROUP, OR CLASS?

The distinction between philosophical (or normative) versus scientific (or empirical) is one way of explaining the diversity of approaches to political inquiry (leaving aside the point that one can be philosophical *and* scientific). Another basis for different approaches is perspectives about what constitutes the most basic unit of analysis. What is our starting point? What is the most fundamental level on which we should focus?

ATOMISM (POLITICS IS ABOUT THE ACTIVITY OF INDIVIDUALS)

A prominent approach to studying politics in Western cultures has been to treat the *individual* as the fundamental unit; in fact, there have been several different approaches based on the individual as a political atom (**atomism**). Classical liberalism, in both politics and economics, is based on a view of individuals as rational, self-interested actors seeking to maximize their position (economic or political) within society. One interesting application of economic liberalism to the political sphere has been the development of **public choice theory**. This theory combines the economic liberal idea of the individual as a rational, self-interested maximizer with aspects of game theory to explain how different political actors seek to improve their position within a particular institutional setting by bargaining and trading with the resources at their disposal. For example, citizens give (or withhold from) politicians the resources they control (votes, campaign contributions, civil obedience) in return for specific public policy outcomes. Program administrators seeking more program dollars (which elected politicians control) bargain with the resources they have, such as information and expertise (which elected politicians need). Politicians want favourable publicity; journalists want inside stories or advance notice of events. The possibilities of a mutually beneficial exchange are clear.

Not all individualist approaches to politics stress the competitive, acquisitive dimensions of human nature. For example, Canadian political scientist Ron Manzer has applied Abraham Maslow's categories of human needs to a discussion of political *goods*. Maslow argued that *needs*, which are properties of being an individual, can be understood as hierarchically organized. It is only as each level of need is satisfied that we can

turn our attention to the next level. If our basic physiological needs for food and shelter are not adequately satisfied, we will remain focused upon their attainment, unable to give proper attention to our safety or belongingness needs. At the highest level are self-actualizers, who realize an ideal character of autonomous individuality (a level that Maslow believes only a small proportion of us are capable of attaining).

Manzer has defined a political good as "a condition we have some reason to regard as agreeable, beneficial, commendable, right, proper, or morally excellent," and one which "represents a public virtue realizable at least in part through collective action" (8). Public education, effective health care, and development of the arts and sciences are concrete examples of such a political good. The good is grounded in our nature as individuals but requires our collective or co-operative activity for its realization; we cannot provide these goods for ourselves but depend, to at least some degree, upon the resources of the community (or the state). In a relatively brief space, Manzer presents a plausible association of each of Maslow's categories of need with a traditional political good and, in doing so, generates "a useful framework for analyzing the purposes and assessing the results of the political arrangements in a community" (7).

CLASS ANALYSIS (POLITICS IS DRIVEN BY THE CLASS SYSTEM)

Atomism is criticized as being too abstract (i.e., removed from reality), divorcing the individual from all the contexts where he or she is not alone (most atoms, after all, are bound up in molecules). It also assumes an equality between individuals that is contradicted by the very real structures within society that determine advantage and opportunity. Central among

NEEDS AND POLITICAL GOODS

MASLOW'S HEIRARCHY OF NEEDS	MANZER'S SET OF POLITICAL GOODS
self-actualization ↑	liberty
esteem ↑	equality
belongingness ↑	fraternity
safety ↑	security
physiological	welfare

Figure 2.1

these structures is **class**, the existence of a hierarchical structure of levels that provide varying degrees of access to scarce resources. For some, then, class is the fundamental unit of analysis because they believe it is class that determines individuals' outcomes, not individuals who determine class. These levels may be determined by different factors, such as **status**, land ownership, or level of education. The most famous proponent of class analysis is Karl Marx, but one does not have to be a Marxist or seek, as Marx did, the overthrow of the class structure, to recognize that class is an important variable in political explanations.

PLURALISM (POLITICS IS ABOUT THE COMPETITION OF GROUPS)

A third position argues for neither individuals nor classes but for something intermediate: the *group* as the fundamental unit of analysis. Atomism may be too focused on the trees to recognize there is a forest, but the class model is guilty of abstraction in its own way and—from the pluralist perspective—oversimplifies social reality. Individuals act neither alone nor as class-conscious workers or capitalists but as members of any number of groups with shifting memberships. Some of these will be very much concerned with securing power and influence; some will not. The pluralist argues that power is neither concentrated in one class nor dispersed equally among all individuals. Which groups have the advantage in getting their way depends on a number of factors and circumstances and is often if not always changing. Individuals may belong to many (even competing or conflicting) groups or have little involvement at all, but it is only through their association with the organization, expertise, and information of the group that individuals have influence in society. So **pluralism** argues.

WHICH APPROACH IS RIGHT?

Pluralists do not deny the existence of class or of individuals apart from groups, and Marxists do not dispute the reality of individuals or groups. In each case the argument is that these other units are less significant or even *in*significant in the final analysis. It is also interesting that while the rivalry seems to be about the proper orientation of empirical research, it also reflects normative judgments. The pluralist is not simply saying that it is a fruitful research strategy to focus on groups but also that groups *are* what is paramount. Similarly, the Marxist who envisions a classless society is not going to argue that it is individual self-interest or the pluralist competition of interest groups that gets in its way. The way we see the world is very often closely related to the way we think the world should be.

ECLECTICISM

(from Greek *eklektikos*, "selective"), in philosophy and theology, the practice of selecting doctrines from different systems of thought without adopting the whole parent system for each doctrine. It is distinct from syncretism—the attempt to reconcile or combine systems—inasmuch as it leaves the contradictions between them unresolved. In the sphere of abstract thought, eclecticism is open to the objection that insofar as each system is supposed to be a whole of which its various doctrines are integral parts, the arbitrary juxtaposition of doctrines from different systems risks a fundamental incoherence. In practical affairs, however, the eclectic spirit has much to commend it.

"eclecticism." © Encyclopaedia Britannica/eb.com. 14 November 2010. www.britannica.com/EBchecked/topic/178092/eclecticism

BROADENING HORIZONS

Two articles in the June 2010 issue of *Perspectives on Politics* discuss at greater length two themes touched upon in this chapter.

ECLECTICISM

Rudgra Sil and Peter J. Katzenstein (in "Analytical Eclecticism in the Study of World Politics") discuss the development of "research tradition," a more formal terminology for talking about what this chapter has called competing "approaches" to the study of politics. They suggest this competition persists because of "convictions about what kinds of social phenomena are amenable to social analysis, what kinds of questions are important to ask, and what kinds of processes and mechanisms are most likely to be relevant." In the process of doing this, research traditions "bypass aspects of a complex reality that do not fit within the ... parameters they have established" (413). By analogy, each tradition understands one type of tree, but none are able to explain the forest. They illustrate this point by drawing on a well-known observation made by Albert Hirschman: "Ordinarily, social scientists are happy enough when they have gotten hold of one paradigm or line of causation. As a result, their guesses are often farther off the mark than those of the experienced politician whose intuition is more likely to take a variety of forces into account" (341).

The aim of "analytical eclecticism," as Sil and Katzenstein present it, is to build on the success of research traditions and engage "substantive issues of policy and practice" (i.e., real-world problems).

SCHOLASTICISM

Lawrence Mead (in "Scholasticism in Political Science") accuses political science of becoming "*scholastic*," by which he means "academic work that is over refined at the expense of substance." Noting the roots of the term in the Middle Ages when, it was said, scholars would debate "how many angels could dance on the head of a pin," Mead continues: "Similarly, today's political scientists often address very narrow questions, and they are often preoccupied with method and past literature. ... Scholars are focusing more on themselves, less on the real world. That has harmed the realism of their work and the audience for it" (453).

Mead identifies four trends that constitute what he identifies as scholasticism:

- (over) specialization (which includes interacting intellectually only with specialists in the same area)
- methodologism (to the degree that many scholars "often are interested mainly in methodology or statistics, rather than in the subject of analysis")
- non-empiricism (hypotheses are "based on past research or on academic theory, usually economics, rather than contact with actual politics")
- literature focus (to the degree that "scholars are expert primarily about the literature on a subject ... much of what they study and talk about is this body of past work, rather than politics or government directly") (453–55).

The solution, Mead suggests, is to re-emphasize relevance to real-world issues and audiences as a research priority.

What are the implications of different approaches to the discipline? Must students choose one or another, and if so, what should guide their choice? This book is written from the perspective of methodological **eclecticism**, in the belief that there is something to be said for each of the methods (and other perspectives not yet discussed, such as gender studies). Alternative methods for studying politics exist and persist because each focuses on a different portion of the political world; each is valid but partial. In certain respects and situations, the focus should be on the individual, but in other cases or for other questions, class, or group, or gender may well be more relevant—given the over-determined character of social phenomena, noted above, this should not be surprising.

The diversity of approaches to the study of politics also reflects the interdisciplinary nature of social science. In other words, the concepts and methods of any one discipline (such as economics, anthropology, psychology, or sociology) may be applied in another discipline (such as politics) to generate new insights. Classical economics is concerned with the activities of individuals in the market system. Political economy approaches to economics and sociology are more likely to focus on class. Psychology begins with the conscious and unconscious formations of the individual mind; anthropology investigates small social wholes such as the band or tribe. Each of these fields of study borrows and learns from the others.

The challenge is to put all the pieces together, drawing the insights from each methodological stream into one coherent whole, a task that is perhaps impossible in this age of specialization. Nonetheless, we ought to remain open to the possible contribution of each sub-field or sub-discipline to our knowledge of the political world. The intense focus that specialization requires is best left to the graduate student or to post-graduate research.

POLITICS AS ANTHROPOLOGY

References were made in the previous chapter to insights from political anthropology, in which the fundamental unit of analysis is the social whole, the society or community, considered as an organic body. Anthropologists usually study societies described as pre-industrial or pre-technological—societies at a level of development where stratification and differentiation are at least initially not present or remain less advanced. However, the anthropological method has also been applied to artificial communities in contemporary society, including a study of the members of the US Senate (Weatherford).

Anthropological observations suggest that the less complex a society is—or more precisely, the smaller and more cohesive a community is—the less likely its politics will involve government, or what we recognize as "the state." Anthropologists use a typology to classify pre-industrial political systems and, following Elman Service, distinguish between bands, tribes, chiefdoms, and states.

Bands, the smallest type of society, usually number fewer than 200 individuals. They are marked by a lack of specialization; the tasks of survival (such as hunting or locating water) are carried out collectively by band members. Typically, these foraging (hunting and gathering) societies establish a more or less stable equilibrium with their environment. Describing their politics, Lewellen notes: "Decision-making is usually a group enterprise and access to leadership positions is equally open to all males within a certain age range. Leadership, which temporarily shifts according to the

AUTHORITY IN PRE-INDUSTRIAL SOCIETIES

AUTHORITY IS...	PRE-INDUSTRIAL SOCIETY
DECENTRALIZED & EGALITARIAN	**BAND** refers to a small group of related people occupying a single region **TRIBE** refers to a group of bands occupying a specific region, that speak a common language, share a common culture, and are integrated by some unifying factor
CENTRALIZED & HIERARCHICAL	**CHIEFDOM** refers to a ranked society in which every member has a position in the hierarchy **STATE** refers, in anthropology, to a centralized political system with the power to coerce

(Haviland, 530–537)

Figure 2.2

situation, is based on the personal attributes of the individual and lacks any coercive power" (28).

This last point is crucial: in the absence of coercive power exercised by (or at the command of) a leader, all decisions must ultimately reflect a consensus, including any decision to punish a band member. An individual who refuses to accept the collective judgment risks expulsion from the community and, insofar as survival requires a mutual effort, the threat of death. More importantly, though, because individuals in such societies are unable to conceive of life outside the community, they are unlikely to refuse to accept its ways.

Moreover, a common culture reinforces the cohesion of the society: "the unity of the wider group is ... based on custom, tradition, and common values and symbols" (27).

The band provides a clear example of the homogeneous, shared life that we indicate with the term community. It demonstrates Laver's point (noted in Chapter 1) that where community is strong, government is superfluous. Decisions are the result of a consensus of the group, a consensus that may be preceded by considerable discussion or even debate but is a unity the group requires in order to get on with the necessary tasks of survival. There is no need for a government separate from the group as a whole (nor are there resources to sustain one), and because authority is not permanently placed in the hands of one or a few, all members are generally equal in power or status. For this reason, bands are characterized as **egalitarian** (meaning marked by equality, an absence of strata or classes), and uncentralized (authority or power is diffused among the group).

The tribe is a society in which, for practical reasons such as defence against other people, bands have joined into a larger group by means such as **kinship**. Tribal kinship systems vary tremendously and can be based on blood relationships and descent from common ancestors (consanguinity), relationships to a spouse's blood relatives (affinity), or mythological relationships such as a clan identified by its animal symbol (totem). Tribal peoples are often agriculturalists, and the tribe coordinates or regulates a much larger population than the band. As with bands, authority and power are dispersed throughout the community. The headman position, where it exists, often fulfills formal functions, such as providing a symbolic focus for tribal unity, rather than operating as a government. The authority of the tribal leader is mostly a product of personal traits; it is not institutionalized. In tribes, as in bands, there is often little to distinguish politics from the general life of the community.

In chiefdoms and states, authority has become a permanent feature of the social structure through its centralization in the hands of one or a few individuals and its institutionalization in political offices. Kottak defines an **office** as "a permanent position which must be refilled when it is vacated by death or retirement" (125). Authority belongs to the position, independent of whoever holds the position. This is the beginning of government.

EMERGENCE OF THE STATE

Why do peoples exchange egalitarian, uncentralized social forms for the centralized, inegalitarian chiefdom and state? Evidence suggests that it is a change brought about by circumstances, rather than one made deliberately. **Political centralization** or specialization accompanies (or is produced by) several other social changes:

- increasing population density
- stratification by rank or class
- new productive technology
- specialized social and occupational roles
- economics based on centralized redistribution

In other words, the state emerges where society has become larger, inequality has become a regular feature of the social structure, a division of labour has been employed, and the tasks of production have become more individual and specialized. Redistribution of products (i.e., taxing and granting) reflects these changes and can serve a variety of purposes—from stimulating production, to making scarce products available to all, to guarding against famine. This redistributive function is one reason for the centralization of political authority in chiefdoms and states, but there is also a crucial difference in how each of these societies uses redistribution.

The chiefdom seems to be a transitional stage between tribes and states, in which leadership is vested in an individual and is typically hereditary. The power of the chief comes from control of economic resources such as land or goods, or from leadership of a military force. However, enforcement of decisions is dependent on the ability of the chief to acquire loyalty by granting goods and benefits to individuals.

The egalitarian character of earlier societies is compromised not only by the concentration of public authority but also by a system of ranking, generally on the basis of kinship or lineage: "Every individual is ranked according to membership in a descent group: those closer to the chief's lineage will be higher on the scale and receive the deference of all those below" (Lewellen 37). While the former equality of the tribe or band has been eroded, there is as yet no sharp distinction between elites and non-elites in the chiefdom. While this inequality is manifested in a differential access to resources, as Kottak points out, "even the lowest-ranking person in a chiefdom was still the chief's relative. In such a kin-based context, everyone, even a chief, had to share with his or her relatives" (126).

In the move from tribe to chiefdom, authority and the power to enforce decisions cease to be exercised by the community as a whole and are placed instead in the hands of one or a few. In this transitional stage, the offices of government appear to be the personal property of those who occupy them. The further transition to the state brings about a **depersonalization** of this authority and an increase in the coercive resources that enforce decisions. Whereas the chief's ability to regulate was largely confined to withholding or bestowing

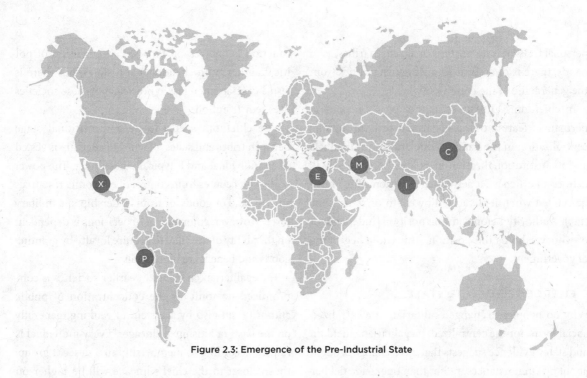

Figure 2.3: Emergence of the Pre-Industrial State

valued goods upon citizens, the state is characterized by its ability to apply physical sanctions against those who do not obey its decisions. This in turn requires the establishment of institutions and public employees to carry out these sanctions.

The first states appear to have emerged about 5,500 years ago, with an exchange of regulation through kinship networks for a "permanent administrative bureaucracy" (Lewellen 47). Another source defines the state as follows: "an autonomous political unit encompassing many communities within its territory, having a centralized government with the power to collect taxes, draft men for work or war, and decree and enforce laws" (Carneiro 735).

Three points are worth emphasizing here. First, permanent staffing of institutions of government changes the nature of redistribution. In earlier chiefdoms, or tribal "big man" systems, what was collected from the

people was largely returned to the people. By contrast, in permanently staffed institutions some of what the state collects must be kept to maintain the state.

Second, the stratification of society increases as we move from chiefdom to state; kinship is replaced by social strata based on differential access to wealth, power, and social status. Structures of inequality broaden and stiffen.

Third, as Lewellen notes, increased social complexity necessitates a depersonalization of decision making: "Because of the vast range of individual and class interests within a state, pressures and conflicts unknown in less complex societies necessitate some sort of rule of impersonal law, backed by physical sanctions, for the ongoing maintenance of the system" (40–41).

Haviland suggests that this is a move from internalized controls ("beliefs ... so thoroughly ingrained that each person becomes personally responsible for his or her own good conduct") to sanctions or externalized controls, a prime example of which is **law**, defined as "a social norm, the neglect or infraction of which is regularly met, in threat or in fact, by the application of physical force on the part of an individual or group possessing the socially recognized privilege of doing so" (544).

There is a good reason for the depersonalization of the authority that governs social life: social life itself has become depersonalized. The emergence of early (or archaic) states is in part a signal that societies have reached a stage where they can no longer be regulated solely by the mechanisms of community. The stratification and centralization that accompany the state are, in turn, evidence that what is held in common has diminished.

The state represents a revolution in terms of social organization, one that occurred independently in at least six different places: Mesopotamia(M), Egypt(E), India(I), China(C), Peru(P), and Mexico(X). Many explanations have been offered for the emergence of the state, from the idea that states emerged to build, maintain, and regulate irrigation systems, to Carneiro's theory that the state originates as the product of environmental pressures, population increase, and warfare. In other words, as the population of the tribe grows, the territory it inhabits is no longer able to sustain it. As the tribe expands its territory, it moves onto land used by others, creating conflict over scarce resources.

Over what may have been considerable periods of time, the state emerged to deal with problems posed by population growth, the persistent encounter with other peoples, and increasing economic and technological complexity. Given evidence that the human species has been around for between 150,000 and 200,000 years, the state is a relatively recent invention.

There are several general insights we can take from the anthropological record:

- As societies transition from band to state, they become *less* egalitarian and *less* participatory. That is to say, as population density increases, and as pressure on existing resources increases, political centralization also increases, and by the same token, popular input to and control over decisions decrease.
- As societies become more complex, the role of community (the *common life* that individuals share) in social organization is diminished, and that of the state (or government) increases.
- As societies become more populous, complex (differentiated by occupation and class), and technologically advanced, their political organizations become centralized, political offices become divorced from other social roles and occupations, and authority is more likely to require justification in turns of some set of public norms (see Chapter 1).

BACK TO BISMARCK: POLITICS AND THE STUDY OF POLITICS

A chapter about methods and approaches seems the best place for a reminder that the study of politics and the pursuit of politics are very different. The study of politics does not train one to be a political candidate, no more than a detailed, even academic study of baseball or music notation equips one to be a shortstop or a composer). The student whose interest in politics is *immediately* practical—wanting to *be* a politician or political aide—is best advised to become politically active: join a political party or interest group, become an intern, work in a political campaign, make political friends, allies, or contacts, and gain the experience that comes from participating in political life. This is not to suggest that the study of politics has no value for someone seeking a political career, just that studying politics will not by itself lead to such a career.

The study of politics should lead to an *understanding* of political institutions, processes, and behaviour, and understanding a thing always requires a degree of detachment from it. Someone with a very intense set of political beliefs may not be the best student of politics. As political scientists we are observers or spectators, but as political partisans or candidates, we are participants. The perspective of the participant may be important for our understanding of political activity, but it is also possible that the interest the participant

has in the outcome of political activity may blind him or her to important facts or considerations.

Such distinctions are, of course, more easily made than maintained. The study (and teaching) of politics is in many ways itself a political activity, one that may have or seek to have some impact on how authority is ultimately exercised. To put it another way, in theory, the study of politics is "disinterested" and political activity is "interested"; in practice, the study of politics often turns out to be "interested" too. Presumably, we engage in political activity to change the world in ways beneficial to ourselves and others, or to prevent others from changing the world in ways detrimental to ourselves and to others. In this way, we have an "interest" in outcomes that change or maintain the status quo, and insofar as each of us is likely to have a set of such interests, it is difficult not to bring them to our study of politics.

The dilemma, then, is that the study of politics invites us to adopt the "impartial" standpoint of the spectator, while the practice of politics and our situation as social actors make inevitable reference to our interested characters. The challenge is to fashion a proper compromise between these two elements. One approach is to attempt the pursuit of a disinterested political discourse *to the degree this is possible*, recognizing in the attempt that there are limits to its feasibility. Another is to discard the notion of disinterested analysis and simply pursue a frankly interested politics, in keeping with Karl Marx's dictum, "The philosophers have only *interpreted* the world, in various ways; the point, however, is to *change* it" (*Theses on Feuerbach*). It may well be that the previous path—the attempt at disinterested analysis—must be travelled first, in order to arrive at the places where the world may be changed.

APPLIED POLITICS

At least three postsecondary institutions in the United States offer a graduate degree (master's level) in Applied Politics: the American University in Washington DC, the University of Akron, and Florida State University. These courses are designed for those who wish to be directly engaged in political life, either as candidates for office, or, more likely, working for elected politicians or political parties. Courses in these programs include the following: Fundamentals of Political Management; The Campaign Process; Campaign Finance; Survey Research Methods; Political Communication and Message Development; Lobbying; and Interest Groups, Advocacy Organizations, and Think Tanks.

REFERENCES

Barabas, Jason, and Jennifer Jerit. "Are Survey Experiments Externally Valid?" *American Political Science Review* 104.2 (2010): 226–242.

Carneiro, R.L. "A Theory of the Origin of the State." *Science* 69 (1970): 733–738.

Easton, David. *A Systems Analysis of Political Life*. Chicago: University of Chicago Press, 1965.

Haviland, William A. *Anthropology*. 6th ed. Orlando, FL: Holt, Rinehart and Winston, 1991.

Hirschman, Albert. "The Search for Paradigms as a Hindrance to Understanding." *World Politics* 22.3 (1970): 329–343.

Judson, Olivia. "The Selfless Gene." *The Atlantic Magazine* (October 2007): 89–98.

Kottak, Conrad Phillip. *Cultural Anthropology*. 5th ed. New York: McGraw-Hill, 1991.

Lavine, Howard. "On-line versus Memory-Based Process Models of Political Evaluation." *Political Psychology*. Ed. Kristen Monroe. Mahwah, NJ: Lawrence Erlbaum Associates, 2002. 225–247.

Lewellen, Ted C. *Political Anthropology: An Introduction*. 2nd ed. South Hadley, MA: Bergin & Garvey, 1992.

Manzer, Ronald. *Canada: A Socio-Political Report*. Toronto: McGraw-Hill Ryerson, 1974.

Mead, Lawrence. "Scholasticism in Political Science." *Perspectives on Politics* 8.2 (June 2010): 453–464.

Paun, Akash, and Robert Hazell. "Hung Parliaments and the Challenges for Westminster and Whitehall." *The Political Quarterly* 81.2 (April-June 2010): 213–227.

Service, Elman. *Primitive Social Organization: An Evolutionary Perspective*. New York: Random House, 1962.

Sil, Rudgra, and Peter J. Katzenstein. "Analytical Eclecticism in the Study of World Politics." *Perspectives on Politics* 8.2 (June 2010): 411–431.

Weatherford, J. McIver. *Tribes on the Hill*. New York: Rawson, Wade, 1981.

FURTHER READING

Alford, John R., and John R. Hibbing. "The Origin of Politics: An Evolutionary Theory of Political Behavior." *Perspectives on Politics* 2.4 (December 2004):707–723.

Dryzek, John S. "Revolutions without Enemies: Key Transformations in Political Science." *American Political Science Review* 100.4 (November 2006): 487–492.

Gunnell, John G. "Dislocated Rhetoric: The Anomaly of Political Theory." *The Journal of Politics* 68.4 (November 2006): 771–782.

Hochschild, Jennifer L. "APSA Presidents Reflect on Political Science: Who Knows What, When, and How?" *Perspectives on Politics* 3.2 (June 2005): 309–334.

Lewelln, Ted C. *Political Anthropology*. 3rd ed. Westport CT: Praeger, 2003.

Milner, Henry. "Are Young Canadians Becoming Political Dropouts?" *IRPP Choices* 11.3 (June 2005): 1–26.

Ware, Alan. "Old Political Issues and Contemporary Political Science." *Government and Opposition* 38.4 (October 2003): 517–535.

CHAPTER 3

From *The Republic* to the Liberal Republic— History and Ideas

"Governments have never learned anything from history, or acted on principles deducted from it."

—GEORG WILHELM FRIEDRICH HEGEL, PRUSSIAN PHILOSOPHER

"Those who cannot remember the past are condemned to repeat it."

—GEORGE SANTAYANA, SPANISH-AMERICAN PHILOSOPHER

...WHICH PROVIDES THE READER WITH

- an overview of the major periods of political history in the West
- brief sketches of representative political philosophers from these eras
- a look at the religious, intellectual, and economic transformations accompanying the transition from feudalism to the modern nation-state
- an explanation of the revolution that led to liberal government

It is easy to overlook the contribution that historical knowledge brings to political studies. The pace of change in our lives today makes it difficult to understand the world our parents grew up in, let alone life in centuries past. Nonetheless, every institution and every political idea has a history. So, especially, do our common law and constitutional **jurisprudence**, which rest (in the Anglo-American world) on **precedents** (the principle of *stare decisis*—for a longer explanation, google "stare decisis Perell"). Without history, we are perpetually in the present, like someone whose memories vanish each time he or she sleeps, waking to amnesia each day. History relates where we have been, how we got here rather than somewhere else, and some idea of our possible tomorrows. It can provide insights into the forces that shape our lives, as well as

HISTORY AS A REALITY CHECK FOR POLICY-MAKERS

In the aftermath of the defeat of the Iraqi army and the fall of Saddam Hussein, many US policy-makers seemed to believe that the institutions and practices of democracy, if not of liberal democracy, would be embraced by the Iraqi people, who had been suppressed by dictatorship for so long. In an article originally published in *Society* and excerpted in *Harper's Magazine*, noted anthropologist Robin Fox questioned the general assumption "in the West ... that people everywhere aspire to a state of liberal democratic polity where human rights and the rights of women will be assured and tolerance and religious freedom will be institutionalized. It is to their constant embarrassment that this does not happen" (17).

The problem here, Fox suggests, is that a historical perspective is missing, one that would remind us that "the institutions we so prize are ... the result of many centuries of effort.... We maintain them with constant vigilance and the support of hard-won economic, political, legal, and social structures. These have taken literally thousands of years to put in place" (17).

One theme of this book is the depersonalization of authority that is part of the process involved in developing the institutions of the state, a political process that reflects the social changes that take place as the strength of community diminishes. As an anthropologist, Fox argues that in places such as Iraq, the sociological pre-conditions for democracy are not present:

"Iraq, like the other countries of the region, still stands at a level of social evolution where the family, clan, tribe, and sect command major allegiance, and the idea of the individual autonomous voter, necessary and commonplace in our own systems, is totally foreign" (18).

Interestingly, Fox's description of the historical journey that has brought some regimes to liberal democracy could stand as a synopsis for the rest of this chapter: "In the West we had to move from tribalism, through empire, feudalism, mercantile capitalism, and the Industrial Revolution to reach our present state of fragile democracy (shrugging off communism and fascism along the way)" (21).

Moreover, Fox suggests there is artificiality to our current way of life: "In making this move we had to change the entire communalistic, ritualistic, kinship-dominated society that is natural to us" (21).

a record of our successes and failures in attempting to change our fate.

On the other hand, history is time consuming (small, intended joke), involves much reading, and introduces us to unfamiliar language, ideas, and situations. In our current world of instant information access, we have an abundance of history, literally, in the palms of our hands, but little time for its study.

A serious impediment for students of all ages is that much of history offends our contemporary modern values and sensibilities—history refuses to be politically correct. From the ancient Greeks to nineteenth-century America, enslavement is a theme in history; from the ancient Greeks to twentieth-century Canada, women are not considered to be "persons." Crusades, inquisitions, holy wars, pogroms, exterminations, and assorted imperialisms detail the violent subjugation or elimination of one population by another over the centuries. Hegel once noted that the ages of human happiness are blank pages in the book of history; on the other hand, the voices of the vanquished—women, people of colour, aboriginal peoples on all continents, ethnic and religious minorities in all ages—are also missing on much of history's soundtrack.

Like philosophy and literature, much of political history is the record of **DWEM**s (dead, white European males). So, too, is this chapter a much too condensed and superficial background to political history and the political ideas expressed by some of its influential philosophers. However, it provides a context to the remaining chapters that some may find useful. The following topical notes provide two additional arguments for an attention to the historical dimension of politics, one methodological and one practical.

World historian J. M. Roberts has argued that the principal theme of human history in the last 2000 years has been the rise and fall of Western Europe's world domination. Political models and principles produced by European culture were exported to (or imposed on) most nations, regardless of their unique religious or cultural traditions. His point is not to suggest the superiority of European culture, but simply to note its historical dominance and the political legacy of that dominance; political history *has been* Eurocentric in important ways that cannot be ignored (as opponents of **imperialism** have always recognized). At the same time, themes presented below in their European context, such as empire and feudalism, have also had their part in the history of other nations, such as China, India, and Japan.

Political history can be divided into three broadly defined periods—**classical antiquity**, the **medieval age**, and **modernity** (see *Figure 3.1: Western European Political History*)—and it is the passage from the second to the last that is most relevant. What generally characterizes regimes in "the West," or what the West

HISTORY AS AN AID TO EMPIRICAL RESEARCH

In a May 2010 article, Marcus Kreuzer discusses the importance of paying attention to history for political scientists who are engaged in empirical research. One area where this matters is studying institutions and their effects, a topic of obvious interest to comparative political scientists. We noted in Chapter 2 that it is sometimes not clear if the independent variable is in fact independent, or, like the dependent variable, the product of some other factor. For example, if we wished to measure the degree to which the number of campaign workers influences a candidate's electoral chances, we would face the problem that the number of campaign workers is influenced by the candidate's electoral chances. Candidates perceived as having a reasonable chance of succeeding will attract more volunteers than candidates perceived to have no hope of success. In technical terms this is known as **endogeneity**—when a factor that is supposed to influence a specific result is itself influenced by that result. Kreuzer suggests that attention to the historical beginnings of institutions can clarify their relationship to other phenomena associated with them (i.e., which is cause, which is effect?). The specific case discussed in the article is whether proportional-representation electoral systems have political or economic origins.

Secondly, Kreuzer highlights the belief of scientists that research becomes more scientific the greater the number of observations made. Common sense alone suggests that increasing the sample size would diminish the impact of unusual events on the conclusions of the research. However, Kreuzer notes that critics of this view have argued that "every increase in the number of observations invariably results in a loss of contextual, historical knowledge," so that "quantitative analysis is prone to make mistakes when it turns proper names into variables and words into numbers" (369).

	CLASSICAL ANTIQUITY 400 BCE – 400 CE	MEDIEVAL ERA 400 – 1400 CE	MODERNITY 1400 –
FORM OF GOVERNMENT	from polis to empire	feudal fiefdom to absolute monarchy	representative government to liberal democracy
MORAL-POLITICAL CONCEPTS	virtue citizenship	natural law divine right	popular sovereignty individual rights
ECONOMIC MODES	slavery agrarian military	agrarian military trading	mercantile commercial industrial
RELIGION	pagan	Catholic Christianity Islam	religious pluralism secularism
INTELLECTUAL APPROACH	philosophical	scholastic	scientific

Figure 3.1: Western European Political History

calls the "developed world," is that they are products of the transformation from the feudal kingdoms of the medieval age to modern **nation-states**, a multi-faceted transformation that was not only political but also economic, cultural, religious, scientific, and perhaps even psychological.

CLASSICAL ANTIQUITY

Once upon a time and not so long ago a good education was considered to require the study of Latin or Greek. Ancient Greece and Rome were the epitomes of classical civilization, in which the arts and sciences flourished to a degree not to be seen in Europe for centuries after the demise of these empires. Much of our political vocabulary has its roots here, from terms such as "democracy," "monarchy," "dictatorship," "republic," and "citizen," to institutions such as "Senate" and "Council," to the very word "politics" itself. The ancient texts of Plato, Aristotle, Cicero, Seneca, and others heavily influenced political thought well into

the nineteenth century. This was possible only because classical texts were preserved by Arab and Greek scholars in the Middle East and returned to Europe in sufficient time to influence the period of intellectual and artistic development known as the Renaissance. Two specific points about classical antiquity are noteworthy.

First is the absence of what we would recognize today as the nation-state. Politics in this period was either local or global: the political unit was the city-state, such as Athens or Sparta, or the empire, such as those assembled by Alexander the Great or Caesar Augustus. In the former case, it was possible for politics to be highly participatory, engaging the energies and attention (at least at times) of a considerable portion of the population. In the empire, however, politics was not primarily participatory (except for limited periods in Rome) but military. The organization, extent, and skill of Rome's armies kept Rome's empire together, just as military defeat at the hands of the nomadic warrior tribes from the East ultimately brought the empire to an end.

Missing in either case, local or global, was an adequate civil service (one advantage Chinese dynasties had over their European counterparts). Without it, the city-state could not expand beyond a certain size *except* militarily. Empires could grow so enormous because they were primarily about military security, not about providing public or political goods to their populations. Nation-states would not emerge in Western Europe until the end of the feudal period.

The second point of interest is the sheer diversity of political organizations and types of government in this period. Most of the terms we use to describe different forms of government come from the classical period, a time in which a primary theme was "What is the best form of state?" It is not just that there were so many Greek city-states, but also that within each **polis** there was much upheaval as one form of government replaced another, peaceably or otherwise. Related issues of importance were stability, legitimacy, and obligation.

THINKERS FROM ANTIQUITY: PLATO AND ARISTOTLE

Plato and Aristotle were active in fourth-century BCE Athens, the leading polis of the Greek city-states. The challenges of governing such political entities preoccupied both thinkers in their political writings. The city-states of this period were agrarian, pre-industrial societies, dependent on the continued exploitation of a large class of slaves, many of whom were foreigners captured in war.[1] Primitive by our standards in technology and practical science, these societies were advanced in philosophy and the cultivation of the arts. During this time, Athens was a democracy; the most important decisions were made by an Assembly of all the citizens (this excluded women and children, slaves, and foreigners)—that is, by all those who chose to attend the business of the Assembly. A Council of Five Hundred, chosen by lot, set the agenda for the Assembly. Neither Plato nor Aristotle was a democrat, although Aristotle's objections to democracy were milder than Plato's.

Copy of Bust of Plato by Silanion. Photo by Marie-Lan Nguyeon.

PLATO

Plato's philosophy is presented in conversations between young Athenian noblemen and the philosopher Socrates (who presents Plato's position). In these Dialogues, Socrates challenges the common-sense opinions of his companions by rigorous questioning (the Socratic method), leading the speakers into contradictions that reveal the flaws of their initial positions. Socrates always tries to move his audience from opinion, which is uncritical and conventional, to knowledge, which is critical and discloses the true nature of things.[2] Plato believed that behind the change and chaos of the world presented by our senses lies an enduring reality—the Forms—that can be approached only through thought.

The principal theme of Plato's most famous political work, *The Republic*, is the nature of justice—that is, how the people are to be ruled. After demonstrating the weakness of conventional understandings of justice, Socrates convinces his listeners that the human soul has three parts: a rational part, a spirited or courageous part, and an appetitive part. In the soul, justice consists of each part performing its own function, which means the rational part rules the appetitive part (mind over body, intellect over senses) and does so with the aid of the spirited part.

Justice in the *ideal* city parallels justice in the soul, for the city has three classes corresponding to the three parts of the soul. The Guardians (the rational class) deliberate about the city, assisted by the Auxiliaries (the spirited class), courageous warriors who preserve the city from external foes and internal dissension. The largest class is the Artisans, citizens concerned with the mundane business of acquiring wealth. Justice in the city consists of each class performing its proper function. Plato believes that individuals are determined by nature for one class or another.

Much of *The Republic* concerns the education and training of the Guardians and the nature of their living. Since the Guardians are to put the good of the city ahead of their own desires, Plato recommends a primitive communism (no private property, no monogamy) *for this class*. From the Guardians will come philosophers (or a philosopher) fit to rule, but, because philosophers love knowledge and prefer to spend their time contemplating the Forms, a philosopher-king will have to be forced to rule.[3]

Plato's theory of human nature is obviously not compatible with democracy, since it holds that most people are suited by neither aptitude nor inclination for making wise political decisions. Governing should be left to those whose natures are suited to that role. On the other hand, Plato believes that ruling is an activity undertaken for the benefit of those who are ruled, not to serve the interest(s) of the rulers. While Plato emphasizes the importance of innate character, he also believes that a noble nature remains merely a potential without the proper nurture and education. One of his lasting achievements was the Academy, founded to provide the education that would ennoble character. This school lasted for several centuries.

ARISTOTLE

The most famous student (and later one of its teachers) to emerge from Plato's Academy was Aristotle. Sinclair (210–11) contrasts Aristotle—"a middle-class professional man, a husband and a father, scientific observer and practical administrator"—with Plato—"the Athenian aristocrat, mystic, ascetic, [and] puritan"—and identifies the following non-Platonic features of Aristotle's politics: "the value of family life, the pursuit of health and happiness, property, [and] respect for public opinion." Perhaps most importantly, for Aristotle, politics is the art of the possible.

Aristotle believes that the Forms are inseparable from the matter that is common to particulars. The

Copy of Bust of Aristotle by Lysippus.

dualism between idea and matter, or mind and senses in Plato's metaphysics, is missing. Central to Aristotle's thought is the idea that everything has a *telos*, an end or purpose to which it strives or is destined or develops. This concept provides a more universal or implicitly egalitarian view of humanity—whatever our differences, as human beings we share a common telos. Aristotle's *Metaphysics* begins with a statement that Plato could never have uttered: "All men by nature desire to know." Like Plato, Aristotle does not question that slavery is natural, and he believes in a natural distinction between women and men. However, while accepting hierarchy and patriarchy, Aristotle presents one human essence, which is present in an inferior or superior manifestation in all individuals.

In both his *Ethics* and *Politics*, Aristotle is concerned with how persons realize the telos that is uniquely human. First, he distinguishes between theoretical and practical reason. Suitable for the study of nature, theoretical reason uncovers necessary and universal laws that constitute knowledge or science. Appropriate for human affairs, practical reason is situational or contextual and produces wisdom or judgment. On this view, the reasoning we bring to politics is fallible and gained only through experience; wisdom is as much a product of age as of intelligence.

Our telos, Aristotle argues, is to seek *eudaemonia*, which is often translated as "happiness" but may be more accurately presented by the term "well-being." Well-being, for Aristotle, comes with living in accordance with virtue—the pursuit of intellectual excellence or acting on our desires in a rational way. Realizing our telos requires education, and this rests on a foundation of good laws. In this way Aristotle's ethics leads to his politics; conversely, the purpose of political life is to present the opportunity for us to realize our telos—to live a virtuous life. We cannot be moral beings in a corrupt city or polis. Like Plato, Aristotle puts little value on the pursuit of wealth (which is why it is the business of one's slaves). Properly understood, money or wealth simply provides us with the leisure to take part in civic life, to cultivate our sense of virtue, and to develop and exercise wise judgment. The primary purpose of the state is educative, and we cannot benefit from this education unless we participate in the politics of the state.

The concept of citizenship is central to Aristotle, who notes as follows: "But since we hold that the same qualities are needed for citizen and for ruler and for the best man, and that the same man should be first ruled and later ruler, it immediately becomes an essential task of the planner of a constitution to ensure that all men shall be good men, to consider what practices will make them so, and what is the end or aim of the best life" (286; *Politics*, Book VII, Chapter 14). To be a good citizen it is necessary to fulfil the telos of being human, but not all can be citizens. To be a citizen is to have the right to share in judicial or deliberative office, and Aristotle accepts the common view that certain classes of people (e.g., slaves, women, foreigners) will never possess citizenship. In addition, who qualifies as a citizen varies from one constitution to another (that is, according to the type of government).[4] Whatever the type of constitution, the citizen will be someone engaged in ruling *and* being ruled, and Aristotle defines the excellence

of the good citizen as "understanding the governing of free men by free men" (110; Book III, Chapter 4).

Like Plato, Aristotle believes that political authority, properly exercised, is directed to the common good. Hence, any regime serving the common advantage is just, and any that pursues a partial interest is corrupt, regardless of who rules (see Chapter 1). Aristotle seems to accept that the best regime is determined by circumstances and social conditions, which vary from polis to polis. Unlike Plato, he believes that many heads are better than one (or a few): "For it is possible that the many, no one of whom taken singly is a good man, may yet taken all together be better than the few, not individually but collectively .... there is no reason in any given case we should not accept and apply this theory of the collective wisdom of the multitude" (123; Book III, Chapter 11).

Lastly, Aristotle considers whether we should be governed by the wisdom of wise rulers or by the impartial neutrality of laws. While the modern answer has been to institutionalize the rule of law, Aristotle notes that with the impartiality of law comes inflexibility, an inability to account for differences in circumstance or application. Ultimately, he argues that the rule of law is to be preferred, but matters that law cannot deal with adequately are best decided by many individuals rather than one or a few. As to what these matters might be, Aristotle is less clear.

1 Slavery is slavery, but in classical antiquity Greek slaves could enjoy a considerable amount of freedom and authority *within* the households where they were kept and were probably better off than most medieval peasants or early nineteenth-century proletarians, all things being equal. The *fact* of slavery was not an issue during the time of Plato or Aristotle; as an institution of civil society, it was taken for granted.

2 This view of knowledge and philosophy is very much out of fashion in many circles of contemporary philosophy.

3 The city depicted in *The Republic* seems so unlikely to some commentators that they suggest Plato actually intended the book as an argument *against* political idealism.

4 One of Aristotle's preparations for his *Politics* was a study of 158 Greek constitutions.

FEUDAL SOCIETY
(THE MEDIEVAL ERA)

The end of the (Western) Roman Empire in the fifth century was brought about by the migration of population from Eastern Europe and Central Asia. Nomadic warrior societies, pushed westward by other peoples behind them, defeated the armies of an aging empire. Much of the politics and society of the medieval period reflects a mix of tribal customs and traditional ways with imperial remnants, such as Roman law and the Catholic Church. Pagan tribes converted to Christianity, and tribal customs and rules were incorporated into codified laws. The political product was **feudalism**.

In feudal society, authority was fragmented. Tribes that had united for military purposes under a powerful chieftain or king dispersed after victory. Authority was exercised by local nobles, whose position reflected military rank or prowess. Although there were attempts to reconstitute the Roman Empire, a medieval monarch was at most a "chief of chiefs" rather than someone who personally governed.

Reflecting its tribal roots, medieval authority was largely personal and justified on traditional grounds; **hereditary monarchy**, a product of this period, is a classic example of the selection of leaders based on custom, tradition, and adherence to "accepted ways." At the same time, leaders worked to secure a higher authority, eventually creating the doctrine of the **divine right of kings**, which claims they are anointed and justified by God in their exercise of power.

It is not possible to overstate the significance of religion in the medieval period. The Roman Empire had spread Christianity throughout the areas its legions controlled, and though the Empire died, the Church survived and grew. The religious unification of Europe under Catholic Christianity meant that its rulers claimed justification under the same God and sought the blessing of the Pope (head of the Church), as well as his ruling to settle disputes about title. Medieval politics was often focused on the relationship between the state and the Church, or between political and **ecclesiastical** authority, which were often enough in conflict.

Political authority was fragmented and weak, and the material ability of rulers to exercise power was limited by the relative absence of resources and the difficulty of transporting them. While these rulers may have been "absolute," unchecked by the niceties of constitutions or other limits to their authority, their ability to enforce this authority over any substantial territory (i.e., their *power*) was often quite limited.

Conversely, the influence of the Church reflected a universal authority grounded in a common religious creed. According to Roman Catholic doctrine, believers are re-united with God by means of their participation in the Church's sacraments, which include baptism, marriage, and extreme unction (last rites). By withholding the sacraments (**excommunication**) the Church could deprive individuals of the channels by which they might receive God's grace.

In this context, rulers sought favour from the Church in order to enhance their legitimacy, while the Church relied upon the power of the local state to enforce its pronouncements, eliminate heretics, and provide and protect Church resources. Church and state needed each other, while often disputing which of them should have the final word.

In feudalism, most individuals were engaged in **subsistence agriculture** and the performance of obligations to nobility and to the Church. They did not own the land they worked but were tenants on the estates

Alnwick Castle. Northumberland, United Kingdom.

of the local aristocrat, paying rent from what they produced from the land. In return, they received protection from the lord against assault or invasion and hope for salvation through the mediation of the Church. While the preponderance of obligations fell on the peasantry, the justification for this was the common good of the community, for which the feudal lord was ultimately responsible. The relationship of peasant and feudal lord was mirrored in the relationship between different levels of nobility: what the peasant owed to his local lord, the local lord owed to the duke or prince, who in turn was obliged to the king or emperor. In other words, medieval society presented an **organic hierarchy**—hierarchical because it was a structure of unequal resources and power, but organic because the various components were linked by reciprocal obligations and duties.

Much of the medieval period is marked by struggles among the nobility, usually settled by battle, to establish positions within this hierarchy of claims and obligations. The laws promulgated by a monarch would extend only so far as the ability to enforce them, or as far as the willingness of vassals (the nobles loyal to the monarch) to enforce them on the monarch's behalf. These vassals, in turn, would make and enforce their own laws to the extent of their ability. While law might announce common standards for a kingdom, in practice it was as fragmented as the political power enforcing it and, on a local level, reflected the traditional practices and customs of the community.

The idea of **social mobility** was foreign to feudal society. Social position, high or low, was inherited and came with obligations and rights specific to it. Feudal society reinforced connections between entrenched social positions. This durable form of living lasted for centuries, for almost a millennium, accommodating development and change. However, it could not be reconciled with the more powerful forces of social change that arose in the fifteenth and sixteenth centuries to produce a social and political revolution.

As historical scholarship has improved our knowledge of the feudal era, it has become possible to recognize its often rich cultural life—of which the Renaissance was the highest statement—and to understand how important social and political changes occurred within the static, conservative structure of the feudal order. Chief among these was the gradual development of nation-states out of the assortment of feudal principalities, dukedoms, and fiefs. This required the development and strengthening of real power in the hands of monarchs, enabling them to back up their claims to rule in the face of challenges from subordinates or external rivals. The development of the nation-state and of absolute monarchy

was generally coincident, accompanied by a corresponding decline in the power or influence of the lesser nobility. The ability of monarchs to consolidate and make real their claim to rule varied from state to state. Germany and Italy, for example, were among the last of the large European nations to be effectively united into kingdoms (the first form of the modern European nation-state), with consequences that influenced their politics well into the twentieth century.

The medieval period ended when the forces of social change became strong enough to dissolve the bonds that held together the feudal structure. Sometimes change was gradual, and sometimes it was explosive. The dissolution of feudal society, in formal terms at least (some of its sociological effects, such as the importance of social class, persist in Europe today), was largely accomplished in England by the end of the seventeenth century, but not complete in Germany until well into the nineteenth century, and only came to Russia early in the twentieth century. Three changes accompanying the end of the feudal era had something to do with its demise: the **Reformation,** the **Enlightenment,** and the **market economy.**

THINKERS FROM THE MEDIEVAL ERA: AQUINAS AND MACHIAVELLI

Thomas Aquinas wrote some sixteen centuries after Aristotle, and Niccolò Machiavelli another 250 years after Aquinas. Such gaps imply that nothing much was happening in political philosophy for a very long time, but schools of Greek philosophy such as the Sceptics and Stoics have been skipped over, as well as Roman thinkers such as Cicero and Tacitus, and Augustine, who attempted to join Christian theology to the philosophies of Cicero and Plato. All in all,

though, developments in political philosophy in the medieval period reflect the relatively slow pace of political development in feudal society.

AQUINAS (1225–1274)

With Thomas Aquinas philosophy becomes a dialogue with thinkers from the past that is situated within a tradition. Aquinas synthesizes Aristotelian philosophy with the Christian theology of Augustine.

Since Augustine was indebted to Cicero and Plato, much of the European philosophic tradition was present in Aquinas's system. In the late nineteenth and early twentieth centuries, papal pronouncements confirmed Aquinas's philosophy as a body of thought with which all (Roman Catholic) teachers of "mental philosophy and theology" are expected to agree.

Aquinas also demonstrates how philosophy can reflect the socio-historical context. Just as medieval politics was dominated by the often fractious relationship between Church and state, medieval political philosophy was concerned with the relationships between royal and ecclesiastical (Church) authority. In Aquinas's time, universities were emerging as schools of professional instruction in medicine, law, and the arts, and for the special training of monks and priests. They were generally run by the Church, the main source and support of intellectual life throughout the medieval period. Thinkers like Aquinas, whose teachings received official Church approval and were the basis of university curricula, became known as Scholastics, and medieval philosophy as Scholasticism.

Two important differences between medieval and classical philosophy result from Christianity's presence. One is the devaluation of political life in light of the belief in an ultimate destination beyond this world for all souls. By suggesting that our telos is not realized in this world, Christianity challenges Aristotle's view that political life is our highest activity or calling. Augustine had argued that we may be citizens of two worlds: the worldly polis of men

Medieval time: Sundial on Church of St. Mary and St. Alkeda. North Yorkshire, United Kingdom.

or the heavenly city of God. The true believer will regard secular purposes, punishments, and rewards as secondary to those of the world to come.

The second large contribution Christianity makes is its emphasis on a universal kingdom of all believers, regardless of nation, state, or status.[1] The centrality of the polis in Greek political thought, the ultimate identification of authority with the community, no longer makes sense. Medieval thinkers like Aquinas no longer understood humans to be political animals in the way that Aristotle had proposed.

Medieval philosophy left subsequent generations with the notion of **natural law**. Just as science would identify "laws of nature" (e.g., the second law of thermodynamics), which appear to govern the physical world, thinkers like Aquinas believed there was a natural law to govern the moral and political realm. On this view, natural law is part of how God has structured the universe, and as creatures with reason, we are especially capable of recognizing it and are obliged to follow it. As Fortin (248–275) puts it:

Precisely because he is endowed with reason man participates more perfectly than all other natural beings in the order of divine providence. . . . As dictates of practical reason these principles constitute a "law," promulgated by nature itself, which enables him to discriminate between right and wrong and serves as the infallible criterium of the goodness or badness of his actions. . . . Since they are considered to be laws in the strict and proper sense of the term, the moral principles in question take on a compulsory character they did not have for Aristotle and the philosophic tradition generally. For the natural law ... clearly presupposes both the personal immortality of the human soul and the existence of an all-knowing and all-powerful God who rules the world with wisdom and equity and in whose eyes all individual human actions are either meritorious or deserving of punishment.

Natural law in the moral sense will appear curious to many readers and not particularly helpful in understanding today's political institutions and practices. However, many of the early modern political philosophers who *have* exerted considerable influence on modern political culture began by using or rejecting the language of natural law. It has also contributed to more durable ideas such as "principles of fundamental justice" and "natural rights."

MACHIAVELLI (1469–1527)

Whereas Aquinas followed Aristotle in identifying politics with ethics, Machiavelli is famous (or infamous) for identifying politics with immorality in his doctrine that the end justifies the means. Regarded by many as the first truly modern political thinker, Machiavelli is also linked to classical political thinkers through the Italian Renaissance and his attraction to the **civic republicanism** of ancient Rome. What made Machiavelli's reputation was his rejection of natural law *and* of the classical notion that political rule is ethical activity. The goods that Machiavelli recognizes are power, greatness, and fame; *virtu* represents the qualities that contribute to attaining these goods.

While Machiavelli seems to view political power as a good in itself, the end that he most consistently promotes is the creation, nourishment, and expansion of the nation-state, ideally conceived as a republic. When Machiavelli condones unethical or immoral activity by rulers, it is to stabilize, strengthen, or expand the state, not because it brings personal gain or pleasure to the rulers. This concern for the health of the state makes him, like the nation-state itself, particularly modern, and the last chapter of *The Prince* (his most famous work) is one of the first great statements of nationalism.

Machiavelli stands apart in his focus on the possible; a pessimist (or realist, depending on one's perspective), he does not believe that wisdom, virtue, and good government are necessarily connected. In classical times and during much of the medieval era, the idea that one might choose between being rational and being virtuous would have been nonsense. By Machiavelli's time, and clearly in his thought, this equation of goodness and reason has been broken; the wise man may well choose what is immoral or unethical for the sake of some other (non-moral) good, such as the security of the state or the extension of empire.

The view that reason is **instrumental** (capable of serving any number of purposes—good, evil, or indifferent) is very much part of the culture of the modern world. One factor contributing to the dissolution of the identity of reason and virtue is an increasing diversity of perspectives on what is good, or virtuous, or right. Out of this diversity, in part, comes the modern reliance on institutions and rules to be the guarantor of good government rather than good character. To the degree that Machiavelli remains focused on the character and judgment of rulers—to the degree that he is concerned with "greatness"—he remains typical of late medieval thought and the age of kings.

1 One should not look for evidence that ordinary people benefited from the effect of this doctrine on those with political or ecclesiastical power.

Stone altar. Stiftskirche, Stuttgart, Germany.

THE REFORMATION

The Reformation refers to the end of the religious and cultural domination of the (Roman) Catholic Church. It is usually dated from Martin Luther's rebellion in 1517, but this was only the first in a series of upheavals that established various Protestant sects within Christianity and in doing so produced widespread social unrest, including war between and within states. (Good search terms for background on this matter include "Lutheranism," "Edict of Worms," "Diet of Speyer," and "Thirty Years' War.")

Politically, the Reformation shattered the unity of religious life within Western Europe and undermined the authority of the Catholic Church. Rulers who converted to one of the Protestant faiths could establish their independence from the Church at Rome and shape laws and practices free of ecclesiastical influence. Monarchs often found religion a useful pretence, or the basis of a duty, to go to war against rulers of the opposite conviction. But most immediately, for the ordinary individual, the establishment of reformed Christianity (which did not take hold or was suppressed in some nations, such as France, Spain, and Italy) brought an increased measure of individual freedom. The Reformation brought liberation from the authoritative obligations and duties imposed by the Catholic Church and an increased emphasis on individual conscience and self-direction. For Protestant theology, the idea of "excommunication," discussed above, is meaningless: a person receives God's grace by faith alone.

Notwithstanding this, the demands that a Reformed church placed upon its adherents could often be as unbending as any other doctrine, and the end of the Roman Church's monopoly did not create religious pluralism. In most cases, one established church (Roman Catholic) was replaced with another (e.g., the Church of England in the United Kingdom, or Lutheranism in the Scandinavian countries and many German principalities). For a long time, to be a Protestant in an officially Catholic country or a Catholic in an officially Protestant country was to guarantee discrimination, invite persecution, and risk death.

THE ENLIGHTENMENT

The Enlightenment was a revolution against traditional ways of seeing the world and the approaches to science and natural history that prevailed in the medieval period (i.e., Scholasticism). In an age when education was provided mostly by men of the Church, medieval thought explained the world in a way that was consistent with Catholic theology. For example, the theoretical conclusion of Polish mathematician Nicolaus Copernicus—that the earth and other planets orbit the sun—and the confirming observations of Italian astronomer Galileo, were denounced by the Church for contradicting the biblical account of the creation of the earth. Although Copernicus was long dead, Galileo was forced to recant his findings and spend the rest of his life under house arrest. In place of faith and tradition, the Enlightenment put reason and science.

It is not a coincidence that the Enlightenment followed on the heels of the Reformation, but it flourished because its new explanations of the world could be applied practically to demonstrate their superiority to traditional accounts. When new thinking led to new ways of doing, theology had to give way. The term "Enlightenment" included several (sometimes opposing) approaches to understanding the world, such as idealism, **empiricism**, **rationalism**, **utilitarianism**, and **materialism**. All the same, unity was provided by an emphasis on reason and a scientific approach to understanding the world. Critical reflection on experience was at the heart of the Enlightenment.

Statue of Friedrich Schiller, Enlightenment thinker and poet. Schillerplatz, Stuttgart, Germany.

Complementing the emphasis on the examination of experience was an intellectual skepticism, a disposition to take nothing for granted, to question, probe, and challenge existing ways of thought in order to uncover and eliminate error, weakness, or inconsistency. All traditional theories or explanations, whether scientific, religious, political, or moral, were open to challenge by the Enlightenment. The fundamental premise of all Enlightenment thought was that experience, in the natural world or in social life, is accessible to human reason and explicable in rational terms.

The Enlightenment had a profound impact on feudal society because it challenged all existing ways of living and the justifications offered for them. Skepticism undermines traditional rationales for political institutions; the arrangements of society, like all else, are open to inspection. Understanding matters rationally carries with it the imperative to organize and conduct life rationally; this was a doctrine with revolutionary implications in a society governed by traditional institutions. Many of our key political ideas and public values—liberty, equality, popular sovereignty, the rule of law, and rights (or what we now think these terms mean)—are products of the critical reflection on political experience by Enlightenment thinkers. Ultimately, the Enlightenment proposed that each individual has, in his or her ability to reason, a means for reflecting on the world, for judging that world, and for changing it.

THE MARKET ECONOMY

The Reformation and the Enlightenment were revolutions in the way people thought and believed that changed how they lived their lives. The growth of the market economy was a revolution in the organization of practical life that transformed human culture.

A market is a place, actual or virtual, where individuals exchange goods, services, and labour. A *market economy* exists when the purpose of economic activity is market exchange. While there were markets in feudal towns—often surrounded by villages that had no market—this did not constitute a market economy. Most economic activity was for the purpose of immediate consumption or for authoritative transfer (taxes to the landlord or tithes to the Church), rather than exchange. Individuals engaged in market activity only on a limited basis and only after other ends such as immediate consumption and the payment of feudal obligations had been met. Markets need buyers as well as sellers, and the vast majority of people—feudal peasants—generally had little or nothing to spend or trade within the marketplace. The consuming class consisted mostly of the nobility and those in their employ.

Market activity in feudal society took place largely in towns, or when travelling merchants came to the feudal manor/castle, and was limited principally to basic necessities that required craftsmanship (tools, utensils) or luxury articles imported from other places. About the sixteenth century, this began to change; a market economy could not develop without the erosion of feudal relations, and as the market economy grew, it eroded what remained of feudal society.

A market economy has two fundamental requirements that feudal society could not fully meet: first, that economic production is undertaken for the purpose of exchange in the market, and second, that individuals obtain what they consume through purchases in the market. It was necessary, then, to transform an economy based on the subsistence agriculture of the feudal countryside into an economy of predominantly urban market-oriented production. Agricultural production would be reorganized on capitalist rather than feudal

The Shambles, York, United Kingdom.

lines (agricultural workers would sell their labour to landowners for a wage or, if fortunate enough, become farmers owning their own land, growing crops or raising or livestock for sale). An emerging market thus challenged the very basis of feudal society—the relationship between lord and peasant. Expanding markets required the transformation or elimination of feudal institutions, practices, and structures.

For example, a market economy requires a supply of workers to produce goods or process commodities. Developing a market in labour involves displacing individuals from subsistence agriculture and paying them a wage in exchange for their work in other forms of production; displacing peasants from the land requires freeing them from feudal obligations to the nobility and Church. As with the Reformation and the Enlightenment, the growth of a market economy dissolved the bonds that held together the feudal order and thus tied individuals to their place in an organic, traditional society.

PIONEERS OF LIBERAL THOUGHT: HOBBES AND LOCKE

Thomas Hobbes has been described as the greatest of all English political thinkers: there are few ideas in liberal thought that do not stem from Hobbes, or his critics, the most famous being John Locke. Together, Hobbes and Locke first put into conceptual form the character of modern liberal society and the limited government that seems necessarily (to liberals) to accompany it.

THOMAS HOBBES (1588–1679)

Shaping English politics in the mid-1600s and pro-viding the political context for Hobbes was the struggle between monarch and Parliament, beginning with the English Civil War and concluding with the Glorious Revolution of 1688. These events marked England's adjustment from a feudal, traditional society to a modern, legal-rational polity, a social transformation Hobbes seems to have anticipated and welcomed. His insights into the nature of post-feudal society make him so "radical" for his own time and so relevant to our own. Arguing in the language of his day, he can easily seem archaic to contemporary readers. A conservative dimension to Hobbes is expressed in his fear of conflict, his concern for order and stability, and the paternalism that informs his theory of government.

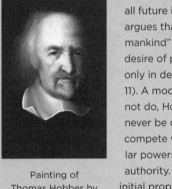

Painting of
Thomas Hobbes by
John Michael Wright.

Individualism

For Hobbes, the individual is logically prior to any group or collective formation. Individuals are bodies in motion, guided by their passions, the strongest of which is the fear of death. Two consequences follow. First, human reason operates to serve the passions in obtaining their object (pleasure or the avoidance of pain); all voluntary actions and inclinations we have are concerned with "securing a contented life" (161; *Leviathan*, Chapter 11). Second, society is artificial: "All society therefore is either for gain, or for glory; that is, not so much for love of our fellows, as for the love of ourselves" (24; *De Cive*, Chapter 1). Others are of value to us only as means to our ends; they have no intrinsic value in and of themselves. We value others for the power they have, power being a present means to some future end.

Because fear of death is our strongest passion, we desire satisfaction not only now but in all future instances. Therefore, Hobbes argues that "a general inclination of all mankind" is "a perpetual and restless desire of power after power, that ceases only in death" (161; *Leviathan*, Chapter 11). A modest or moderate power will not do, Hobbes notes, because we can never be certain it is enough. Humans compete with each other for particular powers such as wealth, status, and authority. Thus Hobbes's basic and initial propositions about human nature place each individual in conflict with every other individual: you are my enemy because you want the same things I want, and presumably both of us cannot have or enjoy them.

The State of Nature and Civil Society

Hobbes famously describes a **state of nature**, a hypothetical condition that would exist if there were no social and political authority. Since each person is the enemy of every other, Hobbes argues that the best defence is a good offence: "there is no way for any man to secure himself, so reasonable as anticipa-tion; that is, by force, or wiles, to master the persons of all men he can, so long, till he see no other power great enough to endanger him" (184; *Leviathan*, Chapter 13). Therefore, the state of nature is a state of war, "and such a war, as is of every man against every man" (185; *Leviathan*, Chapter 13).

This conception of the state of nature as a state of war is one of the most powerful images of political thought: an anarchy of the worst kind, a condition of violent stagnation that recommends itself to no one, and a place where life is "nasty, brutish and short." Nonetheless, individuals in this state are acting rationally on the basis of their appetites, and Hobbes insists that their actions are not sinful or evil or unjust. Good and evil, justice and injustice, right and wrong exist only when there is a commonly agreed-upon standard and a power to enforce it—neither is present in the state of nature.

Hobbes offers an apparent solution: an agreement of every person with every other person to be ruled by a common power ("a Sovereign"), who "shall act, or cause to be acted, in those things which concern the common peace and safety" (227; *Leviathan*, Chapter 17). This is the "great Covenant" (an agreement binding the parties to future compliance) by which **civil** (political) **society** (the Commonwealth) is created so that individuals might escape the state of war. Each individual surrenders his right to defend himself from others and agrees to the protection provided by a Sovereign, who is thereby empowered to make laws and enforce them.

Government and Self-interest

The idea that political society is something that individuals create by means of a contract in order to protect or further their self-interest signals clearly that society is instrumental and artificial for Hobbes. The purpose of government is the security and safety of the individuals governed. Hobbes is not saying that the state provides for the welfare (wellbeing) of individuals, but rather that it delivers a framework of stability (through laws) within which individuals may pursue their own ends. Individuals are no less self-interested and driven by their passions or appetites in civil society than in the state of nature. What has changed is that the law enforced by the Sovereign protects each individual from the self-interested actions of others.

For Hobbes, it does not matter how governments *actually* come into being: their nature, their purpose, and their justification are the same. Because humans are the way they are, a sovereign power is always necessary to keep peace. Therefore, all Sovereigns are justified in exercising power. Without a Sovereign to keep the peace by enforcing law, men would return to the state of nature, which is a state of war. The surest sign of this, Hobbes suggests, is the destruction brought by civil wars when authority is in dispute. For Hobbes, then, all government is legitimate.

The Absolute Sovereign

Hobbes's hypothetical account of the state of nature and the covenant that establishes civil society is intended to establish two points. One, for citizens, is the necessity of an absolute, unlimited Sovereign to enforce the laws required for stability and security. The second, for rulers, is that the justification and purpose of government is to provide for the peaceful pursuit of self-interest. To make the Sovereign anything less than absolute would weaken the ability of the Sovereign to enforce the law. A less effective Sovereign would be unable to adequately protect citizens from each other, and they would eventually revert to the state of nature.

To the question "What form shall the state take?" Hobbes has two answers. The first is that it does not matter, so long as the government has a monopoly of power and is unlimited in its authority. Second, Hobbes believes that democracy is not possible in practice, and that monarchy is preferable to aristocracy. An assembly of men would suffer from internal conflict because its members would be concerned as much or more with their own personal well-being than with that of the Commonwealth.

Hobbes on Liberty

Insistence on an absolute Sovereign seems to contradict Hobbes's reputation as a *liberal* thinker. He defines liberty as "the absence of external impediments" (189; *Leviathan*, Chapter 14). In the Commonwealth, the impediments to liberty are the laws made and enforced by the Sovereign—liberty is not confined by *authority*. It is *law* that limits liberty, and the liberty citizens enjoy depends on the extent of the law made by the Sovereign. Hobbes is famous for stating that the liberty of citizens consists in "the silence of the law." While he insists upon an absolute Sovereign, Hobbes also believes the enlightened Sovereign will permit subjects an extensive sphere of personal liberty by making "good laws," defined as those which are "needful, for the good of the people, and withal perspicuous" (388; *Leviathan*, Chapter 30—"perspicuous" meaning "clearly expressed or presented, easy to understand").

Painting of John Locke by Sir Godfrey Kneller.

On the divide, as it were, between feudal society and modern market society, Hobbes is a radical conservative, a liberal monarchist, a modern thinker at work in an as yet un-modern world. His work should not be evaluated as the last word in modern liberal thought but rather as its initial systematic statement.

JOHN LOCKE (1632–1704)

Compared to Hobbes, Locke's views were much more traditional when it came to human nature, morality, and our relationship to society, but much more modern regarding institutions. Locke is more confident that we can recognize the law of nature, regulate our passions, and live together morally. For this reason, Locke imagines that we might live peaceably, sociably, but without government in a state of nature containing property, money, and other features of social existence. Nonetheless, conflicts over property form the greatest impediment to our peaceful existence in the state of nature, and it is for the protection of property (defined as "life, liberty, and possessions") that we abandon the state of nature and create a political society.

Consent of the Governed

Like Hobbes, Locke puts a mutual agreement among those who wish security and stability at the beginning of civil society. Locke writes as if this **social contract** is not hypothetical but a real, historical event, and in contrast to Hobbes, presents it as a contract *between* the Sovereign and the subjects. The origin of government is literally the *consent of the governed*, which constitutes a theory of **popular sovereignty**. Locke also argues that the people have a right to revolution if the Sovereign becomes a tyrant or abuses the terms of the social contract. Unlike Hobbes, Locke would place limits on the authority of the Sovereign. The unanimity of all participants in Hobbes's hypothetical covenant is replaced in Locke's account by the more practical principle of majority rule.

Separation of Powers

Perhaps Locke's most important contribution is the idea that the Sovereign power *must* be divided, with the executive and legislative powers placed in different hands. He argues that the legislative power should be in the hands of an assembly, a body of men who together make the law but are at the same time subject to it. Locke insists that the legislative power is the supreme power, and that the people have a right to alter the legislature when it acts contrary to the trust placed in it.

By making a series of important modifications to the arguments that Hobbes advanced, Locke presents a picture of government that is much more familiar to us than Hobbes's absolute Sovereign. While Locke was no more a democrat than Hobbes, he articulated the principles of popular sovereignty and of representative government. He simply assumed, as did almost anyone of his day, that the citizens who might vote and sit in the legislature would be adult males holding a significant amount of property.

Hobbes had written within the context of the English Civil War, a struggle—complicated very much by religious issues—between the monarchy and those defending Parliament. In 1688, the Glorious (Whig) Revolution dismissed the Catholic Stuart monarchy and installed William and Mary of Orange on the English throne to guarantee a Protestant succession. Most importantly, the new monarchs agreed to conditions that eventually resulted in the supremacy of Parliament and a steady diminution of the active role of the Sovereign in political affairs.

The outcome of the Whig Revolution was a limited government of the propertied class, represented in an assembly and subject to majority rule; and executive power in the monarch, subordinate to the legislative power. Because this corresponded so well to the basic outlines of Locke's theory, it was once believed that Locke wrote the *Second Treatise* in order to justify the 1688 change of succession. However, evidence now suggests that Locke wrote the *Second Treatise* in 1688 in anticipation of the changes to come.

SYNERGY

The Reformation, the Enlightenment, and the growth of the market economy were mutually reinforcing changes. For example:

- The development and expansion of the market benefited from a revolution in morals acknowledging that it was proper for ordinary individuals to be concerned with the acquisition of wealth; the Reformation helped to accomplish this revolution.
- The diminution of the power of the Church, generally a conservative institution, weakened resistance to social change.
- The market economy benefited from the development of new manufacturing processes and the reorganization of work around production for the market. The Enlightenment initiated an expansion of technology and the inventions that sparked the Industrial Revolution.
- Science provided not only new ways of processing raw materials and new kinds of goods but also a way of problem-solving that allowed for continual innovation, invention, and improvement of existing designs.

The social transformations deriving from the Reformation, the Enlightenment, and the emergence of a market economy combined to replace an organic, hierarchical, traditional society with an increasingly individualistic, dynamic, and pluralistic one. Reason and science replaced custom and divine intention as central standards for evaluating policy and institutions. In contrast to a rigid order of entrenched social positions, the new society was premised on the liberation of individuals from arbitrary, traditional, involuntary bonds and on their replacement with relationships of rational self-interest. Not surprisingly, this new society was not one that could accommodate feudal political institutions—material pressures demanded new structures.

Viewed from another perspective, the arbitrary, involuntary bonds of feudal society were simply exchanged for the arbitrary, involuntary bonds of capitalist society. The feudal tenant lived a familiar, predictable life in a community where one might expect the comfort of the Church or the largesse of the landlord in times of difficulty. The worker in the emerging capitalist economy lived on a subsistence wage in filthy, crowded towns and cities without any support beyond what relatives might provide.

POLITICAL REVOLUTION

In a process that was truly revolutionary, political life was reorganized, new institutions and structures of authority were established, and new ideologies were created to justify these transformations. Political transformation occurred quickly in some cases (e.g., France), more gradually in others (e.g., England), but wherever it occurred, similar changes were accomplished.

OLD	. . . GIVES WAY TO . . .	NEW
Absolute Monarchy	→	Republic or Limited Monarchy
Personal, Arbitrary Authority	→	Rule of Law
Subjects (with obligations)	→	Citizens (with rights)
Executive Government	→	Representative government

Figure 3.2

LIBERAL REVOLUTION IN THE NEW WORLD

The American Revolution was an uprising by societies more modern and liberal than the institution ultimately governing them—the arbitrary authority of the British Crown. In fact, many British parliamentarians were sympathetic to the colonial cause. The US War of Independence inspired subsequent uprisings throughout the Caribbean and Latin America by colonies of France, Spain, and Portugal, starting with Haiti in 1791.

Liberal self-government came to the British colonies in Canada peacefully and gradually, notwithstanding the rebellions of 1837 in Upper and Lower Canada. In the colony of Quebec, which had been settled along quasi-feudal lines by the French, the British initially reinforced existing centres of authority—the Church and the seigneurs (quasi-feudal landlords)—with the *Quebec Act* (1774). The so-called Quiet Revolution of the 1960s may be seen as the belated arrival of the liberal revolution to francophone Quebec society. In this case, modern liberal political structures had long existed, but were mostly controlled and enjoyed by the anglophone minority (see the discussion of Quebec in Chapter 9).

Because of its emphasis (which would increase over time) on "the individual," this was a **liberal** revolution.

Alternatively, this was a revolution on behalf of the capitalist classes—the "individuals" most favoured were those with resources derived from the market economy: merchants buying goods and commodities in one market to sell in another; manufacturers organizing technology labour and raw materials to produce goods to be sold to consumers or other producers; and bankers lending to the merchants and manufacturers.

The liberal revolution did not necessarily or immediately improve the lot of peasant farmers, urban wage labourers, or even those whose wealth was based on owning land and collecting rent.

In short, the liberal revolution was the political restructuring that accompanied the transformation from a traditional, agrarian, organic society to a rational, market-oriented, pluralist society. It is by no means obvious that every society *must* undergo such a transformation, but it is common to all so-called Western nations. The liberal revolution informs modern ideas of legal-rational authority and democracy, and helped create the constitutional systems and governmental institutions examined here and in later chapters.

LIBERAL GOVERNMENT

The liberal revolution created a new form or style of government, dramatically redesigning state institutions (as in France) or changing the rules and conventions governing existing institutions (as in England). In the former, government by a monarch and noble-born aristocracy was rejected for a republican form of government, a republic being a nation of citizens equal in political rank and status (in theory, if not in practice). In the latter, the monarchy was retained, but its power was diminished (and would continue to be reduced).

The common theme is the depersonalization of authority and power. No longer was the power of the state to be seen as a possession or right of those wielding it, but rather as something exercised on behalf of "the people." The essentially "liberal" idea at the core of the liberal revolution was that *government exists to protect the interests of the individuals*

THINKERS IN REVOLUTIONARY TIMES: ROUSSEAU AND BURKE

Jean-Jacques Rousseau and Edmund Burke are two critical voices within the liberal tradition, opposing each other from opposite sides of the French Revolution. Rousseau's thought is concerned with the relationship between liberty and equality; Burke was anxious to preserve inequality in the form of an ordered hierarchy.

JEAN-JACQUES ROUSSEAU (1712–1778)

A citizen of Geneva, Rousseau was a critic of absolute monarchy and of the social, economic, and political inequality of the late feudal and early modern periods. While the liberal focus on the individual contains a latent current of egalitarianism (a theory or movement promoting equality), liberalism has been able to turn a blind eye to considerable levels of economic, political, and social inequality. Rousseau stands out for his uncompromising egalitarianism, which has an elegantly liberal foundation: we cannot be free if we are not equal.

For Rousseau, liberty is not the absence of law but rather the absence of dependence upon another or others. Freedom is independence. Social and economic inequalities create relationships in which some are dependent on others, and unevenly so, an idea that eventually worked its way through German philosophy to the young Marx. Although he was egalitarian, Rousseau was not a socialist: his ideal society is pre-industrial and his hero is the independent farmer/artisan, self-sufficient by means of his own work on the land and the materials it supplies him.

Painting of
Jean-Jacques Rousseau
by Allan Ramsay.

Rousseau's State of Nature

In the *Discourse on the Origin of Inequality*, Rousseau presents a state of nature almost completely opposite to Hobbes's. Here the primitive individual (formed solely by Nature) roams the forest, all wants readily supplied because his or her needs are very simple. This is the famous "noble savage," living at peace with all other creatures, if somewhat indifferent to them. All humans are equal; all are free. The differences between individuals do not yet matter.

Development beyond this initial condition is initially a blessing but contains within it the seeds of a subsequent fall. At first, the solitary human becomes social, living in community with others and enjoying the benefits of collective effort and company, without surrendering the independence of working for oneself. It is in society that humans begin to compare themselves with others and in society that social, economic, and political distinctions arise. Nonetheless, so long as humans are socially united but economically independent, they are in the best of all possible worlds. The central moment where this all begins to unravel is the introduction of private property, conceived initially as ownership of land. Private property leads to a **division of labour**, to exchange, profit, exploitation, and inequality. What began as a relatively equal distribution of resources becomes increasingly and inevitably an unequal concentration in the hands of a few. In this way the natural differences between humans contribute to differences that are lasting because they can be passed from one generation to the next.

Economic and Political Inequality

In the *Discourse*, Rousseau follows Locke in regarding political society as something created by those with property wishing to protect it from those without. The initial degree of political inequality reflects the amount of economic inequality at the time government is instituted. As economic inequality increases over time, so too will political inequality, until a situation is reached of complete despotic rule of one individual over the rest (Rousseau's view of absolute monarchy).

The Social Contract

Pessimism or fatalism is also present in Rousseau's most famous work, *The Social Contract*. This book addresses the question: What conditions must be satisfied for government to be legitimate? Starting from liberal premises, he reaches different conclusions from most liberal thinkers. Rousseau begins with the idea that individuals are by nature free and equal. To be legitimate, any political society must be voluntary, not forced. In agreeing to live in political society, we surrender our natural liberty to the community in exchange for **civil liberty**. Our bond with others is "a form of association which will defend and protect with the whole common force the person and goods of each associate, and in which each, while uniting himself with all, may still obey himself alone, and remain as free as before" (174; Book I, Chapter 6).

An important point here is Rousseau's definition of liberty, seen not as "the silence of the law" but as "obedience to a law we give to ourselves." The absence of law is licence; we are free when we are self-regulating, self-determining beings. In a legitimate political community, we are collectively self-governing by virtue of our participation in something Rousseau calls the **general will**: "Each one of us puts his person and all his power in common under the supreme direction of the general will, and in our corporate capacity, we receive each member as an indivisible part of the whole" (175; Book I, Chapter 6). What this implies is a fully democratic body politic in which all citizens take part collectively in making the laws by which they are governed as individuals. To paraphrase Rousseau, the Sovereign is all the people and never anything less than all the people. Rousseau identifies legitimate government as full popular sovereignty realized through the democratic participation of the people as legislators.

Rousseau's vision of citizen legislators draws upon his knowledge of the constitutions of ancient Greece. Like the ancients, he also believed that laws should be relatively simple and not require great adjustment or supplementation; while the people would be Sovereign, they would not, as Sovereign, be busy. As for administering the law, or applying it to particular cases, this is what Rousseau called "government" or the "executive function," which he expected would be carried out by a small group of deputies acting on instructions from the Sovereign and continually accountable to the Sovereign.

Rousseau's Legacy

There is much more that is interesting and/or controversial and/or puzzling in Rousseau's *Social Contract*. Examples include exactly what he understood the general will to be; whether or not his political theory justifies totalitarian rule; and the reasons why he believed any political community, however wisely constructed, would nonetheless become corrupted and degenerate. At the core is Rousseau's vision of legitimate government as a fully democratic state founded on initial conditions of equality and freedom, and ultimately surviving only so long as it is able to maintain some semblance of these conditions. Rousseau's understanding of the relationship between liberty and equality, and of the collective participation of citizens in a common good (the "general will"), makes him a powerful source of the communitarian strain within modern democratic thought.

While there is evidence that Rousseau (who died in 1778) was wary of revolutions in general and would have disapproved of much of what the French Revolution embodied, it remains the case that many associated the events of 1789 with his political thought—the revolutionary slogan "liberty, equality, fraternity" seems Rousseauian in spirit.

EDMUND BURKE (1729–1797)

Among those who linked Rousseau to the French Revolution was Edmund Burke, the Anglo-Irish thinker and statesman. Although Burke sat in the English Parliament as a Whig for almost 30 years, he was both an aristocratic and a situational conservative, whose writings and speeches still inspire conservatives today. The key to his apparent inconsistency (he could support the American Revolution and condemn the French Revolution) is the gradual way in which England became liberal, so that parliamentary, representative government coexisted with a traditional monarchy, landed aristocracy, and the absence of democracy. Burke supported all the fundamental institutions of his England. His most famous work is *Reflections on the Revolution in France* (1790), written before, but anticipating, those darkest periods of the revolution that became known as The Terror. He laments that "the age of chivalry is gone. That of sophisters, economists, and calculators has succeeded, and the glory of Europe is extinguished forever" (86). In contrast to the revolutionary spirit, Burke preaches loyalty to tradition:

We·know that we have made no discoveries, and we think that no discoveries are to be made, in morality, nor many in the great principles of government, nor in the ideas of liberty, which were understood long before we were born, altogether as well as they will be after the grave has heaped its mould upon our presumption and the silent tomb shall have imposed its law on our pert loquacity. . . . We fear God;

we look up with awe to kings, with affection to parliaments, with duty to magistrates, with reverence to priests, and with respect to nobility … instead of casting away all our old prejudices, we cherish them to a very considerable degree, and … the longer they have lasted and the more generally they have prevailed, the more we cherish them. (97–98)

The Advantages of Aristocracy

In addition to praising traditionalism, Burke's conservatism celebrates the virtue of a natural aristocracy. Burke believes in the hierarchical ordering of society and that the privileged orders, namely the nobility and the clergy, have given society its civilization and refinement:

Nothing is more certain than that our manners, our civilization, and all the good things which are connected with manners and with civilization have, in this European world of ours, depended for ages upon two principles … I mean the spirit of a gentleman and the spirit of religion. The nobility and the clergy, the one by profession, the other by patronage, kept learning in existence, even in the midst of arms and confusions, and whilst governments were rather in their causes than formed. Learning paid back what it received to nobility and to priesthood, and paid it with usury [i.e., interest], by enlarging their ideas and by furnishing their minds. (89)

The Autonomy of Representatives

Last but not least, Burke is remembered for his defence of the autonomy of representatives from their constituents, expressed in a speech still quoted today by legislators seeking to justify taking a position they know is contrary to the opinions of their electorate (see Chapter 4).

it governs. This idea challenges all concentrations of power and is implicitly democratic—who better to protect citizens' interests than citizens themselves?

On the other hand, the modern state of Western Europe and its colonies was liberal first and democratic only later, and when it became democratic, it was through a series of gradual, cautious expansions of the class of persons entitled to vote. These extensions of the democratic franchise were often made in response to agitation from the disenfranchised, but not in every case. It has always been possible to justify these extensions as consistent with the core logic that has driven the evolution from responsible government to representative government to liberal democracy.

BILL OF RIGHTS

From the 1688 **Bill of Rights**, a declaration by the Houses of Parliament of rights and liberties, subsequently affirmed by William and Mary, Prince and Princess of Orange in accepting the English throne:

That the pretended power of suspending of laws or the execution of laws by regal authority without consent of Parliament is illegal.

That the pretended power of dispensing with laws or the execution of laws by regal authority as it has been assumed and exercised of late is illegal.

...

That levying money for or to the use of the crown by pretence of prerogative without grant of Parliament for longer time or in other manner then the same is or shall be granted is illegal.

That it is the right of the subjects to petition the King and all commitments and prosecutions for such petitioning is illegal.

That the raising or keeping a standing Army within the kingdom in time of peace unless it be with consent of Parliament is against [the] Law.

That the subjects which are Protestants may have arms for their defence suitable to their conditions and as allowed by Law.

That election of Members of Parliament ought to be free.

That the freedom of speech and debates or proceedings in Parliament ought not to be impeached or questioned in any Court or place out of Parliament.

That excessive bail ought not to be required nor excessive fines imposed nor cruel and unusual punishments inflicted.

...

And that for redress of all grievances and for the amending strengthening and preserving of the laws Parliaments ought to be held frequently.

Bill of Rights 1688 c.2 1 Will and Mar Sess 2.

PHILOSOPHICAL WORKS

Aristotle. *The Politics*. Trans. T. A. Sinclair. Penguin: Harmondsworth, 1962.

Burke, Edmund. *Reflections on the Revolution in France*. Ed. Thomas Mahoney. Indianapolis: Bobbs-Merrill, 1955.

Hobbes, Thomas. *De Cive (The Citizen)*. Ed. Sterling Lamprecht. New York: Appleton-Century-Crofts, 1949.

_____. *Leviathan*. Ed. C. B. Macpherson. Harmondsworth: Penguin, 1968.

Locke, John. *Second Treatise of Government*. Ed. Peter Laslett. Cambridge: Cambridge University Press, 1960.

Rousseau, Jean-Jacques. *The Social Contract*. Trans. & Ed. G. D. H. Cole. London: J. M. Dent & Sons, 1973.

REFERENCES

Fortin, Ernest. "Thomas Aquinas." *History of Political Philosophy*. 3rd ed. Ed. Leo Strauss and Joseph Cropsey. Chicago: University of Chicago Press, 1987. 248–275.

Fox, Robin. "The Kindness of Strangers." *Harper's Magazine* (November 2007): 15–21.

Kreuzer, Marcus. "Historical Knowledge and Quantitative Analysis: The Case of the Origins of Proportional Representation." *American Political Science Review* 104.2 (2010): 369–392.

Roberts, J. M. *The Pelican History of the World*. New York: Pelican, 1980.

Sinclair, T. A. *A History of Greek Political Thought*. London: Routledge and Kegan Paul, 1959.

FURTHER READING

Boix, Carles. "Electoral Markets, Party Strategies, and Proportional Representation." *American Political Science Review* 104.2 (May 2010): 404–413.

Hill, Christopher. *Reformation to Industrial Revolution*. Harmondsworth: Penguin, 1969.

McLean, Iain. "Political Science and History: Friends and Neighbours." *Political Studies* 58.2 (March 2010): 354–367.

Norton, Anne. "Politics against History: Temporal Distortions in the Study of Politics." *Political Studies*. 58.2 (March 2010): 340–353.

Phillips, John H., and William S. Taylor. "The Great Reform Act of 1832 and the Political Modernization of England." *The American Historical Review* 100.2 (April 1995): 411–436.

Raphael, D. D. *Problems of Political Philosophy*. Rev. ed. London: Macmillan, 1976.

Weale, Albert. "Political Theory and Practical Public Reasoning." *Political Studies* 58.2 (March 2010): 266–281.

CHAPTER 4

The Fall and Reluctant Rise of Democracy

...WHICH PROVIDES THE READER WITH

- an account of the emergence of representative democracy in the modern period
- an examination of the possibilities and limits of democracy in mass societies
- a discussion of the costs and benefits of democracy and its future prospects
- a distinction between electoral and liberal (free) democracies and consideration of their measurement in the world today

The age of democracy has arrived—there is no compelling alternative basis on which a state can claim to be legitimate. Even so, democracy often disappoints—sometimes our institutions seem democratic in name only, a facade behind which a largely undemocratic politics persists. Our political culture is democratic—ideologies that are elitist and anti-democratic remain at the margins—but the unanimous voice for democracy is muted (not too much or too fast), opportunistic (the people voted for me, who are you to criticize?), confused (mistaking freedom for democracy), or begrudging (elections are a bother and an expense). At times, widespread public suspicion of politicians or dissatisfaction with political institutions has led to reforms that, in the process, diminish rather than enhance democracy. In a democracy, all voices are democratic because this is the language of political success, but it is also possible for the words to mask indifference or hostility to public participation in political life.

As noted previously, democracy existed (and was criticized) long ago in the city-states of ancient Greece. Democracy can also be seen as the logical conclusion to some of the premises implicit in liberalism. These two democracies—ancient Greece and liberal democracy—are not the same. The liberal revolution replaced traditional and charismatic grounds of legitimacy with the *consent of the governed*. Within liberal theory, this consent evolved from something hypothetical (Hobbes) to something **tacit** (Locke) to something expressed (Rousseau) to something represented (James Mill and John Stuart Mill—see below). In practice, the category of "those whose consent is necessary to confer legitimacy" was gradually extended from a small class of male property owners to all adults able to think for themselves. The state of democracy within the modern age (the present time included) represents a compromise or trade-off between the logic for democracy and the social and cultural impediments to its actualization.

This chapter examines more closely what democracy is or might be within contemporary societies, identifies the constraints within which democracy is or is not possible, and considers its future prospects.

DEMOCRACY DEFINED

For the ancients, democracy meant the "rule of the many"; today it is usually translated literally as the "rule of the *people*," as in Abraham Lincoln's famous phrase about a government "of the people, by the people, and for the people." Democracy is a form of **popular sovereignty**: the authority of the state derives from the people who are governed. What distinguishes democracy is its insistence that the authority of the state not only *derives* from the public (so, too, on some interpretations does the power of a monarch) but *continues to rest* with the public. In some way, the people must be involved in the exercise of the authority of the state, or those who exercise the authority of the state must be accountable to the people. Democracy is subversive of power by insisting that authority ultimately belongs to the ruled, not the rulers.

How does this work in practice? When societies were smaller and the scope of government was much

FIRST DEMOCRAT?

While many regard Rousseau as one of the first philosophers to advocate democracy, Lee Ward has argued that Benedict Spinoza (1632–1677) is "the first important political philosopher to endorse democracy as the best government .... primarily on the basis of the claim that it is the most natural regime" (55). Unfortunately, Spinoza is not a philosopher commonly studied by students of political thought.

less than it has become today, it was conceivable that "the people" might exercise authority themselves. As communities became larger, more diverse, and the tasks of the state became more complex, the direct participation of the people in government became increasingly impractical; democracy came to mean the popular choice of delegates or representatives to govern *on behalf of* the people. In classical and medieval times, democracy still stood for the direct participation of all citizens in the task of government; since the early nineteenth century, democracy has been understood as a form of representative government in which people choose their rulers in elections.

An alternative to **representative democracy** is **direct democracy**, where matters are decided by a popular vote. Examples are **referenda** (binding on the government) and **plebiscites** (non-binding), where the government places a question before the public; **initiatives**, where a portion of the public successfully petitions the state to place a matter before the entire electorate in a referendum; and **recall**, where voters may force the resignation or re-election of their elected representative (see also Chapter 11). Any or all of these instruments of direct democracy may be used to supplement representative democracy, as they do to varying degrees in countries such as Australia, Italy, and (especially) Switzerland.

Both representative and direct democracy consist of a relatively simple act—marking a ballot or registering one's choice by mechanical or electronic means. Neither engages citizens in the debate and dialogue that Aristotle would have associated with democracy in particular but also with political activity generally. **Participatory democracy**, which involves citizens in the discussion and informed debate that precedes decision making, is the democracy of small societies, of town-hall meetings, and sometimes the workplace. It is a model of decision making that has always encountered practical limits once the scope of its application is enlarged very much; it remains to be seen whether social media can (as some believe) provide for a more widespread participatory system.

Democracy, then, may be present in a political system in different ways and with various degrees of intensity. To qualify as democratic, a system must present its citizens with the opportunity of selecting political elites in competitive, periodic elections. This is the very least, and it is possible for democracy to entail much more. Actual political systems or regimes fall somewhere on a continuum that begins with an absence of public input and ends with a maximum of public involvement. Most of the systems recognized as democratic do not go very far beyond the minimum of holding periodic elections.

MAJORITY RULE?

Some describe democracy as **majority** rule, but a close look at the support received by the governing party or parties in most systems indicates something less than a majority, by most measures. Recent election results for six countries are compared in the following table.

COUNTRY	YEAR (TURNOUT)	VOTES FOR GOV'T ('000)	% , OF VOTERS	% OF ELECTORS	% OF POPULATION	TYPE OF GOVERNMENT
Australia	2010 (98.8%)[1]	6,216	50.1%	46.7%	27.8%	minority (1-party)
Austria	2008 (78.8%)[2]	2,700	55.2%	43.5%	32.9%	coalition (2-party)
Canada	2011 (61.4%)	5,832	39.6%	24.3%	17.0%	majority (1-party)
Netherlands	2010 (75.4%)	4,666	49.6%	37.2%	28.2%	coalition (2½-party)[3]
New Zealand	2008 (79.5%)	1,215	51.8%	41.2%	28.5%	minority (1-party)
United Kingdom	2010 (65.1%)	17,541	59.1%	38.5%	28.4%	coalition (2-party)

1 Australia has compulsory voting.
2 Voting age in Austria begins at 16.
3 Two parties form the coalition government in the Netherlands with the formal support of a third party.

DISTRUST OF DEMOCRACY

It is easy for citizens who have grown up within a democratic political system to take it for granted. It is also easy to overlook how recent the allegiance to democracy is, something perhaps obscured by knowing that a democracy existed in ancient Athens, however different that democracy was from anything we experience today.

Early critics of democracy had two main concerns. First, that democracy is inherently unstable, because eloquent, charismatic orators (**demagogues**) can too easily play upon the fears, prejudices, or vanity of the public in order to exercise power without restraint—democracy gives way to tyranny. Second, critics argued that democracy can become rule by the larger part of the people over the lesser part, what has been called a **tyranny of the majority**. In such a case, instead of being rule by the people for the general welfare, democracy turns into rule by the largest group or class for its own interest, an interest that may include exploiting or persecuting the minority.

Underlying many criticisms of democracy is a low opinion of "the people," that is to say, of ordinary citizens, generally assumed to be ignorant and irrational. Accordingly, power must be retained by an enlightened **elite** to keep government from being usurped by a popular tyrant, to protect minority interests, or simply to preserve the benefits and achievements of culture and civilization. The danger of a "tyranny of the majority" has often been raised by a minority occupying economically, politically, or socially privileged positions. Nonetheless, in ethnically diverse societies, the possibility of a majority (particularly if constituted on religious, linguistic, or ethnic grounds) oppressing a minority *is* a potential social problem for fully participatory models of democracy.

In societies where the unequal exercise of power has ensured that the mass of the population remains poor and uneducated, fears about the weaknesses of democracy may not be entirely unfounded, but obviously the problem here is not democracy but the effects of social inequality. Not surprisingly, then, democracy remained a suspect form of government from the time of Aristotle until the late eighteenth century, when thinkers like Rousseau began to argue for its legitimacy. It took many generations of reform to turn liberal representative government into liberal democratic government. The success of democracy in the United States in the early nineteenth century provided an example for other liberal nations.

FROM LIBERAL GOVERNMENT TO LIBERAL DEMOCRACY

The movement from liberal government to liberal democracy was gradual, involving a series of reforms, often implemented in the face of strong opposition from those in power. Looking back from our own time, these reforms often seem to have been logical if not necessary steps. The English example illustrates this well.

The sketches of Hobbes and Locke in Chapter 3 reveal that neither of these giants of early liberal philosophy was a democrat. The century that followed Locke's writings on government was marked by the development of Parliament into an institution of cabinet government consisting of a prime minister and ministers drawn from the membership of the legislative body. It was also the beginning of England's economic ascendance as the major capitalist power in the world, which it accomplished by taking advantage of new ways of creating wealth in the still emerging market economy. Throughout this time, parliamentary government was open only to the small class of wealthy landowners, whose income largely came from production on their estates, including rent from the tenants who farmed their land. As the market economy expanded, so too did the class of individuals whose wealth came from trade, from commerce and banking, and from manufactures and eventually industry—most of whom were shut out of parliament and many of whom felt their interests were not served by the **landed gentry** who dominated government.

By the late seventeenth and early eighteenth centuries, liberal reformers were beginning to recognize that rule by a small class of propertied males was not consistent with liberal principles, nor, and perhaps more decisively, with the continued well-being of modern market societies.

In England, for example, seats in the **House of Commons** had been granted by royal charter to towns in the Middle Ages, many of which barely existed centuries later. One notorious example was Old Sarum, a

THE *REFORM ACT* (1832)

The first Reform Bill was introduced by a newly elected Whig government in the spring of 1831; its provisions included making a fairer distribution of electoral districts and doubling the size of the electorate (those allowed to vote). When opposition in Parliament stalled the Bill, the government requested **dissolution** and an election on the issue, which it won overwhelmingly. A second Reform Bill was passed by the House of Commons in September 1831, but it was defeated in the more conservative House of Lords. In reaction, rioting took place across the country. After receiving a vote of confidence in the House of Commons, the government opened a new session of Parliament, which allowed it to introduce the third Reform Bill. When the **House of Lords** attempted to amend the Bill, the government asked the King to appoint pro-reform members to the House of Lords. When the King declined this advice, the Whig government resigned, but the inability of the Tories to form a government in the face of public opposition brought the Whigs back to power. The King was able to persuade the Lords opposed to the Bill to abstain from further votes on the matter. The *Reform Act* became law on June 7, 1832.

The Act eliminated many "rotten boroughs" (districts with very small electorates easily controlled by the nobility or landed gentry), created new seats for areas previously with none, lowered and standardized the amount of property requirement for eligible electors, and brought in a system of voter registration. Middle-class males benefited from the lower property requirements, which still excluded the working class and agricultural labourers from voting. For the first time, by explicitly identifying "male" property holders, the electoral law excluded women. The work of reforming the British system of representative government continued through the nineteenth century:

1835 increase in the number of polling places
1836 polling held on one day
1854 provisions to address corrupt parties
1867 extension of voting to male working class, and redistribution of electoral districts
1872 introduction of the secret ballot
1883 campaign expenditure limits
1884 extension of voting to agricultural labourers
1918 property qualifications for voting abolished for males, and for certain females over 30
1928 equal voting rights for women

cathedral city in the twelfth century that contained fewer than 10 voters by 1831. In the election of that year, more than 150 of the 403 seats in the House of Commons were elected by fewer than 100 voters. Many large, thriving communities had no representation at all. The *Reform Act* of 1832 was the first in a series of similarly titled Acts over the next 100 years that were necessary to implement the basic features of *fair* elections (representation by population, a secret ballot, single-member districts) that many would take for granted today. In addition, the system moved ever closer to genuine representative democracy as the class of those eligible to vote was eventually expanded to **full adult suffrage**.

In most regimes the expansion of the right to vote to all adults had to wait for the twentieth century—New Zealand in 1893 being the notable exception. As in Britain, expansion often happened in the face of much opposition and resistance. Extensions of the democratic franchise involved

(a) eliminating property qualifications;
(b) recognizing women as persons equally entitled to political rights;
(c) removing restrictions based on racial, ethnic, or religious grounds; and
(d) lowering the minimum age to vote.

ASSESSING REPRESENTATIVE DEMOCRACY

SIGNIFICANCE OF THE RIGHT TO VOTE

Despite the great resistance that greeted every effort to extend the right to vote to disenfranchised portions of the population, doing so did *not* alter the basic functioning of representative government; the same institutions, conventions, and practices operated as before. Elected representatives gained perhaps even more autonomy from the immediate demands of their constituents as their constituencies became larger and more diverse. While each expansion of the franchise has required elected officials to be responsive to this section of the electorate, those voting for the first time did so within the context of established political institutions, including a party system seemingly capable of absorbing them. An additional reason the act of voting fails to carry more weight is the nature of the relationship between the voters and their representatives.

Elected representatives serve as members of a legislature until, in most cases, the legislature is dissolved and a new election is held. While in office, members represent their constituents but have no legal obligations to them. They require the support of their constituents to be re-elected, and cannot engage in illegal or criminal behaviour but have no additional obligations except of a moral nature. The absence of accountability between elections is called representative autonomy and is a feature of most contemporary democracies. A famous defence of the autonomy of the elected representative was provided by Edmund Burke in a 1776 letter to his constituents and is quoted still by members wishing to justify their vote in awkward circumstances.

It is important to note that Burke made this statement *prior to* the development of strong **party discipline** within parliamentary systems. Legislators may have autonomy from their constituents, but not from their party, which expects them to follow its positions. Individual autonomy comes into full play only when a **free vote** is held on a so-called matter of conscience, such as capital punishment or abortion.

UTILITARIANS—JAMES MILL AND JOHN STUART MILL

Utilitarianism first emerged as a stream of liberalism based on a hedonistic (pleasure-seeking) psychology rather than on arguments from an imagined or hypothetical state of nature. The idea that each of us seeks to maximize our pleasure and minimize our pain was very central to Hobbes, but the utilitarians turned this into an ethical and political theory and looked to maximize social rather than merely individual utility. The most influential utilitarian was Jeremy Bentham (1748–1832), who formulated the principle of the **greatest good of the greatest number** as the maxim on which all rational government should rest. Although intuitively attractive, there are difficulties with realizing this idea consistently, such as assigning values to pleasures or pains, or treating all pleasures as equally deserving of consideration, or acting as if only the consequences of actions and not the intentions or motivations are what matter. It is not difficult to discern in the utilitarian concern for the greatest happiness of the greatest number a path that leads in the direction of democracy.

A friend and disciple of Bentham was James Mill (1773–1836), whose son John Stuart Mill (1806–1873) was a pupil of both. In an essay on "Government," written in 1820 for the *Encyclopaedia Britannica*, James Mill argued that the self-interest that drives us to seek pleasure (and avoid pain) makes it necessary for our security that we have a share in government. Otherwise, we risk being abused by those who have such a share: "Whenever the powers of government are placed in any hands other than those of the community—whether those of one man, of a few, or of several—those principles of human nature which imply that government is at all necessary imply that those persons will make use of them to defeat the very end for which government exists" (54; Part III).

Arguing it would not be practical for the people to exercise the authority of the state directly, James Mill advocated representative government chosen by the people. Then, recognizing how radical a proposal this was, he considered if it would be possible for such a government to be chosen by anything *less* than all the people. By a series of dubious arguments (such as eliminating the need for women to participate because they have either husbands or fathers who will look after their interests), he reduces the electorate necessary for good government to the richest one-third of males older than 40 years of age. Even Bentham found James Mill's arguments ridiculous, but in many circles the criticism was that Mill's proposals went *too far* and would give too much power to the wrong sort of people.

After publishing influential works in logic, political economy, and politics (such as his treatise *On Liberty*) the younger Mill (John Stuart) turned his thoughts to representative government, publishing a work on the subject in 1861. While the older utilitarians had justified democracy to protect the people from the abuse of power, J. S. Mill recommended representative government as a way to involve the public in political life and educate them to nobler purposes: "The most important point of excellence which any form of government can possess is to promote the virtue and intelligence of the people themselves" (193; Chapter II). If this seems rather Aristotelian, so too might his proposal that those with education should be given more votes than those without, skilled workers more votes than unskilled, and so forth. Like the classical thinkers, Mill believed that government should be placed in the hands of the wisest; unlike the ancients, he believed that all have the potential to become wise, and in an ideally constituted society could become so.

An active feminist, J. S. Mill advocates a "perfect equality" between the sexes in his work *The Subjection of Women* (1869), and as a Member of Parliament between 1865 and 1868, he introduced legislation giving women the right to vote, 50 years before Parliament would pass such a measure. Mill's arguments on this topic are typical of his thought: the subjection that women endure in marriage and in society is an impediment to their liberty, which not only limits them from developing their full potential, but, in doing so, impedes the full perfection of *both* sexes.

EDMUND BURKE TELLS HIS CONSTITUENTS HOW HE WILL REPRESENT THEM...

"Certainly, Gentlemen, it ought to be the happiness and glory of a representative to live in the strictest union, the closest correspondence, and the most unreserved communication with his constituents. Their wishes ought to have great weight with him; their opinions high respect; their business unremitted attention. It is his duty to sacrifice his repose, his pleasure, his satisfactions, to theirs and above all, ever, and in all cases, to prefer their interest to his own. But his unbiased opinions, his mature judgement, his enlightened conscience, he ought not to sacrifice to you, to any man, or to any set of men living. These he does not derive from your pleasure; no, nor from the law and the constitution. They are a trust from Providence, for the abuse of which he is deeply answerable. Your representative owes you, not his industry only, but his judgement; and he betrays, instead of serving you, if he sacrifices it to your opinion.

Government and legislation are matters of reason and judgement, and not of inclination; and what sort of reason is that in which the deliberation precedes the discussion, in which one set of men deliberate and another decide, and where those who form the conclusion are perhaps three hundred miles distant from those who hear the arguments?

To deliver an opinion is the right of all men; that of constituents is a weighty and respectable opinion, which a representative ought always to rejoice

Statue of Edmund Burke by Jon Foley. Dublin, Ireland.

to hear, and which he ought always most seriously to consider. But *authoritative* instructions, *mandates* issued, which a member is bound blindly and implicitly to obey, to vote, and to argue for, though contrary to the clearest conviction of his judgement and conscience; these are things utterly unknown to the laws of this land, and which arise from a fundamental mistake of the whole order and tenor of our constitution.

Parliament is not a *congress* of ambassadors from different and hostile interests, which interests each must maintain, as an agent and advocate, against other agents and advocates; but Parliament is a *deliberative* assembly of *one* nation, with *one* interest, that of the whole where not local purposes, not local prejudices, ought to guide, but the general good, resulting from the general reason of the whole. You choose a member, indeed; but when you have chosen him, he is not a member of Bristol, but he is a member of *Parliament*. If the local constituent should have an interest or should form a hasty opinion evidently opposite to the real good of the rest of the community, the member for that place ought to be as far as any other from any endeavour to give it effect. . . . Your faithful friend, your devoted servant, I shall be to the end of my life: a flatterer you do not wish for."

(*Speech to the Bristol Electors*, November 3, 1774)

POLITICAL PARTICIPATION AS RATIONAL ACTIVITY

In classical liberal democratic theory, the selection of representatives through popular periodic elections is a rational activity by which citizens communicate their policy preferences (e.g., to pay more taxes, receive fewer public services) or their position on issues by examining the stated positions or platforms of candidates and/or their parties and choosing the one who most closely aligns with their interests. Liberal theorists have compared voting in the political system to purchasing in the market. Just as companies compete for the consumer dollar, election candidates compete for votes. To the degree that the analogy fits, a number of economic principles are reproduced in the political arena—from the laws of supply and demand, to the importance of marketing, to the principle of *caveat emptor* (buyer beware). What is missing in the voting "transaction" is any warranty, limited or extended.

Moreover, studies of contemporary political engagement often identify features difficult to reconcile with the portrait drawn by classical democratic theory. One such is a lack of interest and involvement in the political process, mirrored by a lack of knowledge about how political institutions actually function (or fail to function). Most citizens participate only by voting, declining to engage in other voluntary activities such joining a political party or advocacy group, writing to a representative, campaigning on behalf of a candidate, or even running for office.

Voter turnout seems to be declining in all political systems, reversed only on occasion by a contest more interesting than normal (e.g., the 2008 US federal election). In a handful of Western democracies (including Argentina, Australia, Brazil, Chile, and Uruguay), voting is not regarded as a privilege or a right but rather as a civic obligation enforced by penalties for non-compliance (**compulsory voting**). Elsewhere, there is much concern about the disengagement of citizens—particularly younger citizens—from the political process. The view—often expressed by younger citizens themselves—that political participation is something they'll "get around to" later in life, is not sustained by voting studies, which show just the opposite: those who do not participate when the opportunity is first presented to them are unlikely to become engaged citizens later on.

Numerous studies have discovered low levels of political knowledge, accompanied by voting decisions that are influenced by "non-rational" factors such as emotion, habit, socialization, peer pressure, misinformation, or manipulation (the same things that influence decision making generally). Behavioural studies discovered some decades ago that a democratic disposition (whatever that might be) is not innate. Some persons seemed to display attitudes identified as authoritarian, such as deference to authority and a desire to exercise authority over others. Typically, such attitudes were identified among the "apathetic," the non-participators.

While all this evidence is usually presented under the heading "the myth of the rational voter," perhaps this could be turned around—is it rational to invest time and other resources in the modern democratic process? Consider the autonomy of elected representatives from their constituents or the lack of direct input by citizens into decision making; is there any reason to take an active, rational interest in politics? The behaviour of citizens might just reflect the opportunities given (or not given) to them. There are at least two sets of impediments to citizen participation: institutional and cultural.

First Meeting of the Ontario Citizens' Assembly on Democratic Reform, September 2006.

Impediments To Political Participation

Among institutional impediments, the electoral machinery of most democracies provides no means to register the reasoning behind any vote. The representative who is elected, or the leader of the party to which he or she belongs, can only speculate about why he or she received more votes than any other candidate. There is no opportunity for the voter to indicate on the ballot that he or she supports this party for its economic and foreign policies but opposes its approach to social programs and legalized gambling. That ballot will look the same as one which supports the same party because of its promises on social programs *in spite of* its foreign policies and support for legalized gambling. The absence of information transmitted by the ballot makes talk by election winners about receiving mandates a bit of a stretch, even when the parties have published detailed and comprehensive election manifestos or platforms. In election campaigns in which the focus is on the relative attractiveness or trustworthiness of party leaders, or which party best masters the art (or survives the onslaught) of negative campaigning, the vote amounts to not much more than writing a blank cheque to the winner. The end result is more a transmission of trust or statement of faith than a set of instructions or directives. In these cases, emotion, habit, or socialization may be just as "rational" a basis for deciding between candidates as any calculation of enlightened "self-interest."

Institutional limitations to democracy are buttressed by cultural messages transmitted from generation to generation. A political culture is an aggregate of the beliefs within a society or community about the political world, and beliefs about democracy feature prominently in many contemporary political cultures. It is often a limited or qualified belief in democracy that prevails, just as the democratic institutions of most regimes offer limited forms of public participation. Belief in the rightness of democracy is accompanied by the age-old suspicion of "the public" or of its competence to judge how authority and power should be exercised. The phrase "too much democracy is dangerous" captures this ambivalence: democracy is fine, when kept within limits, not taken too far. An equivocal stance towards democracy is very often transmitted, if not reinforced, by the socialization process—the mechanism by which we acquire our beliefs.

WHAT LIBERAL (REPRESENTATIVE) DEMOCRACY IS AND ISN'T

If liberal democracy fails to give citizens an actual role in governing, and is unable to recognize (let alone reward) rational activity in the selection of rulers, what *is* it then, and what good is it?

The liberal democratic state (like every other state) is a system of **elite dominance**—that is, it concentrates authority and power in the hands of a few. It differs from other systems in which elites dominate by having periodic elections in which some of those elites must compete with others for scarce positions of power and authority. This seems to be a long way from the characterization of democracy as "rule by

the people"; in the latter half of the twentieth century, liberal democracies were praised less for embodying the popular will and more for their *stability* compared to other forms of government. Effective competition among political elites and their replacement through the electoral process means that unpopular governments can be ousted without revolution or violence. At the same time, what some might call the democratic myth continues to foster the view that popular inputs are closely reflected in the content of the law, of policies, and of programs. Such a view enhances the state's claims to legitimacy and its ability to rely on authority rather than power.

If liberal democracy is distinguished from other political arrangements by the popular selection of elites, much depends upon the nature and significance of this selection process. The modern process definition of democracy makes reference to "periodic, competitive" elections. The three propositions presented above attempt to indicate what makes popular participation in the political process meaningful.

The degree of choice (D1) is concerned not just with the *number* of options presented to the citizen but also with the *ideological diversity* or the range of policy positions represented by the options on offer; the *clarity* of the competing positions advanced; the *responsibility* of candidates for positions advanced or to be implemented (i.e., will the person making a promise in exchange for votes be in a position to keep that promise?); or the availability of *accurate information* about the candidates, the issues, and the policies proposed to address them.

As examined in Chapters 10 and 11, there are very real differences in the electoral and party systems of liberal democracies, differences that may affect all of the considerations just described. The competitiveness of the contest (D2) is also determined by the electoral system, the laws that administer the voting process, and rules about the financing of political parties and candidates.

Finally, the fidelity of outcomes to the inputs delivered is determined in part by the electoral system and any local variations in how that system is employed, and in part by the public-policy process and the degree of public input to that process.

COSTS AND BENEFITS OF DEMOCRACY

The justification of the liberal revolution against medieval authority was to secure individuals from the arbitrary exercise of authority. There are two fundamental ways to do so: to constrain authority/power so that it cannot harm citizens (justice), and to involve citizens in the exercise of authority/power (democracy). The critic of (more) democracy points out that democracy is expensive, that it slows down the work of government, that it is economically inefficient and can burden the marketplace, that it requires a commitment by citizens to activities that may not be attractive or entertaining (or as attractive or entertaining as other pursuits), that it is time consuming, or that it presupposes a level of political knowledge and experience that citizens do not have (and which it would be expensive to provide them with). It is best, on these grounds, to keep government small, manageable, efficient, and in the hands of experts.

Such arguments are more compelling if it can be demonstrated that the justice system secures us from the arbitrary or injurious use of that power by governmental elites. With the establishment of constitutionalism, of the rule of law, and in particular the entrenchment of individual rights in common law and constitutional law, it is tempting to conclude that democracy has become something of a luxury, perhaps even superfluous. Governments may be kept honest by appealing to the courts when rights have been infringed—a remedy more efficient and convenient for the community at large than wholesale political participation.

The latter view overlooks the relationship between democracy and justice. Democracy is a possible way of keeping those who safeguard the citizens' rights accountable to the citizens. Similarly, **social justice** involves difficult decisions about the distribution of public goods, the criteria by which this distribution should take place, what kinds of inequalities should be tolerated, and so on. Even if such decisions could be made by the justice system, they are fundamentally political decisions (as, some argue, are judicial decisions concerning rights). Governments must continually make decisions about the use of the state to regulate the market or manage the economy. Who but citizens of the state should determine its economic management strategies? One reason that individual rights are entrenched in constitutions is to ensure that democracy remains consistent with justice. Justice without democracy risks becoming justice for some, but not all.

DEMOCRACY'S PROSPECTS

The last one hundred years have witnessed some of the greatest advances towards popular democracy and some of its greatest repudiations. At the end of the twentieth century, some argued that democracy was the one great remaining ideology. More than a decade later, it is worth a pause to assess the prospects for democracy.

CHALLENGE: THE (INEVITABLE?) CONCENTRATION OF POWER

In every age and in every political system, democratic or otherwise, there are powerful pressures towards the centralization of power, including the desire of those who have authority for more. Without periodic reforms to strengthen the ability of the public to keep their rulers accountable, there is an almost inevitable erosion of popular sovereignty, *even as* the appearances and rhetoric of democracy are maintained and championed in a way that obscures their superficiality. In the past, democracy was implemented or extended as the result of revolution, or when voices of reform managed to influence or become the government. Any expansion of democracy in the countries where liberal democracy has been established will require the election of political parties committed to that purpose, or circumstances to arise that will make more democracy (enhancing citizens' choices, the competitiveness of elections, and/or the responsiveness of the political process) an attractive option for all parties.

CHALLENGE: TOO MANY PUBLICS?

In contemporary societies, it is almost impossible to speak in any meaningful way about "the people" or to identify *a* public will—there are several or many publics, each with their own interests and purposes.

Pluralism presents at least three challenges for democracy. One is the possibility that a democratic majority may systematically exclude a people or peoples, with destabilizing results over the long term. The legitimacy of the state diminishes quickly for those who are consistently excluded from shaping its policies. A second challenge is when the political process is unable to secure the consent of a majority, and a minority ends up deciding for all, with potentially destabilizing tendencies over the long term. Finally, as the plural character of society grows more sharply defined, compromises between competing interests may become more difficult to reach; instead of enabling collective decision making, democracy becomes the battleground for irreconcilable, competing voices seeking outright victory.

CHALLENGE: THE LEARNING CURVE OF INFORMED PARTICIPATION

The increasing complexity of societies in the face of population growth, the ever-expanding consumption of finite resources, and constantly changing technology present challenges that have fuelled the growth of the state over the last two centuries or so. Recurring rhetoric about making government smaller and simpler has been matched with limited success at best, and the benefits remain uncertain. Reducing the capacity of the state to respond to unforeseen catastrophes or crises is not wise public policy. Apart from its volume, the work of government has become increasingly technical. Informed decision making requires informed decision makers, and democratic decision making requires an informed citizenry. Citizens may be better educated on average than previous generations and have more information at their fingertips, literally, but they are not always informed or educated about government, politics, or the substance of political decisions. When most public information is delivered by companies whose primary business is entertainment (see Postman), it is reasonable to suspect that most citizens are not as adequately prepared for democratic decision making as they might be. Other means of acquiring information are available to those with the interest and time, but both seem to be scarce commodities.

CHALLENGE: DISENCHANTMENT WITH POLITICS

Democracy endorses the political sphere; by inviting or even requiring citizens to participate in the exercise of authority and power, we indicate that this is an important, worthwhile activity. Such an approach and attitude are at least as old as Aristotle's view that politics is a noble, worthy human activity, unlike making

HOW MANY POLITICIANS IS ENOUGH?

No occupation has gathered less respect in recent times than that of "politician." This suggests that, collectively, politicians are not doing a very good job. Either the wrong kind of people are going into politics, or there are structural reasons why well-intentioned people who have generally been successful in their previous lives consistently disappoint once elected to office. In either case, there are several reasons for thinking that reducing the number of politicians will not make it easier for those who remain to perform adequately as representatives.

The fewer representatives there are, the more constituents each must serve, and the ability of legislators to give voice to or respond to constituents' concerns is compromised in more than one way. First, as constituencies grow, the diversity of interests they contain may also increase, and the proportion of the representative's attention that any particular group can hope to receive will diminish. Those who are better organized or have more resources will often move to the head of the line, to the detriment of less advantaged groups. Second, as the number of legislators is reduced, their parliamentary duties increase, leaving less time for addressing constituency concerns. Third, in smaller legislatures, the margin that the government holds over the opposition may also be smaller, magnifying the importance of keeping

all representatives consistent with the party line, regardless of whether that position meets the needs of all its members' constituents.

Contraction in national or sub-national legislatures is not common. However, reductions in the machinery of democracy have taken place in countless municipalities, school boards, and other elected bodies across North America. In some cases, these are excellent examples of "symbolic" politics: having fewer politicians is presented as eliminating "waste" and "duplication." While the budgets of parliaments and the salaries of representatives are not small change compared to the budget of the average citizen, they are dwarfed by the state's expenditures on programs and the departments that administer them.

Combining population growth with a legislature whose size is fixed or otherwise static has the same effects on representation as reducing the number of representatives—what matters is the number of constituents per representative. In 2010, the average population of a Congressional District in the United States was more than 700,000. The comparable population represented by a member of the lower chamber in Ireland was about 27,300. It would not be difficult to argue that the former is too high, and the latter too low.

money, which is fit for servants or slaves. It is no exaggeration to say that in most contemporary democracies the situation is reversed; making and spending money are celebrated, while politicians and political activity are distrusted and sometimes despised.

Ironically, much of the public disenchantment with the political realm stems from its failure to be more democratic, or to be as democratic in practice as it is in theory. People hear political promises made to entice their support; people become cynical when office holders backtrack or renege on their commitments. Political actors seek to control public opinion in order to sidestep the minimal accountability to which they are subject, and manage to alienate a wary public. The political process is discredited, and instead of agitating for more democracy, citizens turn away from the limited democracy they have.

CHALLENGE: SELF-DEFEATING REACTIONS

In rejecting "big government" or calling for "less government," actions may be taken that threaten the institutions and processes of democracy rather than address the operations of government bureaucracies or put an end to wasteful spending. The decade of the 1990s was one in which the growth of the state was slowed, halted, or in rare cases reversed. This was also the period in which the trend began towards smaller governments, in the strictest sense. In parliamentary countries this meant smaller cabinets and leaner structures to support them, and in some jurisdictions a move to smaller legislatures. While the intent of the former may be to reduce pressures for public spending, the effect of the latter is to diminish representation as each legislator must represent a larger constituency. While cabinets have grown again in many cases (as seems their inevitable tendency), the size of legislatures has not. The

ability of the legislature to keep the executive accountable is diminished and democracy is not improved.

A second backlash that hurts democracy is the turn away from political parties, inspired largely by their tendency to function better as machines for collecting money and organizing modern election campaigns than as vehicles of representation for their members and supporters. The alternative approach is to work towards improving the ability of political parties to involve citizens in thinking about, debating, and even deciding on the policy positions to be placed before the larger public.

CONSOLIDATING DEMOCRACY

The number of regimes in which democracy is so firmly established that its overthrow or suspension is unthinkable is somewhere around 60 (including at least a dozen micro-states—those with a population of less than 1 million). The number of countries that qualify as "democratic" today is about twice that, and much larger than it was only 30 years ago. In many of the more recently democratic regimes, the real challenge is not the machinery of democracy but establishing the habits and norms within the political culture that will make other forms of government unacceptable. This is the work of consolidating democracy.

In 1991, Huntington noted that the growth of democracy in the world had occurred in three waves, from 1828 to 1926, from 1943 to 1964, and most recently after 1974. He also observed that the first two waves of democratization were followed by reverse waves in which democratic regimes suffered breakdown, returning to authoritarian or dictatorial rule. Some indication of movement in that direction is shown in the results for 2010 in Figure 4.1. Hence the importance

YEAR	REGIMES	DEMOCRACIES	% DEMOCRACIES	AVERAGE FREEDOM SCORE
1974	145	39	26.9	4.47
1990	165	76	46.1	3.84
1997	191	117	61.3	3.58
2005	192	123	64.1	3.27
2010	194	115	59.3	3.30

Data: Freedom House (www.freedomhouse.org)

Figure 4.1

of strengthening, if possible, a democratic political culture in newly democratized regimes.

The extent of the **third wave** of democratization is clear: 49 new regimes in 36 years, 76 more countries considered democratic, and a corresponding increase in the proportion of democracies from 1 in 4 countries in 1974 to 3 of every 5 in 2010. The table also indicates a loss of eight democracies between 2005 and 2010, bringing the number to 115, its lowest level since 1995.

MEASURING DEMOCRACY

The table provided above is based on the definition of democracy as a regime with regular, contested elections. "Regular," because elections must have a constitutional or legally prescribed regularity that is beyond the control of those in power; "contested," because to be democratically meaningful, elections must also be competitive—there must be more than one party with a legitimate opportunity of winning. Diamond has defined authoritarian regimes as those that lack "legal, independent opposition parties" (17) and **pseudo-democracies** as regimes that lack "an arena of contestation [competition] sufficiently fair that the ruling party can be turned out of power" (15).

If the rules are stacked in favour of (or can be manipulated by) the party in power, it may be impossible for a legal, independent opposition party to win, ever. At various times, Mexico, Senegal, and Singapore have been cited as classic examples of pseudo-democracy.

The 115 countries listed as democratic in 2010 represent regimes which, at that time, were considered to have competitive, periodic elections, satisfying the criteria of **electoral democracy**. Schmitter and Karl have labelled the idea that having elections is sufficient to establish democracy the fallacy of "electoralism" (78). In addition, they and others suggest, democratic choice must be meaningful, informed, unforced, and free of personal repercussions. These (and other) key variables have nothing to do with the machinery of elections and much more to do with the environment in which elections are contested. Incorruptible, independent electoral officials, a free press, gender equality, confidentiality, public literacy, and civilian control of the military are just a few of the ingredients that must accompany elections if democracy is to be meaningful.

Many of the conditions of democracy are closely associated with the values, institutions, and practices of the liberal state. On this basis, Diamond and others

Score*	STRONGLY LIBERAL DEMOCRATIC		WEAKLY LIBERAL DEMOCRATIC		PARTLY FREE
	1	1.5	2	2.5	3 – 4
>1 million population	Australia, Austria, Belgium, Canada, Chile, Costa Rica, Czech Republic, Denmark, Estonia, Finland, France Germany, Hungary, Ireland, Lithuania, Netherlands, New Zealand, Norway, Poland, Portugal, Slovakia, Slovenia, Spain, Sweden, Switzerland, United Kingdom, United States, Uruguay (28)	Croatia, Ghana, Greece, Israel, Italy, Japan, Mauritius, Panama, South Korea, Taiwan (10)	Argentina, Benin, Brazil, Bulgaria, Dominican Republic, Latvia, Mongolia, Namibia, Romania, Serbia, South Africa, Trinidad and Tobago (12)	Botswana, El Salvador, India, Indonesia, Jamaica, Mali, Montenegro, Peru (8)	3: Albania, Bolivia, Ecuador, Lesotho, Macedonia, Mexico, Moldova, Paraguay, Philippines, Senegal, Sierra Leone, Tanzania, Turkey, Ukraine (14) 3.5: Bangladesh, Bosnia and Herzegovina, Colombia, East Timor, Liberia, Malawi, Maldives, Papua New Guinea, Zambia (9) 4: Guatemala, Nicaragua (2)
<1 million population	Andorra, Bahamas, Barbados, Cape Verde, Cyprus, Dominica, Iceland, Kiribati, Liechtenstein, Luxembourg, Malta, Marshall Islands, Micronesia, Nauru, Palau, St. Kitts and Nevis, St. Lucia, St. Vincent and Grenadines, San Marino, Tuvalu (19)	Belize, Grenada, Monaco (3)	Samoa, São Tomé and Principe, Suriname, Vanuatu (4)	Antigua and Barbuda, Guyana (2)	3: Seychelles, Tonga (2) 3.5: Comoros (1)

* Average of Freedom House rankings on Political Rights and Civil Liberties, 2011 Report.

Figure 4.2

distinguish between minimally democratic regimes, which contest periodic elections (electoral democracies), and more completely democratic regimes, in which elections are contested within an environment of civil and political freedom (liberal democracies). Interestingly, the most stable and long-lasting democracies have been those that qualify as liberal democracies, and those democracies most likely to backslide into pseudo-democracy or authoritarianism have been electoral democracies in which the institutions that provide citizens with liberty have yet to become firmly established in the state or in civil society. Diamond lists 10 conditions of liberal democracy, ranging from the vesting of authority in elected officials to whom the military is subordinate,

to conditions of cultural, ethnic, and religious liberty, to an independent media, to freedom of association and expression.

Since 1972 an organization called Freedom House has measured the status of political and civil liberties in countries around the world and published an annual report entitled *Freedom in the World: The Annual Survey of Political Rights and Civil Liberties.* The table in Figure 4.2 has been compiled from the rankings contained in the *2011 Report*, which reports on conditions in calendar year 2010. Freedom House ranks each country on the basis of its political rights from 1 (best) to 7 (worst), and similarly for its civil freedoms. The score which heads each column reflects the average of the countries' rankings for political rights and civil freedoms. Countries with an average score of 1 are those with the highest ranking in both political rights and civil freedoms (1, 1). The regimes in the table are the 115 countries recognized by Freedom House as "electoral democracies." Freedom House divides countries into three categories: Free (average score of 2.5 or lower), Partly Free (average score of 3 to 5), and Not Free (average score of 5.5 to 7). The 87 regimes Freedom House categorizes as Free are described in the table as either "strongly" liberal democratic or "weakly" democratic. The 28 electoral democracies that are Partly Free are listed in the final column. Not listed are the 79 regimes that are not electoral democracies.

Whether democracy spreads and become more stable in the future depends on the ability of formally democratic regimes to foster the liberal conditions noted above. As yet, most of the world's population still lives in non-liberal democratic regimes. In addition, in some countries considered to be liberal democratic (e.g., India, the Philippines), large portions of the population live in poverty, illiteracy, and under the influence of societal norms (e.g., patriarchal cultures) that discourage democratic citizenship for many. In many cases, the most certain guarantee of a future for democracy will be economic growth, but also, *and this is as true of established as of growing democracies*, a greater equalization of wealth and economic opportunity.

In the longest established democracies (which, because of restrictions on the ability of women to vote *and* hold office, did not really exist until the twentieth century), liberal political institutions and a civil society embodying at least moderate levels of tolerance, middle-class affluence, and widespread literacy *preceded* the reforms that constituted democratization. In many of the world's newer democracies, another experiment is under way—namely, to establish democracy without, or prior to, creating the liberal foundations that most citizens in the West have come to take for granted.

Monument to the People's Heroes. Tiananmen Square, Beijing, China.

REFERENCES

Diamond, Larry. *Developing Democracy: Towards Consolidation*. Baltimore: Johns Hopkins University Press, 1999.

Huntington, Samuel P. *The Third Wave: Democratization in the Late Twentieth Century*. Norman, OK: University of Oklahoma Press, 1991.

Mill, James. *An Essay on Government*. Ed. Currin Shields. Indianapolis: Bobbs-Merrill, 1955.

Mill, John Stuart. *Utilitarianism, On Liberty*, and *Considerations on Representative Government*. Ed. H. B. Acton. London: J. M. Dent & Sons, 1972.

Postman, Neil. *Amusing Ourselves to Death: Public Discourse in the Age of Show Business*. New York: Viking, 1985.

Schmitter, Philippe C., and Terry Lynn Karl. "What Democracy Is ... and Is Not." *Journal of Democracy* (Summer 1991): 75–88.

Ward, Lee. "Benedict Spinoza on the Naturalness of Democracy." *Canadian Political Science Review* 5.1 (January 2011): 55–73.

FURTHER READING

Coppedge, Michael, and John Gerring, with David Altman et al. "Conceptualizing and Measuring Democracy: A New Approach." *Perspectives on Politics* 9.2 (June 2011): 247–267.

Dahl, Robert A. "What Political Institutions Does Large-Scale Democracy Require?" *Political Science Quarterly*. 120.2 (Summer 2005): 187–197.

Huntington, Samuel P. "How Countries Democratize." *Political Science Quarterly* 124.1 (Spring 2009): 31–69. [Originally published in the Winter 1991 issue of the *Quarterly*.]

O'Flynn, Ian. "Deliberative Democracy, the Public Interest and the Consociational Model." *Political Studies* 58.3 (June 2010): 572–589.

Putnam, Robert. *Making Democracy Work*. Princeton, NJ: Princeton University Press, 1994.

Schmitter, Philippe C. "Re-presenting Representation." *Government and Opposition* 44.4 (October 2009): 476–490.

CHAPTER 5

Roadmap to the Rest (a Comparative Framework)

...WHICH PROVIDES THE READER WITH

- an overview of the comparative institutional framework that informs the rest of the book
- facts and figures on the 45 regimes that constitute the data set to which subsequent chapters refer (and from which further comparisons may be generated)

This (admittedly simplistic) diagram maps a simple political system indicating a flow consisting of inputs from civil society to the state, and a flow of outputs from the state to civil society. The political process makes up the input side of the political system; the output side consists of public policy and administration. Accordingly, the three main sections of this book, following this chapter, focus on three elements:

- the state
- the political process
- governing (public policy and administration)

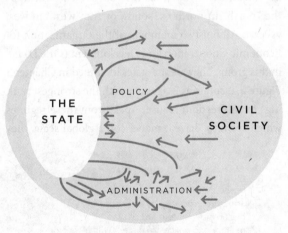

Figure 5.1

Because it is a political *system* that is being studied, understanding fully any one of these sections requires reference to the others. For the same reason, *any* starting point is arbitrary. This chapter offers the briefest guide to the institutional framework of the political system. Readers may then approach the remaining sections of this book in the order that interests them.

WHO'S IN AND WHO'S OUT

A long-distance view of the political system high-lights features common to all regimes. Every country has a state, even the most authoritarian state has a political process (dominated perhaps by negative elements such as the suppression of opposition, the manipulation of public political activity, and the avoidance of a *coup d'état*), and no totalitarian state has succeeded in completely suffocating civil society. This framework *could*, in theory, be used to compare all regimes, but the focus here is narrower, on regimes with political systems that have the following characteristics in common.

Regimes sharing these characteristics are identified as "liberal democratic," as the "developed" world, as the "north" in north vs. south, or the "west" in west vs. east. All but two members of the Organization for Economic Cooperation and Development (OECD) fall in this group. They are the states identified in Chapter 4, Figure 4.2, columns 2, 3, and 4 with the strongest rankings from Freedom House. Apart from these regimes, which seem to "have it made" (on a global scale, they

are the haves rather than the have-nots), there are two other sets of regimes with which a contrast will be made from time to time.

One group comprises the most weakly liberal democratic regimes (column 5 of the same figure) and the electoral democracies considered to be "partly free" (listed in column 6). The former have made strong moves towards liberal democracy but have not yet consolidated the institutions, habits, and culture that would provide the regime with long-term stability, or are unable to guarantee these conditions in all parts of their jurisdiction. The "partly free" regimes have adopted the machinery of democratic elections but have not as yet achieved the necessary conditions of civic liberty. In some states, political corruption still exists, or the threat of a military coup remains strong. Because these regimes are often changing from one type to another, or have the potential to move in either direction—towards or away from greater levels of democracy—they can be described as **transitional**.

The final group consists of regimes with little immediate prospect of change because they are locked

THE STATE	CIVIL SOCIETY
• based on rule of law • structure is defined by a constitution • has an independent judiciary • military and police are under civilian control	• universal public education • religious toleration and freedom of association • private property and markets • competitive, independent mass media • freedom from discrimination
POLITICAL PROCESS	PUBLIC ADMINISTRATION / POLICY
• universal adult suffrage • regularly scheduled, fair elections • system of competitive political parties	• professional, merit-based public service • mechanisms/offices of oversight and appeal • stakeholder involvement in policy formation

Figure 5.2

LEGISLATIVE FUNCTION	EXECUTIVE FUNCTION	JUDICIAL FUNCTION
making authoritative decisions in the form of laws (i.e., **legislating**)	carrying out, enforcing, or administering the content of the law (i.e., **executing**)	resolving disputes over the execution of the laws or interpreting their content (i.e., **judging**)

Figure 5.3

in the grip of an authoritarian government. As events in North Africa in 2011 (unforeseen by most observers) serve to remind, when authoritarian regimes lose their grip, the pace of change can seem breathtaking. Unfortunately, sometimes when the dust settles, the reins of power have simply been taken up in a new set of authoritarian or unaccountable hands.

LAW VERSUS POLICY

The importance of "law" (as noted in Chapter 4) was its origin in Parliament, in contrast to the prerogative of the Sovereign. Decisions that are singular, such as declaring a state of emergency, or particular and personal, such as appointing an ambassador or recognizing a citizen's outstanding bravery, may still be made by the modern political executive, in distinction from the universal rules passed by the legislature. While laws are often statements about what *may* or may not be done, or about what *must* or must not be done (i.e., they "permit" or "prohibit", "prescribe" or "proscribe"), many authoritative decisions establish benefits (such as pensions or student loans), provide public goods (such as education or health care), or encourage economic activity (through measures such as subsidies, tax rebates, or low-interest loans). Because the state's decision-making is broader than making law (but is almost always grounded *in* law), this function is often referred to as **policy-making**.

FUNCTIONS, INSTITUTIONS, SYSTEMS

The three basic functions of the state, performed in all regimes—liberal democratic, transitional, and authoritarian—consist of

· making authoritative decisions
· carrying out or enforcing authoritative decisions
· settling disputes related to authoritative decisions

Authoritative decisions take various forms, including commands, decrees, and proclamations, but in the modern world, in almost all regimes, they take the form of (or are based in) *law*. In this context, the three basic operations are described as the **legislative**, **executive**, and **judicial functions**. (Such functions are not only basic to the state, but they are also mirrored in other settings where decisions are intended to bind persons, as in the family, the religious body, the military, even the street gang.)

FUNCTIONS, *INSTITUTIONS*, SYSTEMS

Institutions such as the **legislature**, the **executive**, and the **judiciary** are the specific parts of the state that exist to perform its functions—recalling that institutions are practices or routines organized to accomplish identifiable purposes such as legislating, executing, and

THE LEGISLATIVE	THE EXECUTIVE	THE JUDICIAL
legislators gather in a parliament or assembly to propose, debate, amend and decide on bills (proposed laws)	head of state/government leads a cabinet/council of ministers/secretaries in managing departments of the government bureaucracy	judges preside over a court, applying legal principles to evidence and arguments to arrive at a verdict or judgment

Figure 5.4

judging. Those practices and routines are carried out by individuals who have specific roles or offices, such as legislator, executive, or judge, and take place in buildings designated and/or designed for that purpose, such as a legislative building or a courthouse.

FUNCTIONS, INSTITUTIONS, *SYSTEMS*

A system is the way in which the basic institutions of the state are organized, perhaps by the constitution, perhaps by custom and the accidents of history, to perform the functions of the state. What interests political scientists most is how different systems manage to be more or less effective, or efficient, or representative, or, at times, even dysfunctional.

The simplest system is absolute monarchy or personal dictatorship, in which one person decides, administers, and judges any dispute (assisted in each of these capacities by loyal and/or fearful followers). In medieval times, such a concentration of authority in one set of hands became less and less practical as kingdoms grew. The idea emerged of dividing up the responsibility for the functions of state and assigning them to institutions or branches of government, and eventually this became the norm.

The separation of powers to perform each function, and their assignment to distinct institutions, creates as well the challenge of organizing them. Allowing each to do its own thing could lead to a dysfunctional, if not ungovernable, state. The seventeenth and eighteenth centuries provided two solutions to this problem: the Westminster system (parliamentary) and Madisonian (separated powers) system.

The principal difference between these systems is the relationship of the executive and legislature. In the Westminster system, the political executive—the cabinet, headed by the prime minister—is a small group of members of the elected legislature. This is known as a **fusion of powers**. In addition, the executive (often just described as "the government") must maintain the support of a majority of the members of the elected legislature. This is the principle of **responsible government**.

In the Madisonian model, the executive—the directly elected president and the officials of his or her administration, including a cabinet—is entirely separate, distinct from the legislature. This is known as a **separation of powers**. In this model the judiciary, or the judicial branch—headed by the Supreme Court—also has a more independent role than in the Westminster system. The relationship of the three branches of government in the Madisonian model is one of **checks and balances**, safeguards intended to ensure that no one branch is able to become too powerful.

The differences in these two models also affect who is responsible for public policy, how law is made, how public budgeting is approved, how government departments are administered, and even the basis for foreign-policy decisions.

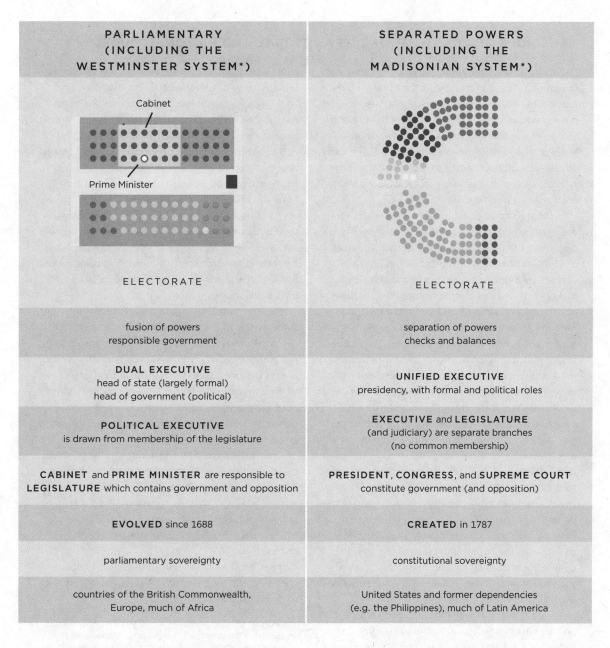

PARLIAMENTARY (INCLUDING THE WESTMINSTER SYSTEM*)	SEPARATED POWERS (INCLUDING THE MADISONIAN SYSTEM*)
ELECTORATE	ELECTORATE
fusion of powers responsible government	separation of powers checks and balances
DUAL EXECUTIVE head of state (largely formal) head of government (political)	**UNIFIED EXECUTIVE** presidency, with formal and political roles
POLITICAL EXECUTIVE is drawn from membership of the legislature	**EXECUTIVE** and **LEGISLATURE** (and judiciary) are separate branches (no common membership)
CABINET and **PRIME MINISTER** are responsible to **LEGISLATURE** which contains government and opposition	**PRESIDENT**, **CONGRESS**, and **SUPREME COURT** constitute government (and opposition)
EVOLVED since 1688	**CREATED** in 1787
parliamentary sovereignty	constitutional sovereignty
countries of the British Commonwealth, Europe, much of Africa	United States and former dependencies (e.g. the Philippines), much of Latin America

* Ironically, neither the Westminster nor the Madisonian system is now typical of the majority of regimes in the parliamentary and separated powers categories, respectively.

Figure 5.5

THE ROLE OF CONSTITUTIONS: TRADITIONAL AND RATIONAL MODELS

The way that a system is put together, its design or blueprint, is found in its *constitution*. Every regime has a constitution—the basic rules that describe the powers of the institutions of the state, their relationship to each other and to the people, which may be more or less formal, more or less detailed, and more or less difficult to change. To employ another analytic distinction, it is possible to contrast *traditional* and *rational* constitutions.

In the traditional constitution, rules are less formal and may not even be written in one specific document identified as *the* Constitution. The rules describe existing and past practices and have evolved over time into their present shape. The informality of these rules does not make them optional—adherence to them is necessary for the regime to function. Unwritten rules that are binding in this way are known as **conventions**, and in this case, as constitutional conventions. Conventions work because it is commonly understood that they prescribe a necessary relationship or set of circumstances. When a convention is blatantly broken or set aside, it either causes a crisis or reflects a widespread understanding that practice requires a new rule. One example of a convention that seems close to losing its meaning is the doctrine of **ministerial responsibility**, intended to define the relationship between a member of the political executive and the administration of the department over which he or she is the nominal head. A successful constitution has the flexibility to evolve as the needs of the regime change. The conventional basis of the traditional constitution suggests it might have that flexibility, but experience shows that this isn't necessarily the case.

The description of the English Constitution as an "unwritten constitution," although somewhat misleading, reflects the primary importance of conventions in that basic body of rules. It is a traditional constitution, and many regimes that were formerly British dominions, such as Canada, Australia, and New Zealand, have areas in their constitution that are substantially traditional, particularly with respect to responsible government.

By contrast, the Constitution of the United States is one of the oldest written constitutions in use today and a good example of a rational constitution—the product of a deliberate effort by its authors to design and create institutions of state for a regime. Such a document is revolutionary because it sets aside what was in place before and establishes something new from constitutional first principles.[*] Such an exercise in constitution-making often follows a political revolution.

A written constitution is a body of law, the supreme law of the regime, literally the Basic Law (as the German constitution is named), from which the authority of all other laws is derived. It is almost always designed so as to be difficult to change, either by requiring a higher level of support than is necessary to pass ordinary law, or by requiring multiple approvals (e.g., by national *and* sub-national governments, or popular ratification in a referendum of a proposal passed by legislatures). In some cases, the protections built into the constitution to prevent it from being too easily changed by those in power make it all but impossible to change—and therefore inflexible. The US Constitution is regarded as one of the most inflexible because it is so difficult to change.

It has become commonly understood, almost a convention, in fact, that any new regime will have a written or rational constitution.

[*]The current US Constitution is actually the second attempt; an earlier constitution (the *Articles of Confederation and Perpetual Union*), which created a confederal state, was the basic law from 1777 to 1789.

THE JUDICIARY AS A BRANCH OF GOVERNMENT

In the Madisonian model of the United States, the judiciary is the third branch of government in a way it has never been in the Westminster model in the United Kingdom. The US Constitution defines the powers of the executive and legislative branches, as well as the powers of the states, the powers reserved to "the people," and the rights that belong to citizens. This provides a basis for the judiciary to consider whether an action by a branch of government is consistent with the powers granted to it and/or consistent with the rights protected in the Constitution. If the action is ruled "unconstitutional," it is not valid. The ability of the courts to consider an action of the executive or legislative branch and rule on its validity is known as **judicial review**.

By contrast, and notwithstanding the 1688 Bill of Rights (see Chapter 3), at Westminster there was no written constitution setting out the powers of the executive or the legislature—their relationship evolved over time and became embedded in constitutional conventions. Nor was there a bill of citizens' rights. Not only was there no basis on which a high court could rule an act of the government unconstitutional, but the judiciary itself was not separate from the executive and legislature. The highest court in the UK consisted of either the Judicial Committee of the Privy Council (part of the executive) or the Law Lords (part of the legislature). Only in 2009 was the United Kingdom Supreme Court made the highest court for most judicial matters.

Common to all systems based on the rule of law is the principle that all citizens, rulers, and those who are ruled are subject to known, impartial rules. No one, not even the highest political official, is above the law. To ensure this is possible, conditions of **judicial independence** are necessary; officers of the courts must be free from political interference or influence. Specific rules about the appointment and removal of judges, the determination of their salary, and other conditions of employment are among the practical means by which judicial independence is realized.

BICAMERALISM—DO TWO HOUSES MAKE A HOME?

Most legislatures, it seems, consist of two houses or chambers (hence **bicameral**) and important decisions made in one legislative chamber must be ratified or confirmed by the other house. In some regimes the two chambers are referred to as the "upper" and the "lower" (or senior and junior) houses, reflecting a time when one house was for the upper classes (the Lords) and the other for the lower classes (commoners, or the Commons), as it remains at Westminster. The upper chamber was expected to act as a check against any radical legislation from the lower house (such as the *Reform Act* of 1832 or any other bill threatening the status quo).

As representative government and then representative democracy advanced and became a principal condition of legitimacy, the "lower" or popularly elected houses became the **confidence chamber** in most parliamentary regimes, and the body from which most of the cabinet was selected. The powers of upper houses to second guess the lower houses were often diminished and in some cases (e.g., Canada's first provinces) these upper chambers were abolished.

From the start, the United States demonstrated another use for second chambers—to represent the sub-national units of the state. Under the US Constitution, representation by population in the House of Representatives is balanced by equal representation of the states in the Senate. Similar considerations inform the composition of the upper house in other **federal** regimes such as Australia, Canada, and Germany (see Chapter 8).

It is useful, then, to distinguish, first, between regimes with bicameral or **unicameral** legislatures (i.e., with one chamber, as in New Zealand and the Scandinavian countries), and, second, among bicameral regimes, whether they have strong or weak bicameralism. In strong bicameralism, the powers of the two legislative chambers are identical. As the powers of one House diminish relative to those of the other House, the effect of bicameralism is progressively weakened.

DEGREES OF FEDERALISM

The particular role of second legislative chambers in federal countries introduces another important dimension: the degree of centralization or decentralization of the state. Formally, or constitutionally, a permanent level of decentralization exists in federal states such as Argentina, Australia, Belgium, Brazil, Canada, Germany, Switzerland, and the United States. In these regimes, the state exists at (at least) two levels—national and **sub-national**—as do the political process, the public policy and administration systems, and even civil society. While the two levels of government are, by definition, autonomous from each other, this does not mean that each can go about its business without interacting with the other. Therefore, in federal regimes, intergovernmental politics is particularly significant, whether this is the vertical relationship between the national state and the sub-national units (e.g., **provinces**, **states**, **cantons**, or ***Länder***), or the horizontal relationships between the sub-national bodies.

Regional and municipal governments provide additional layers, as do local bodies such as school boards, police service boards, social service councils, and the like. An important difference is that in most regimes, local governance has no independent constitutional standing. It is created by a higher level of government—usually by the sub-national units in a federal system, like Canada's provinces, or by the national government in a **unitary** state such as the United Kingdom—and remains subject to the legislation made at the higher level of the state.

A useful distinction in this regard is between the division of powers (federalism) and the **delegation of power** (sometimes known as devolution). As implied above, municipalities and local boards exercise delegated power, authority that is on loan, as it were, even if it seems to be permanently on loan. Canada's northern territories, for example, differ from provinces in that their authority is delegated by (i.e., devolved from) the national government.

DIVISION OF POWERS	DELEGATION OF POWER (DEVOLUTION)
The assignment of spheres of jurisdiction (i.e., powers) between autonomous (independent) levels of state, such as between Canada and its provinces, the United States and its states, Australia and its states, Germany and its *Länder*, usually requiring a constitutional amendment to alter, subject to the agreement of both levels of state.	The assignment of power from one body to another, usually revocable by the body assigning the power (at least in theory*). The powers exercised by the Scottish Parliament and the Northern Ireland and Welsh Assemblies are devolved from the national Parliament at Westminster. *Any power, once surrendered, becomes more difficult to reclaim the longer it is exercised by the body to which it was surrendered.

Figure 5.6

Devolution serves to remind us that decentralization can occur in regimes that are not federal—that is, in unitary states—but usually on terms set by the senior level of the state. Belgium is a regime where the decentralization of power to its principal divisions went so far that a new federal constitution was finally required. Historically, the dynamic was usually the opposite: states would join together into a larger whole in which (and sometimes *by* which) their individuality would be preserved, in other words, to **federate** or **confederate**. Many modern nation-states have their origin in a confederation, including Canada, Germany, Switzerland, and the United States. "Confederation" is still used to describe the creation, in 1867, of the Dominion of Canada with the union of three British North American colonies. However, the term **confederal** is also used to describe a regime in which the national government remains subordinate to the subnational units (see Chapter 8).

ELECTORAL AND PARTY SYSTEMS

The comparative framework also incorporates variables from the **political process**, which is focused on, but is not exclusively about, elections and the system of political parties. The most important factor is the **electoral system**, the set of rules that translates citizens' preferences (votes) into results (seats in the legislature, an executive office) that determine, directly or otherwise, who will govern and who will not.

Although there are many types of electoral rules, the most basic distinction is between those designed to produce *a* winner (**majoritarian systems**) and those intended to ensure the result matches as closely as possible the diversity of choices expressed in the votes (**proportional systems**)—see *Figure 5.7*.

ELECTORAL SYSTEMS	
MAJORITARIAN	PROPORTIONAL
FIRST PAST THE POST (FPP) Canada, United Kingdom	**MIXED MEMBER PROPORTIONAL (MMP)** Germany, New Zealand
ALTERNATIVE VOTE (AV) Australia	**SINGLE TRANSFERABLE VOTE (STV)** Ireland
TWO ROUND SYSTEM (TRS) France	**LIST SYSTEMS (PR LIST)** Netherlands, Sweden, Switzerland

(See Chapter 10)
Figure 5.7

The type of electoral system is related, in turn, to two other regime variables: the **party system**, and the **type of government** that forms in the legislature.

TWO-PARTY VERSUS MULTI-PARTY

Political parties exist in a system (see Chapter 11). While each regime's party system is unique in some respects, party systems share similarities that are often related to the electoral system and to other features of the regime's constitution. For example, two-party systems tend to be associated with majoritarian electoral systems (especially FPP) and multi-party systems with proportional-representation systems. (Regimes without competitive elections often have a one-party system.) The distinction between two-party and multi-party systems matters because parties behave differently in each environment and display characteristics specific to that environment; these differences have significance for voters and for the quality of democracy in the regime.

STRONG VERSUS WEAK PARTIES

A second distinction is between strong and weak parties, measured by the discipline displayed by a party's elected membership. In strong parties, the elected members vote as a bloc and may be disciplined by the party leader or leaders for failing to adhere to the party's official position on any issue. In weak parties, there may be no official party line and leaders have insufficient means at their disposal to force a common vote. Strong parties are associated with parliamentary systems, having developed under the conditions of responsible government. Weak parties are associated with the separated powers of the Madisonian model where there is no government in legislature.

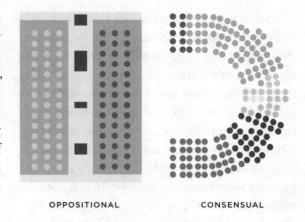

OPPOSITIONAL   CONSENSUAL

Figure 5.8

OPPOSITIONAL VERSUS CONSENSUAL LEGISLATURES

Combining variables, the legislative behaviour of strong parties in a two-party system tends to be **oppositional**. Because one party (usually) has a majority of seats, it does not need to co-operate with its opposition, and in such systems the roles of government and opposition have become institutionalized in a manner that is reflected in the seating of legislators in the legislative chamber.

On the other hand, legislative activity in a two-party system with weak parties often requires **bipartisan brokerage** politics. This is reinforced by the additional circumstance that systems with weak parties often have separated powers with strong bicameralism. The passage of any law usually requires the support of members of both parties, and alliances are made on an issue-by-issue basis.

The behaviour of parties, strong or weak, in multiparty systems is more typically co-operative or even **consensual**, particularly in those regimes where coalition government is the norm. A typical European parliament is configured so that parties sit side by side facing the Speaker or President of the Assembly rather than opposite one another. Both chambers of the US Congress are also arranged in a semi-circular fashion facing the presiding officers and their staff.

TYPE OF GOVERNMENT

Electoral systems also tend to produce specific types of government. A majoritarian system combined with a two-party system results in **majority government**; the addition of another party or parties may produce short-lived **minority** governments. Proportional-representation systems reflect or support multi-party systems and usually generate **coalition** governments (majority or minority). The differences between majority, minority, and coalition governments are explored at greater length in Chapter 6.

RECAPPING

A large number of distinctions have been made in this chapter, including those in *Figure 5.9*. While there is no necessary correspondence between all the items on one side of the table or the other, the positions on the right-hand side are all less likely to concentrate power in one set of hands. The most powerful figure within democratic regimes is the prime minister in a Westminster-style parliament. He or she typically heads a majority government in a strong party system, guaranteeing control of the policy process. If she or he is in office in a regime with no judicial review, a unicameral legislature, and a unitary state, the only effective challenge she or he faces during the period between elections will come from within the party she or he leads. Such was the status of the New Zealand prime minister prior to that regime adopting a proportional representation electoral system in 1996.

The combination of these variables in any regime constitutes, in large part, its institutional setting. The institutions in place present certain possibilities for the political process. So, too, do other factors, such as how **interest groups** interact with policy-makers, the absence or presence of instruments of direct

democracy (referendums, initiatives, and processes for recalling elected representatives), the role of (and rules for) lobbyists, the influence that private economic power has on elected representatives and/or public opinion, and the strength of trade unions and popular **social movements**.

At same time, the type of government, the party system, the degree of judicial review, and whether the constitution is parliamentary or otherwise (perhaps the biggest variable) will influence the way that **public policy** is formulated, and how it is administered. The differences between regimes that have a legal system based on common law and those with **civil law**, or, similarly, the distinction between **adversarial** and **inquisitorial** justice systems, have yet to be noted and added to the mix.

APPENDIX: COMPARATIVE DATA SET

The regimes in Figure 5.10 make up the comparative data set for this text. They are, with two exceptions, countries listed in the top half of *Figure 4.2* (in Chapter 4) in columns 2, 3, and 4. The first exception is the inclusion of Iceland, which has less than one million people, but a land mass greater than 100,000 square kilometres. Apart from Suriname, none of the other countries in the bottom half of columns 2, 3, and 4 has a land mass over 23,000 square kilometres, and the average size of these regimes is under 3,000 square kilometres. The second exception is a group of countries with Freedom House scores that qualify them as electoral democracies, but that also have United Nations Human Development rankings that indicate serious deficiencies in literacy, years of education, and life expectancy, and very often high levels of economic inequality. These countries are Benin, Dominican Republic, Ghana, Mongolia, Namibia, South Africa, and Suriname.

CONSTITUTIONAL SYSTEM

parliamentary ↔ non-parliamentary
dual executive ↔ unified executive
fusion of powers ↔ separation of powers
responsible government ↔ checks and balances

JUDICIAL REVIEW

no review →limited review → full judicial review

LEGISLATURE

unicameral → weak bicameral → strong bicameral

FEDERALISM

unitary → federal → confederal

ELECTORAL SYSTEM

majoritarian ↔ proportional representation

PARTY SYSTEM

two-party ↔ multi-party
strong parties ↔ weak parties

TYPE OF GOVERNMENT

majority/minority ↔ coalition

Figure 5.9

	1	2	3	4	5	6	7	8	9	10	11	12
	ALL REGIMES (45)	MONARCHY/REPUBLIC	U/F	UNI/BI	TERM (YRS)	ELECTORAL SYSTEM	GOVERNMENT	LAST ELECTION	TURNOUT (%)	PARTY SYSTEM (ENLP)	SEPARATE CONSTITUIONAL COURT	CIVIL OR COMMON LAW SYSTEM

PARLIAMENTARY (36)

PROPORTIONAL (27)

	1	2	3	4	5	6	7	8	9	10	11	12
Austria	R (6)	F	Bi	5	List PR(C)	C (2)	2008	78.8	4.27	Y	Civil
Belgium	M	F	Bi	4	List PR(O)	C (6)	2010	89.2	8.43	Y	Civil
Bulgaria	R (5)	U	Uni	4	Parallel[1]	Min	2009	61.0	3.34	Y	Civil
Croatia	R (5)	U	Uni	4	List PR(C)	C (4)	2011	56.3	2.35	Y	Civil
Czech Republic	R[PAR] (5)	U	Bi	4	List PR(O)	C (3)	2010	62.6	4.51	Y	Civil
Denmark	M	U	Uni	4	List PR(C)	C (3)	2011	87.7	5.61	N	Civil
Estonia	R[PAR] (5)	U	Uni	4	List PR(O)	C (2)	2011	62.9	3.84	N	Civil
Finland	R (6)	U	Uni	4	List PR(O)	C (6)	2011	67.4	5.83	N	Civil
Germany	R[PAR] (5)	F	Bi	4	MMP(FPP)	C (2)	2009	70.8	4.83	Y	Civil
Greece	R[PAR] (5)	U	Uni	4	List PR(O)	Maj	2009	70.9	2.59	N	Civil
Hungary	R[PAR] (5)	U	Uni	4	MMP(TRS)	Maj	2010	64.4	2.00	Y	Civil
Iceland	R (4)	U	Uni	4	List PR(C)	C (2)	2009	85.1	4.18	N	Civil
Israel	R[PAR] (7)	U	Uni	4	List PR(C)	C (6)	2009	65.2	6.77	N	Civil
Italy	R[PAR] (7)	U	Bi	5	List PR(C)	C (3)	2008	80.4	3.05	Y	Civil
Latvia	R[PAR] (4)	U	Uni	4	List PR(O)	C (3)	2011	59.5	4.52	Y	Civil
Netherlands	M	U	Bi	4	List PR(C)	C min (2)	2010	75.4	6.74	N	Civil
New Zealand	M	U	Uni	3	MMP(FPP)	Min	2011	73.5	2.98	N	Common
Norway	M	U	Uni	4	List PR(O)	C (3)	2009	76.4	4.07	N	Civil
Poland	R (5)	U	Bi	4	List PR(O)	C (2)	2011	48.9	3.00	Y	Civil
Portugal	R (5)	U	Uni	4	List PR(C)	C (2)	2011	58.1	2.93	Y	Civil
Romania	R (5)	U	Bi	4	List PR(C)	C (2)	2008	39.2	3.23	Y	Civil
Serbia	R (5)	U	Uni	4	List PR(C)	C (9+)	2008	61.4	3.48	Y	Civil
Slovakia	R (5)	U	Uni	4	List PR(O)	C (4)	2010	58.8	4.01	Y	Civil
Slovenia	R (5)	U	Bi	4	List PR(O)	Forming	2011	65.6	4.52	Y	Civil
Spain	M	U	Bi	4	List PR(C)	Maj	2011	71.7	2.60	Y	Civil
Sweden	M	U	Uni	4	List PR(O)	C (5)	2010	84.6	4.53	N	Civil
Switzerland	R[PAR] (1)	F	Bi	4	List PR(F)	C (4)	2011	49.1	5.57	N	Civil

SEMI-PROPORTIONAL (3)

	1	2	3	4	5	6	7	8	9	10	11	12
Ireland	R (7)	U	Bi	5	STV	C (2)	2011	70.1	3.46	N	Common
Japan	M	U	Bi	4	Parallel[3]	Min	2009	69.3	2.10	N	Civil
Lithuania	R (5)	U	Uni	4	Parallel[4]	C (4)	2008	48.5	5.79	Y	Civil

	1	2	3	4	5	6	7	8	9	10	11	12
	ALL REGIMES (45)	MONARCHY/REPUBLIC	U/F	UNI/BI	TERM (YRS)	ELECTORAL SYSTEM	GOVERNMENT	LAST ELECTION	TURNOUT (%)	PARTY SYSTEM (ENLP)	SEPARATE CONSTITUTIONAL COURT	CIVIL OR COMMON LAW SYSTEM
MAJORITARIAN (6)												
Australia	M	F	Bi	3	AV	Min	2010	93.0	2.95	N	Common
Canada	M	F	Bi	4	FPP/SMP	Maj	2011	61.4	2.40	N	Common
France	R (5)	U	Bi	5	TRS	Maj	2007	60.4	2.49	Y	Civil
Mauritius	R^{PAR} (5)	U	Uni	5	Block Vote	C (3)	2010	78.0	1.91	N	Hybrid
Trinidad and Tobago	R^{PAR} (5)	U	Bi	5	FPP/SMP	C (5)	2010	69.5	1.71	N	Common
United Kingdom	M	U	Bi	5	FPP/SMP	C (2)	2010	65.1	2.58	N	Common
PARLIAMENTARY (9)												
PROPORTIONAL (5)												
Argentina	R (4)	F	Bi	4	List PR(C)	n.a.	2009	72.4	7.39	N	Civil
Brazil	R (4)	F	Bi	4	List PR(O)	n.a.	2010	81.9	10.44	N	Civil
Chile	R (4)	U	Bi	4	List PR(C)	n.a.	2009	86.7	5.64	Y	Civil
Costa Rica	R (4)	U	Uni	4	List PR(C)	n.a.	2010	69.1	4.04	N	Civil
Uruguay	R (5)	U	Bi	5	List PR(C)	n.a.	2009	89.9	2.65	N	Civil
SEMI-PROPORTIONAL (3)												
Panama	R (5)	U	Uni	5	Parallel[1]	n.a.	2009	70.0	3.65	N	Civil
South Korea	R (5)	U	Uni	4	Parallel[2]	n.a.	2008	46.0	2.93	Y	Civil
Taiwan	R (4)	U	Uni	4	Parallel[3]	n.a.	2008	58.5	1.75	Y	Civil
MAJORITARIAN (1)												
United States	R (4)	F	Bi	2	FPP/SMP	n.a.	2010	76.4	1.97	N	Common

1 FPP/SRP=31/List(C)=209　2 FPP/SMP=300/List(C)=180　3 TRS=71/List(C)=70　4 FPP/SMP=26/List(O)=45　5 FPP/SMP=254/List(C)=45　6 FPP/SMP=73/List=40

Figure 5.10

EXPLANATORY NOTES

(1) All Regimes: regimes from table in Figure 4.2 averaging 1, 1.5, or 2 on the 2011 Freedom House scores; with population >1,000,000, plus Iceland (>100,000 km²); scoring Very High or High on 2011 UN Human Development Index

(2) Monarchy or Republic: constitutional status of regime; (#)=length of presidential term; R^{PAR} =president is elected by the parliament

(3) U/F: U=unitary state, F=federation

(4) Uni/Bi: Uni=unicameral legislature, Bi=bicameral

(5) Term: fixed (or maximum) term of the legislature

(6) Electoral System: electoral system used to elect the legislature, or, in bicameral systems, the lower house of the legislature (see Chapter 10 for details)

(7) Government: (applies to parliamentary systems) type of cabinet (as of December 2011); Maj=single-party majority; Min=single-party minority; C(#)=majority coalition with number of partners, except where C min; new government not yet formed in Slovenia at year's end

(8) Last Election: date of last legislative election, mid-term in Argentina and United States

(9) Turnout: proportion of registered electors voting in (8)

(10) Party System: ENLP=effective number of legislative parties (see Chapter 10), based on results in last election

(11) Separate Constitutional Court: existence of dedicated court for constitutional cases (see Chapter 13)

(12) Civil or Common Law System: nature of private law system (see Chapter 13)

FURTHER READING

Böckenförde, Markus, Nora Hedling and Winluck Wahiu, eds. *A Practical Guide to Constitution Building*. Stockholm: International Institute for Democracy and Electoral Assistance (International IDEA), 2011. [Book in whole or by chapter may be downloaded from the International IDEA website.]

Gandi, Jennifer. *Political Institutions under Dictatorship*. Cambridge: Cambridge University Press, 2008.

Heffernan, Richard. "Why the Prime Minister Cannot be a President: Comparing Institutional Imperatives in Britain and America." *Parliamentary Affairs*. 58.1 (January 2005): 53–70.

Lundell, Krister. "Accountability and Patterns of Alternation in Pluritarian, Majoritarian and Consensus Democracies." *Government and Opposition*. 46.2 (April 2011): 145–167.

Marquand, David. "The Once and Future Constitution." *Government and Opposition*. 46.2 (April 2011): 274–292.

Systems of Government: Parliamentary Options

Most of the world's successful democracies are parliamentary, whether success is defined in material terms or as the absence of authoritarian interruptions (military **juntas** or civilian dictatorships). Parliamentary democracies vary in important respects, and this chapter focuses on the differences between majoritarian and proportional parliamentary regimes. These, in turn, have much to do with the types of electoral system in use and the party system produced or reinforced by the electoral rules. It is necessary, first, to review the basic features of the parliamentary type of government.

COMPONENTS OF PARLIAMENTARY GOVERNMENT

The essence of parliamentary government is the relationship between the executive and the legislature, expressed as *responsible cabinet government achieved through a fusion of powers*. This has several components.

CABINET GOVERNMENT

First, the government in power (i.e., those who control the state) consists of a committee—the cabinet—of persons exercising executive power both collectively and individually. Headed by the prime minister, the cabinet, as a body, is the author of all government policy and is responsible to the legislature. A cabinet/ government remains in power only as long as it maintains the *confidence* of the legislature—the support of a majority of its members. Individually, each member of cabinet (minister) is the executive or head of a government department or is responsible for an area of public policy. The minister's area of responsibility is known as a **portfolio**. Ministers are expected to shepherd legislation relating to their portfolio through the **legislative process** and answer to the legislature (and its committees) for matters in their department.

Second, in the evolution of the Westminster Parliament, the principle of responsible government motivated prime ministers to appoint an ever larger proportion of the cabinet from the membership of the lower house (in a bicameral legislature)—that is, from the chamber elected on the basis of representation by population. While there are parliaments where ministers do not or cannot hold seats in the legislature, such as those in Norway and the Netherlands, the cabinet is still required to have the support of the legislative body.

Third, the **collective responsibility** of the cabinet to the legislature is shared by all its members. The principle of **cabinet solidarity** requires every member of the cabinet to support each of its decisions. This is one reason why cabinet meetings are held *in camera* (without observers) so that a full discussion of issues can contribute to the consensus that emerges, and why cabinet minutes and other documents often remain secret for a prescribed period of time.

PRIME MINISTER

The head or chair of the cabinet is the prime minister, sometimes described as a "first among equals," which is misleading because the prime minister is in fact preeminent among ministers. In systems with traditional constitutions, the prime minister may determine not only the membership of the cabinet, but its size, structure, and style of decision making. In some regimes, such as the United Kingdom, there is a distinction between what is called "the Ministry" (which includes all members with a ministerial role) and "the cabinet," which is a much smaller committee composed of the prime minister and senior ministers acting as the collective executive. In such a setting it is the prime minister who determines how small or large the cabinet may be. In regimes with a rational constitution, the number of cabinet ministers and their portfolios may be prescribed by law.

As head of cabinet, the prime minister is the head of government and the chief *political* executive. Parliamentary systems have a **dual executive**: someone *other* than the prime minister holds the position of head of state, a *formal* executive performing mainly formal and ceremonial functions, but also holding powers that are critical at certain times in the political cycle and used under very specific circumstances. The exercise of these powers may be prescribed in greater or lesser detail in the constitution, and is the most important part of what remains of the royal prerogative in regimes where the head of state is a monarch.

PARTY POLITICS

Parliamentary government is also about party politics. The fusion of powers and the requirements of responsible government made it inevitable that political parties would become highly structured, disciplined bodies, an institutional imperative now supported by the cost of conducting a modern political campaign. The focus in this chapter is a political party's elected members in the legislature, collectively identified as its **caucus** (or the parliamentary party). The parliamentary setting provides a number of opportunities for party leaders to reward loyalty or punish disloyalty within the caucus. Promotion to cabinet is perhaps the chief prize, but favoured committee assignments, or even opportunities to participate in parliamentary debate or question period, can be granted or withheld from ordinary members (whom the Westminster tradition labels as "backbenchers").

Strong, unified parties and the competition between them are central to what happens in the legislature, in the cabinet, and in the relations between cabinet and legislature in parliamentary systems. Since the prime minister is often also the head of his or her party, in addition to being the head of government, he or she has a particularly central position within the parliamentary system. However, the relationship of the prime minister to the cabinet; of the cabinet to the legislature; and of cabinet, legislature, and prime minister to the political parties can be very different under different types of parliamentary government and within majoritarian and proportional systems.

MAJORITY, MINORITY, OR COALITION

The level of support that the government can command in the legislature and the number of parties that are part of government are the primary variables in determining whether a parliament has a majority government, a minority government, or a coalition government [*Figure 6.1*]. "Majority" government and "minority" government both indicate a single-party government. A coalition government may control a minority or a majority of the members of the legislature.

Why do these distinctions matter? Consider the contrast between majority and minority governments in *Figure 6.2*. In short, minority government is susceptible

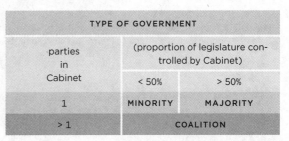

TYPE OF GOVERNMENT		
parties in Cabinet	(proportion of legislature controlled by Cabinet)	
	< 50%	> 50%
1	MINORITY	MAJORITY
> 1	COALITION	

Figure 6.1

to the observations (or criticisms) that it is inherently unstable (because it cannot control the outcome of any vote) and indecisive (it must always negotiate and compromise to secure the support of other parties). Majority government is vulnerable to the observation (or criticism) that it may be unrepresentative and/or unresponsive to constructive criticism.

Coalition governments can display the characteristics of majority *and* minority governments—the best coalition governments combine their strengths, the worst coalition governments combine their weaknesses. A coalition exists when there is a formal agreement between two or more parties to govern together; this compact involves three elements:

· a division of the cabinet seats between or among the parties;
· agreement about which cabinet posts (including the prime minister and deputy prime minister) each party will hold; and
· a list of policies that the parties have agreed to implement (i.e., the government's agenda).

WHY COALITION?

Apart from situations of national emergency (which can prompt parties in any system to govern collectively), coalition governments usually form in systems

MAJORITY governments, because they control a majority in the legislature, are unlikely to be defeated and will serve out their full term—in this respect they are very stable.

WHICH MEANS THAT

MINORITY governments constantly face the possibility of defeat and may not be able to serve out their full term—in this sense they can be quite vulnerable.

A MAJORITY government will control the policy and legislative agendas, and be free do to whatever it wishes, subject to its sensitivity to public opinion, its desire to be re-elected, and the effectiveness of any delaying or blocking measures available to the opposition.

WHICH MEANS THAT

WHICH MEANS THAT

A MINORITY government can only survive with the co-operation of another party or parties, making deals on an issue-by-issue basis, or in sustained legislative partnership with a like-minded party.

Majority governments promote oppositional legislative politics—any party excluded from government, with limited input to the policy process and no control over the legislative agenda, must settle for the frustrating task of opposing all government policy while waiting for the next election.

WHICH MEANS THAT

WHICH MEANS THAT

A MINORITY government may also promote oppositional legislative politics, if it has reason to believe that its defeat is unlikely, or, if it wishes to engineer its own defeat in order to bring about an election it believes it can win. A minority government that intends to govern for any length of time, though, may find it is better served by seeking partnerships and making compromises that accommodate other parties' positions to gain their support—in short, pursuing a more consensual politics.

While a MAJORITY government sounds democratic, it very well may not be. At the very least, it limits the popular input to government to the segments of society that supported the governing party. How representative the government is will be influenced by how much its support reflects the different interests in civil society.

WHICH MEANS THAT

Government by a party with a MINORITY of the seats may seem undemocratic, but if such a government remains in power because it receives a majority of votes in the legislature, a majority that is composed of the votes of two or more parties, it may be more representative of the population at large than a majority government.

Figure 6.2

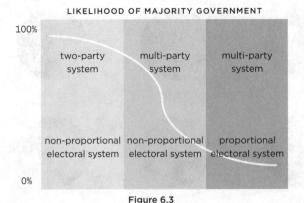

LIKELIHOOD OF MAJORITY GOVERNMENT

100%

two-party system

multi-party system

multi-party system

non-proportional electoral system

non-proportional electoral system

proportional electoral system

0%

Figure 6.3

in which it is unlikely that any party will form a majority on its own. The likelihood that one party will win an outright majority of seats is itself a product of two factors—the number of political parties and the electoral system. As a general rule, the greater the number of parties winning seats, the less likely it is that any one of them will win a majority. Also as a general rule, the more proportional the electoral system, the less likely it is that one party will win a majority.

The order—from left to right—of the electoral systems in *Figure 6.3* is a rough guide to their evolution. Many systems started out with a basic two-party system (e.g., Whigs vs. Tories, Democrats vs. Republicans, Liberals vs. Conservatives), in which all that is necessary is a First Past the Post (**FPP**) electoral system— the candidate with the *most* votes wins. If there are only two parties, the winner will necessarily have a majority of the seats, and the parliament will have a majority government. The addition of another small party or two will usually not make a difference. For reasons explained at greater length in Chapter 10, an FPP system tends to give a premium to the party that finishes first in the election. This means it receives a larger share of seats than its share of votes. Related

characteristics of FPP tend to preserve a two-party system by making it difficult for new parties to succeed.

If a multi-party system emerges, the odds that the winning party will have a majority are greatly diminished. At least two factors can lead to a multi-party system. One is social: a diversity of interests that cannot be accommodated within a two-party system. The other is institutional: the presence of a proportional-representation system that (a) does not provide the premium that winning parties rely on to get their majority, and (b) allows smaller parties to become established because it treats all parties fairly.

Since 1993, Canada has provided an example of a regime with a multi-party system in a majoritarian (or non-proportional) electoral system. During this period there were three straight minority governments (after the 2004, 2006, and 2008 elections), and the majority after the 1997 election was by a slim margin (*Figure 6.4*). It remains to be seen whether the 2011 majority government is a return to "normalcy," or a temporary

Throughout this book, reference to a coalition should be understood to mean an **executive coalition**, as described in the bullet points above. An arrangement whereby the party in government has the formal support of a party in the legislature—a *pact*—is sometimes called a **legislative coalition**. An arrangement whereby two parties agree to provide mutual support in an election campaign, including an agreement not to run candidates in the same constituencies, is an **electoral coalition**; it signals a high probability that the parties will continue to work together after the election in a legislative pact or a coalition government.

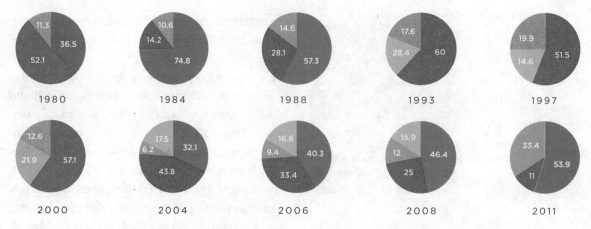

Charts present share of seats in House of Commons after each general election.

■ Progressive Conservative, then later, Conservative Party ■ Liberal Party ■ New Democratic Party
■ Bloc Québecois ■ Reform Party, later Canadian Alliance ■ Green Party 2011

Figure 6.4

deviation from the trend towards minority government. Such a trend, if it were to last, could lead in one of two directions:

· the formation of a coalition government, the first in the national Parliament since 1917; or
· increased support from parties in Parliament and/or the public for moving to a proportional representation (PR) electoral system.

WHY NOT A COALITION?

With minority government accounting for nine of the last 19 administrations in Canada, it might be asked why a coalition government was not formed in any of these situations.

SYSTEM EXPECTATIONS. Each electoral system generates expectations about what type of government is "normal." Because FPP systems tend to produce majority governments, the expectation preceding each election is that a majority government will result. Whenever a minority government is produced, it is treated as a temporary state of affairs that will disappear after the next election.

COMPATIBILITY OF PARTNERS. Coalitions require that parties are able to work with each other. As noted above, regimes with majoritarian systems tend to produce oppositional legislative politics, which means parties develop long-standing antipathy towards one another, even when their ideological positions, in another system, would make them logical partners. In Canada, the strongest rivalry (going back to Confederation) is between the Liberals and Conservatives, each of which is perhaps the most natural ally for the other.

Coalitions can also be difficult to form when there is a party with which no other party is willing to risk an alliance—a **pariah party**. Such describes the Communist Party in Italy during the years after World War II and, arguably, the position of the Bloc Québécois in Canada's Parliament from 1993 to 2011.

ABSENCE OF CRISIS. Coalitions often form to create a controlling majority in the legislature in order to be able to take decisive, even unpopular, measures in response to a crisis or serious set of policy challenges. Canada's only coalition at the national level was during World War I, and it was the country's longest-serving parliament. The coalition that formed after the 2010 election in the United Kingdom was that country's first since World War II, and the decision to go that route was described in part as a response to the economic challenges left over from the 2008–09 recession.

In short, Canada provides an example of a multi-party system persisting with a non-proportional electoral system normally associated with two-party systems. When a proportional representation (PR) electoral system is in place, a multi-party system is reinforced. By design, a PR system delivers to each party a share of seats in the legislature that matches its share of votes—an outcome so obviously consistent with basic ideas of fairness that in countries with long experience of PR, any other way of determining outcomes is basically unthinkable. It means that any party that can attract some minimum level of support—how small a measure will depend on whether there is a **legal threshold**—will gain a corresponding share of seats in the legislature.

In some cases, PR systems originate because of the existence of multi-party systems, not vice versa. In New Zealand, for example, having more than two parties in an FPP electoral system contributed to outcomes that were clearly contrary to the preferences expressed by a majority of voters. These events led to the eventual adoption of a PR electoral system in the mid-1990s. Joseph Colomer has argued that in a multi-party FPP setting, most parties eventually realize that the odds of being part of the government (i.e., in coalition) in a

PARLIAMENTARY BASICS
ELECTION DAY a week or two is required to validate the results and publish them officially
FORMATION OF GOVERNMENT* a prime minister is nominated by the head of state and asked to assemble a cabinet (government)
SWEARING IN OF GOVERNMENT* cabinet is sworn in by the head of state (or rep.) and ministers take office
FIRST MEETING OF PARLIAMENT* head of state issues proclamation summoning Parliament to meet for the first time and elect or appoint a Speaker to preside over its meetings **INAUGURAL (THRONE) SPEECH* & VOTE** head of state reads government's outline of its plans for the coming legislative Session, followed by debate and a vote to test the legislature's confidence
PARLIAMENT SITS a parliamentary calendar determines when the legislature meets to do business or stands recessed
PROROGATION* [1] having finished the agenda set out in the inaugural speech, or wishing to set new goals, the government ends the Session by asking the head of state (or rep.) to prorogue parliament, which ends the Session
PROCLAMATION OF OPENING* head of state issues proclamation summoning Parliament to meet and open the new Session **INAUGURAL (THRONE) SPEECH & VOTE** head of state reads government's plans for the new Session, followed by debate and vote
PARLIAMENT MEETS according to the parliamentary calendar, the legislature meets to do business or stands recessed until Prorogation or Dissolution
DISSOLUTION* head of state (or rep) ends parliament and starts election period
ELECTION DAY . . .

*indicates involvement of head of state (or representative, such as a Governor General)

[1] it was once common for parliaments to have one Session per year, beginning with a speech setting out the legislative agenda for the year and ending with Prorogation, a practice that made great sense when Parliament sat for only two or three months a year

Figure 6.5

proportional system are greater than the odds of winning a majority on their own. Once parties with that understanding control a majority of seats in the legislature, electoral reform is all but inevitable.

WHERE COALITION IS THE "NORM"

To the degree that social diversity in modern regimes is unlikely to be adequately represented by any two-party system, Colomer's argument suggests that the long-term future of democracy is one of proportionality and coalition. At present, a majority of developed democracies incorporate proportionality as a key characteristic of the design of their electoral system. Of the 45 regimes in the Chapter 5 data set, 32 use a PR system to elect their legislature and another six use a semi-proportional system.

In such countries, the expectations about what is "normal" parliamentary government are quite different. A single-party majority is an oddity, possible but unlikely. Minority government is quite common, not as a temporary measure until an election can be forced that will return a majority but as a viable option for governing until the next scheduled election. The "norm" in such countries is coalition government, with two or more parties sharing the reins of power.

When coalition government is the "norm," an entirely different set of practices and expectations develops around the behaviour of political parties and their relationships with each other than is the case in majoritarian FPP parliaments. Compromise and co-operation become routine because they are required to form and maintain a working coalition. Such an approach also helps minority government to survive: instead of governing as if it has a majority (as is typical in a majoritarian parliament), the minority will govern as if it is in a coalition by making deals with other parties on an issue-by-issue basis, or by securing the regular legislative support of a party not in government. Whereas majoritarian systems such as those created under FPP tend to produce oppositional legislative politics, coalition governments have long been linked to a more **consensual** approach to governing.

> "The unwritten rules of the game in British politics are deeply intertwined with the assumption that one party will win a clear majority and rule the roost. If that assumption is no longer valid, a very large proportion of the normal conventions of government would come under challenge."
>
> David Butler (qtd. in Institute for Government, April 2010)

THE GOVERNMENT-FORMATION PROCESS

Contrary to countless post-election broadcasts, citizens in a parliamentary democracy do *not* elect the government. The government is *formed* out of the individuals elected to the legislature. However, since the development of strong parties during the nineteenth century it has been more accurate to say that the government is formed out of the political parties in the legislature.

ROLE OF THE HEAD OF STATE

Responsibility for overseeing the formation of government in a parliamentary system rests with the **head of state**. While the distinction between head of state and **head of government** originates in the distinction between the monarch and his or her chief minister, a *dual executive* is a constitutional necessity in all parliamentary systems, republics, and constitutional monarchies alike.

Long before the development of disciplined political parties, it became, and remains, the duty of the head of state to nominate an individual to form a government—in other words, to serve as prime minister and assemble a cabinet of ministers capable of receiving and sustaining the support of a majority in the legislature. Responsibility for key decisions about the formation of government and the dissolution of the legislature remains the most important power exercised by the head of state, someone occupying what is otherwise a largely formal (but not for that reason unimportant) position.

In countries like Canada, with a traditional constitution, the role of the head of state is often a matter defined by convention. Where the activity of the head of state is infrequent, it may not be generally understood, even by the political actors, let alone the general public. In parliamentary republics, or regimes with a rational constitution, the steps that the head of state is to take in the government-formation process (or following a vote

Arendt Lijphart used nine variables, only some of which refer to parliamentary characteristics, to distinguish between "majoritarian" and "consensual" democracies.

of non-confidence, or when the government resigns) may be set out in considerable detail in the constitution.

It is necessary that there always be a cabinet in office, even when the government has formally resigned or an election has been called. Normally, the prime minister and ministers remain responsible for their offices until they are re-elected or a new government is sworn in to replace them (this is described as the **demissionary phase** of their administration). When a coalition government falls apart, or the members of the executive refuse to remain in their posts, the head of state will usually appoint an interim government to serve as a caretaker administration until an election is held and the new government formed.

NO MERE FORMALITY

The head of state is often described as performing a *formal* role, which is true to a point but risks giving the impression that this half of the dual executive is unimportant, perhaps even expendable. This chapter describes several moments in parliamentary government when the head of state may be called upon to exercise powers attached to his or her office that are not fully prescribed by rules and conventions (as would be any purely formal exercise of authority).

The importance of formal authority should be acknowledged, primarily for the legitimacy it confers. For example, having a diploma or a driver's licence signed by the proper authority (the university chancellor, the Minister of Transportation) and printed in

an official manner are formalities that matter, because they signal to others the validity of the document. Where the exercise of power is formally contained in rules and precedents, someone is required to recognize and apply the rules, and not just anyone, but a person properly occupying that position.

Several of the duties of the head of state serve to provide legitimacy to the actions of government, and he or she serves as a representative of the state (but not its government) on the world stage. The individual who serves as head of state should be capable of commanding the respect of all citizens and all parties.

POST-ELECTION SCENARIOS

RE-ELECTION. The simplest situation is the re-election of a majority government (strictly speaking, the election of a legislature with a majority of its members supporting the government still in place from the previous legislature). No discretionary activity is required by the head of state. The prime minister may "shuffle the cabinet" (i.e., revise its membership) in response to the retirement or defeat of current ministers and the election of new members.

ONE-PARTY MAJORITY. If the newly elected legislature does not contain a majority of members whose support is committed to the government still in place from the previous parliament, then a number of possibilities arise. If there is a party that has won control of a majority of the seats, the head of state will invite its leader to form a government and schedule a meeting with the outgoing prime minister to make arrangements for the transfer of power.

NO MAJORITY. If the election returns a parliament in which no party has a majority, it may be unclear which party should be given the opportunity to form a government. The strongest claims will be made by the party with the largest number of seats and by the party that was in office when the election was called. If the party that was previously in power *is* the party with the largest seat total (Party D in *Figure 6.6*), the head of state will likely be required (by convention or constitutional rules) to invite the leader of this party to form a government. In some parliaments with traditional constitutions, this is true even when the other parties have made it clear that they will vote to defeat this government.

Party A	9
Party B	42
Party C	4
Party D	**45**

Figure 6.6

In some regimes, once the individual invited to form the government has finalized a possible cabinet, the head of state polls the parliament as a whole to determine whether the proposed government has the support of a majority of its members. This is known as an **investiture vote**; the head of state will not (or cannot) appoint a cabinet that loses an investiture vote.

In countries with a multi-party system, it is often possible for a party that falls just short of a majority to govern by working out partnerships with other parties on an issue-by-issue basis. The likelihood of coalition government increases where an investiture vote is a constitutional requirement. The investiture vote asks the legislature to evaluate the government as a whole, prior to its presentation of any policy proposals.

If the party that most recently governed (Party B in *Figure 6.7*) is *not* the party with the largest number of seats, the head of state must decide which party should have the first opportunity to form a government—unless an existing provision directs the head of state one way or another. A constitution could require that the leader of the party with the largest number of seats be given the first chance to form a government, and if unsuccessful, the leader of the second-place party be given a chance, and so on. Another set of rules might require the leader of the previous government to be given the first opportunity, followed by the party leader controlling the largest number of seats.

Party A	9
Party B	**42**
Party C	4
Party D	45

Figure 6.7

LESSONS FROM THE 2010 UK ELECTION

Long before the 2010 general election in the United Kingdom, many observers anticipated a "hung parliament" (what the British call it when no party has a majority). Striking, but not surprising, is how many of the experts believed that minority government was the most likely (if not the only) possible outcome. The title of a report, "Making Minority Government Work," published just six months before the election by a major think tank, reflects that judgment: (www.instituteforgovernment.org.uk/pdfs/making-minority-gov-work.pdf).

Four days after the election, it was reported that senior Conservative officials were urging leader David Cameron not to go full out into coalition with the Liberal Democrats and, in particular, to resist any demand by the Liberal Democrats for proportional representation as the price of their support. Another analysis suggested that only 16,000 more votes, distributed among the 19 electoral districts where the margin by which the Conservatives lost was the smallest, would have given them a majority government (www.dailymail.co.uk/news/election/article-1275917/UK-ELECTION-RESULTS-2010-David-Cameron-urged-to-LibDem-demands.html). This is an example of the mind-set that a new election could easily restore majority government.

To be equally hypothetical, any leader in David Cameron's position might calculate that the concessions made to get a coalition with a smaller party and long-term stability in government might be preferable to the ongoing vulnerability of minority government. As noted in a PowerPoint presentation still available on the Institute for Government website in early 2011: "Coalition (majority) rule makes life difficult within government but simple in parliament. Minority government is the other way around" (www.instituteforgovernment.org.uk/images/files/understanding_hung_parliaments.ppt).

A coalition controlling 363 seats (of 650) emerged two months after the election, composed of the Conservatives (306 seats) and Liberal Democrats (57 seats). The coalition agreement gave the Liberal Democrats 5 of the 22 cabinet seats, including leader Nick Clegg as Deputy Prime Minister (www.cabinetoffice.gov.uk/news/coalition-documents).

Two other specific outcomes of this process are worth noting. First, long-term stability was enhanced by the agreement of the partners to set the date for the next election (subject to the consent of the Queen) as May 7, 2015—legislation to bring in a fixed-term of five years for parliamentary elections was introduced. Second, the coalition agreement committed to holding a referendum on changing the electoral system to the Alternative Vote (AV) system, which is the majoritarian system used in Australia, Malta, Papua New Guinea, and Fiji.

In some places, the individual invited to form a government is called the **formateur**. The Greek constitution requires the head of state to invite the leader of the largest party to act as *formateur*, and if this individual is unsuccessful, the leader of the second-largest party, and so on, in order. Where there is discretion for the head of state and where the choices are less clear-cut, there is a danger that the head of state might appear to be involved in the struggles of partisan politics. To avoid this, some constitutions designate the use of an *informateur*—a senior statesman or retired politician—whose role is to conduct informal inquiries and negotiations leading to the designation of a *formateur*.

THE CONCLUSION OF A GOVERNMENT AND ITS IMPLICATIONS

In a parliamentary system, the government may end at any time, for one of the following reasons:

LOSS OF LEGISLATIVE CONFIDENCE. The principle of responsible government requires a government to resign if it loses the support of a majority in the legislature. What counts as a **loss of confidence** can vary considerably. In traditional Westminster parliaments, in addition to a direct motion of non-confidence in the government, defeat of the motion following the presentation of the government's agenda (the Speech from the Throne) and the defeat of Budget measures are considered to indicate a lack of confidence. Nonetheless, some government leaders treat every vote on government business as a vote of confidence, if only to keep their members in line. Such a threat is more effective in those systems in which the loss of confidence is assumed to lead automatically to an election.

In Westminster parliaments, the rules about which votes count as a measure of confidence are often a matter of convention. Other countries have constitutionalized rules concerning confidence. France and Sweden require the vote of an absolute majority of legislators, not simply a majority of those present at the time of the vote. In Spain, the motion of non-confidence must specify who is to replace the prime minister. Germany only permits a *constructive* vote of non-confidence—the motion must specify the composition of the government that would replace the current one. There are many cases when opposition parties are united in their desire to bring down the government but unable to agree on a workable partnership to replace it. In Switzerland, a vote of non-confidence in the Executive is not an option (see Chapter 7).

THE CABINET IMPLODES. This is most likely where internal dissension, personality clashes, or changing circumstances cause one or more of the coalition partners to pull out of the government. It is also possible that an internal party division could split a minority or majority government, conceivably after a change (or seeking a change) in leadership. What is left of the government may not control enough support in the legislature to continue.

THE GOVERNMENT VOLUNTARILY RESIGNS. The most common reason for an unforced resignation is to seek an early election. There are three strategic reasons for doing so: (1) to capitalize on high levels of popularity that may not last until the next election is scheduled, (2) to demonstrate there is popular support for a policy that the opposition has been blocking, and (3) to seek a new mandate after a change in leadership.

THE TERM OF PARLIAMENT ENDS. Every parliament has either a set term of office with fixed-date elections, or a maximum term of office and flexible elections. Either way, the last *possible* day that the government will enjoy the confidence of the legislature is known well in advance.

The end of a government means that it must be replaced by another. This requires forming a new government from the current parliament or dissolving the legislature and holding a general election to return a new parliament, from which a new government will be formed. At the end of a parliament's term of office, the legislature is dissolved and a new election follows—there is nothing to be decided by the head of state. But, if the government resigns early, prior to the scheduled end of the parliament, the head of state must decide between inviting another party leader to attempt to form a government, or dissolving the legislature and issuing the call for an election. The possible scenarios

WITH PREMATURE END OF GOVERNMENT, THE HEAD OF STATE . . .	TYPE OF GOVERNMENT		
	MAJORITY	MINORITY	COALITION
1 . . . invites current prime minister to form a new government	never	never	common
2 . . . invites another party leader to form a government	never	possible	common
3 . . . appoints a "caretaker" government to govern until the next scheduled election	rare	possible	possible
4 . . . dissolves Parliament and calls an early election	normal	common	possible

Figure 6.8

depend on circumstance and on the type of government in power (see *Figure 6.8*).

1—If a coalition government falls apart, it may be possible for the existing prime minister to put together another coalition, replacing one partner with another, or working out a new agreement with the previous partner or partners.

2—If a minority government falls apart or is defeated, it may be possible for the leader of an opposition party to form a viable government. If the minority government of Party D (*Figure 6.9*) were to be defeated, the potential of Party B to govern with the support of Party A would merit careful consideration. On occasion, with defections and deaths, a government with a small majority has, during the course of the parliament, been turned into a minority government (e.g., the UK Conservative government in 1996–1997). In such a case, the former majority government could be defeated *and* replaced with an alternative government.

Party A	9
Party B	42
Party C	4
Party D	**45**

Figure 6.9

Where a coalition government fails, it is even more feasible that an alternative government can be formed, led by a different prime minister from one of the parties in the just-dissolved coalition, or from one of the parties previously excluded from the coalition.

3—Most regimes with rational constitutions (and an increasing number of those with traditional constitutions) have fixed electoral terms, running on a three-, four-, or five-year cycle. In at least one case—Norway—an early election is not constitutionally possible. In many cases, particularly in regimes with three-year cycles, or where elections for all levels of government are held on the same day, early elections are not desirable. Where the defeat or resignation of a government occurs within a few months of the next scheduled election, the head of state may appoint a *caretaker government* to serve out the interval. This role may be taken by the existing government or the senior coalition partner, but it does not matter too much who is governing—a caretaker cabinet is pledged to take no new policy initiatives except in response to urgent circumstances. If significant steps are required, the caretaker government is expected to consult with the opposition parties on an appropriate remedy. All parliamentary regimes have *de facto* caretaker governments during the election period (from the dissolution of the

Interior of the House of Commons, Parliament of Canada. Ottawa, Ontario.

parliament until the swearing-in of the post-election cabinet).

4—If a majority government resigns, requesting dissolution of the parliament and a new election, there is little choice but to grant the request, since the party with majority is in a position to defeat any alternative government. In regimes with FPP, where majority governments are the norm, this is also understood to be the normal way that parliaments end and elections are called. Any other set of events (as in 1, 2, and 3) seems to be largely unknown.

Accordingly, in such a regime, when a minority government requests dissolution because it is ready to take its chances on an election, it, too, normally gets what it wants, even though an alternative government might be found among the opposition parties. One study of 20 democracies over a 33-year period found that defeat in the legislature was the most frequent cause of termination for minority governments, and that of all types of government, minority governments were the most likely to be terminated by legislative defeat (Budge and Keman). The study did not show how many times this defeat was engineered by the government rather than the opposition.

A CLOSER LOOK AT COALITION GOVERNMENT

The most common parliamentary government in liberal democracies is coalition government. In the overwhelming majority of cases it is associated with PR electoral systems and multi-party governments.

The popularity of PR electoral systems is explained at greater length in Chapter 10, but the briefest explanation is their success in meeting proposition D3 (noted in Chapter 4: a regime is more democratic the more exactly the outputs generated by the political process reflect the inputs made by citizens). PR systems are designed to give each party a share of seats that matches its share of votes. The societal and political pressures that work towards multi-party systems (see Chapter 11) are also better accommodated by the correspondence of outputs to inputs in PR systems than by the winner-take-all dynamic of FPP systems. As the proportion of majoritarian democracies declines worldwide, a comparative approach to politics requires greater attention to coalition government.

By definition, as noted, coalition government has three elements:

1. Two or more parties share the role of government.
2. The partners agree on the allocation between them of cabinet seats, including the prime minister and deputy prime minister(s).
3. The partners negotiate a program of policies on which they will govern, based on their election campaign manifestos.

In *Making Minority Government Work*—the Institute for Government report on the prospects for a hung parliament in the United Kingdom—the authors (Hazel and Paun) suggested a fourth element: "Agreement on procedures to consult and resolve disputes within the coalition is as important as agreement on policies" (6).

FORMING A PARTNERSHIP

The first matter to be determined is how many parties will share the role of government, and any other arrangements with parties that are necessary to provide the coalition with stability.

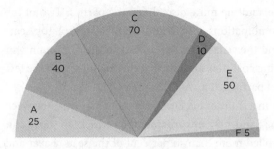

Figure 6.10

Putting together a *winning* coalition—a partnership that controls a majority of seats in the legislature—is the first goal. Formal coalition theory, which draws upon the branch of mathematics called game theory, suggests that of all the possible winning coalitions, the one that is formed will be a **minimal winning** coalition. A minimal winning coalition has only as many parties as is necessary to control a majority of seats, but would cease to do so if it lost any one of its members. In the hypothetical result (*Figure 6.10*) for a 200-seat legislature, there are at five minimal winning coalitions:

COALITION	ABE	ACD	BC	BDEF	CE
SEATS	115	105	110	105	120

Figure 6.11

Some of these combinations may seem more likely than others, although even BDEF could describe a situation where Party C is a pariah party that none of the other parties will partner with. Among minimal winning combinations, some suggest the best outcome is the **minimum winning** coalition, the smallest among the minimal winning conditions. The reasoning here is that the fewer members there are to share the advantages of government, the more loyal the members will be, and the more disciplined the parties. Two of the combinations—ACD and BDEF—control 105 seats, and the same logic that points to the minimum winning coalition suggests that the coalition with the fewest partners (i.e., ACD) is preferable.

In a study of 196 European cabinets formed between 1945 and 1987 in parliaments in which no party controlled more than 50 per cent of the seats, Laver and Schofield (70) found that minimal winning coalitions were the most common (39.3%), but only just ahead of minority governments (37.2%). The remaining 23.5 per cent were **surplus majority** coalitions, where at least one party *more* than was required to control a majority of seats was included in the partnership. Several factors may explain surplus coalitions, not least the possibility that an extra party in the coalition may diminish the ability of any party to exert pressure on the others by threatening to withdraw from the partnership.

Two other considerations may play a role in determining which combination of parties makes up the coalition, as well as its stability. Coalition formation is about more than putting together enough seats to control the legislature; it is also about finding an agenda with which to govern. The ease with which policy agreements can be negotiated and the likelihood that the parties will support these over the life of the parliament depends on the compatibility of the parties. To reach a policy agreement, all parties in a coalition will have to put on hold or even abandon some of the positions on which they campaigned and attracted votes. The closer the parties are ideologically, the more acceptable any trade-offs they make may be to their core supporters.

Election results in multi-party systems are often presented in a half-pie chart like the hypothetical result presented in *Figure 6.10*. The parties are arranged on

the basis of their ideologies from one end of the spectrum to the other. Looked at in this light, some of the minimal winning coalitions look much less likely (e.g., ABE or BDEF) than others (e.g., BC or CE). The affinity or compatibility of parties in this sense is captured by the term **connected coalition**, which indicates that all the partners are ideologically adjacent to each other. Adding a party to create a connected coalition is another reason for the high proportion of surplus winning coalitions. CE, for example, is a minimal winning coalition with the partners separated only by the relatively small party D. Incorporating D into a CDE coalition could be a sound strategic move, especially if D can help the two larger parties find a middle ground on some difficult issues.

Finally, any combination containing Party C has a greater chance of forming a viable coalition, because C controls what is called the **median legislator**. If all the legislators are arranged in a series from the most right wing to the most left wing (or from most conservative to most radical; or from most interventionist to most laissez-faire), the representative in the exact middle is the median legislator. There is some reason to think that coalitions or minority governments containing the median legislator might be more stable than other combinations, probably because of the tendency for public opinion to cluster at the centre.

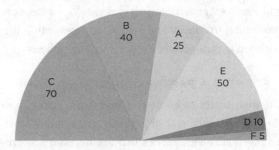

Figure 6.12

In *Figure 6.12* the parties' seat totals are the same as above, but their ideological order has been shuffled. Here, B controls the median legislator and is in the most favourable position; it can partner with C on the one side, or with A and E on the other side, in either case forming a connected minimal winning coalition.

In short, coalitions are less about numbers and more about which parties can work together. Where public opinion is polarized, or there are dimensions other than ideology shaping policy preferences, the median legislator may have no significance. Coalitions form in the rough and tumble of political life, not in the abstract. Theory can only guide expectations in the absence of knowing anything about the parties themselves, their history, their leaders, their past successes or failures in government, the issues that are driving the political agenda, or the nastiness that might have inhabited the election campaign. These real-world considerations explain why so many coalition outcomes are not quite (or even radically unlike) what game theory might have predicted.

SHARING THE GOVERNMENT

The coalition agreement to govern jointly requires the partners to negotiate several distinct, but ultimately related, matters. The first concerns the actual division of the cabinet, starting with who will be the prime minister and finishing with the most junior minister or secretary of state. Certain general rules seem to apply, although there are exceptions to each of these:

(a) Each party's share of seats at the cabinet table will be proportionate to its share of legislative seats.

(b) The prime minister will be the leader of the largest party in the coalition.

(c) Leaders of other parties in the coalition will hold senior portfolios (such as deputy prime minister, attorney general, or finance minister) and/or positions of particular interest to their parties and/or to themselves. The leader of a Green party might prefer to head the environment ministry or the energy department; the leader of a party with a rural base may want control of the agriculture ministry.

(d) Parties, generally, negotiate for responsibilities that are consistent with the interests of their supporters, or that, traditionally, have been "theirs."

The coalition agreement will include a statement of policies that the new government will pursue or support during its time in office. This may be the most difficult part of the exercise because the platform presented to the legislature must be one that all coalition partners can support publicly (unless a party negotiates the right to dissent from a measure that is fundamentally contrary to its historic positions). All partners need to show a willingness to compromise, modify their positions, or even accept defeat on some issues in order to secure victories elsewhere. Junior coalition partners will have to be content with less, so long as there is some gain at the policy table to take back to supporters.

As noted earlier, a major concession that the UK Liberal Democrats were able to secure as the price of their participation with the Conservatives after the 2010 election was the holding of a referendum on electoral reform (albeit for a system that was not their preferred option). The subsequent failure of the referendum may have left some Liberal Democrats second-guessing their party's support for the rest of the government's agenda.

Interior of Landtag of Baden-Wurttemberg. Stuttgart, Germany.

Interior of the Scottish Parliament. Edinburgh, United Kingdom.

In regimes where coalition government is common, if not the norm, a consideration in designing the election **manifesto,** and during the election campaign, is awareness of the possible partnerships that could form after the election. These manifestos are comprehensive explanations of the party's positions on all the salient issues. Pre-election party conventions can play a significant role in their drafting.

The strong influence of the party membership means that sometimes the compromises agreed to by the parliamentary leaders in order to join the coalition may backfire. A departure from party policy that proves too difficult for the party's members to accept can lead to pressure on the parliamentary leaders to withdraw from the coalition. For those who are troubled by the fact that coalitions sometimes fail, it should be noted that sometimes they fail because they are more, rather than less, democratic.

Similarly, unforeseen events may put a coalition government on the spot because they require a policy response not anticipated in the coalition agreement negotiated by the partners. Failure to find common ground may cause the coalition to break apart (in February 2010, for example, the Dutch coalition government collapsed over the inability of its partners to agree on extending the Dutch involvement in Afghanistan). To order to minimize the likelihood of that happening, a well-constructed coalition agreement will contain provisions for ensuring good communication between the parties and a dispute-resolution mechanism.

GOVERNING WITH A COALITION

There are now more liberal democracies with coalition government than not (28 of the 36 parliamentary regimes in the data set in Chapter 5), and it is instructive to consider why, given the suspicion of coalition government by many who have never experienced it. Is this anything more than a reluctance to share power?

From a democratic perspective, a majority coalition represents a majority of voters, which, paradoxically, is usually *not* the case in regimes with majoritarian electoral systems (as is explained in Chapter 10). The style of governing is also more cooperative than competitive, and this is not just between the coalition partners but, to a certain degree, between the parties in government and the parties in opposition (opposition today, but potential coalition partners tomorrow). This stands in contrast to the oppositional character of politics in Westminster-style parliaments, a difference captured (as noted in the previous chapter in *Figure 5.8*) in the parliamentary seating arrangements.

This contrast is also reflected in the way that political parties approach issues. In a majoritarian system, a party stakes out its policy position(s), and then seeks a mandate to proceed with implementation. In consensual regimes, when parties establish their policy positions, they do so with awareness that the support of another party or parties will be required for their implementation. This awareness involves thinking about possible partners and developing fallback positions that might be required in order to reach partnership agreements, in or out of coalition.

While a change of government is always significant, its effects may be less dramatic when a coalition government turns over than when one single party majority succeeds another. In the latter case, relatively total control of the policy agenda shifts from one party to another, sometimes leading to complete reversals in policy direction. By contrast, the probability is high that a new coalition government contains one or more of the partners from the previous government.

- Germany has had 16 general elections since 1953, and a change of government between elections on three occasions; only once has the new government not contained one of the coalition partners from the previous government: in 1998, the Christian Democrat/Free Democrat coalition was succeeded by the Social Democrat/Green Party coalition.
- The same four parties have comprised the seven-member executive in Switzerland since 1959. Until 2003, the composition was two Free Democrats, two Social Democrats, two Christian Democrats, and one Swiss People's Party member. In 2004, the composition was altered by taking one position from the Christian Democrats and giving it to the Swiss People's Party. By Swiss standards, this was a very radical change.
- Considerable levels of continuity can be found in the composition of governments in Denmark, Italy, the Netherlands, Norway, Sweden, and elsewhere.

Continuity of one or more coalition partners may be accompanied by continuity of policies. At the very least, there will be strong resistance to completely undoing the work of the previous government. Policy making in coalition systems generally is *incremental*, proceeding in gradual and limited steps away from the status quo. Such a reformist approach is consistent with a political style that is consensual rather than confrontational. Radical change is much more likely to be undertaken by a majority government willing to turn the policy of the previous administration upside down. This is especially likely if the party system is marked by polarization rather than convergence.

CRITICISMS OF COALITION GOVERNMENT

Criticisms of coalition government tend to focus on instability, indecisiveness, the inordinate influence of minor parties, and the length of the government formation process.

"Coalitions Are Unstable ..."

This argument always talks about the worst performers, such as Italy and ... well, Italy, which had, in the second half of the twentieth century, almost as many governments as there were years. [Note: the author was unable to find any other regime consistently identified with unstable coalitions, but in the process found many commentators who treat "coalition" and "unstable" as synonyms.] The discussion should be broadened to include those regimes where coalitions have regularly served out the full term between scheduled elections, including Austria, Denmark, Finland, Germany, Sweden, and Switzerland. In some cases, factors contributing to coalition instability have little to do with coalitions *per se*, but reflect a poorly designed electoral system that allows too many parties into parliament (Israel), or parliamentary practices that weaken party discipline (Italy), or the presence of a pariah party that has enough strength to require parties of quite dissimilar natures to form partnerships, which, by their nature, are inherently fragile (again, Italy).

Where governments are short-lived, elements like the continuity of coalition partners from one government to the next, caretaker governments, and the ability of the professional public service to administer programs and laws in the absence of parliament provide more stability than the frequent change in governments suggests. Finally, the "instability" of coalition is often stated without any explanation of the dangers that lurk there. The preference of the business community for predictable government is well known, and some concerns about unstable coalition government may be historical leftovers from the **Cold War era** of the late twentieth century.

"It Takes So Long to Form a Government ..."

Closely related to the criticism of instability is the concern with the length of time that it may take for the government to form. Depending on the particular configuration of parties left by the election and the negotiations required to complete a coalition agreement, government formation can last from a few weeks to months.

The German election of 2005, for example, produced a set of results from which several possible coalitions could have formed, not all of which had been anticipated or considered likely prior to the vote. It was not even clear who should get the first opportunity to try to form a coalition. It took nine weeks for the two largest parties, each unable to find a workable partnership with a combination of the smaller parties, to join in a **grand coalition**, with 50 per cent of the cabinet apiece. In the meantime, while some German citizens were reportedly "anxious" (mainly the business classes and the press), neither the country nor its economy was staggered by the delay.

Belgium recently demonstrated the ability of the modern state to function without a government by doing so for 541 days between its June 2010 election and the formation of a new government in December 2011. (As is the norm, a caretaker government was in place during that time, led by the previous prime minister, but without a mandate to make any new decisions.) This situation has almost nothing to do with coalitions and instead reflects the basic division in

COUNTRY	CABINET SIZE
Canada	38
Israel	30
Trinidad and Tobago	28
Croatia	27
Mauritius	25
Sweden	25
United Kingdom	22
Italy	21
Serbia	21
Finland	20
Netherlands	20
Norway	20
Australia	20
Denmark	19
Greece	19
New Zealand	19
Poland	19
Slovenia	19
Austria	18
Japan	18
Bulgaria	17
Portugal	17
Romania	17
Germany	16
Ireland	16
Spain	16
France	16
Belgium	15
Czech Republic	15
Estonia	14
Lithuania	14
Slovakia	14
Latvia	13
Hungary	10
Iceland	10
Switzerland	7

Figure 6.13

Belgian society that threatens to create two independent regimes. The largest party in the Belgian parliament after the 2010 election was a Flemish independence party, which is *not* one of the six parties that eventually became the government. As with the defeat or collapse of coalitions, a lengthy government-formation process may turn out to have few negative consequences in otherwise stable societies.

"Coalition Government Is Indecisive ..."

This criticism is most valid when the coalition government must respond to unforeseen circumstances or address issues not negotiated in the coalition agreement. Each party in the coalition may need first to work out with its members a position on the issue that has arisen, as well as the compromises it might be willing to make, if necessary, prior to consulting with its coalition partner(s) on possible solutions. The formulation of a policy response, all things being equal, will occur more quickly in the cabinet of a single-party government.

"Coalition Government Gives Too Much Power To Minor Parties ..."

Like other points, this is a valid criticism in specific circumstances, but not a proposition that applies to all coalitions. One such circumstance is the formation of a minimal winning coalition that includes a very small party. Able to bring the government down by itself, such a party may demand a greater say in matters (generally or on specific issues) than its strength otherwise warrants. These are circumstances in which forming a surplus majority coalition might be preferable. The critical factor is to design an electoral system that makes it difficult for very small parties to proliferate.

THE MINISTRY

In Canada, **the Ministry** refers to all members appointed to cabinet by a prime minister (or provincial premier) for the period that he or she is uninterruptedly in office (i.e., until he or she resigns, is defeated, or dies in office). For example, Canada's seventh prime minister, Wilfrid Laurier, won four consecutive elections and was prime minister for 15 years spanning four parliaments. The Laurier Ministry (the 7th Ministry of the Parliament of Canada) remains its longest, encompassing all the cabinet appointments made by Laurier during those 15 years.

In PR systems, setting a minimum threshold of support that must be reached in order to benefit from the mechanisms that ensure proportionality will eliminate many small parties. The regime best demonstrating how coalitions may fall hostage to very small (and extremist) parties is Israel, which elects its parliament (the Knesset) on a national basis. With 120 seats and strict proportionality, only 2 per cent (previously 1 per cent) of the vote is required for a party to be guaranteed its share of seats. The lower house of the Netherlands parliament is also elected on a national basis, with 150 seats, full proportionality, and no threshold; each seat requires the equivalent of 0.67 per cent of the national vote. However, while Israeli cabinets have tended to include very small, extremist parties (often with a religious base), Dutch cabinets have not. The difference here is cultural, not institutional.

More recently, the negotiation of confidence and supply agreements has become an alternative to including a small party or parties in cabinet. In exchange for concessions on some of its policy positions, a small party agrees to support the government on its financial legislation and on motions testing the legislature's confidence in the government. The arrangement seems to have originated in New Zealand after the adoption of a PR electoral system in 1996, but it has since been used in the Scottish Parliament and elsewhere.

CABINETS: SIZE AND STRUCTURE

It should be clear at this stage that the cabinet is the central institution of the parliamentary system and that the central figure in the cabinet is the prime minister. Under the leadership of the prime minister, the cabinet makes policy decisions, brings supporting legislation to parliament, and remains responsible for the implementation and administration of policy by departments and agencies of the state.

The size, structure, and working styles of cabinet government vary from country to country, reflecting some of the differences in political culture, circumstances, and expectations noted earlier. In traditional (i.e., Westminster) parliamentary systems, the size and organization of the cabinet are almost entirely at the discretion of the prime minister and will reflect his or her own style and philosophy of decision making. In some regimes the size of the cabinet is fixed in the constitution.

SIZE OF CABINETS

Two factors bearing on the size of cabinets are the size of the legislature and the size of the state. The larger the legislature, the more supporters on whom the life of the government depends. It is always wise to ensure enough of them are rewarded for their loyalty with cabinet posts, parliamentary secretary positions, or other offices that provide elevated status and extra pay.

Having a sufficient number of discretionary appointments also provides those not receiving one with reason to hope for a promotion in the future. Shuffling bodies in and out of such positions is one of the principal means of ensuring party discipline.

The size of the contemporary state helps in this regard by providing a broad range of ministries, departments, agencies, and programs that may be assigned as areas of responsibility. It is surprising, sometimes, that cabinets are as small as they are.

Political factors can also play a significant role in the size of cabinets. Why, for example, does Canada top the list, in *Figure 6.13*, ranking the cabinets (2010–11) of the 36 parliamentary regimes in the data set? A large part of the answer is the role of regionalism in Canadian politics. Prime ministers are expected to construct a cabinet in which every region of the country is represented, and represented in the right proportions, as well as one reflecting all other aspects of Canada's diversity. It is a welcome bonus if this also permits a mix of individuals with abilities that suit their portfolios.

Too large a cabinet makes collective decision making more difficult and can lead to a less efficient and less responsive policy process. Two different approaches are taken to deal with these challenges. In the United Kingdom, there is a clear division between the cabinet (the group of 20 or so senior ministers chaired by the prime minister) and the Ministry. The latter is a larger body that includes junior ministers and secretaries of state who assist the senior ministers with large portfolios, or have charge themselves of more limited portfolios.

ORGANIZING CABINETS

A second approach, much favoured in Canada, has been to structure cabinets by means of committees, including a "priorities and planning" (P&P) committee or one that serves such a function under another name. Operating like an "inner" cabinet, the P&P committee makes the key decisions about policy, and the other cabinet committees receive direction from and report to P&P. Structuring the cabinet is supposed to increase its efficiency by allowing smaller groups to make decisions, reducing the number of decisions to be made by the cabinet as a whole. Evidence that such a cabinet architecture achieves its purpose is mixed, not least because success has as much to do with the personalities involved as it does with the organizational features.

Where there is a distinction between cabinet and Ministry, there is also a need to coordinate the work of the Ministry with the priorities of the cabinet. In the UK government that formed in 2010, the coalition agreement not only involved dividing the cabinet posts between the coalition partners but also assigning places in the Ministry. An important consideration was the creation of "pooled" ministries where, if one party holds the senior portfolio (i.e., cabinet position), the other party occupies at least one of the junior positions supporting that portfolio in the Ministry. This decision was made in recognition of the added importance of good communication in a coalition executive.

HOW PRIME IS THE PRIME MINISTER?

The "prime" or "first" minister is the first to be sworn in by the head of state *and* is responsible for the selection of the other ministers, who serve at his or her pleasure. The prime minister may fire a minister at any time, decide to "shuffle" the cabinet by reassigning ministers to new portfolios, or choose to drop ministers from the executive and replace them with others from the legislature. This degree of control is unfettered in regimes with traditional constitutions

under conditions of single-party government (minority or majority). The prime minister's control is much reduced under the conditions of a coalition agreement, where any changes to the structure or membership of cabinet may require negotiation with the coalition partner or partners. The size and/or composition of the cabinet may be prescribed or limited by the constitution in some regimes. One example is constitutions that provide for the attorney general to be designated by the head of state, not the prime minister—presumably to preserve the justice system (for which the attorney general is responsible) from political influence.

EXECUTIVE DOMINANCE

In anticipation of Chapter 12, the role of the cabinet and prime minister in policy making deserves emphasis. In most parliamentary systems the cabinet monopolizes policy making. Responsible government has been identified as the defining element of parliamentary government, requiring the cabinet to maintain the confidence of the legislature. Given the presence of strong parties, this confidence is virtually guaranteed for any party (or combination of parties) that controls a majority of the legislators in parliament. The result is that responsible government can easily mean that the cabinet is "responsible" for everything. Deciding what government will do, or not do; when it will be done and how; drafting regulations or legislation and presenting the latter to parliament; overseeing the implementation and ongoing administration of policy: all of these are in the control of the cabinet, with not much left over. Accordingly, parliamentary legislatures are usually described as being characterized by executive dominance. (It may be true that in *all systems* the executive is dominant, but it is not the case that the executive is dominant in all *legislatures*.) As a result, parliamentary government, all else being equal, is *strong* government, capable of putting the power of the state behind the problem solving it undertakes. The ability of parliamentary government to act decisively (if not quickly) is one of its advantages among possible democratic models.

Possible challenges to or checks upon the monopoly of the cabinet over policy making can be found in **strong bicameralism**, enhancing the powers of the head of state (**semi-presidentialism**), the possibility of **judicial review**, and processes of **direct democracy**. Each of these is addressed in the chapters that follow, as is the ultimate check on any government—the judgment delivered by its citizens in periodic, competitive, fair elections. Some would argue that the powerful centralization of power in the hands of cabinet government can only be justified today if the political process delivers effective control over cabinet government. Otherwise, there is little that parliamentary government cannot do, and as in earlier days, citizens must rely on the wisdom and moral restraint of their rulers.

REFERENCES

Budge, Ian, and Hans Keman. *Party and Democracy: Testing a Theory of Formation, Functioning, and Termination of Governments in 20 Democracies*. Oxford: Oxford University Press, 1993.

Butler, David. *Governing Without a Majority: Dilemmas for Hung Parliaments in Britain*. Basingstoke: MacMillan, 1983.

Colomer, Joseph. "It's the Parties that Choose Electoral Systems (or Duverger's Laws Upside Down)." *Political Studies* 53.1 (2005): 1–21.

Institute for Government. "Understanding Hung Parliaments; and How Minority Governments Work." PowerPoint Presentation. April 2010. Web.

Laver, Michael, and Norman Schofield. *Multiparty Government: The Politics of Coalition in Europe*. Oxford: Oxford University Press, 1990.

Lijphart, Arend. *Democracies*. New Haven: Yale University Press, 1984.

FURTHER READING

Bale, Tim, and Torbjörn Bergman. "Captives No Longer, but Servants Still? Contract Parliamentarism and the New Minority Governance in Sweden and New Zealand." *Government and Opposition*. 41.3 (July 2006): 422–449.

Debus, Marc. "Portfolio Allocation and Policy Compromises: How and Why the Conservatives and Liberal Democrats Formed a Coalition Government." *The Political Quarterly* 82.2 (April–June 2011): 293–304.

Dewan, Torun, and Arthur Spirling. "Strategic Opposition and Government Cohesion in Westminster Democracies." *American Political Science Review* 105.2 (May 2011): 337–358.

Duch, Raymond M., Jeff May, and David A. Armstrong II. "Coalition-Directed Voting in Multiparty Democracies." *American Political Science Review* 104.4 (November 2010): 698–719.

Fox, Ruth. "Five Days in May: A New Political Order Emerges." *Parliamentary Affairs*. 63.4 (October 2010): 607–622.

Hazell, Robert, and Akash Paun, eds. *Making Minority Government Work: Hung parliaments and the challenges for Westminster and Whitehall*. London: Institute for Government/The Constitution Unit, 2009. [Book may be downloaded from the Institute for Government website.]

Lees, Charles. "How Unusual Is the United Kingdom Coalition (and What Are the Chances of It Happening Again?)" *The Political Quarterly* 82.2 (April–June 2011): 279–292.

Schleiter, Petra, and Edward Morgan-Jones. "Constitutional Power and Competing Risks: Monarchs, Presidents, Prime Ministers, and the Termination of East and West European Cabinets." *American Political Science Review* 101.3 (August 2009): 496–512.

Siaroff, Alan. "Varieties of Parliamentarianism in the Advanced Industrial Democracies." *International Political Science Review* 24.4 (October 2003): 445–464.

Tavits, Margit. "The Role of Parties' Past Behavior in Coalition Formation." *American Political Science Review* 102.4 (November 2008): 495–507.

CHAPTER 7

Systems of Government (2): Degrees of Presidentialism

All of the democratic alternatives to the classic model of parliamentary government presented in the previous chapter are characterized by having an executive that cannot be defeated by the legislature. In each case this executive is headed by a president.

MADISONIAN PRESIDENTIALISM

The dominant alternative to organizing the democratic state on a parliamentary basis has employed a strict separation of powers (sometimes called a "three-branch" system). The 1789 Constitution of the United States outlines the best known (and the oldest) of these, but variations of the **Madisonian model** remain in place throughout Latin America and in regimes that were once under US control or influence, such as the Philippines and South Korea. Two features define this system, and in each there is a potential for regime instability, if not possible regime failure.

SEPARATION OF EXECUTIVE AND LEGISLATIVE POWERS

The first element is the separation of the executive from the legislature, a separation in three respects:

1. The president (or chief executive) is elected independently from the legislative branch: either directly by popular vote or through an indirect process such as the Electoral College (see *Presidential Elections*, p. 154) used in the United States.
2. No member of the executive, including the cabinet, may hold a seat in the legislature.
3. The executive is not responsible to the legislature, neither collectively nor individually (nor is it necessary that all members of the executive—cabinet—be from the same political party). Conversely, the executive may not initiate legislation and has no control over its passage through the legislature.

In other words, the system gives its president control over the machinery of state, including the military (of which he or she is Commander-in-Chief), but no legislative power or direct access to it. In a regime based on the rule of law, this is rather remarkable, as well as the basis for observing that the president in a three-branch system can be a relatively weak executive compared with a prime minister. A president in this system must rely on the support of allies in the legislative branch, support that does not always come easily or cheaply. If the legislature is controlled by a party or parties other than the president's own, support for the president's initiatives may not come at all. In addition, the judicial branch stands apart from both the legislature and the executive, wielding considerable power of its own.

The absence of legislative power provides an incentive or temptation for a president to install loyalists in the legislature, rule by decree, seek a popular mandate with which to oppose the legislature, or try to control the judiciary—in each case subverting the democratic process. Unless there are strong legislative and judicial branches, firmly rooted in civil society, the presidency will overshadow the rest. It is important, if the powers are to be separate, that they be balanced. In the United States, this has managed to be sufficiently the case, over the long haul. In many Latin American countries in which the Madisonian model was adopted, presidents grew too strong and became presidents-for-life, or remained weak and were replaced by military rule.

REGIME FAILURE

Regime failure occurs when a government is removed by a non-legal process (is overthrown) or is usurped from within (one element within the state takes control of the rest). Although the term sounds negative, it need not necessarily be seen as such. Regime change that replaces a dictator with an accountable representative government might be regarded as a positive case of regime failure. It is of more concern when regime failure turns a democratic regime into an authoritarian one.

Regime failure was not discussed in the previous chapter because parliamentary systems seem generally to be immune, although this is not entirely the case (the regime failure of the Weimar Republic—Germany, 1930s—was both parliamentary and calamitous). Nonetheless, regime stability has been more of a concern in non-parliamentary democracies.

The prominence of an independently elected chief executive has led most to simply call the model of separated powers (a.k.a. the three branch system or the Madisonian model) the *presidential* system. Lijphart, for example, distinguishes **presidentialism** with a political (and not merely formal) executive that is *not* drawn from the legislature and is *not* responsible to the legislature, from the parliamentary executive that *is* drawn from and remains responsible to the legislature. Sartori identifies a system as presidential "if, and only if, the head of state (president) (i) results from popular election, (ii) during his or her pre-established tenure cannot be discharged by a parliamentary vote, and (iii) heads or otherwise directs the governments that he or she directs" (84).

CHECKS AND BALANCES

The framers of the US Constitution might not have approved of calling their creation "presidential," given their attempt to create a system in which the three branches of government operate within a set of checks and balances. "Presidential" fails to recognize the independence of the legislature from the executive, an independence designed to prevent the re-establishment of autocratic rule by one individual—the very condition the colonists had fought a war of revolution to escape. The point of building in checks and balances between the three branches of government was to ensure that power could not become concentrated in any one of them.

A system of checks and balances works by ensuring that each institution (executive, legislature, judiciary) cannot fully perform its functions without being subject to the approval of one or both of the others. Some examples include the following:

- Legislation must be passed by both chambers of the bicameral Congress (the House of Representatives and the Senate) in an identical form, which then goes to the President who may (a) **veto** the bill, (b) sign it into law, or (c) do nothing, in which case it becomes law after 10 days.
- The Congress may overturn the presidential veto with a vote of two-thirds in both chambers (the House of Representatives and the Senate).
- The President appoints numerous senior administrative officials as well as nominees to fill vacancies in the Supreme Court, but many of the appointments, including those to the Supreme Court, require confirmation by the Senate.
- The Supreme Court hears appeals against laws and can declare them unconstitutional and thereby invalid, or shape their application with its interpretations.
- Through a complicated process involving the legislatures of the states, the Constitution may be amended.
- Congress passes legislation, but the departments that oversee its implementation or enforcement are headed by members of the cabinet (Secretaries) appointed by the President.
- Congressional committees have extensive powers to inquire into matters of policy and public administration.

Influencing the design of this system was the idea of **mixed government**, which can be traced back to Aristotle but was the central element in the political writings of the French philosopher Montesquieu (1689–1755). It was Montesquieu's ideas, along with those of John Locke (see Chapter 3), that most influenced the framers of the US Constitution, such as

James Madison and Alexander Hamilton. Mixed government means combining the monarchic, aristocratic, and democratic elements—rule by one (the President), rule by the few (the Supreme Court), and rule by the many (Congress)—into one balanced system.

The positive function of checks and balances is to counteract the tendency for power to concentrate anywhere, but particularly in the office of the chief executive. The negative by-product of checks and balances is that they can make it difficult for the state to provide timely solutions to the social and economic problems that citizens expect government to address. In some countries, when such a system has become paralyzed and in some very real senses has been unable to govern, the result has been suspension of the constitution, military overthrow of the civilian administration, or revolution and civil war.

Unlike the parliamentary system, the three-branch system has no accountable, responsible government. There is "government" in a general or all-encompassing

> "We the people of the United States, in order to form a more perfect union, establish justice, insure domestic tranquility, provide for the common defense, promote the general welfare, and secure the blessings of liberty to ourselves and our posterity, do ordain and establish this Constitution for the United States of America."
>
> —Preamble to the *Constitution of the United States of America*

sense, but the activity of governing is a by-product of the activity and interaction of the chief executive, his or her cabinet, the two houses of the legislature, the Supreme Court, and the various agencies, departments, and other bureaucratic pieces of the state, with no one body or group of persons providing central coordination. Deprived of legislative power, the president's cabinet meets infrequently as a collective body. This system creates issues of accountability and transparency (it is no wonder that conspiracy theories are so prevalent in the popular culture): who *should* the voters hold responsible for public-policy outcomes (or failures)?

STAGGERED TERMS OF OFFICE

The designers of this system were worried not just about keeping power from concentrating with one branch of the state; they also worried about the power of the people (a cautious attitude toward democracy typical of the eighteenth century). "We the people" should not become a tyranny of the majority, or mob rule.

PRESIDENT			4 years		4 years		4 years		
HOUSE OF REPRESENTATIVES	2 years	2 years	2 years	2 years	2 years	2 years	2 years	2 years
SENATE ⅓			6 years			6 years		
⅓	6 years		6 years			6 years		
⅓	6 years			6 years			6 years	

Figure 7.1

The US Capitol Building. Washington, DC.

One solution was to stagger the terms of the various elected offices, eliminating the possibility that a faction or party dominant at one point in time could control all the institutions (see *Figure 7.1*).

In a year when the president is elected to a four-year term, the entire membership of the House of Representatives is elected to a two-year term, and one-third of the Senate to a six-year term. At the halfway point in the president's term, the entire House of Representatives and a different one-third of the Senate comes up for election. If the president seeks a second term in office, he or she will do so at the same time as the House of Representatives and the final one-third of the Senate. The makeup of the Congress can change quite dramatically during, and sometimes in response to, a president's administration.

When this staggered timing of the renewal of the executive and legislative branches is combined with weak party discipline, it is not easy to assign responsibility for what policy gets made or doesn't. For this reason, interest groups and organizations are quite active in tracking how members of Congress vote on issues of relevance to their supporters. It is certainly possible for the president and the two houses of Congress to work together, but Madison's intention of setting "ambition against ambition" has worked often enough to ensure that this is as much the exception as the rule.

WEAK GOVERNMENT

The military and economic power of the US state and the role of the president as head of a world power sometimes work to obscure the *domestic* weakness of the US government and the limits on the ability of any of its presidents to determine the outcomes of ordinary policy making. A prime minister in a parliamentary system has a much greater chance of being able to achieve his or her domestic agenda.

To say that the three-branch system offers weak government is not necessarily a criticism, no more than noting the strength of single-party majority government in a parliamentary system is to praise it. Weak government may be a good thing; strong government may be dangerous or unrepresentative. In either case, it depends on context and on the perspective(s) that prevail in the political culture about the role of government.

As noted earlier, the checks and balances in the US Constitution were not unintended accidents of history and circumstance, but written in deliberately by its framers. These men could not have foreseen in 1789 the growth of the state and the challenges that governments would face on the other side of industrialization, urbanization, and globalization. The fact that the most powerful state in the world is governed by a constitution designed in the eighteenth century is not only remarkable, but quite possibly problematic. More than a few observers have suggested that the longevity of the US Constitution may be as much a weakness as a strength.

A weak or less active state certainly appeals to those with a **libertarian** perspective. This dimension of US political culture has always been strong, and it is no coincidence that the growth of the state characteristic of advanced industrial societies in the twentieth century was less dramatic in the United States than

AMENDING THE US CONSTITUTION

The US Constitution is not an easy document to amend; since the passage of the Bill of Rights (the first 10 Amendments) in 1789, the US Constitution has been amended only 17 times in more than 220 years. The most recent amendment to be ratified, in 1992, was originally proposed in 1789, taking only 203 years to be approved by the necessary number of states. (This amendment—"No law, varying the compensation for the services of the Senators and Representatives, shall take effect, until an election of Representatives shall have intervened"— gives the electorate a chance to pass judgment on any measure to increase the pay for members of Congress *before* it comes into effect.)

elsewhere. This difference is even more pronounced when military spending is removed from the picture.

WEAK PARTIES

The Madisonian legislature is also known for its weak political parties, "weak" in terms of disciplined behaviour, which can be measured by the tendency of party members to take a common position on issues, vote together, and follow their leader(s). In each of these respects, the Democratic and Republican Parties, strong organizations in and of themselves, are weak compared to parliamentary parties. This has been true in the past in several respects and for several reasons.

Lack of Internal Agreement

It has not been unusual for either or both parties to contain groups of members with very different approaches to issues. Sometimes this has reflected regional political cultures, such as when many Democrats elected

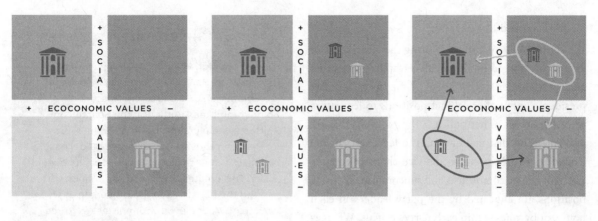

| Figure 7.2 | Figure 7.3 | Figure 7.4 |

in southern states held very conservative positions in a nominally liberal or progressive party, or when New England Republicans commonly took positions that would be described today as socially liberal. While these geographical distinctions have evaporated considerably in the past few decades, each US party has always tended to be more a collection of factions than a congregation of ideological conformity.

It is also difficult to accommodate all issues within a two-party system (as discussed more completely in Chapter 11). By way of illustration, *Figure 7.2* shows a hypothetical situation where the Blue Party is +E +S (+ on both the economic and social dimensions) and the Red Party is –E–S.

However, in the real world, it is more likely that some Blues will be +E–S and some Blues will be –E+S, while some Reds will be +E–S and some Reds will be –E+S. This possibility is pictured in *Figure 7.3*.

Bipartisan Voting

In a parliamentary system, with its strong party discipline, the Blues or Reds in the top right or bottom left quadrants would likely be compelled to vote with the majority of their party. In a three-branch system such as the United States, where party discipline is weak, it is possible that the Blues and Reds in the bottom left quadrant will vote with the Red Party on social issues and with the Blue Party on economic issues, while the Reds and Blues in the top right will vote with the Blues on social issues and the Reds on economic matters—see *Figure 7.4*.

There are a number of reasons for thinking that a two-party system is better served by conditions that encourage bipartisan voting over uniform party-line voting that puts the party with the majority in a constant winning position over the minority party. As noted in Chapter 6, strong party discipline developed in parliamentary systems because the survival of a cabinet government depends upon maintaining the support of a majority in the legislative chamber (satisfying the convention of responsible government). The separation of powers in the three-branch system means that the executive is not responsible to the legislature or for the legislation it considers. The passage or defeat of a bill is just that and has no additional constitutional significance.

Constrained Leadership

The ability of party leaders to bring their members in line is constrained by the relative scarcity of rewards and punishments. Unlike a prime minister, the president cannot offer cabinet positions to legislators who support his or her policies. The positions that are available (and that matter most) to legislators in the United States are the chairs and vice-chairs of congressional or Senate committees and subcommittees. These positions are allocated by the party leaders in each house, or by votes within each party's caucus. Whereas the task of ordinary legislators in parliamentary systems is to support (or oppose) the executive (the cabinet), in the three-branch system, the job is to build the alliances required to get any legislation passed, or drum up support for proposals that will benefit the legislator's constituents, or please those interests willing to contribute to the legislators' election campaign funds.

JUDICIAL REVIEW

When the US executive and legislative branches *are* able to work together, they remain subject to review by the courts. The tradition of judicial review dates back to a case heard by the Supreme Court in 1804 (*Marbury v. Madison*), only five years after the ratification of the Constitution. This decision was the first case in which the Supreme Court judged an act of Congress to be unconstitutional and established the principle that the courts could overturn legislation that conflicts with the Constitution.

In addition to the Articles of the Constitution, the Bill of Rights (the first ten amendments to the Constitution) provides criteria which the courts can apply to their review of legislation and executive orders. However, the willingness of the courts to act is not a given. It took until the 1950s and 1960s for a liberal

Supreme Court to make landmark rulings putting an end to legal racial segregation, paving the way for significant civil rights legislation. That court was "liberal" because of appointments made to it by Democratic presidents Franklin Roosevelt and Harry Truman. Supreme Court judges serve for life, and some have been especially long-lived.

The life tenure of the Justices is another element in the system of checks and balances; a president and/or Congress of one political disposition may co-exist with a Supreme Court appointed by previous administrations of an opposing disposition. The Supreme Court, however, is composed of a mix of judges, with court watchers identifying the balance of liberals and conservatives or, on occasion, which judge provides a "swing vote" between the two camps. Every appointment to fill a vacancy is watched carefully for its potential to change the balance from one side to the other.

An individual nominated to the Supreme Court (by the president) is subject to hearings by the Senate Judiciary Committee, and then confirmation by the Senate as a whole. The hearings provide an opportunity to question nominees about their previous rulings and uncover any existing predispositions. Sometimes, when it has appeared that the Senate is unlikely to approve an appointee, the president has withdrawn the nomination before it could come to a vote. Filling a vacancy on the Supreme Court provides an excellent example of checks and balances in play, involving all branches of the three-branch system.

SUMMING UP

In short, in contrast to the relative coherence or concentration of authority within parliamentary systems, the separation of powers in the United States leads to a fragmented and often weak government. Its supporters, however, celebrate the US system as the epitome of pluralist democracy. While parliamentary systems tend to manufacture a majority government or create coalitions, power is exercised in either instance by a relatively static majority from one election to the next. Those who are not in government, the minority, are often left with very little voice in the policy-making process and, thus, with ineffective representation. At its worst, this can become a tyranny of the majority over the minority. Fearing that men of property and substance would be submerged in the democratic mass, the designers of the US Constitution hoped to avoid this outcome by fragmenting power through the checks and balances of separated powers. As the term "pluralist" implies, power is centred nowhere within the American state but is dispersed among various institutions and diluted by being placed in many hands. As critics point out, the fragmenting of political power may enhance the concentration of private power and allow those with wealth and influence in civil society to have a disproportionate share of influence in all three branches of government (see Parenti).

COALITIONAL PRESIDENTIALISM IN LATIN AMERICA

Whereas the weakness of government in a presidential system with separated powers was an attraction for those who designed it, the result is that policy-making is not easy. In many of the countries that have adopted a similar constitution, the inability to take decisive action and govern effectively led to short-lived regimes. In 1994, Giovanni Sartori listed 18 countries outside the United States with presidential democracies; apart from the Philippines, all were in Latin America, and only three—Costa Rica (1949), Venezuela (1958), and Colombia (1974)—had been uninterruptedly democratic for more than 20 years. (In 2011, rated "not free" by Freedom House, Venezuela is no longer considered to be an electoral democracy, and Colombia is rated "party free," with an average score of 3.5 on political rights and civil liberties.) Sartori concluded as follows:

> Ironically, then, the belief that presidential systems are strong systems draws on the worst possible structural arrangements—a divided power defenseless against divided government—and fails to realize that the American system works, or has worked, *in spite* of its constitution—hardly *thanks to* its constitution (89).

In 2011, five of the Latin American presidential regimes rated as "free" by Freedom House—Argentina, Brazil, Chile, Panama, and Uruguay—have joined

Costa Rica in having been uninterruptedly democratic for more than 20 years.

The largest number of regimes with a separated-powers system are in Latin America, but significant differences have emerged between these regimes and the Madisonian presidentialism of the United States. Most Latin American democracies employ a proportional-representation electoral system for legislative elections, which means that multi-party systems are the norm. It is unusual for any party, including the president's party, to have a majority in the legislature.

With a two-party system, US legislatures contain a majority party and a minority party; there is at least a 50 per cent chance that the majority is of the president's party. When it is not, the support of only a few representatives from the other party may be all that the president requires to have a workable legislative majority. In Latin American regimes, the opposition to the president usually consists of several parties. When democracy was restored to many Latin American regimes in the 1980s and 1990s, many observers predicted that the combination of multi-party systems and "presidentialism" would not work, and recommended adopting arrangements that would provide for a two-party format (Pereira, Power, and Raile, 1). Since that time, though, and especially in the largest regimes—Brazil, Argentina, and Chile—the combination of a strong president with a proportional legislature seems to have been stable and productive.

Many Latin American presidents, unlike the US president, have a degree of legislative power, whether it is the ability to legislate by executive decree, a measure of control over the legislative agenda, or a broad range of veto powers. As in the United States, the president determines who will sit in cabinet, but with two important differences. First, in some regimes it is possible that members of the legislature may sit in cabinet. Second, the cabinet is often assembled with representatives of various parties in the legislature, so that it resembles a European-style coalition government. This is one of the ways in which Latin American presidents, facing multi-party legislatures in which their own party is a distinct minority, are able to assemble the level of support necessary to govern successfully. Coalition cabinets in Latin American presidential systems now seem to be the norm rather than the exception.

Lawrence has suggested that the Latin American systems are much more complex than the Madisonian model of US presidentialism, requiring presidents to "become effective managers of inter-party alliances." (29) Other observers have noted that the tools available to presidents for managing multi-party legislatures vary from regime to regime. The Brazilian president has the exclusive right of budgetary initiative, for example. Legislators may propose amendments, but the executive determines which ones are adopted, a power that provides important leverage when seeking the support of legislators (Pereira, Power, and Raile 13). The federal executive (the presidency) in Brazil also has control over "who will fill about twenty thousand jobs that are kept exempt from merit-based selection criteria" (Sola 40).

It is not difficult to conclude that the dominance of the president is much more pronounced in Latin American systems, compared to the United States. The powers provided to the president, coupled with multi-party legislative chambers, have worked to diminish the role of legislators in the policy process (Morgenstern, Negri, and Pérez-Liñán 161), redirecting their focus to the oversight of the executive or to

National Congress of Brazil. Brasilia, Brazil.

brokering deals for their constituencies. Executive dominance may not seem problematic in regimes that have, with few exceptions, a recent authoritarian past. It also seems to be accompanied by high levels of "pork barrel" politics (delivering government funding to projects in districts of those who support the executive) and other uses of executive power that can range from the questionable to the corrupt. (Look up, for example, the "Mensalão scandal" that occurred in Brazil in 2005.)

The combination that has become known as **coalitional presidentialism** has been much more stable and successful than many observers thought it might prove to be. It is as yet unclear, though, just what sacrifices to democracy, transparency, and to rule of law may be required to sustain it over the long term.

SEMI-PRESIDENTIALISM

If coalitional presidentialism combines a strong president with a multi-party legislature in a system of separated powers, **semi-presidentialism** combines a strong president with a multi-party parliamentary government. The key element here is the presence of a strong president *in addition to* a prime-minister–led cabinet.

The strength of the president in a constitutional system that separates the legislative and executive powers—whether US Madisonian presidentialism or Latin American coalitional presidentialism—is fairly obvious and is rooted in the direct election of the president. On the other hand, most parliamentary republics have a president who serves as head

PRESIDENTIAL ELECTIONS

One of the defining characteristics of a strong presidency (constitutionally speaking) is direct election by the people. This is not enough by itself to guarantee a strong presidency—examples are common enough of popularly elected presidents (e.g., in Ireland, Finland, Portugal, Slovenia) with limited powers. On the other hand, it would be unusual to have a strong president in a democracy who was *not* popularly elected—it is the legitimacy that accompanies election that enables the president to impose a veto or dismiss a government, for example. In those parliamentary republics where the president's role is limited to the largely formal functions of a head of state, the president is usually elected by the members of the legislature (as in the Czech Republic, Estonia, Germany, Greece, Hungary, Israel, Italy, and Mauritius).

Direct election may be decided by plurality—whichever candidate receives the most votes—but the farther the winning total drops below 50 per cent, the less legitimacy the presidency may have, or be perceived to have. For this reason, perhaps, the most common means of electing a president is the two round system (TRS), with a run-off taking place if no candidate wins an outright majority, eliminating all candidates but the top two from the first round.

Costa Rica requires a candidate to receive only 40 per cent to avoid a run-off. In the 2006 election, the leading candidates both finished with just over 40 per cent, separated by a margin of less than 3,300 votes. After a recount, the revised results gave the winner 40.92 per cent and the runner-up 39.8 per cent. Argentina requires the winning candidate in its presidential election to reach 45 per cent to avoid a run-off. In the 2007 contest, Cristina de Kirchner won 45.29 per cent, with a winning margin of 22.25 per cent. The Argentinian constitution permits a candidate to win with 40 per cent of the vote, provided that he or she has at least a 10 per cent margin of victory.

Prior to 1995, the Argentinian president was elected by an **electoral college**. Today, the United States is the only regime to elect its chief executive through such an indirect means. The size of the US Electoral College is the same as the number of members of Congress (both houses) plus three for the District of Columbia—a total of 538. To win, a presidential candidate must receive 270 Electoral College votes. Elections in the United States are administered by the state governments; each state has as many electors (Electoral College votes) as its total number of US Senators and Representatives. When voting for president, voters are actually choosing a set of state electors pledged to support that presidential candidate. In all but two states (Maine and Nebraska), this is a winner-take-all contest. Thus, it is possible for the winning candidate (by Electoral College votes) to have finished second in actual votes, as happened most recently in 2000, when Democrat Al Gore finished with more popular votes than George W. Bush, but with 266 Electoral College votes to Bush's 271. It is also possible to win the presidency with the Electoral College votes of only 11 states. These and other characteristics of the Electoral College have prompted calls for its replacement with a form of direct election.

United States—Electoral College Votes, by State

of state—in many cases (14 of the 25 parliamentary republics in the data set) directly elected by the people—but is *not* strong. Except in certain constitutionally significant moments connected with the defeat of government and/or the government formation process, the parliamentary president's powers are largely formal and ceremonial. It is the head of government—the prime minister—who is the primary holder of political power. Semi-presidential systems are parliamentary, but they differ in that a larger discretion than would otherwise be the case is given to a popularly elected head of state.

The semi-presidential system is sometimes described as a *diarchy*, because of its dual executive, but since all parliamentary systems have a dual executive—a formal head of state (monarch or president) and a political head of government (prime minister or premier)—the semi-presidential system is set off by a dual *political* executive: both the president and the prime minister have political authority. One of the determining variables of semi-presidential systems is the nature of the relationship between the president and the prime minister. The semi-presidential system is a *hybrid* system incorporating features of both parliamentary and separated-powers systems. There are many powers that the semi-presidential constitution can allocate to the president, but perhaps the most important are the ability to name the prime minister (and perhaps the cabinet ministers) and the discretion to dismiss the prime minister and/or the legislative assembly. Shugart and Carey have made a useful distinction between two types of semi-presidential systems, the *premier-presidential* and the *president-parliamentary*.

In the premier-presidential version of semi-presidentialism, the president selects the prime minister, but only the legislature is capable of dismissing the prime minister. In this way, responsible government remains in place. The discretion of the president to select the prime minister is greatest when the legislative majority is controlled or headed by the president's party. If the president's party does not control the legislature, then he or she will be forced to choose the prime minister most likely to receive the support of the parliamentary (non-presidential) majority. Shugart suggests this means that "once appointed ... a cabinet that enjoys parliamentary confidence is not subordinated to the president but to parliament, and thus the relationship between president and cabinet is ... transactional" (333). "Transactional," for Shugart, describes a relationship between equals, as opposed to the "hierarchical" relationship of superior and subordinate [*Figure 7.5*].

In the presidential-parliamentary version, the president retains the ability to dismiss the prime minister, and while this is closer to "pure presidentialism," Shugart suggests the arrangement is only semi-presidential because the legislative majority also may dismiss the cabinet, even contrary to the wishes of the president (344). Because the cabinet is doubly accountable, to the president and to the legislature, a transactional relationship is established between the president and the legislature (hence presidential-parliamentary).

SEMI-PRESIDENTIALISM IN FRANCE

The most familiar example of a semi-presidential system is France's current regime, the Fifth Republic, established in 1958, mostly in response to the instability and ineffectiveness of the Fourth Republic. During the 13 years of the Fourth Republic (1946–58), France had 27 governments, partly because an overly fragmented party system led to unstable coalitions, and partly because these governments faced a number of

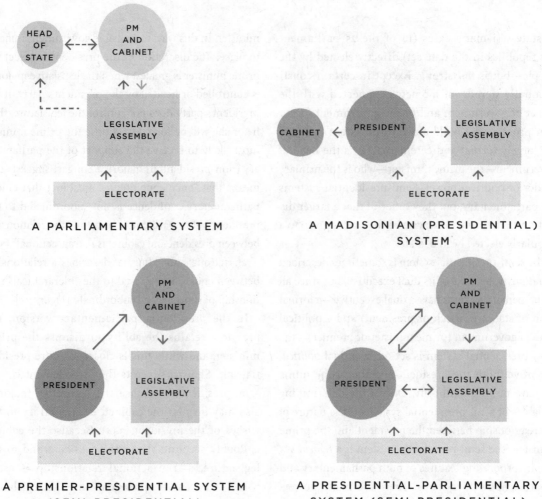

Figure 7.5
(Adapted from Shugart (2005): the solid gray arrows indicate who selects the office holder; the gold solid arrows indicate relationships of accountability; the dashed double arrows represent transactional relationships between offices/institutions.)

divisive policy questions, among them the war over Algerian independence. Where coalitions are fragile, government is often indecisive, paralyzed by the challenge of taking (or even finding) a solution that will satisfy all coalition partners. The constitution of the Fifth Republic, authored by Charles de Gaulle (its first president) and Michel Debré (the future prime minister), weakened the role of parliament and prime minister, and strengthened the presidency in several important ways.

Palais Bourbon, home of the Assemblée Nationale. Paris, France.

Beginning in 1962, the French president was elected to a seven-year term of office—such a lengthy term of office was meant to guarantee an executive institution that is stable and independent of parliamentary turnover or turmoil. (In 2000, a constitutional change limited this term to five years, for reasons explained below.) The president in turn appoints the prime minister and, depending on circumstances, the cabinet ministers. If sitting members of the legislature are appointed to cabinet, they must resign their legislative seats. The government, once installed, is responsible to the first chamber of the legislature, the National Assembly. A motion of censure (non-confidence) must be moved by at least one-tenth of the Assembly's deputies, and to succeed requires the approval of an absolute majority (as opposed to a majority of those present at the time). The president also has the ability to dissolve parliament (no more than once per year) and require elections. The French chief executive also has considerable emergency powers and, like the US president, is commander-in-chief of the armed forces.

The pre-eminence of the French president is greatest when his or her political party also controls a majority in the legislature, a circumstance that has been the norm for most of the Fifth Republic. Like most European regimes, France's party system contains a grouping of parties on the right and a grouping on the left. When the president's party is part of the minority group in parliament, the prime minister will come from the majority grouping and the government will be responsible to the National Assembly, not the president. A period where the president and prime minister are from opposing political parties is known as **cohabitation**. During the early years of the Fifth Republic, some observers doubted if the system could work if there were ever to be a strong parliamentary majority opposed to the president. However, since 1986 there have been three separate and relatively successful periods of cohabitation, the first two with a socialist president and a conservative prime minister and the last between a conservative president and a socialist prime minister. Nonetheless, in 2000, the term of office of the president was limited to five years, the same as the term for the National Assembly. Since the elections for the two institutions take place only a few months apart, this is intended to reduce the likelihood of cohabitation.

It has always been clear that when the government comes from the president's party, the preponderance of policy-making power may rest with the president rather than the prime minister. Cohabitation demonstrated that when the government comes from a party opposed to the president, the ability of the president to express his or her will is constrained, and the prime minister's influence over policy making is enhanced. A study by Samuels and Hellwig came to the general conclusion "that in semi-presidential systems, voters hold the president accountable for economic performance when the president and prime minister are politically compatible, but the prime minister's party when they are not (i.e., under cohabitation)" (quoted in Shugart 345).

OTHER EXAMPLES OF SEMI-PRESIDENTIALISM

Because the semi-presidential system rests on the exercise of discretionary powers by the president, above and beyond what would be exercised by a formal head of state in a parliamentary system, it is difficult to identify the level of presidential power that is sufficient to make a system semi-presidential. It should be noted that popular election of the president is the first step; any president elected by members of the legislature (R^{PAR} in the data set) will have the normal limited discretionary powers of a parliamentary head of state. Direct election, in and of itself, may not mean much either. Two elements that Shugart emphasizes are the power of the president to name the government and to dissolve the legislature at any point (as opposed to dissolution after a vote of non-confidence or the failure to invest a government). Ability to dismiss the prime minister is also a significant variable, as is whether any government appointed by the president can take office *without* an investiture vote (if so, the power of parliament has been diminished). In 2005, Shugart estimated that 12 of the 14 democracies in the post-communist regimes were semi-presidential "in some form," as were seven of the 12 new democracies in Africa since 1980 (quoted in Shugart, 344).

Figure 7.6 combines a list of political powers employed by Shugart with data from Magalhães and Fortes for those parliamentary democracies in the data set that have popularly elected presidents.

regime	names prime minister (PM)	may dismiss PM	cabinet forms without investiture	may dismiss legislature	has a veto	chairs cabinet meetings	has emergency and decree powers	central foreign policy role	has discretion over appointments	total Y
PREMIER-PRESIDENTIAL										
Bulgaria (1991–)	N	N	N	N	Y	N	N	N	Y	2
France (1958–)	Y	N	Y	Y	N	Y	N	Y	Y	6
Lithuania (1992–)	Y	N	N	N	Y	N	N	Y	Y	4
Poland (1997–)	Y	N	N	N	Y	N	N	N	Y	3
Poland (1992-97)	Y	N	N	N	Y	N	N	Y	Y	4
Portugal (2005–)	Y	N	N	N	Y	N	N	N	N	2
Portugal (1984-2005)	Y	N	N	Y	Y	N	N	N	N	3
Portugal (1976-1982)	Y	N	N	Y	Y	N	N	Y	Y	5
Romania (1996–)	Y	N	N	N	Y	Y	N	N	Y	4
Slovakia (1999–)	Y	N	N	N	N	Y	N	N	N	2
PRESIDENT-PARLIAMENTARY										
Austria (1920–)	Y	Y	Y	Y	N	N	N	N	N	4
Taiwan (1946–)	Y	Y	Y	N	N	Y	N	Y	Y	6
NOT RECOGNIZED BY SHUGART										
Croatia (2000–)	Y	N	N	N	Y	N	Y	N	Y	4
Finland (2000–)	N	N	N	N	Y	N	N	N	N	1
Finland (1994-2000)	N	N	N	N	Y	Y	N	Y	Y	4
Finland (1956-1994)	Y	Y	Y	N	Y	Y	N	Y	Y	7
Finland (1945-1956)	N	N	Y	N	Y	Y	N	Y	Y	5
Iceland (1945–)	Y	Y	Y	Y	N	N	N	N	N	4
Ireland (1945–)	N	N	N	N	Y	N	N	N	Y	2
Serbia (2006–)	N	N	N	N	N	N	N	N	N	0
Slovenia (1991–)	N	N	N	N	N	N	N	N	N	0

▪ Categories used by Shugart   ▪ Categories used by Magalhães and Fortes

Figure 7.6

Looking at the last column (total Y), which Magalhães and Fortes used as an index of presidential powers, two things are immediately obvious: the number of free, democratic states with strong presidentialism is limited, and the trend in several states has been in the direction of weakening the powers of the president. Only three of the current regimes have a total Y greater than 4. In many cases, the scores reflect the letter of the constitution, not the existing practice of the constitutional arrangements. Both Austria and Iceland have constitutions that are strongly semi-presidential, but in both regimes the exercise of presidential power is no more active in practice than in any other parliamentary republic. Portugal, Finland, and, to a lesser degree, Poland provide examples of regimes that have successively moved away from semi-presidentialism in the direction of parliamentary republicanism. The regimes in the top two sections of the table are classified as semi-presidential in large part because of the ability of the president to name the prime minister. However, in most cases, the prime minister and cabinet cannot take office without ratification by the legislative assembly (an investiture vote), which limits the president's discretion in nominating a prime minister.

Similarly, while possession of a veto is a common presidential power, in almost all cases that veto can be overridden by a vote of the legislature, sometimes by a simple majority of 50 per cent plus one.

Just as Madisonian presidentialism seems to work in the United States (arguably) but not as well elsewhere, so too, semi-presidentialism has not flourished outside France. With each of these regimes, their prominence on the world stage manages to keep their unique constitutional models on display.

AN EXCEPTIONAL CASE: SWITZERLAND

Among the world's democracies, Switzerland truly is in a class of its own. Most of its constitutional features, considered independently, are not exceptional, but no other country has the combination of elements that Switzerland does. In addition, with many of these elements, there is something unique about the way the Swiss experience it.

COALITION PARTNERS (CABINET SEATS)			
1959 - 1999	SEATS	1999 - 2011	SEATS
Free Democrats	2	Free Democrats	2
Social Democrats	2	Social Democrats	2
Christian Democrats	2	Swiss People's Party	2
Swiss People's Party	1	Christian Democrats	1

Figure 7.7

The first anomaly is that Switzerland is a parliamentary system without responsible government. Like many European parliamentary republics, the members of the executive (the cabinet) do *not* hold seats in either of the Swiss legislative chambers. In addition, the executive is not subject to the confidence of the legislature, making the system at least quasi-presidential. The size of the Swiss executive is fixed constitutionally at seven members, elected by a joint session of the Swiss parliament to a four-year term. There is no prime minister, and each member of this joint executive takes a turn being president (in addition to his or her portfolio) for a period of one year. In keeping with parliamentary tradition, though, the composition of the Swiss executive is determined by the distribution of seats in the legislature among parties.

Although the Swiss have one of the most open proportional-representation electoral systems in the world, it provides them with an unusually stable party system. Coupled with a long-standing convention that requires Switzerland's main linguistic communities (French, German, and Italian) to be represented in cabinet, the country has a history of grand coalition governments (the coalition includes all the major parties in the legislature). As *Figure 7.7* indicates, only one change has been made to the composition of the Swiss executive during the last 52 years. After the 2011 election, the coalition partners still held 74 per cent of the seats in the National Council, despite the emergence of two new parliamentary factions (parties gaining more than 5 per cent of the vote).

The relative permanence of the composition of the Swiss executive, barring any radical shift in party support, and the inability of the legislature to defeat the executive once installed are among the reasons Switzerland is regarded as the epitome of *consensual democracy*. The flip side of this is the lack of an effective parliamentary opposition or mechanism to keep the executive accountable. Instead, the Swiss have a long tradition of **direct democracy** (see Chapter 11) that balances grand coalition government with popular initiatives and referendums. Fittingly, perhaps, in a system in which the people's representatives have little control over the executive, the task of keeping government accountable is one that the people must exercise themselves. Interestingly enough, in Switzerland they do so in ways that are often strikingly conservative. For example, it was not until 1971 that a referendum finally passed to permit women to vote in federal elections. On the other hand, in September 2010, Switzerland joined Finland, Norway, and Spain as countries in which the majority of the cabinet members are women.

CONCLUSION

This chapter and the previous have presented a variety of constitutional arrangements existing in systems that otherwise have a great deal in common. Common to the systems in this chapter is a political executive that is neither drawn from nor responsible to the legislature. In these systems the president replaces, rivals, or dominates the prime minister. Among presidential regimes, the United States remains unique in the strength of its separation of powers, particularly the independence of the legislative branch from the executive. In Latin American presidential systems, the existence of multi-party legislatures elected on a proportional basis has led to an arrangement called coalitional presidentialism. Semi-presidential systems offer the hybrid of a dual executive—a strong president and a prime minister accountable to the legislature. In almost all cases *except* France, semi-presidential regimes, too, have multi-party legislatures elected on a proportional basis. It is tempting to hypothesize that the evolution of many semi-presidential systems (e.g., Portugal, Finland) in the direction of a parliamentary system may have something to do with the control of coalition government by the prime minister. At the end of the day, the strongest distinction between democratic systems may be between systems that put power in the hands of one party (majoritarian) and those that tend to produce coalitions (proportionate or consensual). This distinction, in turn, rests on the political process, and in particular on the electoral system. The next chapter considers a wholly different basis for distinguishing among democratic regimes, namely, the division of power between different levels of government, or what is commonly known as federalism.

REFERENCES

Lawrence, Christopher N. "Regime Stability and Presidential Government: The Legacy of Authoritarian Rule, 1951–90." 2000. Web.

Lijphart, Arend. *Democracies: Patterns of Majoritarian and Consensus Government in Twenty-One Countries*. New Haven: Yale University Press, 1984.

Magalhães, Pedro C., and Braulio Gómez Fortes. "Presidential Elections in Semi-Presidential Systems: Presidential Powers, Electoral Turnout and the Performance of Government-Endorsed Candidates." *Digital CSIC* [Institutional Repository of the Spanish National Research Council] 2008. Web.

Morgenstern, Scott, Juan Javier Negri, and Aníbal Pérez-Liñán. "Parliamentary Opposition in Non-Parliamentary Regimes: Latin America." *The Journal of Legislative Studies* 14.1–2 (March /June 2008): 160–189.

Parenti, Michael. *Democracy for the Few.* 3rd ed. New York: New York University Press, 1980.

Pereira, Carlos, Timothy J. Power, and Eric Raile. "The Presidential Toolbox: Executive Strategies, Coalition Management, and Multiparty Presidentialism in Brazil." 2006. Web.

Sartori, Giovanni. *Comparative Constitutional Engineering.* New York: New York University Press, 1994.

Shugart, Matthew Søberg. "Semi-Presidential Systems: Dual Executive and Mixed Authority Patterns." *French Politics* 3 (2005): 323–351.

Shugart, Matthew Søberg, and John. M. Carey. *Presidents and Assemblies: Constitutional Design and Electoral Dynamics.* Cambridge: Cambridge University Press, 1992.

Sola, Lourdes. "Politics, Markets, and Society in Lula's Brazil." *Journal of Democracy.* 19.2 (April 2008): 31–45.

FURTHER READING

Church, Clive H., and Adrian Vatter. "Opposition in Consensual Switzerland: A Short but Significant Experiment." *Government and Opposition* 44.4 (October 2009): 412–437.

Colomer, Joseph M., and Gabriel L. Negretto. "Can Presidentialism Work Like Parliamentarism?" *Government and Opposition* 40.1 (Winter 2005): 60–89.

Conley, Richard S. "Presidential Republics and Divided Government: Lawmaking and Executive Politics in the United States and France." *Political Science Quarterly* 122.2 (Summer 2007): 257–285.

Elgie, Robert. "Semi-presidentialism, Cohabitation and the Collapse of Electoral Democracies, 1990–2008." *Government and Opposition* 45.1 (January 2010): 29–49.

_____. "Presidentialism, Parliamentarism and Semi-Presidentialism: Bringing Parties Back In." *Government and Opposition* 46.3 (July 2011): 392–409.

Huneeus, Carlos, Fabiola Berrios and Rodrigo Cordero. "Legislatures in Presidential Systems: The Latin American Experience." *The Journal of Legislative Studies* 12.3–4 (September-December 2006): 404–425.

CHAPTER 8

Dividing the State: Federalism and Other Options

...WHICH PROVIDES THE READER WITH

- a look at various ways in which the state may be decentralized
- an explanation of the distinction between federal, confederal, and unitary states
- a closer examination of the elements (and varieties) of the federal state, including
  - the division of powers: legislative, administrative, and fiscal
  - bicameralism
  - amending a federal constitution
- a consideration of options for decentralizing powers in a unitary state

Previous chapters have been primarily focused on *the* state, or *the* government. In fact, almost everywhere, the state operates at several levels from immediate to remote. The complete duties of citizenship in Canada, for example, include electing national, provincial, and municipal representatives, and may also involve choosing members of local boards, such as school trustees. Clearly, in many regimes the state is multiple and governments are many.

With the exception of Mauritius, the countries in the data set used here occupy thousands or even millions of square kilometres, areas that are often too large to be administered from one centre or capital, wherever it might be located. From the time when modern nation-states were being consolidated out of the patchwork of feudal principalities and duchies, and from the high days of imperialism when European powers believed they could govern colonial "possessions" halfway around the world, to today, when significant parts of nation-states have no effective law enforcement or are controlled by rebels or warlords (from Mexico to the Democratic Republic of the Congo to Afghanistan), the extension of the power of the state to all parts of the regime is a central challenge of establishing and maintaining **sovereignty**. Canadians are often reminded just how lightly sovereignty over their nation's Arctic lands and seas is exercised.

All developed states have addressed the problem of localizing administration, that is to say, bringing the power to enforce statutes and regulations *and* the ability to deliver programs and benefits to *all* citizens. The greater the territorial range of the regime, the larger the challenge of administering all of its population. However, the several hundred years of Roman rule of Mediterranean regions and Western Europe (ending in 476 in the western half that was ruled from Rome) gave the hint it might be done—a feat all the more remarkable given the absence of the technologies that would be required to accomplish the same today. The solution then was to divide the empire into provinces, establish centres of administration for enforcement of Roman law in each province, station enough soldiers in each province to maintain security, and strengthen lines of communication with Rome. At that time, effective communication required building good roads (some of which may still be used today). Each new province added through conquest or annexation would be administered on the same model (admittedly, the

Figure 8.1 The Roman Empire in the year 117 CE

model changed over time), enforcing Roman law and collecting taxes to support the Empire.

UNITARY, FEDERAL, CONFEDERAL

When nation-states began to emerge, after the fall of the Roman Empire and almost a thousand years of feudalism, they were only as strong as their ability to extend the power of the monarchy from the centre (e.g., London, Paris, Lisbon, Madrid) to all locales, establishing the supremacy of national law over the often considerable powers of the local or regional aristocracy. Today, a regime in which the national law and parliament are supreme over every subnational and municipal body is known as a unitary state.

As experience demonstrates, government is always local. Annexing local territories and putting them under a common, centrally directed government is one model (*imperial*) of state building. The reverse is also possible, when local governments combine to create a central authority. In this model (*federal*), the constituent states or provinces recognize the need to combine their authority and resources into one body that can protect and promote their collective interest. At the same time, they may not be willing to surrender all their authority. Instead, the state exists at two levels—the *national* and the *sub-national*.

The origin of federal regimes in the joining together of (what have become) sub-national units is reflected in language that persists today. The creation of Canada from three British North American colonies is known as Confederation, and those who were responsible for drafting the terms of that arrangement as the "Fathers of Confederation." Australia's national state is commonly known as the Commonwealth government, in distinction from the states and territories. The official

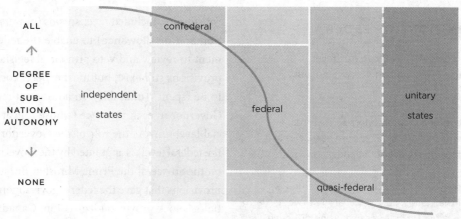

Figure 8.2 Sub-National autonomy

name of Switzerland is the Swiss Confederation; and—something that is not always known outside the United States— the first US constitution (1777–1788) was called the Articles of Confederation and Perpetual Union.

Technically, there is an important difference between the terms **federal** and confederal. In a proper confederation or confederacy, the national government is not only created by the sub-national units, but it remains under their control. In a confederal state, the national government exercises only the powers that the sub-national states have delegated to it, powers that collectively they could revoke, revise, or limit. The national government in a confederal system almost inevitably turns out to be weak, limited in its ability to act in a way (such as imposing a tax) that benefits the national whole at the expense of the sub-national components. In addition, the threat exists that one or more of the sub-national units might *secede* (withdraw) from the confederation.

The weaknesses of the original confederal constitution of the United States were apparent soon enough, and it was replaced in 1789 by the federal constitution, which is still in place today. The confederal status of the Swiss Confederacy, dating back to the thirteenth century, ended for good in 1848 with the adoption of a federal constitution (known nonetheless as the Swiss Confederation) at the conclusion of a civil war. For a short time, Serbia and Montenegro existed in a confederal arrangement until 2006, when Montenegro and then Serbia declared their independence from the union.

In a federal design, four elements are present (see also Definitions of Federalism, p. 166):

1. the regime has a national (or central) state and sub-national (or regional) states;
2. the regime's constitution divides the powers of government between the national and sub-national states;
3. each level of state has autonomy from the other—neither one can dissolve the other nor unilaterally adjust the **division of powers** between them; and
4. a majority (if not most) of the regime's people live under the jurisdiction of both levels of state.

DEFINITIONS OF FEDERALISM

(provided respectively by an Australian, a Canadian, a Swiss, and an American political scientist)

The method of dividing powers so that the general and regional governments are each, within a sphere, co-ordinate and independent. (Wheare, 11)

A political system in which . . . the structural elements of the state . . . are duplicated at two levels, with both sets of structures exercising effective control over the same territory and population. Furthermore, neither . . . should be able to abolish the other's jurisdiction over this territory or population. (Stevenson, 8)

A federal system of government consists of autonomous units that are tied together within one country. (Steiner, 123)

In a federal system there are two levels of government above the local level, each enjoying sovereignty in certain specific areas. (Mahler, 31)

The last point recognizes that many federal states (including Australia, Canada, and the United States) also have regions (territories) with sub-national administration that is *not* autonomous from the national government.

That Canada's founding moment is called "Confederation" is somewhat ironic, given the intention of the arrangements of 1867 to place the preponderance of power with the new national government of Canada. Believing that the provinces should be little more than expanded municipal governments, the constitutional architects assigned what they believed were the most important powers to the national state. The new constitution included mechanisms (powers of **reservation and disallowance**) to enable the federal government to review and veto provincial legislation. These provisions still exist, but most experts consider them to be "spent" (unusable). In addition, the Lieutenant Governor in each province (whose role at the provincial level mirrors the role of the Governor General at the federal level) is appointed by the Governor General on the advice of the Prime Minister. Because of these provisions that gave the federal government the potential to block provincial legislation, Canada has sometimes been described as a **quasi-federal** state, although in practice it ceased to be one a long time ago.

Accidents of history, judicial decisions, and social and technological change have tipped the balance so that the powers exercised today by the provinces make Canada one of the world's most decentralized federations. Conversely, the United States has moved in the opposite direction; the balance in what was established as a relatively decentralized federation has tilted in favour of the national government. One lesson here is the inability of constitution designers to control what history and circumstance will do with their design; a second is that federations evolve, and not always in the same direction.

As *Figure 8.4* indicates, with the exception of China, the world's geographically largest regimes are federal states. Some, like Mahler, regard China's system of government as having federal characteristics (31).

The data set introduced in Chapter 5 contains nine of the 22 federal states identified on the map in *Figure 8.4*, including two small states that are organized federally—Belgium and Switzerland. These two (along with Bosnia and Herzegovina) illustrate the attraction of a federal constitution for safeguarding the interests of ethno-linguistic minorities by providing a measure of

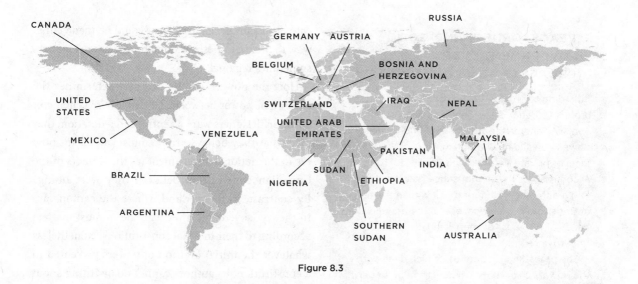

Figure 8.3

political autonomy to the geographic regions in which they are located. Such considerations clearly had a part in the original design of the Canadian federal state.

COMPONENTS OF FEDERALISM

Several institutional features are required or created by a federal system, including a written constitution, a division of powers, a bicameral legislature, and a constitutional amending formula.

WRITTEN CONSTITUTION

If federalism is to preserve the autonomy of both levels of state, the basic facts of federalism must be described and protected in the constitution. One of those key facts is a division of powers, which identifies the responsibilities of each level of state. Among the powers to be divided are the ability to legislate in specific policy areas, the power to administer laws, and the capacity to raise and spend money. Sometimes referred to as the "federal bargain" between the two levels of

government, the division of powers is, in a genuine federation, a set of arrangements that neither party can alter without the consent of the other.

DIVISION OF POWERS—LEGISLATIVE

Stevenson calls the division of legislative powers the "heart of any federal constitution" (30), perhaps because it is the source of most federal disputes. These arise not only because all governments are likely to challenge any encroachment of their powers, but also because the division of powers is almost impossible to get right. Deciding what powers should belong to each level of state is not as simple as assigning matters with a "national" dimension to the national state and those with a "regional" character to the sub-national states. What constitutes a "national" matter? While some subjects, like defence, foreign trade, treaties, banking and currency, and the postal service, seem obviously national in character, other subjects are not so clear cut. For the environment, labour relations, education, highway construction and maintenance, and health

"PEACE, ORDER, AND GOOD GOVERNMENT" VERSUS "PROPERTY AND CIVIL RIGHTS"

Intending to provide for a strong national government, section 92 of Canada's *Constitution Act, 1867* enumerated 16 "heads" of provincial power, concluding with "all matters of a merely local or private Nature in the Province." To accommodate the circumstance that Quebec had a different system of civil law than the rest of British North America, one of the provincial heads of power is "property and civil rights in the Province."

The preceding section (91), which dealt with the powers of the national government, began as follows: "It shall be lawful for the Queen, by and with the Advice and Consent of the Senate and House of Commons, to make Laws for the Peace, Order and Good Government of Canada, in relation to all Matters not coming within the Classes of Subjects by this Act assigned exclusively to the Provinces [i.e., section 92]." Known as the Peace, Order and Good Government clause (or just POGG), this paragraph *seems* to provide a straightforward division of powers. Nonetheless, perhaps in order to emphasize the dominant role of the national government, the section then lists 29 heads of powers assigned exclusively to it.

The effect of providing *two* lists of enumerated powers was to make it more difficult in later cases to interpret the application of POGG. Complicating matters was the very broad interpretation that some judges applied to the provincial power over "property and civil rights." The consequence was rulings in some key constitutional cases that shifted the balance of power in the Canadian federal system towards the provinces.

care, for example, an argument could be made either way. In practice, these are sometimes national matters, sometimes regional.

How the powers are divided also determines the *balance* of power between the two levels. When constitution designers want a centralized federation, they give what they believe are the most important powers to the national government (as the framers of the Canadian constitution believed they were doing). By contrast, in Switzerland, where the cantons are in theory "sovereign," they legislate in most matters according to their internal constitutions. Nonetheless, whatever the initial division of powers presented in a constitution, its authors cannot do anything about three developments.

UNINTENDED CONSEQUENCES. The first is the changing significance of the various powers assigned to either level of state. The balance of powers between Canada's provinces and the federal government shifted towards the former as several powers originally assigned to the provinces, such as education, health care, and natural resources, were transformed by social and economic change and advances in technology.

UNANTICIPATED DEVELOPMENTS. The second is the impossibility of foreseeing the emergence of new areas of activity that will require regulation. Automobiles, aeronautics, electrification, telecommunications, radio, television and film, urbanization, modern medicine, computers, and the digital revolution are but some of the developments that eighteenth- and nineteenth-century constitution framers could not have imagined. In some cases, the courts have had to decide which level of state should exercise jurisdiction in these areas.

UNEXPECTED INTERPRETATIONS. The third is how the courts over the years will interpret the

Landtag of Baden-Wurttemberg. Stuttgart, Germany.

division of powers as it applies to concrete cases. In the early days of the Canadian federation, the division of powers was at the heart of many of the leading constitutional cases, often the result of a party adversely affected by a law challenging whether the level of state that made the law had the authority to do so. The significance is this: a ruling that a law is intra vires (within the powers) or ultra vires (beyond the powers) might affect not just the specific legislative power exercised in a particular case, but also provide a template or argument to be applied to other cases and other powers. During the Great Depression of the 1930s, in both Canada and the United States, social and economic legislation enacted by the federal government was repeatedly ruled unconstitutional by the Supreme Court on the basis that it encroached on the powers of the provinces or states.

How the division of powers is presented in the constitution may affect its later application or construction (i.e., interpretation). The simplest method is to list the powers assigned to one level and provide all other powers to its counterpart. This approach was taken in the US Constitution and, much later, the Australian. (The Australians considered, but rejected, the Canadian example of listing the powers of the provinces.) A clause indicating which level of state has responsibility for powers not expressly assigned is known as a **residual clause**. Section 51 of the *Act* to constitute the Commonwealth of Australia assigns 39 headings of power to the Commonwealth government and any powers not included in this list are considered to be residual powers that rest with the states, unless there is an explicit assignment of power somewhere else in the constitution. (In the *Canadian Constitution*

Act, 1867, for example, jurisdiction over education is addressed in a separate clause.) In the United States, the enumeration of the powers of the federal state in the Constitution, with a residual clause (the Tenth Amendment) reserving all other powers to the states or to the people, reflects the intent to limit the powers of the national Congress. However, one of the enumerated powers of the national government gives it any power required to carry out its other enumerated powers; this is a very broad grant of power that has become known as the "elastic clause."

Being newer, and building on experience in other federations, the German constitution treats the division of powers in a more complicated fashion. The constitution lists the powers of the national (federal) state, and provides that the sub-national governments, the *Länder*, hold the residual power (the ability to legislate in all other matters). The constitution also provides that federal law takes precedence over *Land* law (as it does in Australia, Canada, and the United States). In fields of *exclusive* federal competency (jurisdiction), the *Länder* can legislate only if a federal law expressly states that they may do so. In fields of *concurrent* jurisdiction, the *Länder* can legislate only if the federal state has made no use of its legislative powers in the relevant field. Finally, in *framework* legislation, the federal state establishes legal requirements and conditions (the framework) concerning a policy matter, with the *Länder* filling in the details according to their own needs and regional differences.

DIVISION OF POWERS—ADMINISTRATIVE

Responsibility for administering a law usually sits with the level of state that has made the law. This is reflected, generally, in the constitutions of Australia, Canada, and the United States. In some cases, though, it makes sense for law to be administered at the sub-national level, even though it was made by the national legislature. In Canada, the provinces are responsible for the administration of justice, but criminal law and procedure in criminal matters are matters of federal jurisdiction. Arrangements whereby one government delegates to another the responsibility for administering legislation (known technically as "federal interdelegation") are not uncommon.

In Germany, by contrast, the Basic Law (the constitution) establishes that the *Länder* will implement and administer laws passed by the federal government and empowers them to execute federal laws "as matters of their own concern" (Mény, 209). *How* a program is delivered is sometimes more critical than the legislation establishing it—a consideration that really matters in regimes in which the legislative and executive powers are controlled by different parties. In Germany's case, the legislative superiority of the German federal government is balanced by the administrative powers of the *Länder*. Public servants employed by the *Länder* outnumber their federal counterparts by about 4:1; in Canada, by comparison, the ratio is somewhere between 2:1 and 1:1, depending on the definition of public servant.

DIVISION OF POWERS— FISCAL FEDERALISM

It is said that George Washington blamed the failure of the first (*con*federal) US constitution on a lack of money. The national state in a confederal system depends on the funds the sub-national states are willing to grant it. In a federal system, logic suggests that the degree of autonomy enjoyed by each level of state should also extend to fiscal (financial) matters and be reflected in a division of revenue powers such as taxes, tariffs, royalties, and fees. In a properly designed system, it might be argued, both the provinces and the nation would have the capacity to raise the revenue required to exercise their legislative and administrative responsibilities. Almost inevitably, this is not the case, and instead, there is a **vertical** fiscal **imbalance**.

A vertical (national versus sub-national) fiscal imbalance arises because the constitution fails to provide each level of state with the revenue authority it requires to fulfill its responsibilities. It may be, as in Canada, that certain types of taxes are reserved for one level of government or restricted for the other (provinces, for example, may collect only *direct* taxes). Most commonly, the fiscal imbalance favours the national government, with its revenue authority and capacity exceeding the authority and capacity of the sub-national states. This places the federal government in a position where it is able to subsidize the provincial governments, and sometimes in a position where it *must* assist them. In return, the senior government may gain influence over public policy at the state/provincial level, even in areas that otherwise fall outside its jurisdiction. It can do this by setting conditions on the design of specific programs or the program areas for which it is willing to transfer funds. The *Canada Health Act,* which allows the federal government to penalize provinces by withholding transfers for health care if certain specific conditions are not met, and the US *No Child Left Behind Act,* which required states to develop standardized tests to assess students' skill levels as a condition of receiving federal funds for education, are well-known examples.

A tug-of-war often takes place where intergovernmental transfers are concerned. The sub-national governments, obviously, would like as much stable, long-term funding from the national government as possible, and as few strings attached as can be managed.

The national government, to the degree that it is willing to make transfers, needs something in return, such as a degree of control over how the transferred funding is spent. If the provinces insist on maintaining control over how funds are used, the national government may decide to use transfers that provide it with flexibility in how much it spends. In Canada today, most federal transfers are either unconditional or consist of **block funding** for provincial programs.

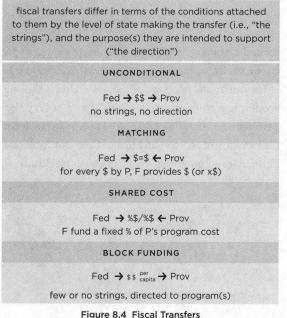

fiscal transfers differ in terms of the conditions attached to them by the level of state making the transfer (i.e., "the strings"), and the purpose(s) they are intended to support ("the direction")
UNCONDITIONAL
Fed → \$\$ → Prov no strings, no direction
MATCHING
Fed → \$=\$ ← Prov for every \$ by P, F provides \$ (or x\$)
SHARED COST
Fed → %\$/%\$ ← Prov F fund a fixed % of P's program cost
BLOCK FUNDING
Fed → \$\$ $\frac{\text{per}}{\text{capita}}$ → Prov few or no strings, directed to program(s)

Figure 8.4 Fiscal Transfers

A **horizontal imbalance** arises when the provinces or states have unequal **revenue capacity**. For example, all Canadian provinces levy a corporate income tax, but the contribution that such a tax makes to the provincial treasury varies greatly. This can be the result of policy decisions made concerning the levels of such a tax, but it also reflects the differences in the corporate tax base in each province. Likewise, revenue from

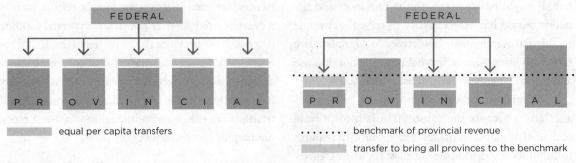

TRANSFERS FOR VERTICAL IMBALANCE | TRANSFERS FOR HORIZONTAL IMBALANCE

FEDERAL

P R O V I N C I A L

▬▬ equal per capita transfers

FEDERAL

P R O V I N C I A L

········ benchmark of provincial revenue

▬▬ transfer to bring all provinces to the benchmark

Figure 8.5

natural resource development has been a bigger contributor to some provinces' treasuries than to others.

The horizontal fiscal imbalance also reflects shifting economic fortunes in the regions. The discovery and development of offshore oil and gas helped transform the province of Newfoundland and Labrador from one of the poorest provinces to one of the more positively

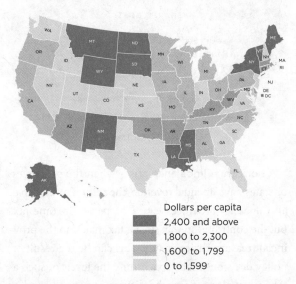

Dollars per capita
■ 2,400 and above
■ 1,800 to 2,300
■ 1,600 to 1,799
□ 0 to 1,599

Figure 8.6: US to Aid to Federal States, Fiscal Year 2005
(source US Census Bureau)

situated. The so-called rust belt in the United States, a stretch of northern and midwestern states where much of the nation's heavy industry and manufacturing once underpinned general prosperity, is awash today with abandoned plants and empty factories. It has become common to hear of abandoned land, residential as well as industrial, in large US cities such as Detroit being reclaimed by nature or returned to agricultural use.

While the horizontal fiscal imbalance highlights regional disparities, it has national significance. Over time, it can create regional tensions that may contribute to divisive regional politics and, in extreme cases, actions that undermine regime stability. At a more immediate level, governments in poorer provinces or states will find it difficult to provide education, health care, policing, environmental protection, libraries, parks, and all other public services to the same standard as other provinces or states. Since 1957, Canada has formally recognized the principle of **horizontal equity** (i.e., that all Canadians should receive comparable levels of public services at comparable levels of taxation) with a system of equalization payments, and in 1982 enshrined the principle of equalization in the constitution.

In theory, the wealthier provinces could decide to share some of their revenue with the less favoured provinces. In practice, redistribution for the purposes of equalization is carried out by the federal state in the transfers it makes to the provinces or states. In Canada, for example, the federal government makes several transfers to the provinces, but the largest two consist of transfers to correct the vertical fiscal imbalance (specific program grants) and transfers to address the horizontal fiscal imbalance (**equalization** grants).

Note that in *Figure 8.5* there are no arrows from the provinces to the federal state, or between the provinces. All of the federal transfers are funded by *federal* revenues (taxes, fees, and tariffs), which are collected in *every* province, including those that receive equalization grants. While the greatest part of the federal revenue is collected in the wealthiest provinces, equalization consists of compensatory payments from federal revenues to the poorest provinces. Equalization is *not* a straight transfer from richer provinces to poorer provinces.

In some jurisdictions, such as Australia, Austria, and Germany, the goal is full equalization, described by the Australian Commonwealth Grants Commission as "offsetting interstate differences in revenue raising capacity and the costs of providing services and acquitting infrastructure." The same body contrasts Canada's program as "one-sided revenue equalization (provinces with low revenue capacity receive extra resources with no adjustment for those with high capacity)." The United States is one of the few federal states not to have equalization grants, although some of its transfers provide a measure of compensation to the poorer states. (See *Figure 8.6*).

In Canada in 2009, revenue from intergovernmental transfers accounted for 20.3 per cent of provincial revenue. By comparison, the proportion of provincial (state) revenue accounted for by transfers in other jurisdictions was 38.8 per cent in Austria, 70.3 per cent in Belgium, 16.1 per cent in Germany, 29.8 per cent in Switzerland, and 20.6 per cent in the United States (OECD, Fiscal Decentralization Database). The proportion in Australia, according to the Commonwealth Grants Commission, was 49.8 per cent in 2009–2010.

INTERGOVERNMENTAL RELATIONS

A by-product of the measures devised to address fiscal imbalances has been an increase in the importance of **intergovernmental relations**. *Figure 8.7* depicts a continuum: at one end (autonomous federalism), the two levels of state go about their own business with a minimum amount of interaction with each other. At the other end (integrated federalism), there is scarcely anything that one level might do without consultation, negotiation, or agreement with the other level. The more complicated the federal fiscal arrangements, the more integrated the model of federalism will be.

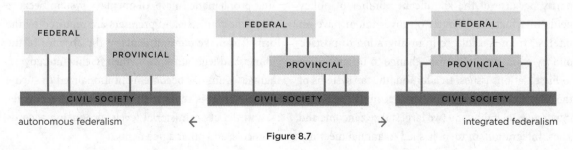

autonomous federalism ← → integrated federalism

Figure 8.7

Interior of dome of the British Columbia Legislative Building. Victoria, BC.

Canada's federal system has evolved in the direction of an integrated model, partly because of the scope of fiscal transfers between the two levels of state and partly because of the significant number of policy fields in which both levels of government have an interest, from agriculture to immigration to postsecondary education to climate change to urban transit to First Nations issues. In addition, the tax systems of the two levels of government have become increasingly integrated, including the two largest taxes: income and sales. Integration, in turn, has led to annual meetings of the federal, provincial, and territorial First Ministers, meetings capable of producing agreements and commitments of some significance. They are also somewhat problematic in a parliamentary system because the prime minister and premiers are required by the format to make commitments in the absence of the cabinet and legislature. Nonetheless, this intergovernmental forum has become institutionalized to such a degree that it is replicated regularly at the ministerial and deputy ministerial levels, producing accords, protocols, and other agreements.

ASYMMETRICAL FEDERALISM

The considerable degree of integration that character-izes federal systems today means that changes to pro-grams that both levels of state have an interest in (such as health care or employment and skills training) often require negotiation. This can involve the federal state bargaining with all the states or provinces, but often means an agreement between *a* province/state and the federal government. Provinces that do not want to participate in a program may opt out, and partici-pating provinces may reach agreement on terms that meet their own specific needs or interests. The result is **asymmetrical federalism**, where powers exercised by the sub-national states are not identical.

In Canada, Quebec's civil-code legal system (a carry-over from its French colonial past) is a built-in asym-metry that has existed since before Confederation (and continues to require that three of the justices on the Supreme Court are members of the Quebec bar). In the 1960s, when the Canada Pension Plan (CPP) was established, Quebec opted to create its own Quebec Pension Plan (QPP). On issues such as the treatment of natural-resource revenue for equalization purposes, control over immigration, and tax harmonization, other provinces have negotiated their own deals with Ottawa. Since 1982, Canada's constitution has permit-ted the federal government and a province to amend the constitution regarding that province without affect-ing or consulting other provinces.

The United States exemplifies a federation with symmetry—each state has exactly the same pow-ers. Spain, which could not be any closer to being a federation without becoming one, has considerable variation in the powers it has ceded to its various autonomous regions, most notably Catalonia and the Basque region.

BICAMERALISM

All federal states have bicameral legislatures in which the second chamber has the role of representing the interest of the sub-national states and/or their popu-lations, in contrast to a first chamber elected on the principle of representation by population. Under a First-Past-the-Post (FPP/SMP) electoral system, rep-resentation by population favours the larger provinces; under proportional representation (PR) it reflects the political parties' national strengths. Either way, the second chamber is intended to give a more equitable representation to sub-national interests.

There are at least three dimensions on which federal second chambers may be compared:

(a) Who elects the members?
(b) How equally are the provinces/states repre-sented in the second chamber?
(c) What is the status of the second chamber rela-tive to the first chamber?

REGIME	STATES/ PROVINCES (#)	2ND CHAMBER	# SEATS
Argentina	Provinces (23)*	Senate	72
Australia	States (6)	Senate	76
Austria	Länder (9)	Federal Council	62
Belgium	Regions (3) /Communities (3)	Senate	71
Brazil	States (26)*	Federal Senate	81
Canada	Provinces (10)	Senate	105
Germany	Länder (16)	Federal Council	69
Switzerland	Cantons (26)	Council of States	46
United States	States (50)	Senate	100

* plus one federal district (i.e., the capital)
Figure 8.8

ELECTION

Direct election of the second chamber deputies (hereafter Senators, for the sake of convenience) by the sub-national populations occurs in five of the federations in *Figure 8.8* (Argentina, Australia, Brazil, Switzerland, and the United States) and for a portion of the Belgian Senate (see *Doubly Federal* on p. 177).

In most cases, the term of office for a Senator is longer than that of a Representative or Member of Parliament (MP), and only a fraction of the second chamber's membership is elected at any election. For example, in Argentina and the United States, one-third of the Senate is elected every two years; in Brazil, where the term of office is eight years, the election of two-thirds of the Senate is followed four years later by the election of the remaining one-third. Australia elects one-half of its Senators every three years. In Belgium and most of Switzerland, all the second-chamber seats are elected at the same time, and at the same time as the election for the first chamber.

Indirect election occurs in Austria, where the Landtag (the Land parliament) elects the Federal Council (Bundesrat) deputies on a proportional basis (the equivalent would be having Canadian Senators elected by the provincial parliaments). The composition of the Federal Council changes every time an election alters the composition of a Landtag.

In Germany, the Bundesrat deputies are not elected by each Land's parliament but *selected* by its *government*. Normally, each Land's delegation consists of the First Minister plus other cabinet ministers, depending on the number of votes that the Land has in the Federal Council (see *Figure 8.9*). It is also possible for one of the delegates to exercise all of the Land's votes.

In short, the second chamber can represent the sub-national populations, the sub-national legislative assemblies, the sub-national governments, or a mix of any or all, as in Belgium. Similarly, quasi-federal Spain's second chamber contains 204 Senators directly elected in the provinces and 55 Senators elected by the legislative assemblies of its 17 autonomous communities.

While Canada's second chamber is not unique in being an appointed body, the appointment of its Senators (who serve until age 75) by the Governor General (on the nomination of the Prime Minister) makes it one of the most undemocratic of second chambers. Among federal nations, it is arguably the least effective second chamber in representing sub-national populations (and was never intended to represent their governments).

AUSTRIA	GERMANY	
1. the largest Land (LL) is assigned 12 seats	Land Population	No. of Seats
2. other Länder (OL) receive the number of seats that corresponds to the ratio of their population to that of the LL:	< 2 million	3 seats
Seats(OL) = [pop(OL)÷pop(LL)] X 12	> 4 million	4 seats
for example, an OL with a population one-half of the population of the LL gets 6 seats	> 6 million	5 seats
3. no Land gets fewer than 3 seats	> 7 million	6 seats

Figure 8.9

EQUALITY

In chambers elected on the basis of representation by population, the emphasis is on each citizen's vote carrying the same weight in the political process. This means that states or provinces with the largest populations will elect the largest number of representatives. If the second chamber is to represent the interests of the sub-national units, the units need to be put on a more level footing. In the United States Senate, each state is equal, electing two Senators, whether California with 37 million inhabitants or Wyoming with 540,000. (Several states now have more seats in the Senate than they do in the House of Representatives, where representation is based on population.) Equal representation also characterizes the sub-national states' representation in the second chambers in Australia, Argentina, Brazil, and Switzerland.

In Austria and Germany, representation of the Länder in the second chamber strikes a compromise between

DOUBLY FEDERAL

Belgian federalism is one of the most complicated systems, the result of successive reforms intended to accommodate challenging linguistic and ethnic divisions. At present, the Belgian federation has *two* levels of sub-national state/government: regions and communities, each with its own areas of responsibility (called "competencies"), and each with its own elected assembly and government.

Belgium's regions have powers relating to the economy, employment, agriculture, water policy, housing, public works, energy, transport, the environment, town and country planning, nature conservation, credit, foreign trade, supervision of the provinces, communes, and intercommunal utility companies. ("Commune" is the French word for municipality and is often used in Europe to refer to municipal governments.)

Belgium's communities, which are language-based, have powers for culture, education, the use of languages, and certain powers pertaining to health policy and social assistance. Each community has its own elected parliament and government, as does each region. However, because the Flemish (Dutch-speaking) community and region are identical, regional competencies are exercised by the government of the Flemish community (i.e., there are five sub-national governments, not six).

The Belgian Senate consists of 40 directly-elected Senators (15 elected by voters in the Walloon region and 25 by voters in the Flemish region, with voters in Brussels choosing to vote for one or the other); 21 Senators appointed by *and* from the governments of the communities (10 from the Flemish community, 10 from the French-speaking community, and one from the Germany-speaking community); and 10 Senators chosen by the other 61 Senators (six by all the Dutch-speaking Senators and four by the French-speaking Senators).

BELGIUM'S REGIONS
■ Flemish ■ Walloon
■ Brussels-Capital

BELGIUM'S COMMUNITIES
■ Flemish ■ French ■ German

DIVISION	SEATS
Maritime Provinces	24
New Brunswick	10
Nova Scotia	10
Prince Edward Island	4
Ontario	24
Quebec	24
	72

1864: Resolutions adopted by the Fathers of Confederation in Quebec called for a Senate with three Divisions of 24 Senators each, and contained provisions for the later entry of Newfoundland, British Colombia, and the Northwest Territory.

DIVISION	SEATS
Maritime Provinces	24
New Brunswick	12
Nova Scotia	12
Ontario	24
Quebec	24
	72

1867: Prince Edward Island did not agree with the Quebec resolutions, unhappy with the unequal allocation of Senate seats, among other matters, and did not join the federation. In the original Senate, New Brunswick and Nova Scotia had 12 seats.

DIVISION	SEATS
Maritime Provinces	24
New Brunswick	10
Nova Scotia	10
Prince Edward Island	4
Ontario	24
Quebec	24
Manitoba	2
British Columbia	3
Northwest Territory	2
	79

1870–1879: During this decade, Manitoba (1870), British Columbia (1871), and Prince Edward Island (1873) became provinces with initial Senate allocations of 2, 3, and 4 seats respectively. In 1879, the Northwest Territory was allocated 2 seats.

DIVISION	SEATS
Maritime Provinces	24
New Brunswick	10
Nova Scotia	10
Prince Edward Island	4
Ontario	24
Quebec	24
Western	24
British Columbia	6
Alberta	6
Saskatchewan	6
Manitoba	6
	96

1903–1915: In 1903 the Northwest Territory received an additional 2 seats. Two years later, the new provinces of Alberta and Saskatchewan were created out of the Territory and given 4 seats each. In 1915, the Western Division was formally created, each western province having 6 seats. Regional equality had been achieved.

DIVISION	SEATS
Maritime Provinces	30
New Brunswick	10
Nova Scotia	10
Prince Edward Island	4
Newfoundland	6
Ontario	24
Quebec	24
Western	24
British Columbia	6
Alberta	6
Saskatchewan	6
Manitoba	6
Territories (1 each)	3
	105

1949–1999: The Quebec resolutions had provided that Newfoundland would have its own representation of 4 seats; upon joining Canada in 1949, it received 6 seats. Constitutional amendments gave 1 seat each to the Northwest Territories and Yukon (1975), and Nunavut (1999).

Figure 8.10: Building the Canadian Senate

strict equality and full representation by population. In Austria, the Land with the largest population has 12 Councillors and the number for each of the remaining *Länder* ranges between three and 12, as determined by the formula described in *Figure 8.9*. In Germany, each Land's representation is determined by its population, according to the scale shown in *Figure 8.9*.

At first glance, the distribution of Canada's Senate seats appears to have been an entirely arbitrary or haphazard affair, but it is explained by history and a focus on regional, rather than provincial, equality. The elevated status of provinces in forums such as First Ministers conferences reflects a shift in the Canadian political culture that has added to historic regional perspectives and grievances a contemporary layer of expectation that provinces will be treated equally. This expectation is not met by a Senate in which New Brunswick has 10 Senators and British Columbia has six.

A big issue in Senate reform proposals is the distribution of seats among the provinces. While some proposals advocate equality of representation, as in the United States, critics question allocating the same number of seats to Ontario (13 million) and to Prince Edward Island (less than 150,000).

Broadening the comparative focus to include Europe, the approaches taken in Austria and Germany are worth considering in the search for a formula that produces a fair distribution that stands somewhere between formal equality and the status quo (see *Figure 8.11*).

EFFECTIVENESS

Second chambers also vary in terms of their status compared to the first chamber, which, in practical terms, means the extent of their powers. These include the ability to initiate legislation, to amend or defeat legislation originating in the first chamber, and whether they have a veto in the constitutional amending process.

At one end of the scale are chambers like the US Senate, which is in most respects equal, and in some, perhaps, superior to the House of Representatives. Lijphart calls legislative equality of the two chambers **symmetry,** which he identifies as one of the ingredients of strong bicameralism (the other being **incongruence**, which exists when the electoral districts used to elect the two chambers are different). Of the five federal systems in his data set of 21 democracies, Lijphart considered four regimes to be strongly bicameral—Australia, Germany, Switzerland, and the United States; the system he considered weakly bicameral was Canada's (99).

SENATE SEATS UNDER THE ...	AUSTRIAN FORMULA	GERMAN SCALE*
Newfoundland and Labrador	3	3
Prince Edward Island	3	3
Nova Scotia	3	3
New Brunswick	3	3
Quebec	7	6
Ontario	12	6
Manitoba	3	4
Saskatchewan	3	4
Alberta	3	5
British Columbia	4	5
Yukon	1	1
Northwest Territories	1	1
Nunavut	1	1
	47	45

* scale modified to reflect Canada's population
Figure 8.11

In parliamentary systems, where the government must maintain the confidence of the legislature, it is generally accepted that the first chamber is the "confidence chamber"—the government is not considered to be defeated by the loss of a vote in the second chamber. In some parliamentary constitutions the status of the first chamber as the confidence chamber is made explicit; it may be accompanied by a requirement that bills approving the expenditure of public funds are introduced in the first chamber (which is also true in the non-parliamentary US Congress). The refusal of the Australian Senate to approve a bill authorizing government expenditures in 1975 led to a constitutional crisis when the Governor General dismissed the government and called for elections to both houses of parliament.

At the other end of the scale, opposite to symmetry, is the situation where the second chamber may only delay the passage of any matter approved by the first chamber—what is known as a **suspensive veto**. A suspensive veto has the effect of delaying the passage of a matter by requiring the first chamber to vote a second time on the matter after a specified interval. In the (non-federal) United Kingdom, the House of Lords has been limited to a suspensive veto since 1911. Since 1949, the delay that it places on the second passage of the bill by the House of Commons has been 12 months. (However, for money bills, the delay is only one month; for bills to extend the life of a parliament and delegated legislation, the veto is absolute [Russell, 1].) In Germany, the approval of the second chamber is required for any laws that would affect the interests of the Länder. On other matters, the second chamber has only a suspensive veto, which the first chamber may overturn with the vote of an absolute majority. Russell notes that it is common for there to be a limit on the amount of time that the second chamber has to consider legislation passed by the first chamber; a bill not

considered in that time passes automatically. In cases where this is so, including Austria and Belgium among the federal regimes, the first chamber is able to overturn a decision made by the second chamber (2).

The Canadian Senate's powers are almost equivalent to those of the House of Commons. Money bills must originate in the lower house, and since 1982 the Senate's veto over constitutional motions has been limited to a six-month suspensive veto. In all other respects, though, the Senate has full legislative power, and its defeat of any legislation from the House of Commons cannot be overturned. This legal power must be balanced with the reality that as an appointed chamber, its legitimacy to block the will of the democratically elected first chamber is suspect. To block or overturn legislation from the House of Commons on a regular basis would likely increase the calls for the Senate's abolition. As currently constituted, the Senate does not fulfill the role of a second chamber in a federal system—namely, to provide a voice in the national legislature for provincial interests, as either an ally or alternative to the provincial parliaments or governments.

AMENDING FORMULA

The definition of federalism—that each government is autonomous from the other—is satisfied only if certain features are present in the constitution. In particular, any amendment that would affect both levels of government, national and sub-national, should require the consent of both levels of government or of a majority of citizens polled directly on the issue. Where the consent of both levels of government is necessary to approve or *ratify* an amendment, the degree of consent from each must also be specified. As noted, the inability to agree on an **amending formula** kept Canadians from controlling their own constitution for decades.

The amending formula (which may include exempting certain matters from amendment) is a critical feature of any federal system.

VARIATIONS: SIMPLE BUT RIGID

Amending formulas may be simple or complex and they may be rigid or flexible. The amendment process for the US Constitution is simple and rigid: of the thousands of amendments proposed since 1787, only 27 have been ratified. This total includes the first 10 amendments (constituting the Bill of Rights), ratified in 1791. A constitutional amendment can be proposed by a state legislature or by the federal Congress, where it must receive a two-thirds vote in both houses. (An alternative method of holding a national convention to approve a proposal if requested by two-thirds of the states has never been used.) Ratification of an amendment requires approval by three-quarters of the states, either by the states' legislatures or by constitutional conventions held in the states. It is up to Congress to choose the method of **ratification**, and ratification by conventions was used only once (to end Prohibition). The margins of approval—two-thirds vote in Congress, three-quarters of the states—are much greater than a simple majority; this is common to constitutional votes and reflects the belief that the basic rules should not be too easy to change.

VARIATIONS: SIMPLE AND FLEXIBLE

The Basic Law of Germany has a simple and flexible amending procedure: a vote of two-thirds of the members of both houses of the federal legislature. Because the second chamber is composed of delegates of the *Länder* governments, this procedure secures the consent of both levels of state. Although less than 50 years old, the German constitution has been frequently amended. At the same time, some parts cannot be amended, including the federal character of the regime, and certain individual rights.

VARIATIONS: COMPLEX AND RIGID

Among federal regimes, Canada's constitutional amending formula is one of the newest, in effect since 1982 when the constitution was **repatriated** from the United Kingdom. It includes the following provisions:

· A proposal may be put forward by the Parliament of Canada or any provincial legislature.
· The general rule for ratification is the support of Parliament and the legislatures of at least seven (two-thirds) of the provinces that have between them at least 50 per cent of the population of all the provinces.
· Ratification under the general rule must take place within three years of the proposal first being adopted by Parliament or a provincial legislature.
· If the amendment under the general rule affects the powers of the provinces, it has no effect in a province where the legislature has expressed its dissent.
· Certain matters require unanimous consent: ratification by Parliament and all 10 provincial legislatures.
· Some changes may only be made by the general rule, but without the provision that permits dissenting provinces to opt out.
· Any matter that affects some but not all provinces requires the support of Parliament and the legislatures of the provinces affected.

Except for amendments made under the latter provision, Canada's amending formula has proven to be very

AUSTRALIA'S CONSTITUTIONAL REFERENDUMS REQUIRE A DOUBLE MAJORITY						
	YES	NO			YES	NO
			New South Wales		✓	
			Queensland			✓
			South Australia		✓	
			Tasmania		✓	
The States	✓		Victoria		✓	
The Territories		✓	Western Australia		✓	
National Total:	✓		State Total:		✓	
1. A Majority in the National Vote			2. A Majority in a Majority of States			

Figure 8.12

rigid. This has been aided by the tendency to address constitutional issues in First Ministers' meetings, which, by their nature, produce complex proposals that contain something for everyone at the table, and (therefore) many reasons for those not at the table to reject the package). Canada's already complex formula might have been improved with a clause limiting the number of its sections that could be amended at any one time.

POPULAR RATIFICATION

Australia and Switzerland both provide the public with a direct role in the constitutional amendment process. In Australia, the normal procedure is that a proposal receiving a majority in both houses of parliament is submitted to the people for ratification in a referendum. The states have no role in initiating constitutional change. To succeed, the proposal must receive a majority of all votes cast, as well as a majority of the votes in a majority of the states (a **double majority**). Of 44 proposals put to the public between 1906 and 1999, eight were ratified in the referendum vote. In the 1999

referendum asking Australians whether they wished to replace the Queen as head of state and adopt a republican constitution, the measure was defeated nationally by a margin of 55 per cent to 45 per cent, and in five of the six Australian states.

In Switzerland, procedures are much more complicated, in part because of the possibility that a full or

"REPATRIATED" VS. "PATRIATED"

To *repatriate* means to return something or someone to its country of origin. Since the Canadian Constitution was a statute passed by the Parliament of the United Kingdom in 1867 (the *British North America Act, 1867* or the *BNA Act, 1867*), some—including justices of the Supreme Court—felt a new word was necessary: *patriation*. This Canadian contribution to the English language was unnecessary if one considers that the provisions in the *BNA Act, 1867* were based on the 72 resolutions agreed to by colonial delegates at conferences in Charlottetown and Quebec City in 1864.

partial revision of the constitution may be requested by a portion of the public through an initiative (see Chapter 11). At the end of the day, though, constitutional change requires popular ratification, and as in Australia, must receive a double majority: a national majority, and a majority in a majority of the cantons.

In Belgium, only the federal parliament can initiate a constitutional amendment, which it does by passing a motion indicating its intention to revise the constitution, listing the changes to be made. Both houses of the parliament are then dissolved, elections held, and the new parliament is considered to have a mandate to carry out changes. Adoption of a revision requires a two-thirds majority in each chamber. The public can reject constitutional change by voting for parties opposed to the proposed measures.

NON-FEDERAL OPTIONS

ADMINISTRATIVE DECENTRALIZATION

Just as a considerable degree of centralization is possible within federations when sub-national units become or remain limited in their legislative and/or fiscal powers (Austria being an example of where this is so), considerable decentralization is possible in unitary states, when administrative responsibility is delegated to regional and/or municipal authorities. While delegated authority is always provisional, meaning that it may be revoked or altered at any time, the longer a power is exercised or administered by subordinate governments, the more difficult it may be for the central government to "re-occupy" this area of jurisdiction. Over time, popular expectations, local knowledge, and political traditions may be created that impose practical limits on any "uploading."

CANADA'S CONSTITUTIONAL CHRONICLE

1867 The **BRITISH NORTH AMERICA ACT, 1867** is passed by the UK Parliament, creating the Dominion of Canada, a federal state with four provinces.

1931 The **STATUTE OF WESTMINSTER** is passed by the UK Parliament, relinquishing any legislative authority over the self-governing Dominions (Australia, Canada, Ireland, Newfoundland, New Zealand, and the Union of South Africa).

1982 The **CANADA ACT** is passed by the UK Parliament, containing the **CONSTITUTION ACT, 1982** (which includes seven new sections, among them the **CANADIAN CHARTER OF RIGHTS AND FREEDOMS**, and provisions for amending the constitution, termination of the power of the Parliament of the United Kingdom to legislate for Canada, and provisions re-naming the **BRITISH NORTH AMERICA ACTS, 1867-1975** as the **CONSTITUTION ACTS, 1867-1975**).

1987 Canada's First Ministers agree to the Meech Lake Accord (MLA), which contains significant constitutional changes, including recognition of Quebec as a "distinct society."

1990 The MLA fails to be ratified by all ten provinces before the three-year deadline, required under the amending formula, expires.

1992 Canada's First Ministers agree to the Charlottetown Accord (CA), containing significant constitutional changes and much broader in its scope than the MLA. The government decides to hold a non-binding national vote on the Accord (which is binding in two provinces under their own legislation, passed after the MLA) and Quebec holds its own (binding) vote. The CA fails to receive a majority nationally, and fails in six provinces (including the three in which the vote is binding).

Scottish Parliament. Edinburgh, United Kingdom.

DEVOLUTION

Devolution, or what is sometimes called **home rule,** is a means of allowing some (but not all) areas within a unitary state to have their own autonomous institutions of state (including a legislature and executive) and a division of powers to be exercised by that region's government. The usual reason is to recognize and accommodate the desire of a nationality or ethnic fragment within the regime for a measure of self-government. Among the most obvious examples today are the Scottish Parliament, the Welsh Assembly, and the Northern Ireland Assembly, all established in the late 1990s by the UK government. In Scotland and Wales, devolution was preceded by a referendum vote establishing the support in those historic nations of Great Britain; in Northern Ireland, devolution was part of an agreement to end long-standing hostilities. The powers exercised by each devolved legislature vary,

with the Scottish Parliament having jurisdiction over a wide range of policy fields from health, education, and economic development to criminal and civil justice. Each of these parliaments is elected on the basis of proportional or semi-proportional representation systems, a reform that Westminster has been unwilling to take for its own election. The Irish Assembly Executive is uniquely consensual in being drawn on a proportional basis from all parties in the parliament.

Devolution differs from asymmetrical federalism in two respects. First, the devolved assemblies do not have a constitutional basis, but are created by legislation passed by the national parliament. For that reason their existence is at the pleasure of the national government. On at least two occasions, the Irish Assembly has been suspended by Westminster. On the other hand, the Scottish Parliament has established itself so well that its repeal seems unthinkable.

Figure 8.13

Second, only some parts of the regime fall under devolved assemblies. In the United Kingdom, citizens in Scotland, Wales, and Northern Ireland continue to elect representatives to the Parliament at Westminster. Those living in England elect representatives *only* to Parliament. A similar situation exists with Denmark and its territories of Greenland and the Faroe Islands, which are now largely self-governed under devolved institutions.

Reference has been made to Spain and asymmetrical federalism. Although Spain is not a federal system in the strictest sense, each of its 17 autonomous regions (and two autonomous cities) has its own state structure of executive, legislature, and supreme court. The powers that the regions exercise vary, being outlined in each region's Statute of Autonomy. Four regions—Andalusia, the Basque Country, Catalonia, and Galicia—have a considerable degree of autonomy (the latter three being categorized as "historic nationalities"), exceeding that of the other regions. Each region, in turn, consists of one or more provinces, except for the two cities of Ceuta and Melilla (which are located on the Moroccan coast).

SOVEREIGNTY-ASSOCIATION

In Canada, since the 1960s, support within Quebec for a separate, sovereign state has had a significant impact on politics, public policy, and constitutional negotiations. Among the various political solutions proposed to meet this challenge has been devolving greater power to Quebec's National Assembly. Both the Meech Lake and Charlottetown Accords would have recognized Quebec as a "distinct society," a provision that would not have given Quebec new powers but would have established a criterion for the courts to consider in any jurisdictional or constitutional dispute involving Quebec's exercise of its existing powers.

The goal of the first separatist Premier of Quebec, René Lévesque, was an arrangement called **sovereignty-association**. In sovereignty-association, Quebec and (the rest of) Canada would, as equal sovereign partners, share a common currency and central bank, a common market and external tariff, a customs union, agreements on employment and immigration, and institutions to administer and adjudicate the sovereignty-association treaty. It might be conceived of as a proper confederation of two partners. A referendum held in Quebec in 1980, seeking consent to negotiate sovereignty-association with Canada and the other provinces, lost by a vote of 60 per cent to 40 per cent. In 1995 a second referendum that emphasized sovereignty as the primary goal—with an association with the rest of Canada being a possible outcome of achieving that sovereignty—lost by a much narrower margin (50.6 per cent to 49.4 per cent).

REFERENCES

Australian Commonwealth Grants Commission. "The Australian framework for federal financial relations." *2010–11 Update Report.* Web.

Lijphart, Arend. *Democracies: Patterns of Majoritarian and Consensus Government in Twenty-One Countries.* New Haven: Yale University Press, 1984.

Mahler, Gregory S. *Comparative Politics: An Institutional and Cross-National Approach.* Englewood Cliffs, NJ: Prentice-Hall, 1995.

Mény, Yves. *Government and Politics in Western Europe.* 2nd ed. Oxford: Oxford University Press, 1993.

Organization for Economic Co-operation and Development. *OECD Fiscal Decentralization Database.* Web.

Russell, Meg. "Resolving Disputes between the Chambers." Paper to Royal Commission, The Constitution Unit, University College London, 1999. Web.

Steiner, Jürg. *European Democracies.* 3rd ed. New York: Longman, 1995.

Stevenson, Garth. *Unfulfilled Union.* 3rd ed. Toronto: Gage, 1989.

Wheare, K.C. *Federal Government.* London: Oxford University Press, 1963.

FURTHER READING

Bogdanor, Vernon. "The West Lothian Question." *Parliamentary Affairs* 63.1 (December 2009): 156–172.

Bonney, Norman. "Looming Issues for Scotland and the Union." *The Political Quarterly* 79.4 (October–December 2008): 560–568.

Bradbury, Jonathan, and James Mitchell. "Devolution: Between Governance and Territorial Politics." *Parliamentary Affairs* 58.2 (April 2005): 287–302.

Brock, Katy L. "The Politics of Asymmetrical Federalism: Reconsidering the Role and Responsibilities of Ottawa." *Canadian Public Policy—Analyse de Politiques* 34.2 (June 2008): 144–161.

Bulmer, W. Elliot. "An Analysis of the Scottish National Party's Draft Constitution for Scotland." *Parliamentary Affairs* 64.4 (March 2011): 674–693.

McEwan, Nicola, and André Lecours. "Voice or Recognition? Comparing Strategies for Accommodating Territorial Minorities in Multinational States." *Commonwealth & Comparative Politics* 46.2 (April 2008): 220–243.

Stepan, Alfred. "Comparative Theory and Political Practice: Do We Need a 'State-Nation' Model as Well as a 'Nation-State' Model?" *Government and Opposition* 43.1 (January 2008): 1–25.

CHAPTER 9

Who Wants What?
The Political Process

...WHICH PROVIDES THE READER WITH

· an introduction to the political process
· that focuses on what expectations and demands are brought to the state
· arising out of the divisions known as societal cleavages and
· informed by the systematic sets of political ideas known as ideologies.

What do people want from the state? Who gets it and how? Who does the state serve? Who controls the state? Is it the rich and famous? The dominant economic class? A small, closed elite? The forces of globalization and technological transformation? The people, or, the enemies of the people?

Earlier chapters have noted the deep roots of the idea that the state should serve the public good, the good of the community, rather than the private or partial interests of the few who control the state. And much experience has suggested that relying on the enlightened moral sense of those in charge is not enough to guarantee general well-being.

Political reforms over the centuries have aimed at limiting the arbitrariness with which the state serves some interests and not others and have sought to make rulers accountable to the broader public. This is the purpose of responsible government, representative government, democratic government—however well or poorly they accomplish it.

In any regime, the **political process** describes how those in control of the state come to be there, whose interests they are likely to serve, and any feedback mechanisms that punish or reward them for their use of the government. It should not be necessary to justify focusing on the *democratic* political process, particularly if that focus is critical (in the best sense of that word). The alternatives are the inertia of tradition, the violence of revolution, or the oppressive weight of authoritarianism, each of which has its champions, but none of which offers a means by which the reasonable demands of ordinary citizens can be heard, let alone force a response from those in power.

People bring their expectations to the state in a representative democracy by lending support to those who have been able (or those who promise to be able) to meet those expectations. The people punish those who have failed (or cannot be trusted) to meet their demands by withholding support from them. Elections are only one of the arenas in which this happens.

At the risk of oversimplifying matters, the political process can be boiled down to a two-part question:

What do people want from the state? What can they do to get it?

Well-being; security of life, limb, and property; the opportunity to prosper, materially and/or spiritually; a sociable, peaceful community—these are the easy, abstract answers to the first question. In practice, people hold vastly different notions about what is conducive to well-being, about what activities are acceptable in a peaceful community, or about how opportunities can be created or sustained. They have different ideas about what constitutes political goods and private goods, varying convictions not only of what the state should do, but of whether the state should do anything at all.

Citizens don't form their expectations of the state in the abstract; they hold them from their particular place in time, from their situation in society, and within a particular political culture. Expectations of what the state might do—from defence to environmental protection to social programs, infrastructure, and the arts—have changed dramatically through the past century. Students today have a vastly different idea of the "basics" of well-being and perhaps a more heightened awareness of environmental security than their parents did. Most are at least one generation or more away from the experience of living through a time of war—hot or cold.

Expectations of government that today's students share will change throughout the stages of their lives—there *will* be a time when pensions matter more than student debt load, a day when concern about the quality of their own children's education or their own access to health care services will be at the forefront of any political judgments they form (for those who will make such judgments on the basis of policy considerations).

The remainder of this chapter examines why, or from what sets of circumstances, people are mobilized to become engaged in the political process. This discussion includes the awareness that many citizens do *not* engage in the political process, even when their right to do so is protected and guaranteed. Such disengagement (or more precisely, non-engagement) is as important to understand as its opposite. Some of the underlying answers may come in the following two chapters where the opportunities for engagement are examined. At this point, the focus will be on two elements:

(a) the societal bases of engagement (**social cleavages**); and

(b) the political ideas and belief systems that people adopt (**ideology**).

SOCIAL CLEAVAGES

A recurring theme in definitions of politics is the resolution of conflict, but conflict between whom, and over what? The conflict that states must resolve certainly includes disputes between individuals, but it is as often (and more importantly) about competition between different segments of society for influence, if not control, over public policy outputs. Cleavages, the societal sources of the competition and conflict that are resolved through the political process, are captured by Lane and Ersson's description: "the so-called raw materials of politics which political parties mould by aligning themselves in a party system facing the electorate in competitive elections. Public institutions offer decision-making mechanisms for handling issues that somehow relate to the cleavages in the social structure" (11).

Gallagher, Laver, and Mair describe cleavages as "the actual substance of the social divisions that underpin contemporary ... politics," and identify three dimensions to a social cleavage:

- a "social division" between people in terms of some central characteristic;
- a collective identification in terms of this social division; and
- an organization that gives "institutional expression" to this collective identification (210–11).

The first point suggests that people identify themselves in terms of a common characteristic *and* use this identity to distinguish themselves from others. Of the many bases on which such divisions may rest, the strongest are often traits that are (at least to some degree) **ascriptive**. This means characteristics that are in some way innate (ethnicity), or inherited (mother tongue), or (for at least one's formative years) involuntarily assigned (religion, class). Ascriptive factors contrast with identities more consciously adopted, such as adopting an ideology, making a lifestyle choice, or supporting a social movement. These voluntary identifications may

also sometimes have close links with cleavages (ideology and class, for example).

The second point clarifies how the distinction between ascribed and acquired identities is not merely analytic—while one could hardly belong to a political party or interest group and *not* be aware of it, it is entirely possible *not* to identify ourselves in terms of our ethnicity, mother tongue, religion, or class. Having such characteristics does not necessarily mean that they determine who we are and what we want. Often such characteristics become "visible" to us only in the presence of others whose traits are different. In this sense, a cleavage rests not on the fact of difference but on the *perception* of difference. (Northern Ireland is not the only country divided between Catholics and Protestants, but it is one where the difference—reinforced by other factors—has been profoundly divisive.)

The third point is that the collective identification of people in terms of their common characteristic must express itself in a form of organization that leads to political action. This is where cleavages link up with ideology, or political parties, or interest groups. Some members of the working class, conscious of their collective identity and interest, may adopt a socialist ideology, establish trade unions, and/or support a social democratic political party. Other members of the working class may adopt an ideology and support political parties more reflective of the class to which they would prefer to belong.

These last examples point to a fourth element that is necessary to explain the link between collective identity and political engagement—*interest(s)*. To be conscious of a religious or ethnic or class identity has no political significance unless there is also an interest connected to that identity, an interest that is not being met, or is threatened, or requires protection by the government. The division at the basis of a social cleavage is not simply a difference in identities but a *difference in interests,* where "interest" directs us to what a group wants. Differences in interest (real or perceived) are critical to the movement from collective identity to organization for political action. Where a collective identity fails to mobilize people politically on behalf of some common interest, the cleavage remains *latent,* in contrast to those that are *manifest* in the activity of other groups.

RELIGION

Historically, religion has been one of the strongest cleavages. This division has typically consisted of a conflict between

- *two different faiths*—such as clashes between Christianity and Islam during the Crusades, in medieval Spain, during the Austrian-Turkish wars of the seventeenth and eighteenth centuries, or in twentieth-century Bosnia; between Christianity and First Nations spirituality in North America from the seventeenth century onward; Muslim-Hindu conflicts on the Indian subcontinent; and conflict between African animist beliefs and Christian or Muslim monotheism;
- *two sects of the same faith*—all the instances of Catholic-Protestant conflict since the 1500s, or the conflict between Shias and Sunnis within the Islamic world; or
- *believers and secularists*—the conflict between those supporting a separation of religion and government versus those who defend public policy informed by particular theological

positions. Some Christian democratic parties in Europe, the religious Right in North America, and Islamists in Turkey provide examples of challenges to the wholly secular state.

The clash between believers (who are politically evangelical) and secularists (who may or may not also be believers) can arise only in a society that permits religious non-fundamentalism and tolerance of non-believers. Toleration is a relatively modern idea, particularly for those peoples who are adherents of a monotheistic religion, such as Judaism, Christianity, or Islam. (The contribution of the Reformation/Enlightenment to the development of liberal ideas of tolerance in Europe should not be overlooked.) Without some moderation of literal interpretations of scripture and doctrine, it is too easily believed that to defeat or even annihilate the "apostate" (those who do not follow the "true" faith) is to do the will of God (or the gods).

Theocracy describes a state where the ultimate *and* active authority is divine (God, Yaweh, Allah), realized in practice by the rule of a religious leader (high priest, prophet, pope, ayatollah). The Islamic Republic of Iran is the pre-eminent example of a modern-day theocracy, with the Supreme Leader uniting in one person the ultimate religious and political authority.

Outright theocracies have been less common than states in which the political rulers have the blessing of the highest religious authority. While the practical importance of this blessing depends wholly on the strength of the religion within the regime, in some constitutional monarchies, it is still traditional for a new monarch to be blessed by the highest religious authority. Much of Western European political history (discussed in Chapter 3) was about the eventual separation of political authority from religious authority and the creation of the secular state. The legacy of that struggle is the continued opposition of liberals, reformers, or anti-clericals to any role for religion in the institutions of the state or in public policy.

Finally, it should be obvious that the religious cleavage is often as much about a social identification as it is about a commitment to a particular spiritual creed. In many cases, the conflict between adherents of rival faiths has little to do with theology and everything to do with the struggle for power or scarce resources. In the pluralistic societies that characterize the larger developed democracies, religious adherence is regarded as simply a matter of personal choice. Nonetheless, religion can mobilize its adherents around public morality issues, such as the status of marriage, the availability of abortion, and the regulation of prostitution and pornography, or social justice issues such as the elimination of poverty, the protection of the vulnerable, and the prevention of addiction.

ETHNO-LINGUISTIC

This label applies to several related but sometimes distinct variables, such as the scientifically discredited but still socially relevant concept of racial difference; in some parts of the world, it refers simply to a person's colour. Many of these cleavages are the unhappy legacy of colonialism and imperialism, whereby peoples with little in common were placed within artificial borders as the result of treaties signed by European powers. In other cases, political unions, conquests, or dynastic marriages have joined different ethnic and linguistic communities (which are not so distinct "racially") in one society. English and French in Canada; Flemish (Dutch-speaking) and Walloon (French-speaking) in Belgium; and French, German, and Italian in Switzerland are examples of

· Figure 9.1

significant ethno-linguistic cleavages in developed democracies, but countries such as Spain, France, and Italy also have significant amounts of ethnic diversity. The Balkans have long been a region where ethno-linguistic cleavages have led to war, most recently with the conflicts following the dissolution of the former Republic of Yugoslavia into what has become seven sovereign states (see *Figure 9.1*).

These cleavages are never just about language, but are also about cultural differences rooted in or sustained through linguistic difference. In some cases, like the Scottish or Welsh in Britain, the cultural differences may have survived the demise or decline of the native tongue. Ethno-linguistic cleavages rarely exist in isolation but are often linked to one or more others, such as religion and class. In and of itself, the ethno-linguistic cleavage mobilizes supporters around issues relevant to the survival of the culture, such as preserving the use of language, education, and other cultural supports. In some cases, freedom from discrimination or redress for historic injustices is high on the agenda.

Most important for ethno-linguistic minorities is some degree of self-government, or guaranteed representation in decision making, to increase the likelihood of obtaining favourable policies.

CENTRE-PERIPHERY

Virtually all societies—city-states or micro-states excepted—have a centre. It is the largest city or most populous region; it may be the political capital and/or the most economically developed and productive region. In many cases, this centre is resented by people in other regions who feel disadvantaged or excluded by not being at the centre.

Metropole and **hinterland** have also been used to characterize this cleavage, usually with the inference that the hinterland is exploited or used for the benefit of the metropole. During the 1980s, when "Western alienation" was at its height in Canada, Owram described the western Canadian provinces as a "reluctant hinterland." Although the centre-periphery cleavage is often fuelled by a sense of economic disparity or deprivation, the strongest expressions of western Canadian discontent have come from two of the country's wealthiest provinces. Alienation seemed more about being excluded from economic and political decision making, dominated by the central Canadian voices of Ontario and Quebec. Over the past three decades, arguably, the centre of power in Canada has been shifting westward.

In any society where the potential for a strong centre-periphery cleavage exists, particularly in large countries with federal regimes, sub-national leaders (provincial premiers, state governors) are often tempted to emphasize grievances with the centre as a means of boosting their own support. Many provincial election campaigns have been fought as much against the government in Ottawa as against actual opponents on the provincial ballot.

A hinterland or periphery that feels consistently excluded and/or exploited may conclude that it would be better off on its own. In Italy in the 1990s, there was considerable growth in support in the northern provinces for political movements with separatist agendas. Italy is governed from Rome, which is situated in the more populous, but also poorer, southern half of the country. The Italian state performs a redistributive function, which means that the industrialized urban north subsidizes the south. In this case, northern support for separatist parties seems to signal resentment of a needy metropole by a wealthy hinterland.

The centre-periphery contributes greatly to political regionalism, which exists whenever the identification with a particular territory within a larger geographic whole becomes a factor in political activity. By itself, identification with a particular territorial region is not the basis for political action; something else must unite and motivate the people within this region.

URBAN-RURAL

The urban-rural is a similarly one-sided cleavage, where the outside (rural areas, hinterland, or "have not" regions) has a grievance that the inside (cities, the political centre) may not notice (let alone understand). Grievances are often economic in nature—rural areas tending to be less wealthy and receiving fewer services—but may also result from broader patterns of policy-making in which the interests of the minority (such as rural dwellers) are ignored or overwhelmed by the interests of the majority.

Environmental or planning regulations that satisfy the concerns of urban voters can make life more difficult for farmers, foresters, or others making their living

BLUE	WHITE	PINK	GOLD	GREY	GREEN
wage-earning skilled or unskilled labourers	salaried office workers or professionals	workers in jobs typically held by women	highly skilled knowledge workers and professionals	workers in jobs with white and blue collar elements	workers in jobs in the environmental field

Figure 9.2

off the land. Licensing or registration requirements designed to address the problems that plague cities, such as traffic congestion and gun crime, may simply seem to rural dwellers like annoying intrusions by the state.

Over time, with the nearly complete urbanization of some societies or political units, divisions within cities—urban versus suburban, inner city versus bedroom-community commuters—may become more relevant than the urban-rural cleavage. Similarly, the rise of environmental consciousness, combined with an increase in the number of people who work from a home outside the city, has changed the interests of the rural component that was once primarily—if not uniformly—agricultural in its interests. The replacement of traditional family farming with technology-intensive agribusiness creates additional fractures in the rural population.

CLASS

Many would argue that class is the most significant of the cleavages in contemporary politics—for some it is the only cleavage that matters, the real cause of division underlying religious or ethnic or regional cleavages. Not all countries are characterized by ethno-linguistic divisions, or religious distinctions, or centre-periphery conflicts, but all have socio-economic classes. Two quibbles are in order: deciding *how* to define and identify class; and recognizing that class divisions may be latent or manifest.

In any society, class represents social stratifications that give differential access to resources and other societal goods. How these classes are to be defined and identified depends, in part, on perspective. As a political economist, Karl Marx defined classes *structurally,* in terms of the organization of the means of economic production. He believed that the capitalist mode of production created two essential classes—owners and workers—and that modern politics is about the struggle between these two classes (with the eventual victory of the working class).

In modern industrial (or post-industrial) economies, the structure of capitalism is more complicated. In addition to owners (of particular means of production) and workers (those who sell their labour to an owner for a wage), there are the self-employed, the unemployed, those who work in public or quasi-public institutions, farmers, and students. Division *within* classes, or class fractions, can be as significant as the divisions between classes. Different segments of the business community (manufacturers, merchants, bankers) have different needs and interests, above and beyond what they share in common. Similarly, blue collar, white collar, and workers with collars of other colours may be in as much competition and conflict with each other as with their bosses. The considerable fragmentation of the classes, considered structurally, puts impediments in the way of an oversimplified class struggle.

Sociologically, class is more likely to be considered today in terms of measures such as income, education, status, or composites combining several of these. So, to the extent that class becomes an analytic construct, it is less likely to form the basis of the identities on which politics will be based. As noted, it is possible that class remains a latent cleavage, and there are several reasons for this. One was the growth of a relatively affluent middle class in economically developed democracies, and the strength in such societies of a political culture ignoring or minimizing the significance of class. Evidence suggests that most people view themselves as members of the middle class (despite evidence that the middle class has been shrinking in many of these societies); this may reflect the structural fragmentation noted above, as well as the relative affluence of these societies. It also means that most people would be unlikely to identify class as the basis for their politics (even though it may be just that). As with all cleavages, there must be a significant "other" for the basis of identity to become politicized.

In societies with strong cultural beliefs that individuals' social positions (despite evidence to the contrary) are the product of hard work, intelligence, and initiative, to be disadvantaged in class terms is a sign of failure, not a product of the structure of the economy (i.e., a "class" issue) and therefore *not* a basis for political mobilization. In most European democracies class is a significant cleavage, but in North America it remains more latent. Political parties that campaign on behalf of a particular class are rare, and are rarely successful. This is not to say that class is not an important variable in North American society and politics, only that it is not the primary identity that informs the political consciousness and actions of large segments of society.

THE STRUCTURE OF CLEAVAGES

Any society will have a cleavage structure that reflects some, but not likely all, of the preceding. The cleavages that matter shift as technological, social, and demographic change take effect. Other cleavages (like age) remain latent, with the potential to become manifest at some future date. The constellation of cleavages operating in any given society has two significant relationships, one external and one internal.

The external relationship is between cleavages and the political organizations and institutions where behaviour occurs. A cleavage may account for support given to a political party, to an interest group, or to the strength of an ideology within a political culture. Political parties, interest groups, and other vehicles of representation attempt to obtain policies that respond to the interests of the segments of society they represent. In this way, cleavages are accommodated more or less well within a regime. When a cleavage is most fully accommodated by responsive policies, the division represented by the cleavage ceases to be a basis for political mobilization. In other words, it becomes less politically *salient*. At worst, a cleavage that cannot be accommodated leads to civil war (see Yugoslavia) or partition (as when the former Czechoslovakia divided into the Czech Republic and Slovakia, a fate that increasingly seems likely for Belgium). The ability of a society to accommodate, or at least contain, its cleavages depends on features of the political process, in particular the electoral and party systems, which shape the nature of party government.

The second relationship is internal: how the cleavages present in a society relate to each other. Consider *Figure 9.3*: Example 1 depicts a society in which there is one dominant cleavage between those who identify as X and those identifying as O. Example 2 adds a second

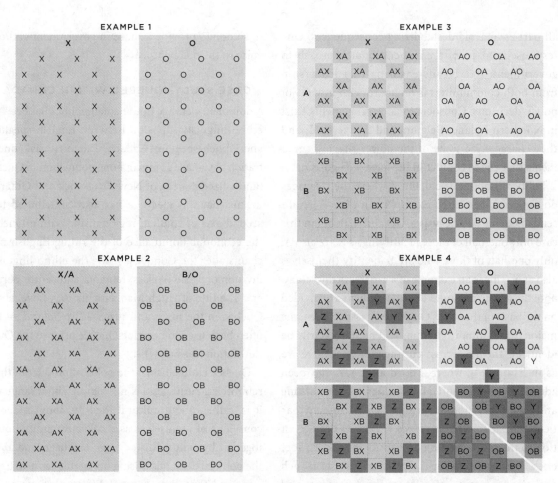

EXAMPLE 1

EXAMPLE 2

Figure 9.3

EXAMPLE 3

EXAMPLE 4

Figure 9.4

cleavage: those who identify as A or as B, and in this society it happens that all those who are X are also A, while all who are O are also B. This is an example of **reinforcing cleavages**: two or more bases of identity (or difference) shared by the same segments of the population. On virtually every issue the lines of opposition separate the same groups from each other. In Austria, a division between the Catholic middle class and the **anti-clerical** working class led to civil war in the 1930s.

Reinforcing cleavages are even more striking in Belgium, dividing the generally more affluent Flemish population in the north and west from the Francophone Walloons in the south and east parts of the country. Differences between these two groups exist on at least three levels, and the effect has been a steady decentralization of the Belgian political system. Generally speaking, reinforcing cleavages lead, all else being equal, to fragmentation of the polity. At the very least, reinforcing cleavages require a special effort by all parties to avoid destabilizing consequences. One response is to adopt a **consociational** approach to government; this means ensuring that leadership from both communities is on board with any major policy decisions. Consociational arrangements exist in Northern Ireland, Belgium and Switzerland, and they characterize some of the power-sharing agreements that ended conflict in the former Yugoslavia.

Political stability is enhanced where the cleavages do not coincide neatly. Example 3 in *Figure 9.4* presents the same two cleavages X/O and A/B, but in this case only one-half of those identifying as X are also A; only one-half of those who are B identify themselves also as Y. This is an example of a **cross-cutting cleavage**: those who are united by one element are divided on the basis of the other. On different issues, then, the majority and minority groups will not necessarily be identical. The more cross-cutting cleavages there are, as in Example 4, where a third axis, Y/Z, has been added, the more political majorities will be shifting and temporary, not favouring or alienating any particular group on a regular basis. Cleavages draw attention to the fragmentation of identity in modern societies. A central task for the political system in such societies is to contain or defuse the differences and contests of interest that emerge out of these various identities. This is the element of politics identified as the resolution of conflict, the engineering of consent, or the art of compromise. If one side of any division is always the "winner" in battles over policy, the "losing" party will soon feel aggrieved, exploited, alienated. The long-term consequences of such a situation are rarely good for a political community. What goes far in determining whether such outcomes are likely is the capacity of the political process to provide representation to the various segments of society and, in so doing, provide a share in government and/or a voice in the policy process.

CASE STUDY—QUEBEC WITHIN CANADA

A dominant cleavage in Canadian politics has been the ethno-linguistic division between English-speaking and French-speaking Canada. The territorial concentration of Canada's Francophone population in Quebec (and adjacent areas of New Brunswick and Ontario), means that this cleavage has also contributed to a second axis of conflict: regionalism. Within Quebec, the economic dominance of the ruling English merchants after the Conquest made the ethno-linguistic division one also of class, religion, and centre-periphery. The title of Hugh MacLennan's 1945 novel about Quebec in the 1920s and 1930s—*Two Solitudes*—has often been used to describe Quebec prior to the Quiet Revolution (see below).

Quebec nationalism—the political product of these reinforcing cleavages—is not simply about language; it is, rather, about cultural identity, about a people conscious of themselves as a collective entity bound together by culture, history, *and* language, and about the political demands arising out of this sense of being "a nation." Thus, there are real differences between the political demands of Francophones *outside* Quebec, largely focused on language and education rights, and the quest of the self-identified Québécois for self-government or greater autonomy within the Canadian state. Responding to Quebec nationalism with a strategy of bilingualism and biculturalism—which treats the cleavage as primarily a question of language—failed because it ignored the respects in which Quebec constitutes a "distinct society."

One type of nationalism is the demand of a people (a "nation") for the political autonomy necessary to preserve their culture and way of life. Nationalism in Quebec has taken two forms. *French-Canadian* nationalism, which covered the period from 1763 to 1960, emphasized survival: maintaining the integrity of language, culture, and custom, and avoiding the pressures for assimilation into a larger Anglophone society. With the passage of the *Quebec Act* in 1774, Quebec received special status in British North America: the *Quebec Act* preserved the civil law code of New France and strengthened the status and power of the local seigneurs (quasi-feudal lords) and of the Catholic Church. In these ways the British engaged in **elite accommodation**—whereby a people are ruled by co-opting (accommodating) their existing leaders.

When Lower Canada (Quebec) and Upper Canada (Ontario) were united in the colony of Canada in 1840, an element of consociational power sharing was introduced. Most historians would agree that the survival of French Canadian culture through two centuries, avoiding assimilation into Anglophone North America in the process, came at a price. Prior to 1960, Francophones in Quebec remained second-class citizens in their own homeland, dominated economically by a wealthy Anglo-Canadian business class in Montreal and socially by a conservative Catholic Church. Perhaps the most extreme expression of the sense of inferiority this created for Québécois was captured in the searing title of Pierre Vallières's 1967 book, *White Niggers of America* (*Nègres Blancs d'Amérique*).

In 1960, forces of social, economic, and political change, previously held in check by governments willing to continue the strategy of elite accommodation, launched what has since been called the Quiet Revolution. This was a time of change: the secularization of Quebec society, an expansion of the Quebec state, and the emergence of a new Québécois nationalism. *Les Québécois* were ready to take their place in urban, secular, liberal North American society, to become fully modern, guaranteeing the survival of their culture and language by political means, with new or expanded authority.

In the past 50-plus years, Quebec society has been thoroughly transformed with the creation of a modern, activist state (symbolized by the giant projects of Hydro-Québec), the emergence of a Francophone business and entrepreneurial class, and the enactment of Bill 101, the *Charter of the French Language in Quebec,* designed to make Quebec, so far as possible, a unilingual, Francophone society. The Quiet Revolution began with a slogan "*Maîtres chez nous*"—"masters in our own house"—which expressed succinctly the political ambition of Francophone Quebecers. The past five decades have shifted the debate to Quebec's place within Canada, a debate conducted by federalists and sovereigntists.

Since the Parti Québécois (PQ) came to power in 1976, support for Quebec sovereignty has been a key variable in Quebec and, at times, Canadian politics. Since 1976, with the exception of the period between the 2007 and 2008 general elections, the PQ has either formed the government in Quebec or been the official opposition. Sovereigntists believe that Quebec's survival as a distinct society in North America depends on becoming a sovereign nation-state. So-called "soft sovereigntists," such as the PQ's first premier, the late René Lévesque, have believed that independence is only feasible if Quebec can remain closely partnered with Canada for economic and defence purposes. Such a partnership ("sovereignty-association" discussed in Chapter 8) would be negotiated with Canada before or after a declaration of sovereignty. Hard-line sovereigntists (such as one-time PQ premier Jacques Parizeau) advocate a unilateral declaration of independence, regardless of the willingness of Canada to negotiate terms or agree to subsequent forms of association. Quebecers have twice gone to the polls for plebiscites that would have authorized the Quebec government to take further steps toward securing independence from Canada. The No/*Non* side won by a 60–40 margin in 1980, but barely eked out a victory in 1995, despite the overwhelming support of non-Francophones.

The "federalist" side argues that Quebec's proper place remains within Canada. This includes the majority of English-speaking Canadians (inside and outside Quebec) that seems comfortable with the status quo. Francophone federalists within Quebec have sought constitutional or legislative accommodation from the rest of Canada as the means of ensuring the survival of Quebec's distinct society. After the 1980 referendum, the federalist position within Quebec was articulated in terms of five "traditional demands" requiring constitutional change. Twice, Canada's prime minister and all ten provincial premiers agreed on the terms of accords that met or went most of the way to meeting these demands: the Meech Lake Accord of 1984 and the Charlottetown Accord of 1992. Neither received the popular support outside of Quebec that its passage required.

In 1998, the Supreme Court of Canada ruled that the rest of Canada would be obligated to negotiate separation with the government of Quebec if it should receive a clear majority in favour of separation in a clearly worded question. In 2000, Parliament passed the *Clarity Act* establishing how the government of Canada would evaluate the clarity of any future referendum questions, the type of majority required before Canada would agree to negotiate, and the matters that would be up for negotiation. The argument has been made in the past that ambiguous questions and a lack of clarity on just what might follow a sovereignty vote have misled many Quebecers who voted Yes in sovereignty referenda.

The strongest arguments against Quebec sovereignty, arguably, are the probable economic costs such a separation would entail, not just for Quebec but for all of Canada. This, combined with the generational shift to a population of Québécois with no memory of being treated as second-class citizens in Quebec, may ultimately weaken the momentum of the separatist movement. Most recently, in the 2011 general election, the Bloc Québécois, formed after the failure of the Meech Lake Accord to be the sovereigntist party in the national Parliament, was reduced from 43 seats to four, and the federalist NDP increased its total (from one) to 59 of Quebec's 75 seats.

IDEOLOGY: THE ROLE OF IDEAS

While the interests generated by cleavages provide one set of explanations for the political orientations expressed through a regime's political process, another

Bagpiper at the Statue of Hume. Edinburgh, United Kingdom.

organized for action, an ideology offers a program designed to transform the world from the way it is now into what (for the ideology) it should be, *or* to protect a valued way of life from change.

An ideology rests on definite notions about what the world *is,* or employs unique concepts to explain or make sense of the world. For example, both radical feminism and Marxism would eradicate inequality, but each identifies inequality differently and seeks a distinct (although not necessarily incompatible) equality. Society is structured for Marxists by *class* relations; for radical feminists, by **patriarchy**: the socio-historical subjugation of women by men through socially constituted gender relations. Feminists do not deny the existence of the economic or material relations indicated by the term "class" but regard them as secondary relationships.

THE CONTEXTS OF IDEOLOGY

Oriented to political action, ideology is sensitive to the politics of particular societies and reactive to contexts of place and time. This explains why conservatives in one country sound like liberals in another, or today's communists sound like the last century's social democrats. Differences in support for public health insurance in the United States and Canada, the contrast between North American and European perspectives on many foreign-policy issues, and the success of far right anti-immigrant parties in Europe reflect distinctly different ideological landscapes. The libertarian strain of distrust in the state in the United States may trace its roots to the country's origins in rebellion against a perceived tyrannical power. The viability of organic conservative and socialist parties in Europe probably owes something to the clarity with which class is still perceived in formerly feudal societies.

basis is the political beliefs of a more or less systematic nature that are present in the regime's political culture, in other words, its ideologies.

WHAT IS IDEOLOGY?

An ideology is defined here as *a consistent set of beliefs about the nature of the society in which individuals live and about the proper role of the state in establishing or maintaining that society.* Informed by philosophy but

JOHN LOCKE

"Men being, as has been said, by Nature, all free, equal and independent, no one can be put out of this estate, and subjected to the political power of another, without his own *Consent.* The only way whereby any one divests himself of his natural liberty, and *puts on the bonds of civil society* is by agreeing with other Men to join and unite into a community, for their comfortable, safe, and peaceable living one amongst another, in a secure enjoyment of their properties, and a greater security against any that are not of it."
—*Second Treatise,* §95

"And thus that, which begins and actually *constitutes any political society,* is nothing but the consent of any number of freemen capable of a majority to unite and incorporate into such a society. And this is that, and that only, which did, or could give *beginning* to any *lawful government* in the world."
—*Second Treatise,* §99

CLASSIC LIBERALISM

Liberalism is the first modern ideology and still dominates today, albeit sometimes in disguise. Originating in reaction to the feudal structures of medieval society, liberalism is a philosophy of individualism; political community is artificial, an arrangement established for the purpose of protecting and furthering personal well-being.

Liberalism is also the ideology of *freedom* or *liberty.* Liberals believe that individuals surrender a portion of their natural liberty to live in society with others, in exchange for security. Government is a necessary imposition, but limitations on personal liberty should be minimal. This liberty has come to be expressed or defined through individual *rights,* claims made against other citizens and (most importantly) against the state. Liberals advocate removing certain subjects from the compass of state authority (limited government) or giving greater control over government to the individuals it is supposed to serve (democracy). Both paths lead to *constitutionalism.*

Constitutionalism

Liberal constitutionalism (expressly limiting the scope of governmental authority or power) was a clear response to the arbitrary, personal nature of absolute monarchy at the end of the feudal period. Uneasy about democracy, early liberals looked

THOMAS JEFFERSON

CONSTITUTIONALISM

"We hold these truths to be self-evident: that all men are created equal; that they are endowed by their Creator with inherent and inalienable rights, that among these are life, liberty, and the pursuit of happiness; that to secure these rights, governments are instituted among men, deriving their powers from the consent of the governed; that whenever any form of government becomes destructive of these ends, it is the right of the people to alter or to abolish it, and to institute new government, laying its foundations on such principles, and organizing its power in such form, as to them shall seem most likely to effect their safety and happiness."
—from *The Declaration of Independence,* 1776

for other constitutional means of keeping rulers in check. In Britain, liberals known as Whigs brought about responsible government with the so-called Glorious Revolution of 1688. A different path to the same goal was the advocacy of mixed government and a separation of powers, as embodied in the American Constitution. In both models liberals agreed on the necessity of representative government, even if their view of who should sit in the legislature or be entitled to vote for such representatives was rather narrow.

Economic Liberty

Equally important to early liberals was economic liberty, or *market autonomy,* where the state does not hinder the private economic transactions of individuals. By contrast, the feudal economy was heavily controlled by church and state, both requiring the transfer of resources from their subjects. The classic liberal statement on economic matters became the *laissez-faire* doctrine of minimal government activity in the marketplace (accompanied by supportive policies such as rules governing exchange, the enforcement of contracts, and a stable currency). In its infancy, liberalism was as much about creating the conditions for a market

society to exist as it was about letting the market do its own thing.

Rationalism

True to its roots in the Enlightenment (see Chapter 3), liberalism promotes a *rational* individualism. This can be seen in three respects:

· the conviction that individuals can be protected from arbitrary authority by rational, predictable government;
· the promotion of an economic system that is supposed to rest on the rational self-interest of buyers and sellers rather than medieval rules and regulations; and
· moral theory that looks for grounding in rational principles rather than tradition and/or received theological doctrines.

In all these ways, liberalism argues that government, politics, and social life generally can be ordered by human reason in ways that will make individuals better off than they might otherwise be.

CONSERVATISM

In the early 1990s in Russia, "liberal" reformers pressed for the kind of economic system favoured by North American "conservatives," while Russian conservatives sought to maintain aspects of the command economy created under Soviet communism. This is one example of how conservatism is sometimes more bound to contexts of place and time than are other ideologies. To the degree that conservatism describes a *disposition to preserve* what exists in the face of change, the content of conservatism is determined by the nature of the status quo. (Those who go further and try to restore

---

JAMES MILL

ECONOMIC LIBERTY

"For though the people, who cannot exercise the powers of government themselves, must entrust them to some one individual or set of individuals, and such individuals will, infallibly have the strongest motives to make a bad use of them, it is possible that checks may be found sufficient to prevent them."
—*Essay on Government,* 1820

what is going or already gone are called *radical conservatives* or, more negatively, *reactionaries*.) In societies where liberal values have become well established or entrenched, conservatism may strive to preserve existing liberal institutions and policies from reform or radical change; in an authoritarian dictatorship, conservatism can support seriously illiberal ideas. The conservatives who sought to preserve the traditional institutions and values of aristocratic society in the face of the liberal revolution, sometimes known as Tories, can be more accurately described as organic conservatives (conservatives°).

MICHAEL OAKESHOTT

"To be a conservative, then, is to prefer the familiar to the unknown, to prefer the tried to the untried, fact to mystery, the actual to the possible, the limited to the unbounded, the near to the distant, the sufficient to the superabundant, the convenient to the perfect, present laughter to utopian bliss. Familiar relationships and loyalties will be preferred to the allure of more profitable attachments, to acquire and enlarge will be less important than to keep, to cultivate and to enjoy; the grief of loss will be more acute than the excitement of novelty or promise."
—"On Being Conservative," *1962*

Organic Conservatives

As liberalism is the ideology of the individual, conservatism° is the ideology of the structured community. Conservatives° believe society is naturally ordered in an organic, hierarchical fashion—an organized community is natural in the way that family is natural. Conservatives° value whatever contributes to the coherence, cohesion, and continuance of this community: its traditions, conventions, time-honoured institutions, structures, and practices. Conservatives° view these institutions (such as monarchy, the church) or practices (traditional morality, deference to authority, performance of duty) as inseparable from a way of life handed down by history; the primary task of the state is to preserve the integrity of the community by sustaining these institutions, practices, and values.

The conservative° accepts individual inequality as natural, confirmed by experience and history. A hierarchical ordering of society is not only inevitable, but proper, so long as the right people are in charge. The aristocracy—whether the hereditary elite of feudal days or the economically privileged classes of modern market society—is regarded as the natural ruling class, especially gifted to lead the rest. The conservative° also understands this hierarchy to be an arrangement that obliges those whom nature has blessed to have regard for the welfare of those less favoured (an idea known as *noblesse oblige*). With privilege comes responsibility.

The organic conception of society regards it to be essential for every individual, regardless of rank or station, to perform the duties and responsibilities associated with their social position. This is because each individual, from monarch to humblest subject, is part of a larger whole *and* serves a larger or nobler purpose than mere self-interest.

The Restrained State

The conservative° has a nuanced position on power and authority. On the one hand, strong (even absolute) authority is necessary to sustain the organic structure of the community. On the other, so far as the community is preserved through custom, convention, and tradition, the active scope or role for government is (or should be) quite small. An activist government is too likely to upset the proper ordering of society with needless or imprudent policies. The conservative^O is skeptical of the power of human reason and its capacity to design social structures and arrangements, preferring the accumulated wisdom of the past to the reforming genius of the present. (Perhaps this is why young conservatives^O are as remarkable as elderly radicals.) Not surprisingly, conservatives^O are more disposed to constitutionalism than democracy, and likely to believe that an agency higher than human minds is present to the world.

The foundation of the traditional aristocracy was the feudal relation between landlord and tenant. The secure identification of an individual with a place, a particular occupation, a clearly recognized set of duties and obligations, and a sound knowledge of one's inferiors and superiors was challenged by market society. Small wonder that Tories (the original conservatives^O) at first resisted the rise of capitalism. Eventually, many realized that the values sustaining the landed aristocracy could also justify an aristocracy of wealth, and that wealth based in land (i.e., rent) could be supplemented with wealth gained in commerce and manufacture. Conservatism^O made its peace with the market economy, and in doing so started down the road to liberal conservatism (conservatism^L).

SOCIALISM

If Toryism was a reaction against liberalism on behalf of a vanishing status quo, socialism responded to the world created by successful liberal capitalism. Socialism was *the* ideology of the nineteenth century, gaining significance after the liberal revolution had succeeded in dissolving feudal society, and after the societal effects of the Industrial Revolution became obvious. Early "utopian" socialists—to use Marx's term—such as Owen, Saint-Simon, Fourier, and Proudhon believed that socialism would result from a moral revolution, transforming what people believe and act upon. The "scientific" socialism of Marx and Engels maintained that socialism would be the eventual outcome of material factors (or "contradictions") embedded within the nature of capitalist society. The revolution would depend on "objective" conditions, not the good intentions of individuals.

Egalitarian Communalism

Like liberals and contrary to conservatives^O, socialists begin with the proposition that humans are fundamentally equal; contrary to liberals but with conservatives^O, socialists see humans as having an essentially social or communal nature. Socialists oppose the inegalitarian beliefs of conservatives^O and the individualism of liberals. Socialists also disagree with liberals about the nature of inequality. While they opposed the inherited or traditional inequalities of a hierarchically ordered society, early liberals accepted a wide range of structural inequalities, seemingly blind to the disadvantages of poverty, social class, and gender under which most of the population laboured. To the socialist, these inequalities were not acceptable; there can be no equality of opportunity in a class-ridden society, and individuals everywhere owe their outcomes as much to chance, inheritance, unequal opportunities, and structural factors as to individual effort.

Class Relations

In practice, the socialist argues, the impersonal market is not impartial but favours those with resources such as capital, information, or education. The social science of the socialist is concerned with how individuals are privileged or disabled by their position within

Statue of Heroes of the Revolution. Tiananmen Square, Beijing, China.

the social structure, a structure understood largely in economic or political-economic terms. For the socialist, the market economy is not about the activity of rational, self-interested individual (as liberals consistently present it), but about the relationships between classes, and primarily about the relationship between the class that owns the means of production (the **bourgeoisie**) and the class that owns nothing but its labour (the **proletariat**).

The Socialist State

Ultimately seeking a society in which all individuals are equal, socialism's immediate concern has been eliminating the exploitation or subjugation of the least privileged classes in society. Socialists believe that the liberal state serves as an instrument (or acts on behalf) of the dominant economic class—the industrial, commercial, and financial interests. The political activities of socialists have been aimed at making the state an instrument employed by, or on behalf of, the exploited or underprivileged classes.

Like conservatives°, but for different reasons, socialists believe in a strong state, not the minimal state of classic liberalism. They note that "rights" tend to be employed mostly to the advantage of those with resources rather than those without, and often to thwart fundamental social change. In theory, socialists have always favoured democracy—after all, the less advantaged are usually in the majority—but, in practice, have faced the persistence of "false consciousness," a term that describes the failure of members of the working class to recognize that their best interest lies with socialism.

The most important task of the state, for socialists, is to regulate, reform, or even replace the private-property market economy of liberal society. The economic liberty or market autonomy that liberals value is responsible for the inequality of capitalist society (socialists argue) and for the consequent absence of genuine freedom for all who are underprivileged. Socialists originally sought to replace private property with *collective* or *public ownership* of the means of production, distribution, and exchange employed

by capitalism (industry, transportation, financial institutions, etc.). In the place of market autonomy and unequal distribution, they promoted central planning and redistribution on rational, egalitarian principles. These were the most contentious parts of the socialist position, and within socialism there was considerable debate about the degree of emphasis that should be put on collective ownership and about adopting those forms of democracy associated with liberal individualism. These issues and others are behind the distinction between revolutionary communists and the less radical democratic socialists (see further below).

SHIFTING CONTEXTS

This account of ideologies in their initial formation may seem strange to the contemporary reader, with a liberalism that does not embrace democracy and a conservatism that is suspicious of capitalism. Moreover, many features of today's society, such as general public education, legal equality between the sexes, the absence of child labour, a minimum wage, health and safety regulations, and income support for seniors, were radical ideas that 150 years ago *only* socialists were likely to support.

Ideologies fall out of fashion when their vision no longer appeals or their perspective no longer makes sense of individuals' social and political realities. Liberalism, conservatism, and socialism have changed considerably since their initial appearances. Liberalism and conservatism°, products of the seventeenth and eighteenth centuries, were re-shaped by events and new ideas (including socialism) in the nineteenth century. Among these were the following:

· The idea of *progress* and the notion of human *perfectibility*: humanity is capable of a

> ### KARL MARX AND FRIEDRICH ENGELS
>
> "The history of all hitherto existing society is the history of class struggles.
>
> ...
>
> The modern bourgeois society that has sprouted from the ruins of feudal society has not done away with class antagonisms. It has but established new classes, new conditions of oppression, new forms of struggle in place of the old ones.
>
> Our epoch, the epoch of the bourgeoisie, possesses, however, this distinctive feature: it has simplified the class antagonisms. Society as a whole is more and more splitting up into two great hostile camps, into two great classes directly facing each other, bourgeoisie and proletariat."
>
> —*Manifesto of the Communist Party*, 1848

progressive development from a primitive state to an increasingly refined and elevated condition (this was, after all, Darwin's century).

· The idea of *determinism*: the development of social sciences such as anthropology, sociology, and psychology provided evidence that individuals are very much the product of social institutions (including educational systems and class structures), kinship systems, and family structures.

· The emergence of *nationalism* as a serious social force: contrary to the universalism of Enlightenment philosophies that had treated all individuals as members of a common humanity, nineteenth-century nationalist movements emerged to celebrate particular ethno-linguistic identities, often with revolutionary enthusiasm and violent results. While there is a conservative element in the nationalist disposition, nationalism can cut across all ideological divisions.

REFORMED LIBERALISM

While liberals continued (and continue) to seek a society in which individual well-being is maximized through the enlightened pursuit of self-interest within a progressively broadening and secure sphere of individual liberty, the breadth and scope of their concerns altered. Liberalism has a progressive streak, in the sense that having secured a gain in one sphere, it moves on to the next goal.

Social Liberty

After political and economic liberty, liberals argued for social liberty. The most celebrated statement on this theme remains John Stuart Mill's essay *On Liberty,* which is about freedom of opinion, belief, and lifestyle. These concerns are consistent with an ideology of individualism, but in discussing these questions, J. S. Mill went further than most previous liberals had been prepared to go.

The concerns of the modern liberal (racial and gender equality; rights for gay, lesbian, or transgendered persons; the provision of education and health care as public goods) would have seemed radical to liberals not so many generations previous. Nonetheless, there is continuity: what the modern liberal seeks is grounded on the same principles with which the classic liberal demanded representative government, the protection of property, and religious freedom.

JOHN STUART MILL

"This then, is the appropriate region of human liberty. It comprises, first, the inward domain of consciousness, demanding liberty of conscience in the most comprehensive sense; liberty of thought and feeling; absolute freedom of opinion and sentiment on all subjects, practical or speculative, scientific, moral, or theological. . . . Secondly, the principle requires liberty of tastes and pursuits; of framing the plan of our life to suit our own character; of doing as we like, subject to such consequences as may follow: without impediment from our fellow-creatures, so long as what we do does not harm them, even though they should think our conduct foolish, perverse, or wrong. Thirdly, from this liberty of each individual, follows the liberty, within the same limits, of combination among individuals; freedom to unite, for any purpose not involving harm to others: the persons combining supposed to be of full age, and not forced or deceived."

—*On Liberty,* 1859

Some liberals recognized that the state (or government) is not the only source of impediments to the freedom of individuals. The institutions of civil society—the capitalist economy, the family, and social norms and attitudes—can also restrict individual liberty. Mill argued in *On Liberty* that personal liberty has as much or more to fear from public opinion and its pressures for conformity as it has from the activities of the state. The negative definition of liberty as an absence of restraints needs to be complemented by the positive definition of being empowered to do this, that, or some other thing. For example, the absence of restrictions on disposing of one's property is irrelevant if the socio-economic system makes it all but impossible for some individuals ever to own property in the first place. In short, continued inequality and the lack of freedom provided the incentive for the reform of liberalism, a reform that took three main directions:

· the incorporation of political democracy;
· an expansion of rights claims by individuals; and
· the abandonment of laissez-faire political economy.

Democracy

Although the basic principles of liberalism were consistent with democracy, early liberals like Locke had expected that representatives would be drawn from and selected by the property-owning classes. The Industrial Revolution created a large class of urban workers with no political rights, a class to which socialists appealed for support. Partly for reasons of principle and partly to head off the socialists, reform liberals came to support extending the right to vote to men, and much later to women, of all social classes.

Rights

A second dimension of liberal reform was an expansion of rights claims on behalf of individuals. The abolition of slavery, the ending of child labour, the extension of legal and political rights to women in the first decades of the last century, the development of the right to strike, the civil rights movement in the United States during the 1960s, and the addition of the *Canadian Charter of Rights and Freedoms* to the Constitution in 1982 are examples of reform liberalism in practice.

Regulation Of The Market Economy

Abandoning the minimal state, reformist liberals looked to an activist state to moderate the inequalities and inequities of the market economy and to act positively to enhance the well-being of all, but most particularly of those most disadvantaged by the

JOHN DEWEY

"The history of social reforms in the nineteenth century is almost one with the history of liberal social thought.

...

[A]n individual is nothing fixed, given ready-made. It is something achieved, and achieved not in isolation, but with the aid and support of conditions, cultural and physical, including in 'cultural' economic, legal, and political institutions as well as science and art. Liberalism knows that social conditions may restrict, distort and almost prevent the development of individuality. ... It is as much interested in the positive construction of favourable institutions, legal, political, and economic, as it is in the work of removing abuses and overt oppressions."
—"The Future of Liberalism," 1935

existing social arrangements. A wide variety of tools was developed and employed by liberals in power, including increasing regulation of economic life and the progressive application of levers of economic management, all moving in the direction of the twentieth-century welfare state. Importantly, reformed liberalism remained committed to the market and to private property. Despite what its critics sometimes allege, the activist state of reformed liberalism falls far short of the interventionist state of socialism.

These reform liberals—sometimes called "social liberals," in contrast to the "classic liberals" of the eighteenth and early nineteenth centuries —are known now simply as (and acknowledge themselves to be) "liberals."

LIBERAL CONSERVATISM

If, then, at some time in the eighteenth and nineteenth centuries in most of Europe and many of its present or former colonies, liberal political and economic institutions became the status quo, it should be no surprise that *conservatism in such societies often developed a markedly liberal character.* Conservatism^O was replaced with conservatism^L. There were two primary ways this happened.

One was conservatives^O embracing the new economic order of liberal market society, recognizing that doing so need not challenge their economic well-being or conflict with their more traditional positions on social and moral (non-economic) issues. Social conservatism, found in notions such as natural inequality, the importance of religion, the value of traditional morality, and pessimism (realism?) about human nature, is not incompatible with the primary institutions of liberal society—constitutional, limited government and a private property market economy. Conservatives embracing liberal economic principles might be described as liberal conservatives.

The second way was classical liberals resisting the developments leading to a reformed liberalism, continuing to support the minimal state and remaining cautious about rights and democracy. These may be described as conservative liberals. Some of the most eloquent spokesmen of conservatism have been conservative liberals, such as Edmund Burke and Michael Oakeshott.

What the conservative liberals and liberal conservatives share is a commitment to the classical liberal economic position—the minimal (or at least less activist) state and (supposedly) balanced budgets. Over time, the classical liberal economic position has also come to be known as *fiscal conservatism.* Today's conservatives are almost without exception fiscal conservatives (i.e., classical liberals) and may or may not also be social conservatives. All conservatives in modern democracies share in the liberal consensus that accords legitimacy to a private property-market economy, the basic institutions of constitutional representative government, and the rule of law. This consensus is so complete in some societies (like the United States) that it is no longer recognized as being specifically "liberal."

Market (Red) Tories

Some readers will have spotted another possible combination—social conservatism combined with (some) reformed liberal economic views. A contemporary conservative with an organic conception of society might find that some of the measures designed to compensate those least advantaged or unable to prosper on their own in a capitalist society appeal to a lingering sense of noblesse oblige (which holds that the fortunate few have a duty to consider the welfare of those less fortunate). These conservatives might be called market tories or (as in Canada) "red" tories.

A European variant of market toryism could once be found in certain Christian Democratic parties, established to give the Roman Catholic perspective a political voice and combat liberal or socialist secularism. Catholic theology and Christian democracy believe that economics should not override social concerns and, for that reason, have supported state policies to protect or give relief to the poor or working classes. The highly developed welfare states of Western Europe have often been the product of a consensus (or compromise) between social democracy on the left and Christian democracy on the right. This also explains why, in many European regimes, a shift from a government led by the left to a government led by the right does not necessarily mean great changes in social policy.

Neo-liberalism and Neo-conservatism

"Neo-liberal" and "neo-conservative" are terms whose widespread use has not made them less confusing. "Neo-liberalism" is best applied to a defence of free-market policies grounded in the theoretical writings of Milton Friedman and Friedrich von Hayek. Writing in the middle of the last century, these economists advocated a return to laissez-faire policies of unfettered free-market capitalism, at a time when most developed economies were moving in the opposite direction by regulating markets and redistributing wealth through taxes and spending. A coherent program of tax reductions, privatization, spending cuts, balanced budgets, and debt reduction characterizes contemporary neo-liberalism. In short, neo-liberalism is what many describe as "fiscal conservatism" and harkens back to nineteenth-century "classic liberalism." In this respect there is nothing "new" ("neo") about neo-liberalism. As a rule, most contemporary conservatives are neo-liberals. So, too, are many liberals: the differences between conservatives and liberals being, often, a matter of degree, and, sometimes, their positions on non-economic issues. Nonetheless, the term "liberal" is now reserved in regimes like the United States for reform ("tax and spend") liberals who support the activist state.

Although adherents of left-wing ideologies sometimes label *all* conservatives "neo-cons," the term "neo-conservative" was first applied to a group of left-wing intellectuals in the United States who drifted rightward during the Cold War to form a more or less evangelical view of their country's role in the world. Many were (or were connected to) followers of the political philosopher Leo Strauss. Neo-conservative positions have included the ideas that the United States has a mission to export its vision of liberal democracy around the world, that the use of military force in achieving American goals is unproblematic, and that the United States should not be fettered by the compromises and trade-offs that accompany multilateralism (working with other states) or membership in international organizations such as the United Nations (UN) or the North Atlantic Treaty Organization (NATO). Fashioned during the Cold War, neo-conservatism became even more fashionable in a world where the United States was the only remaining superpower. The wars against the Taliban in Afghanistan and the war on

Iraq (despite the lack of credible evidence of weapons of mass destruction) have been attributed to the influence of neo-conservatives in Washington.

Both neo-liberalism and neo-conservatism demonstrate how a set of unfashionable ideas can be nurtured and promoted by a dedicated group of intellectuals and sustained by wealthy patrons (e.g., the Olin Foundation for neo-conservatism; the Heritage Foundation for neo-liberalism) until changing circumstances and political events (e.g., 9/11) combine to make them respectable.

FROM COMMUNISM TO SOCIAL DEMOCRACY

Karl Marx had predicted that the socialist revolution would occur in the most developed capitalist societies: there the working class would become aware of its exploitation and, acquiring revolutionary consciousness, overthrow capitalist institutions, both economic and political. This would be a two-stage process: a political revolution by the working class to take control of the state, followed by a social revolution to eliminate capitalist relations of production, thereby creating a classless society. Until the social revolution had been completed, the state would remain a strong instrument of the working classes. Marx called this stage the "dictatorship of the proletariat," and identified it as "socialism." Once the work of eliminating capitalist remnants was complete, the state could "wither away," and only then would society have reached the stage of "communism." At the time of Marx's death in 1883, the proletarian revolution had yet to materialize anywhere.

Evolutionary Socialism

In 1899, Eduard Bernstein published *Evolutionary Socialism* in which he observed that capitalism was not on the verge of collapse, nor was the condition of workers continuing to deteriorate. Marx had failed to appreciate the possibilities of democratic reform within the capitalist state and the fact that the state, as an instrument of regulation and reform, could improve the condition of the working classes. Bernstein argued for a gradual transition to socialism—what he called "evolutionary" socialism— by reforms *within* the capitalist, democratic state. Bernstein's views prevailed among the socialist parties of the Second International, and from that point on, socialism represented the democratic, evolutionary approach to reforming and replacing capitalism.

Communism ≠ Socialism

For more than a century there has been a clear distinction between socialism and communism. Socialism is democratic, reformist, and peaceful; communism is authoritarian, revolutionary, and, if necessary, committed to violent struggle. Communism is authoritarian in two senses: it involves an anti-democratic concentration of power and a commitment to the total employment of the state on behalf of the revolution's ends. The communist party is the *only* party permitted to exist, to organize, to solicit public support, and, most importantly, to hold office. The distinction between party and government is virtually erased, and no opposition to the communist party or its ideas is tolerated or regarded as legitimate. By contrast, democratic socialism accepts the legitimacy of opposition, the inevitability of plurality within contemporary society, and the challenge of competing for public support within electoral democracy. The state and government are and remain separate from the party, even when the party is elected to government.

The communist party's monopoly on power goes hand in hand with a commitment to the total

HOW COMMUNIST IS CHINA?

Five nominally "communist" states remain in the world: Cuba, Laos, North Korea, Vietnam, and China, which has the world's fastest-growing market economy and soon, perhaps, its largest. So, is it still accurate to call China (and possibly Laos and Vietnam, which are following China's example) "communist"?

In the sense that communism stood for a collectively organized alternative to the private-property market economy, China started moving away from

In the sense that communism came to represent a dictatorship by the Communist Party and the absence of liberal democratic rights, China remains very communist. However, if China is to succeed in becoming the world's largest capitalist state, it will have to solve two challenges. One is the environmental pressures created by industrial pollution, the non-agricultural development of arable land, and the increasing consumption of resources. The

Detail from the Monument to the People's Heroes. Tiananmen Square, Beijing, China.

communism in 1978, under Deng Xiaoping ("poverty is not socialism, to get rich is glorious") and Zhao Ziyang. Reforms designed to attract foreign investment and create a private market economy have been described as "socialism with Chinese characteristics," but the institutionalization of property rights and the privatization of state-owned companies confirm that "Chinese socialism" is taking a markedly capitalist route.

other is the pent-up desire for democratic political reform, last crushed *en masse* in Tiananmen Square in June 1989. Capitalist economies create economic classes: China is building a middle class that will, sooner or later, demand political rights in order to protect its interests. Whether China can become the first large-scale market economy to thrive without a liberal democratic political structure remains to be seen.

employment of the power of the state (totalitarianism) on behalf of the ends defined by communism. The distinction between private and public, so central to liberal thought, is regarded as bogus and a barrier to the eradication of liberal capitalism. By contrast, in its commitment to peaceful, piecemeal reform, democratic socialism accepts implicitly, if not explicitly,

that there is a boundary between the public and the private.

From Socialism to Social Democracy

The divorce between communism and socialism was originally rooted in differences over strategy: revolutionary or reformist. Both believed in the replacement of a private-property market economy with a socialized (collective or public ownership) economy under the direction of the state. Over time, though, democratic socialism came to accept the legitimacy of private ownership of property and ceased to call for collectivization of property. Even those elected socialist governments in the twentieth century (in France and the United Kingdom, for example) that nationalized private corporations in sectors such as coal mining and steel production made no attempt to replace the market as the primary means of allocating resources. Such partial (or sectoral) nationalization, long since reversed in most cases, is almost unthinkable today. Socialists still support collective ventures such as co-operatives or worker-owned businesses but are no longer committed to eliminating private corporations or to restructuring the entire economy on an alternative basis.

The retreat of socialism from radical positions to accommodation with private property and the market means that it is increasingly difficult to distinguish socialism from social democracy. (Several democratic regimes have a socialist *and* a social democratic party; Chile has three parties that are members of the Socialist International. The 2010 election of the Brazilian Chamber of Deputies, in which the Workers' Party finished first, also returned deputies for one communist party, three socialist parties, one social democratic party, and five assorted "labour" parties.) Social democracy has differed from socialism in two primary ways. First, it has been a movement that cuts across class lines, appealing to all in the name of social justice or fairness. Second, social democracy has emphasized the regulation of capital and redistribution of its profits through a progressive tax system. In other words, social democrats have been less concerned with transforming capitalism than with its management or

with compensating for its outcomes, on behalf of the greater good.

THE LIBERAL CONSENSUS

In the past two centuries the ideological horizon has become narrower and less clearly defined. The common element eroding these distinctions is the pervasive success of liberalism, a success confirmed by the fact that few of those who are liberals call themselves such today. Liberalism's rivals on both the right and left have accommodated themselves to liberal society to a large, if still varying, degree. Although a number of factors have contributed to the rise of far right political parties in Europe, with positions often informed by strongly xenophobic (anti-foreigner, anti-immigrant) attitudes, the fact that they are so far outside the liberal consensus is frequently demonstrated by the reluctance of other parties to partner with them in government.

OTHER-ISMS

Among the other belief systems encountered, some provide greater depth to the consensus just described and others clearly swim against the tide.

If beliefs about the role of the state are a component of any ideology, then *anarchism* (from the Greek *an* "without" and *archon* "a ruler") is a family of theories organized around the idea of life without a state. The role of the state is replaced by the authority of the community, understood as the unforced, shared decision making of voluntary co-operation (see anarchism. net). This presupposes some common sense of good, a mutual respect and courtesy, and either a shared set of purposes or a willingness to tolerate diverse ends. In other words, it is a vision of a moral community. Anarchist experiments along these lines have been small-scale and short-lived. (Anarchism as a strategy of disrupting the state through acts of random or spontaneous violence is a different matter altogether.)

Closely related to anarchism is *libertarianism,* which opposes almost any activity or regulation by the state. The state, to the degree that it is necessary, is a necessary evil. Libertarians represent extreme classical liberalism where liberty defined as the absence of restraints is applied to both economic and social issues (or as the libertarian would say, personal issues). Historically, the political culture of the United States has had a strong libertarian current.

Another such influence is *populism,* described by Wiles (166) as "any creed or movement based on the following major premise: *virtue resides in the ... people, who are the overwhelming majority, and in their collective traditions.*" Many populist movements, including the Populist or People's Party in the United States in the 1890s, have had an agrarian basis, championing the virtues of the independent farmer against opposing interests represented by banks, railroads, and urban capitalists. In its celebration of "ordinary people" and their values, populism opposes change introduced on behalf of new groups or newly empowered interests in society. In part, populism often reflects an alienation produced by social transformation and modernization. Parties of protest not only draw upon but often fuel popular resentments as a source of their strength. The past two decades have seen a rise in support in many European countries for so-called People's Parties, often characterized by their anti-immigrant policies.

The populist, anti-immigrant parties of Europe are also extreme examples of *nationalism,* a label for any movement to promote, consolidate, or expand the identity of a people who see themselves collectively as a "nation." Nationalism usually takes one of three forms. The first is the goal of achieving political autonomy or

independence for a people, usually situated within a larger society or political unit—what might be called state building. The second form is promoting a sense (or a stronger sense) of attachment among the citizens of a regime that comprises many different peoples— what might be called nation building. The third is an emphasis in policy-making on the integrity or priority of the nation state in opposition to international, supranational, or globalizing forces.

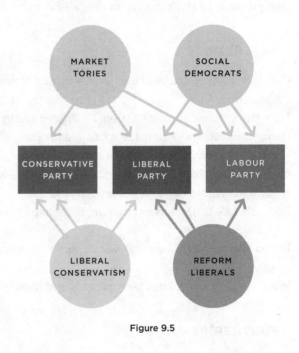

Figure 9.5

IDEOLOGIES AND POLITICAL PARTIES

The names of the dominant ideologies discussed here are often the names of political parties within our political systems. It would be a mistake, though, to assume there is a direct correspondence between party and ideology. Supporters and members of any party could include a mix of ideologies (see *Figure 9.5*). Ideological disposition is only one factor motivating individuals to become active in or support a political party; political parties vary in their ideological "purity" or fervor (which may change over time, or under a particular leader). Ultimately, the test of a party's ideology is not in its name, but in the policies it promises and/or delivers once in office.

Similarly, the degree to which participation in elections and other political activity is motivated solely, or even primarily by ideology is, from all evidence, quite limited. This may be because most people are not conscious or consistent ideologues. A great many of us who are fiscal liberals when it comes to taxes are reform liberals when it comes to the level of public services we expect from the state. Ideologies are there for those who look for principles to organize their political thoughts, and collectively, the ideologies that are dominant in any society determine the menu of choices that citizens consider when addressing political questions.

REFERENCES

Gallagher, Michael, Michael Laver, and Peter Mair. *Representative Government in Modern Europe.* New York: McGraw-Hill, 1995.

Lane, Jan-Erik, and Svante O. Ersson. *Politics and Society in Western Europe.* London: Sage, 1991.

Okin, Susan Moller. "Gender, the Public and the Private." *Political Theory Today.* Ed. David Held. Stanford, CA: Stanford University Press, 1991. 67–90.

Owram, Doug. "Reluctant Hinterland." *The Canadian Political Tradition.* 2nd ed. Ed. R.S. Blair and J.T. McLeod. Scarborough: Nelson Canada, 1993. 153–168.

Rossi, Michèle L. "Democracy and Care Unbound: On Feminism's Abiding Political Value." *Democratic Left* (Spring 2003): 4–10.

United Nations. *Our Common Future.* Report of the World Commission on Environment and Development. 1987. Web.

Wiles, Peter. *Populism.* London: Weidenfeld and Nicholson. 1969.

FURTHER READING

Bale, Tim, Christoffer Green-Pedersen, André Krouwel, et al. "If You Can't Beat Them, Join Them? Explaining Social Democratic Responses to the Challenge from the Populist Radical Right in Western Europe." *Political Studies* 58.3 (June 2010): 410–426.

Berman, Sheri. "The Primacy of Economics versus the Primacy of Politics: Understanding the Ideological Dynamics of the Twentieth Century." *Perspectives on Politics* 7.3 (September 2009): 561–578.

Elff, Martin. "Social Structure and Electoral Behavior in Comparative Perspective: The Decline of Social Cleavages in Western Europe Revisited." *Perspectives on Politics* 5.2 (June 2007): 277–294.

Ferrara, Federico. "Cleavages, Institutions and the Number of Parties: A Study of Third Wave Democracies." *Journal of Elections, Public Opinion, and Parties* 21.1 (February 2011): 1–27.

Judis, John B. "Anti-statism in America: Why Americans Hate to Love Government." *The New Republic* 240.21 (November 18, 2009): 18–20.

Madrid, Raúl L. "The Origins of the Two Lefts in Latin America." *Political Science Quarterly* 125.4 (Winter 2010-2011): 587–609.

Philpott, Daniel. "Explaining the Political Ambivalence of Religion." *American Political Science Review* 101.3 (August 2007): 505–525.

Williamson, Vanessa. "The Tea Party and the Remaking of Republican Conservatism." *Perspectives on Politics* 9.1 (March 2011): 25–43.

CHAPTER 10

Who Gets In?
The Machinery of
Democratic Elections

In democratic regimes, a significant portion of the political process is organized around a single event—the general election. In parliamentary regimes, this contest will elect members of the legislature, out of which a government will be formed. In presidential and semi-presidential regimes there will be the additional election of a president, the chief executive. Most of this chapter is concerned with legislative elections, which occur in all democracies.

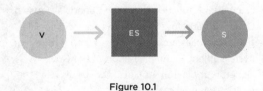

Figure 10.1

WHAT IS AN ELECTORAL SYSTEM?

Each election is held under a set of rules, some of which are *administrative* (dealing with matters such as voting age or party financing—see below), and some of which, the **electoral system**, determine how certain individuals come to be elected, once the votes have

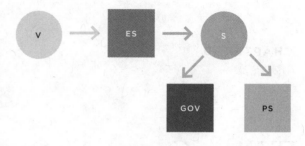

Figure 10.2

FIXED-DATE ELECTIONS

In most democracies, legislative election dates are fixed by law at specified intervals, four years apart being the most common. In parliamentary regimes, where it is possible for the government to be defeated in the legislature (i.e., lose the legislature's confidence), a provision that permits the head of state to dissolve the legislature and call an early election is normal. Such a step will only be taken if there is no possibility of forming a new government that can serve out the time remaining until the next scheduled election. (In Norway, the constitution does not permit an early dissolution of the legislature, so a government *must* be found to occupy the executive offices until the next election.)

Until recently, Canada had no fixed length of parliament, only a constitutionally prescribed maximum (of five years). The decision when to end a parliament and have an election was (within this five-year limit) up to Parliament (the House of Commons and the Governor General). When one party held a majority of the legislative seats (the case more often than not), the timing of elections was effectively the prime minister's call, and a decision made on the basis of political calculations. Election dates for Canada's House of Commons and for most of the provincial legislative assemblies are now set by law on a four-year cycle, subject to the discretion of the Governor General (or Lieutenant Governor) to dissolve the legislature at an earlier date.

been counted. An electoral system (ES) is a mechanism for transforming votes (V) into legislative seats (S).

Out of this transformation, there are two additional by-products. First, the ES creates the distribution of seats from which—in a parliamentary system—a government may be formed.

Second, by establishing a *threshold* of support that a political party must get in order to succeed (i.e., win seats), the ES is the primary determinant of a regime's **party system** (PS). The party system, in turn, has much to do with the range of meaningful options that voters have to choose from.

COMPONENTS OF AN ELECTORAL SYSTEM

There are three basic components of an electoral system, but underlying them is a means of ensuring that the principle of *representation by population* is met as closely as is possible. Representation by population (also known as "one person one vote") holds that for an election to be fair, every citizen's vote should have the same impact. If the 100 citizens of Hamlet elect a member and the 1,000 citizens of Smalltown elect a member, then one Hamlet vote = 10 Smalltown votes. Representation by population suggests that Smalltown should elect 10 representatives. Because populations change over time at different rates, a process of *redistribution* is usually required to ensure that representation by population is maintained. Sometimes this redistribution is built into the design of the electoral system, sometimes it is a separate process that is connected with a national population count or census. The three components of an electoral system are:

(a) District magnitude (D)—the size or magnitude of electoral districts;

(b) Electoral formula (F)—the formula that determines which candidates are elected; and

(c) Ballot type (B)—the type of ballot that voters use to indicate their preference(s).

District Magnitude

District magnitude (size) is not a geographic measure but the number of representatives elected in the electoral district. Canadian citizens are accustomed to $D = 1$ (single member constituencies), as is the case now in federal, provincial, and territorial electoral systems (as recently as 1996, Prince Edward Island had districts that returned two representatives to the legislative assembly). Many municipal elections employ a ward system in which $D = 2$, or simply allow electors to choose as many representatives as there are seats on council. Most of the regimes in the data set have electoral systems in which $D > 1$ (multi-member constituencies). Two countries have only one electoral district: the Netherlands ($D = 150$) and Israel ($D = 120$).

Electoral Formulae (F)

The electoral formula is the mathematical rule or rules that determine which candidate or candidates wins the seats that are to be filled. There are more possible formulae than the average voter might guess—and more than will be discussed here. The principal variations are three:

REPRESENTATION BY POPULATION

Achieving representation by population in Canada is made difficult by both geography and the Constitution. In several provinces, creating electoral districts with a similar population risks leaving vast areas of sparsely inhabited territory with limited representation. The solution of joining parts of these hinterland regions with parts of cities on their borders creates a different problem: ridings split between constituents with very different and perhaps conflicting interests and cultures. The Supreme Court of Canada has ruled that ridings need not be identically sized, given "the primary goal of effective representation," which may require reference to other considerations such as "geography, community history, community interests and minority representation" ([1991] 2 S.C.R. 158 at 184).

In Canada, as in other democracies, a periodic process of redistribution is carried out to adjust boundaries to reflect shifting populations. However, Canada's constitution provides that no province shall have fewer seats in the House of Commons than it has in the Senate. Since 1873, when Prince Edward Island became Canada's seventh province, it has had four seats in the Senate. Strict representation by population would provide PEI with no more than two MPs in the current House of Commons.

In federal systems, generally, the "lower" chamber is the one elected on the basis of representation by population, balanced by an "upper" chamber elected (or, as in Canada, appointed) to represent the sub-national units (or regions). In parliamentary federations the government is usually responsible to the lower chamber, from which it is likely to draw the greatest share of its ministers—both aspects signalling the greater legitimacy of representation by population.

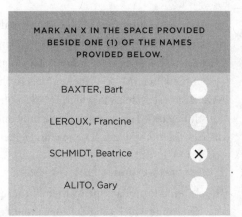

CATEGORICAL BALLOT

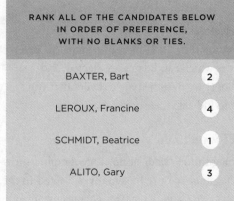

ORDINAL BALLOT

Figure 10.3

1. Plurality—the seat goes to the candidate with the *most* votes (PL)

2. Majority—the seat goes to the candidate receiving at least 50 per cent + 1 vote (MJ)

3. Proportionality—seats are distributed among the candidates according to their share of the vote (PR)

Note that PL and MJ are normally combined with a D = 1, although it is possible to apply the plurality formula to a D > 1. If there are *only* two candidates (as was once common in many systems), the candidate with the most votes (PL) also has a majority of the votes (MJ).

Ballot Type (B)

Whether it is printed paper or electronic, marked by hand or by a machine, the ballot is the record of the voter's choices. The *type* of ballot depends on two ingredients: the number of selections that the elector may choose and the way(s) that the voter is allowed (or required) to make his or her selections. The number of selections on the ballot usually reflects D, and where

D > 1, is a product of F. The marking of the ballots generally falls into one of two categories:

categorical—the voter indicates the candidate or candidates he or she wishes to elect, the number of candidates to be selected being equal to or less than D (CT)

ordinal (or preferential)—the voter ranks the candidates on the ballot in order of preference (first, second, third, etc.) (OR)

In some places, **preferential voting** is optional; in others, such as Australia and its states, it is mandatory. Where preferential voting is mandatory, failure to rank *all* candidates in a proper sequence (e.g., 1, 2, 3, 4, etc.,

BALLOT MARKING RULES

All ballots have rules about how they may or may not be marked, in part to minimize doubts or controversy when they are counted. A ballot that is improperly marked is a **spoiled ballot** (in Australia, an *informal* ballot) and is not added to the count for any candidate.

(D)	D = 1			D > 1			
(F)	F = PL	F = MJ		F = PR			
(B)	B = CT	B = OR	B = CT	B = CT(2)	B = OR	B = LIST	
(ES)	SMP/FPP	AV	TRS	MMP	STV	CLOSED	OPEN
DATA SET	Canada, Trinidad and Tobago, United Kingdom, United States **BLOCK (D>1)** Mauritius	Australia	France	Germany, Hungary, New Zealand **PARALLEL** Bulgaria, Japan, Lithuania, Panama, S. Korea, Taiwan	Ireland	Argentina, Austria, Chile, Costa Rica, Croatia, Denmark, Iceland, Israel, Italy, Netherlands, Portugal, Romania, Serbia, Spain, Uruguay	Belgium, Brazil, Czech Republic, Estonia, Finland, Greece, Latvia, Norway, Poland, Slovakia, Slovenia, Sweden **FREE** Switzerland

LEGEND

SMP/FPP = Single Member Plurality or First Past the Post
AV = Alternative Vote
MMP = Mixed Member Proportional
CLOSED = List PR (closed list)   OPEN = List PR (open list)

BLOCK = Block Vote
TRS = Two Round System
PARALLEL = Mixed Semi- or Non-Proportional
FREE = List PR (free list)

Figure 10.4

with no gaps or ties) creates a spoiled ballot (see *Ballot Marking Rules*, p. 222). The ordinal ballot is also known as a **single transferable ballot (STV)**, because the preferences are used, during the counting, to transfer ballots from one candidate to another, if required.

When district magnitude (D), electoral formulae (F), and ballot type (B) are combined, it creates the galaxy of electoral systems shown in *Figure 10.4*.

CRITERIA FOR EVALUATING ELECTORAL SYSTEMS

It is difficult to compare electoral systems descriptively without evaluating them, or at least appearing to evaluate them. For example, the terms "wasted votes" and "manufactured majority" each measure an objective feature (discussed below) of electoral systems, but are seen by adherents of the systems that display them

as subjectively critical. They are critical only to the extent that what they measure runs contrary to some other characteristics commonly regarded (even by the adherents of these systems) as ones any electoral system should satisfy.

The criteria for evaluating electoral systems can be categorized in terms of the three outcomes identified earlier: a distribution of seats, the possible conditions under which a government might be formed, and a party system. To these, a fourth category can be added: elector-centred variables, such as degree of choice, difficulty of use, and transparency.

Distribution-Based Criteria

The electoral system is a means of transforming a distribution of votes into a distribution of seats. The position taken here is that unless there are good reasons for it being otherwise, the distribution of seats (S) should reflect as nearly as possible the distribution of votes (V). Where this correspondence between the distribution of votes and seats is not identical, it should be clear to voters *why* this happens, and the deviation that results should be predictable given any distribution of votes (for any result of A%, B%, and C% in votes, the corresponding seats shares of X%, Y%, and Z% should be knowable in advance). For example, some regimes (e.g., Greece, Italy) have reinforced PR electoral systems, which boost the share of seats given to the winning party. Everyone in these regimes knows this will happen (or the conditions under which it will happen) and by how much this reinforcement will be.

Where ~ is the distribution of the variable among the
competing political parties

Figure 10.5

The correspondence between distribution of votes and distribution of seats can be viewed as a simple principle of **electoral justice**, to which at least two more may be added. One is an expectation of consistency in the relationship between votes and seats. Inconsistency occurs when a small change in the share of votes produces a large shift in the share of seats for one party but a small shift for another party. Similarly, the system is inconsistent if the change in seats for a given vote share is different from one election to another. A reminder is in order: namely, that the distribution an electoral system makes is (with a minor exception in some MMP systems) of a fixed amount. If one party's slice of the pie increases, then some other party's or parties' share(s) will correspondingly decline. If the electoral system exaggerates the increase in seats for a party with an increase in support, it will exaggerate the decrease in seats for parties for which support declined. The expectation here is that results be, if not proportional, at least proportionate.

The third principle is almost too obvious to state; namely, that an increase in support should lead to an increase in seats, and a decrease in support should lead to a decrease in seats. In some systems, the opposite, what might be labelled "functional inconsistency," has been known to occur. The expectation here is that gains and losses should be *unidirectional* (gains lead to gains, losses lead to losses).

These principles matter because *all* electoral systems are poor at transmitting information about policy options. They function better as feedback mechanisms, allowing electors to reward or punish parties and their candidates for their performance in government or opposition, or in the recent election campaign. If the electoral system is not proportional, is not measured and consistent in its level of volatility, or is functionally inconsistent, its utility as a feedback mechanism is compromised. Voters, the mass media, and political actors focus primarily on the results of the election— namely, the seats won by the parties—rather than on the inputs. What does it matter for a political party to increase its share of votes if that does not lead to at least a corresponding increase in seats? Why should a party that wins a majority government care that its share of the vote declined by 3 per cent or 5 per cent? It will be left to the "experts" to reveal what any given election "really" means.

Government-Formation-Based Criteria

In Westminster-style regimes (Australia, Canada, the United Kingdom), electoral systems seem to be evaluated more on the type(s) of government they are likely to facilitate than for any degree of electoral justice. In the parliamentary world generally, what matters is whether the electoral system is likely to produce majority, minority, or coalition government, accompanied by beliefs about which type of government is more "stable" or "effective." The discussion of these matters is found in Chapter 6.

That being said, some systems are designed (or valued) for their ability to produce a majority government (or to ensure that the winning candidate has a majority of the votes cast). In many cases, these majorities are "manufactured." For example, in SMP/FPP systems it is common for a party to win a majority of seats while receiving a minority of the votes. This is even possible when there are only two parties, if, say, the party with the most seats has won them by a small margin and the losing party has won its seats by a substantial difference. As the number of parties increases in a plurality system, it is almost certain the majority will be manufactured. Both the TRS and the AV are designed to ensure that the winning candidate receives a "majority" of votes, even if this doesn't happen on the first count of the ballots. How they do this, and how well, is discussed below.

Regimes that have adopted systems designed to prevent the manufacturing of a majority—PR systems—are clearly comfortable with the idea of coalition or minority government. The primary question in this context is whether the electoral system promotes the development of stable coalitions or viable minority governments. To the degree that the electoral system can make a difference in the stability of government,

it is by keeping the size of the party system manageable, preventing the proliferation of too many small, extremist, or one-issue parties. This may be as simple as setting a minimum vote share (or threshold of support) that is necessary to guarantee a party its share of seats.

	2008	2011
Conservative	46.4%	53.9%
New Democratic	12.0%	33.4%
Liberal	25.0%	11.0%
Bloc Québécois	15.9%	1.3%
Green	0.0%	0.3%
SEAT SHARES IN THE HOUSE OF COMMONS		

Figure 10.6

Party-System-Based Criteria

The electoral system determines what type of government is likely to prevail because it also contributes to the shape of the party system in a somewhat predictable manner. A party system is not just about the number of parties, but also about their relative strengths. If two parties tend to split the vote and alternate in office, it is fairly obvious that this is a two-party system. But what if a third party routinely wins 15–20 per cent of the vote? Is this a three-party system or a two-and-a-half-party system? To describe party systems more accurately, political scientists have developed measures that attempt to take account of both the number of parties and their size. As *Figure 10.6* shows, four parties won election to the Canadian House of Commons in 2008 and five parties in 2011. According to the measure known as the **effective number of parties**, developed by Laakso and Taagepera, the effective number of legislative parties (ENLP) following the 2008 election was 3.15 and following the 2011 election was 2.41.

The size of the party system matters for citizens for a number of reasons, including the range of choices put before them at election time, the number of sources of policy ideas in the legislature and (potentially) in the executive, and the responsiveness of parties to their members and supporters. The simplest contrast is between electoral systems that sustain a two-party system and those that promote or maintain a multi-party environment.

	2008	2011
Conservative	37.6%	39.6%
New Democratic	18.2%	30.6%
Liberal	26.2%	18.9%
Bloc Québécois	10.0%	6.0%
Green	6.8%	3.9%
VOTE SHARES IN THE GENERAL ELECTION		

Figure 10.7

Another useful contrast is between **electoral parties** (those that put candidates before the electorate) and **legislative parties** (those winning seats in the legislature). In practice, the number of electoral parties will be higher than the number of legislative parties, because the electoral system acts as a filter that allows some parties through to the legislature and effectively screens others out. An important characteristic of any electoral system is the degree to which it refines the party system. For reasons that may already be obvious, the filtering effect of PR systems is weaker than that of majoritarian systems such as SMP and AV. Some PR systems (List or MMP) are more proportional than others (STV). Some PR systems have a legal threshold of support (usually 2–5 per cent of the vote) that a party must win to be awarded a share of seats. The numbers of effective parties in the Canadian House of Commons after the 2008 and 2011 elections noted above represent the effective number of legislative parties (ENLP). It is possible to calculate the effective number of electoral parties (ENEP) on the basis of their vote shares (see *Figure 10.7*). The filtering effect of the electoral system can be measured by subtracting the ENLP from the ENEP.

The filtering effect of the electoral system in Canada in 2011 was to reduce the size of the party system by the equivalent of more than one whole party (see *Figure 10.8*). Note also that while the number of parties with seats in the House of Commons increased by one as a result of the 2011 election (from four to five), the *effective number* of legislative parties dropped from 3.87 to 3.43. This difference reflects the very low seat shares of the two smallest parties after the 2011 election.

	2008	2011
ENEP	3.87	3.43
ENLP	3.15	2.41
difference	0.72	1.02

Figure 10.8

It is important to emphasize that the filtering effect will vary depending on the type of electoral system. *Figure 10.9* demonstrates how a hypothetical distribution of votes might be treated by a SMP/FPP system on the one hand and a PR system with a legal threshold (of five per cent) on the other hand.

An electoral system that works as a strong filter makes it difficult for parties with low levels of support to survive. In a plurality system, a new party faces the challenge that in order to succeed it must finish ahead of all its competitors (all the well-established parties)—there is no prize for finishing second or third, however large an accomplishment that might be. The manner

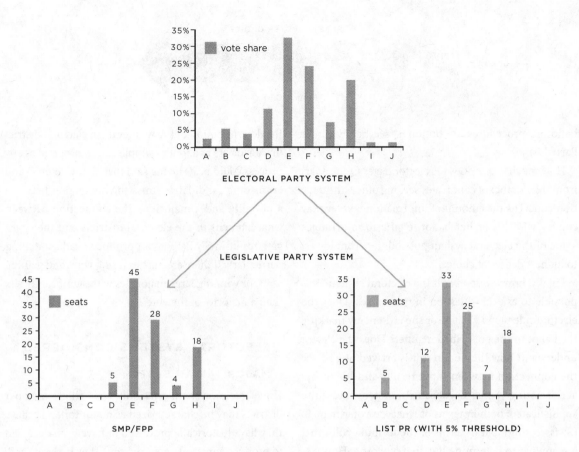

Figure 10.9

in which the plurality formula tends to favour an existing two-party system was described by Duverger as its "mechanical effect." If voters perceive that voting for a new or weak party is a lost cause, at least in the short term, the mechanical effect is compounded by a "psychological effect." An emerging party requires an identifiable social base and/or a compelling ideology to survive under such circumstances. A good example is the Green Party in Canada or Australia, where making the step from electoral party (attracting votes) to legislative party (winning seats) has been very difficult. The table presented at the end of this chapter provides data on the ENEP, the ENLP, and a measure of disproportionality for the most recent election (at the time of writing) for selected regimes in the data set.

Elector-Centred Criteria

What does an electoral system offer to the elector (i.e., a potential voter)? How *difficult* is the act of voting? An ordinal (preferential) ballot requires more work to complete than a categorical one (except that Australia allows parties to provide their supporters with How-to-Vote cards that may be consulted when filling out the ballot). Quite often, the more complicated

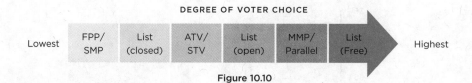

DEGREE OF VOTER CHOICE

| Lowest | FPP/ SMP | List (closed) | ATV/ STV | List (open) | MMP/ Parallel | List (Free) | → Highest |

Figure 10.10

balloting procedures are optional (see below under Party List PR).

How much *choice* does the elector have? Quite apart from the number of candidates seeking office, the question concerns the amount of information a voter may convey with his or her ballot. *Figure 10.10* arranges some of the electoral system possibilities from lowest to highest degree of choice.

Finally, how *transparent* is the electoral system? It is possible to ask this question in two senses: Does the elector understand what he or she is doing by marking the ballot in the prescribed manner? Does the elector understand how the final result is arrived at and see the connection between those results and his or her act of voting? Some European PR systems are quite sophisticated, both in terms of what the voter may do (Swiss voting) and in terms of the formula rules that are applied to determine the final outcome. However, insofar as the seat shares match the vote shares, the end result is fairly transparent. Both the act of voting and the determination of the winner in an electoral district in Canada are as about as simple and transparent as any process could be. (Having said that, many voters—and even some candidates—miss the distinction between a plurality and a majority.) The connection between what happens in the electoral districts and the aggregate result in SMP/FPP can produce head scratching, particularly if there are parties losing votes and gaining seats, or winning large majorities with significantly less than a majority of the vote.

ELECTORAL SYSTEMS CONSIDERED

MAJORITARIAN SYSTEMS

The electoral systems that only have single-member districts may be characterized as **majoritarian** because they have historically produced or have been designed to produce a majority government. They include SMP/FPP, Block Vote, TRS, and AV.

SUMMARY OF CRITERIA			
DISTRIBUTION		**PARTY SYSTEM**	
(a) is outcome proportional?	○	(f) favour two-party or multi-party?	○
(b) are gains/losses proportionate?	○	(g) what is the legal threshold?	○
(c) are gains/losses unidirectional?	○		
GOVERNMENT FORMATION		**VOTER**	
(d) are majorities manufactured?	○	(h) is voting easy or difficult?	○
(e) are stable coalitions supported?	○	(i) how much choice is offered?	○
		(j) is process transparent?	○

Figure 10.11

SMP/FPP

distribution proportional	distribution proportionate	distribution unidirectional	majority manufact'd	stable coalition	party sys. two/multi	legal threshold	ease of voting	voter choices	system transparency
no	no	no	yes	no	two	no	easy	least	D-y/sys-n

Figure 10.12

SMP/FPP

Single Member (D=1) Plurality (F=PL) is perhaps more commonly known by its English label of First Past the Post (**FPP**). This phrase uses a horse-race analogy to describe plurality: the winner is whichever horse (candidate) finishes ahead of all the others. The margin of victory (the number or proportion of votes) is irrelevant; finishing first (having the highest total) is all that matters. If there are only two candidates, the winner will also have a majority, but once the number of candidates increases, the share of votes with which it is possible to win decreases.

The other central feature of **SMP** is its "winner-take-all" awarding of seats. The candidate finishing first wins the seat, regardless of how many votes this represents, and all the other votes count toward nothing. For this reason they are often referred to as **wasted votes**. It is entirely possible, although unlikely in a competitive election, that a party could finish first in every district and still not have the votes of a majority of the electorate. In the New Brunswick election of 1987, the Liberal Party won all 58 seats with 60.4 per cent of the vote. The four out of every 10 voters who voted for the other parties ended up with no representation, or rather (since elected members usually claim to represent *all* their constituents) representation by someone they did not support.

As *Figure 10.12* suggests, SMP does not score well on any of the electoral justice criteria. The strongest arguments made by its supporters are that it produces stable majority governments and is easy for voters to use and understand. It has produced stable majorities by tending to over-compensate the winning party in what was originally a two-party system, a system that its characteristics have historically reinforced. This history also means that coalitions or minority governments are unlikely to serve a full term in office. No system provides less choice for voters, and while winning in the district is straightforward, system-wide results are sometimes not so easily explained.

Block Voting, which is plurality voting in multi-member districts, exhibits the same weaknesses and strengths as SMP/FPP, except in an exaggerated manner. Only one regime in the data set—Mauritius—employs it. It is called "block" voting because the typical result is that the same party will win all the seats in the district.

AV

Alternative Vote (sometimes called Instant Run-off Voting) differs from SMP/FPP in its use of an ordinal (preferential) ballot in a single-member district. In **AV**, ballots are assigned to each candidate on the basis of the first preferences and counted. If a candidate has received a majority of the votes cast, he or she is elected.

WASTED VOTES

SMP/FPP generates the highest number of wasted votes: ballots that are counted but do not contribute to the election of anyone. Some include in this category not only the votes for unsuccessful candidates but also the surplus votes of the winning candidate, as the accompanying calculation illustrates. The preference here is not to include the surplus votes, because the point of identifying wasted votes is to indicate how many voters have no subsequent direct representation of their vote (which they might well have under another system). It is neither possible to identify which voters cast the "surplus votes" for the winning candidate, nor is it likely one could find many supporters of the winning candidate who feel their vote was surplus. (The inclusion of surplus votes in the total may reflect the practice in STV systems, in which the surplus votes of a winning candidate are redirected to the support of other candidates.)

To term any votes "wasted" is not to suggest that they shouldn't have been cast, or that they should have been cast otherwise. Instead, it serves two purposes: first, to explain the psychological effect noted earlier. Suppose the result shown is representative of historic patterns in this district; three questions then arise: What motivates supporters of parties C and D to continue to make the effort? What would it take to motivate supporters of A or B to switch to C or D? Why should the central campaign managers for Party C or D spend any resources in this district? Second, it explains the basis for the disproportionalities created by SMP, because wasted votes have not contributed towards *any* party's seat total. It is not uncommon in a plurality system for the wasted votes to be a majority of the votes.

By contrast, most PR systems have a minimum of wasted votes. They are designed to ensure that the seat shares reflect as closely as possible the vote shares. Some systems even reserve a second tier of "adjustment seats," which are used to correct any disproportionalities created by the initial allocation of seats. This means that *every* vote contributes to the final allocation of seats, quite apart from whether it helps elect a candidate in a district. The supporters of *every* party, including parties like C and D, have an incentive to cast their ballot. Parties have an incentive to seek *all* the votes they can, not just in districts where their history or their polling tells them they might do well.

PARTY	VOTES		WASTED VOTES
Party A	13,133		
Party B	9,466		*9,466*
Party C	4,821		*4,821*
Party D	1,774		*1,774*
			16,061 minimal
	(13,133 – 9,467	= +3,666 *surplus votes*)	
			19,727 maximal

(In the 2010 Australian election—see *Figure 10.14*—this was the case for 64 of 150 districts.) If no candidate has a majority, the ballots of the candidate with the smallest number of first preferences are now transferred to the candidates ranked *second* on each of these ballots.

If that does not produce a majority for any candidate, the process is repeated.

In *Figure 10.13*, candidate A, who would have had a clear victory under plurality rules, is eventually defeated when most of the transferred ballots from candidate D and then candidate C go to candidate B. In the third count, the second preferences on ballots originally sitting with candidate C are counted, *as well as* the third preference on the one ballot that came to candidate C from candidate D in the second count. It is also possible, even likely, that some of the ballots sitting with candidate C have candidate D marked as their second choice, which means that they, too, were transferred on the basis of whichever candidate was marked third. (This is the basis of Winston Churchill's famous criticism of AV: namely, that too many outcomes are "determined by the most worthless votes given for the most worthless candidates." This statement was quoted widely during the debate preceding the May 2011 UK referendum in which voters rejected AV.)

Because voters *must* rank all candidates, there is always a third (and fourth, etc.) preference to which a ballot may be transferred. In Ireland, where the same type of ballot is used to elect up to five representatives but there is no requirement to rank *all* the candidates, it is not uncommon for some ballots to be exhausted—there are no more preferences indicated on them or the remaining preferences are for candidates already elected or eliminated. These are called "spent ballots," which is another way of describing wasted votes.

Australia, under AV, has a virtual two-party system, in which the Labor Party (on the left) is opposed by

what is known as "the Coalition" (on the right). The Coalition is an alliance of the Liberal and National Parties, which, for historical and strategic reasons, have not merged but have institutionalized a voting arrangement whereby supporters of one party make the candidate of the other party their second preference. The use of how-to-vote cards reinforces this arrangement.

It is very difficult for a new party to break into the legislative party system, as it needs to gather more first preferences than one of the leading parties on either the left or right to be around for the second or third count. Such a party cannot count on a wave of support of disaffected Australians who vote for neither of the traditional options—voting in Australia is *compulsory*. The experience of the Australian Greens in the 2010 election illustrates the difficulties that a new party faces.

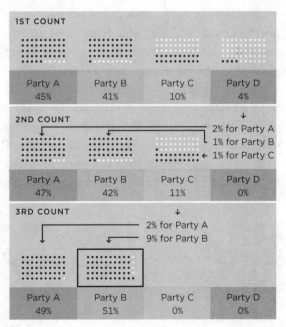

Figure 10.13

With almost 12 per cent of the first-preference vote, the Greens managed to elect only one Member. With the support of this Member and three of the Independents, the Labor Party was able to form Australia's first minority government in 70 years.

AV does not score much differently than SMP/FPP on the criteria indicated in the scorecard below. It does offer voters a greater degree of choice, but the trade-off is that voting is more difficult, particularly since the voter is required to rank all candidates in a proper sequence. It is possible to argue that given the long-standing rivalry of Labor and the Coalition, voting in the electoral district is fairly transparent, but the occasional presence of another party, such as the Greens, which is able to attract a substantial level of support, undermines this clarity. As the final election results show, there is no clear relationship between first-preference vote share and final seat totals.

The bias of the system towards the two leading parties (Labor and the Coalition) is shown in the practice, undertaken by the Australian Electoral Commission, of counting the full distribution of all preferences—even on ballots that did not require to be transferred, and on ballots for a winning candidate for another party—in terms of their ultimate support for Labor or the Coalition. This is known as the "two-party preferred results." Calculating the two-party preferred result for the 2010 election, for example, would have

required taking the ballots for the winning Green Party candidate and for each of the Independents who won and transferring them, for statistical purposes, to whichever party—Labor or the Coalition—was ranked highest on those ballots. The 2010 two-party preferred result was 50.12 per cent for Labor and 49.88 per cent for the Coalition.

AUSTRALIA (HOUSE OF REPRESENTATIVES) 2010

PARTY	SEATS	VOTES	%V
Labor Party	72	4,711,363	37.99
The Coalition	72	5,408,630	43.62
Liberal Party	*44*	*3,777,383*	*30.46*
Liberal National Party (Queensland)	*21*	*1,130,525*	*9.12*
National Party	*6*	*462,387*	*3.73*
Country Liberal Party	*1*	*38,335*	*0.31*
The Greens	1	1,458,998	11.76
National Party (Western Australia)	1	43,101	0.34
Independents	4	312,496	2.52
Totals	150	11,934,588*	96.23

*first preferences

Figure 10.14

AV

distribution proportional	distribution proportionate	distribution unidirectional	majority manufact'd	stable coalition	party sys. two/multi	legal threshold	ease of voting	voter choices	system transparency
no	no	no	yes	no	two	no	difficult	high	D-?/sys-n

Figure 10.15

PARTY		1ST ROUND			2ND ROUND			TOTAL SEATS
		V	%V	S	V	%V	S	
Union for a Popular Movement	UMP	10,289,737	39.5	98	9,460,710	46.4	215	313
New Centre	NC	616,440	2.4	8	433,057	2.1	14	22
Miscellaneous Right	DVD	641,842	2.5	2	238,588	1.2	7	9
Movement for France	MPF	312,581	1.2	1	-	-	-	1
Total Right		11,869,600	45.6	109	10,132,355	49.7	236	345
Socialist Party	PS	6,436,520	24.7	1	8,624,861	42.3	185	186
French Communist Party	PCF	1,115,663	4.3	0	464,739	2.3	15	15
Miscellaneous Left	DVG	513,407	2.0	0	503,556	2.5	15	15
Left Radical Party	PRG	343,565	1.3	0	333,194	1.6	7	7
The Greens	VEC	845,977	3.3	0	90,975	0.5	4	4
Total Left		9,255,132	35.6	1	10,017,325	49.1	226	227
Democratic Movement	MoDem	1,981,107	7.6	1	100.115	0.5	2	3
National Front	FN	1,116,136	4.3	0	17,107	0.1	0	0
Others winning seats	DIV	401,233	1.5	0	139,552	0.7	2	2
Totals		24,623,078	94.6	111	20,406,454	100	466	577
Turnout		60.4%			60.0%			

Figure 10.16

TRS

The Two Round System employs what is known as a **run-off** for any contest in which no candidate receives the required level of support (usually a majority); this means that some candidates are eliminated and voters go to the polls a second time with a shorter list. In a purely majoritarian scenario, only the top two candidates from the initial round remain on the second ballot. Although France is the only country in the data set to use **TRS** to elect its legislature, it is the most common system used for presidential elections (see *Presidential Elections* p. 154), including in France. Party-leadership votes often employ multiple run-offs, whereby the candidate with the lowest total is dropped and everyone votes again, repeating the process if necessary until someone has a majority of the votes.

In France, in the TRS used to elect the National Assembly, any candidate who receives a majority of the vote in the first round (which must also equal at least 25 per cent of the registered voters in the district) is immediately elected. In 2007, only 111 of the 577 seats were decided at the first round of voting (see *Figure 10.16*). If a second round is required, any candidate who has received votes equal to at least 12.5 per cent of the registered electors in the district may remain on the ballot. The candidate finishing first in the run-off (second round) is the winner, which makes the National Assembly TRS a majority-plurality system.

Like many European regimes, France's party system has historically been dominated by a group of parties on the right and a group on the left. While every party wants to win, all parties will assess their chances in a second round, including not only the odds of losing, but the likelihood of taking votes from a like-minded party and ensuring victory for a party from the opposing ideological faction. It would be unusual to find two parties from the right remaining in the race

TRS

distribution proportional	distribution proportionate	distribution unidirectional	majority manufact'd	stable coalition	party sys. two/multi	legal threshold	ease of voting	voter choices	system transparency
no	no	yes	yes	no	multi	no	easy	low	D-y/sys-n

Figure 10.17

against one party from the left, or vice versa. In the second round, more commonly, the party from the left with the highest total in the first round faces the party from the right with the similarly highest total. This dynamic is complicated when other parties that don't fit in with the traditional right and left groupings, such as the far-right National Front or the centrist Democratic Movement, attract significant support in the first round.

It has been observed that the TRS in France produces some of the most disproportionate results in Europe (which is not difficult given that all other European regimes except for the United Kingdom and Malta employ some form of PR). However, just as the Westminster model and FPP were exported to many British colonies, so too is TRS used to elect legislatures in many former French colonial possessions (mostly in Africa), and in several republics that were once part of the Soviet Union.

Several points about TRS are illustrated in the 2007 election results (*Figure 10.16*). The system's ability to manufacture a majority by giving a premium or bonus to the winning party is clear. So, too, is the drop-off in support for the minor parties in each grouping (right or left), parties which, nonetheless, won most of their seats at the second round (reflecting the arrangements between parties in each grouping to support each other in the second round). The large vote total for the UMP in the second round, despite having won 98 seats in the first round, and the very small drop in turnout between the two rounds indicates that many people voted in the second round who had not voted in the initial stage. The drop in support for the Democratic Movement and National Front, from 11.9 per cent of the vote in the first round to 0.6 per cent in the second, suggests that very few of their candidates survived the first round.

In the end, the TRS, like AV, requires many voters to give their support to a candidate/party that is not the

	Seats if D=	1	2	3	4	5	6	7	8	9	10	11	12	13	14	15	16
Party A	14,123 (36.7%)	1	1	1	2	2	3	3	3	4	4	4	5	5	5	6	6
Party B	9,456 (24.6%)	-	1	1	1	2	2	2	2	2	3	3	3	3	4	4	4
Party C	7,890 (20.5%)	-	-	1	1	1	1	1	2	2	2	2	2	3	3	3	3
Party D	4,089 (10.6%)	-	-	-	-	-	-	1	1	1	1	1	1	1	1	1	2
Party E	2,921 (7.6%)	-	-	-	-	-	-	-	-	-	-	1	1	1	1	1	1
Gallagher Index of Disproportionality		51.0	26.6	14.5	13.6	14.5	14.8	9.0	6.4	7.9	7.0	2.9	4.8	3.2	3.9	4.0	2.1

Figure 10.18

Sweden (Riksdag) 2010							
	Votes		Constituency seats		2nd	Total Seats	
Party	No.	%	No.	%	Tier	No.	%
Moderate Party	1,791,766	30.1	107	34.5		107	30.7
Centre Party	390,804	6.6	21	6.8	2	23	6.6
Liberal People's Party	420,524	7.1	17	5.5	7	24	6.9
Christian Democrats	333,696	5.6	11	3.5	8	19	5.4
Social Democrats	1,827,497	30.7	112	36.1		112	32.1
Left Party	334,053	5.6	9	2.9	10	19	5.4
Green Party	437,435	7.3	19	6.1	6	25	7.2
Sweden Democrats	339,610	5.7	14	4.5	6	20	5.7
Others	85,023	1.4					
Totals:		100.1	310	99.9	39	349	100

Figure 10.19

one they would most prefer to support. In the French result shown here, 88.7 per cent of the votes cast in the second round went to the two largest parties.

PR SYSTEMS

Most of the world's democracies employ one or another of the systems characterized by proportional representation. Instead of using a winner-take-all principle of allocation (common to SMP/FPP, AV, and TRS) the system seeks to divide seats among the parties according to their share of the vote. This means employing multi-member districts (D>1) for at least some portion of the seats, if not all of them.

All electoral systems involve trade-offs of one sort or another; multi-member constituencies present a trade-off between personal representation and proportionality. As *Figure 10.18* shows, the larger D is the more proportionality is possible, but the connection between the elected representative and his or her constituents becomes less immediate. The personal accountability of representatives is diminished. Also, as D increases, the share of vote necessary to win a seat decreases, which encourages more parties to participate. The larger the number of parties winning votes, the larger the constituency must be to provide proportionality, and so on.

Sweden's parliament (the Riksdag) is elected on the basis of 29 constituencies averaging more than 10 members each, for a total of 310 constituency seats. Even with constituencies this large, the overall results may not be fully proportional. All systems for allocating seats in a multi-member district have a bias towards or against parties with smaller vote shares. Like many PR systems, Sweden's reserves a **second tier** of seats that serves as a national constituency. These seats are awarded on the basis of the parties' *national* vote shares in such a way as to compensate for disproportionalities that remain after the constituency seats have been allocated. In Sweden, there are 39 **adjustment seats**, or 11 per cent of the Riksdag's 349 seats. The size of the second tier of adjustment seats usually reflects the degree of disproportionality that is typical of the constituency results. The more proportional the results generated by the constituencies, the smaller the second tier needs to be.

In addition, the legal threshold that many PR systems have in place to restrict the proliferation of minor parties may also apply (or primarily apply) to the second tier. In Sweden, to be eligible to participate in the allocation of seats, a party must win at least 4 per cent of the national vote. Any party with support exceeding the threshold will be entitled to receive adjustment seats if its constituency seat total falls short of the seat share corresponding to its vote. Sweden's system also permits a party with less than 4 per cent of the national vote to participate in the allocation of seats in any constituency in which it received at least 12 per cent of the vote.

MMP

Mixed Member Proportional is the variety of PR most often proposed in Canada as an alternative to SMP/FPP and was the model voted on in the 2007 referendum on electoral reform in Ontario, proposed in draft legislation placed before the Quebec legislature in 2004, and voted on in a plebiscite in Prince Edward Island in 2005. The New Brunswick Commission on Legislative Democracy called its 2004 proposal MMP, although it was actually a parallel system (see below). MMP was adopted in New Zealand in 1994 (and first employed in 1996) following significant dissatisfaction with results produced under the SMP/FPP system that had been in place; in a November 2011 referendum, Kiwis voted to retain the system by a margin of 58 per cent to 42 per cent.

In **MMP**, at least half of the seats are elected in single-member districts, usually by FPP (although TRS is used in Hungary and Lithuania, and AV *could* be used). This makes MMP attractive for any regime with a majoritarian system contemplating the move to a proportional system; there would be no change in how at least one-half of the representatives are elected. The remaining seats serve as "adjustment seats," allocated

in such a way that the total seat shares reflect (as much as possible) the total vote shares, regardless of the constituency seat results, and subject to any "threshold" provisions. Citizens under MMP have the advantage of a single, accountable constituency representative *and* the benefit of proportionality in the overall results.

In practice, MMP requires the use of a double ballot that allows the voter to choose between the local constituency candidates on one side, and express a preference for one of the national parties on the other side. This doubles the choices a voter has and allows one to vote for a candidate without automatically supporting the candidate's party (or vice versa). Known as **vote-splitting**, this reduces considerably the number of wasted votes.

YOU HAVE 2 VOTES		
VOTE FOR ONLY ONE PARTY		**VOTE FOR ONLY ONE CANDIDATE**
♣ Party Club	◯ ◯	Candidate A ♣
♦ Party Diamond	◯ ◯	Candidate B ♦
	◯ ◯	Candidate C
♥ Party Heart	◯ ◯	Candidate D ♥
♠ Party Spade	◯ ◯	
🃏 Party Joker	◯ ◯	Candidate F 🃏

Figure 10.20

In a true MMP system (Germany, New Zealand), the party vote determines the final composition of the legislature and the party list (adjustment) seats are awarded in such a way as to ensure that the overall result is proportional. *Figure 10.21* shows a result for a 200-seat parliament with 100 constituency seats and 100 party-list seats. The party vote (column 1) determines the total seats each party should receive (column 2). The number of constituency seats won (column 3) is subtracted from the total seats to determine the number of party-list seats to be awarded (column 4).

MMP: EXAMPLE 1

Party	col.1 %V	col.2 #S	col.3 #S(con)	col.4 #S(list)
A	40	80	65	15
B	32	64	21	43
C	17	34	10	24
D	8	16	3	13
E	3	6	1	5
	100	200	100	100

Figure 10.21

In *Figure 10.22*, the same results are shown with the added assumption that there is a 5 per cent threshold that a party must receive in its vote share in order to qualify for party-list seats. Because Party E's vote share falls below the threshold, it is entitled only to the one constituency seat that it has won. The five party-list seats that it would have won if there were no threshold are distributed among the other parties according to their share of the vote (in this example, A and B each get two more seats, C gains one seat). In Germany, the threshold is 5 per cent or winning three constituency seats; in New Zealand, the threshold is 5 per cent or winning one constituency seat—many have felt the latter requirement to be too low.

MMP: EXAMPLE 2

Party	col.1 %V	col.2 #S	col.3 #S(con)	col.4 #S(rev)	col.5 #S(list)
A	40	80	65	82	17
B	32	64	21	66	45
C	17	34	10	35	25
D	8	16	3	16	13
E	3	-	1	1	-
	100	194	100	200	100

Figure 10.22

In *Figure 10.23*, without a threshold, the added wrinkle is that Party A has won three more seats at the constituency level than its vote share entitles it to. If the other parties receive the entire complement of seats to which their vote share entitles them, the system ends up allocating more seats than there are in the parliament. There are two ways of dealing with this situation. One is to keep the number of adjustment seats at 100 and adjust the distribution among Parties B to E (penalizing them for Party A's success). The other is to temporarily increase the size of the parliament to accommodate Party A's surplus seats, as is done in Germany, where the extra seats are known as **overhang seats**.

MMP: EXAMPLE 3

Party	col.1 %V	col.2 #S	col.3 #S(con)	col.4 #S(list)
A	40	80	83	-
B	32	64	11	53
C	17	34	4	30
D	8	16	1	15
E	3	6	1	5
	100	200	100	103

Figure 10.23

TWO CHANCES TO WIN

To those accustomed to a winner-take-all system (which is also a losers-get-nothing system), the idea that up to one-half of the seats will be filled by individuals who failed to win their constituency seat may seem strange. On the other hand, it allows parties to run very strong candidates head-to-head and know that losing in the constituency will not necessarily keep these individuals from gaining a seat. On average, all districts end up with two representatives, and in some cases, three or even four.

GERMANY (BUNDESTAG) 2009

PARTY	CONSTITUENCY			PARTY LIST			TOTAL		
	VOTES	%	SEATS	VOTES	%	SEATS	SEATS	%	
CDU	13,852,743	32.0	173	11,824,794	27.3	21	194	31.2	PARTIES ABOVE THRESHHOLD
CSU	3,190,950	7.4	45	2,830,210	6.5	0	45	7.2	
SDP	12,077,437	27.9	64	9,988,843	23.0	82	146	23.5	
FDP	4,075,115	9.4	0	6,313,023	14.6	93	93	15.0	
The Left	4,790,007	11.1	16	5,153,884	11.9	60	76	12.2	
Alliance'90/Greens	3,974,803	9.2	1	4,641,197	10.7	67	68	10.9	
Pirate	46,750	0.1	0	845,904	2.0	0	0	0	PARTIES BELOW THRESHHOLD
National Democratic	768,175	1.8	0	635,437	1.5	0	0	0	
HEAW	16,881	0.0	0	230,572	0.5	0	0	0	
The Republicans	30,045	0.1	0	193,473	0.4	0	0	0	
Ecological Democrats	105,276	0.2	0	132,395	0.3	0	0	0	
Family	17,837	0.0	0	120,716	0.3	0	0	0	
Others	298,798	0.7	0	447,094	1.0	0	0	0	
Totals:	43,235,817	99.9	299	43,357,542	100	323	622	100	

NOTES:

CDU = Christian Democratic Union
CSU = Christian Social Union of Bavaria
The CDU and CSU are sister parties: they do not run candidates against each other and form one group in the Bundestag.

SDP = Social Democratic Party
FDP = Free Democratic Party
HEAW = Human Environment Animal Welfare Party

Figure 10.24

The adjustments seats (col. 4) are filled from party lists, which may be national (New Zealand) or regional (Germany), but in either case contain all of the party's candidates ranked in the order the party has determined. If a party is entitled to adjustment seats, the names of those who will fill them come from its list, starting at the top and excluding any candidates who have been elected at the constituency level.

Some have criticized MMP for giving too much power to the party. Admittedly, the ranking of candidates on the party list is a powerful tool for enforcing party discipline, and the fact that a party can ensure that a particular candidate is elected by ranking him or her high enough on the party list removes much of the accountability of candidates, including Members seeking re-election, to the electorate (another electoral system trade-off). On the other hand, the guarantee of proportionality for any party with support above the legal threshold makes *parties* very accountable—every rise or drop in its support results in a corresponding rise or drop in its seat share. The list also allows a party that is inclined to do so to ensure that it elects candidates who, for reasons of prejudice or other biases, might be less likely to win in a winner-take-all contest. The public has the ability to reward or punish the party for how it ranks its candidates.

The 2009 federal German election (*Figure 10.24*) produced several interesting outcomes. The CSU won

distribution proportional	distribution proportionate	distribution unidirectional	majority manufact'd	stable coalition	party sys. two/multi	legal threshold	ease of voting	voter choices	system transparency
yes	yes	yes	no	yes	multi	5%	easy	med	D-y/sys-med

Figure 10.25

all its seats at the constituency level, and won six more seats than its entitlement (according to its vote share on the party-list portion of the ballot). This helped contribute to a record number (24) of overhang seats in this election. All other parties with support above

ORDERING THE PARTY LIST(S)

In Germany, all elections, from local to national, are administered by the *Länder*. This means that the party lists are determined and the party-list seats are awarded at the sub-national level. Under German electoral law, the party lists are drawn up at open conventions held for that purpose by each party at a specified interval prior to the election. Party members vote in a secret ballot on the ranking of the candidates. This ensures that the electorate knows well in advance what the ranking of candidates is on each list (and thereby, some idea of who is likely to be elected from that list). It also means that the decision of who gets in on the party list is not made in some backroom by party officials, but is something that any party member has the opportunity to influence.

In one *Land*, Baden-Wurttemberg, the adjustment seats are filled by the parties' unelected candidates according to the number of votes they received—what has been called a "best losers" allocation rule. This means it is the voters who, however indirectly, determine who gets an adjustment seat.

the threshold (red line) were awarded party-list seats; these accounted for *all* of the Free Democrats' seats and all but one of the seats for Alliance'90/The Greens. The top three parties (and the National Democrats) received more votes on the constituency side of the ballot than on the party-list side, while for all the other parties the situation was reversed. Voters who recognize that the candidate from their preferred party is unlikely to win at the constituency level will support that party on the party-list side of the ballot, but attempt to influence the local outcome by voting for a candidate from one of the parties that has a chance of winning (usually the CDU/CSU or the SPD). The most telling example of this is the 46,750 votes for Pirate Party local candidates compared to 845,904 votes for the Pirate Party itself. The total vote share for all the parties failing to reach the threshold was 6 per cent of the vote, the equivalent of roughly 34 seats, distributed among the parties above the threshold in proportion to their shares of the vote. (While this system is not perfectly proportional, the disproportionality produced—seats not awarded to parties under the threshold—is shared among the parties in the legislature in a proportional way.)

Because MMP elects representatives in two ways, the possibility exists that one or the other will be seen to be more legitimate, or that there may be confusion about the respective roles (if there is any distinction). Partly, this is a matter of political culture and electoral

GERMANY (BUNDESTAG) 2009 — PARALLEL SYSTEM

PARTY	CONSTITUENCY			PARTY LIST			TOTAL		
	VOTES	%	SEATS	VOTES	%	SEATS	SEATS	%	
CDU	13,852,743	32.0	173	11,824,794	27.3	87	260	43.5	
CSU	3,190,950	7.4	45	2,830,210	6.5	21	66	11.0	PARTIES ABOVE THRESHHOLD
SDP	12,077,437	27.9	64	9,988,843	23.0	73	137	22.9	
FDP	4,075,115	9.4	0	6,313,023	14.6	46	46	7.7	
The Left	4,790,007	11.1	16	5,153,884	11.9	38	54	9.0	
Alliance'90/Greens	3,974,803	9.2	1	4,641,197	10.7	34	35	5.9	
Totals:	43,235,817	99.9	299	43,357,542	100	299	598	100	

NOTES:

CDU = Christian Democratic Union
CSU = Christian Social Union of Bavaria
SDP = Social Democratic Party

FDP = Free Democratic Party
HEAW = Human Environment Animal Welfare Party

Figure 10.26

history. When the new Scottish Parliament came into being with an MMP electoral system, some conflict arose between the constituency representatives and the regional (party-list) members in terms of their responsibility for dealing with constituents' concerns. Section 8 of the Code of Conduct for Members of the Scottish Parliament was drafted to address the expectations for the two sets of MSPs.

Parallel Systems

Parallel systems resemble MMP in that there is a tier of constituency seats and a second tier of proportional seats. However, the two tiers are independent; the second-tier seats are not adjustment seats. The parallel system is used in Bulgaria, Japan, Lithuania, South Korea, and Taiwan. Mauritius also has a small second tier filled by the "best losers" method to ensure that there is greater balance in representation of the ethnic communities than might be the case under the block voting system used in the country's three-member constituencies. The parallel system provides representation to parties that may have failed to elect constituency members, and ensures that their share of the second-tier seats is proportional, but it also

STV-PR BALLOT (MODELLED ON THE AUSTRALIAN SENATE)

A	B	C	D	E	F	G	
⚪ Conservative	⚪ Liberal	⚪ Independent	⚪ Green	⚪	⚪ Pirate	⚪ Social democrats	Ungrouped
⚪ McNey, T.	⚪ Faizal, A.	⚪ Khan, O.	⚪ Jones, W.	⚪ Toure, C.	⚪ Zark. B.	⚪ O'Malley, M.	⚪ Viets, S.
⚪ Rawls, Q.	⚪ Gemini, I.		⚪ Wiley, J.	⚪ Bell, V.		⚪ Boulanger, N.	⚪ Hynes, S.
⚪ Bourq, E.						⚪ Mugabe, A.	⚪ Swift, S.
						⚪ Fitzgerald, J.	

Figure 10.27

awards proportionate shares to the parties that were over-represented in the constituency results. *Figure 10.26* illustrates how the German results might have played out under a parallel system. In the end, a parallel system adds an element of proportionality, but does not, considered as a whole, provide proportional representation.

STV-PR

The Single Transferable Vote PR system can be understood as AV applied to multi-member constituencies. It is used most famously in Ireland, but also for elections to the Australian Senate and in some Australian state legislature elections. Ireland's electoral districts elect three, four, or five Members; Australian voters are usually electing six Senators (but sometimes 12). In Ireland, voters may rank as many (or as few) of the candidates as they choose, and in some districts this may be 20 candidates or more. In Australia's Senate elections, voters must either rank *all* the candidates individually, or vote "above the line," which involves selecting one party (or group) and allowing its ranking

of all the candidates (registered in advance with the Electoral Commission) to be followed in the counting of this ballot. As the sample ballot in *Figure 10.27* demonstrates, to rank *all* the candidates below the line in any thoughtful way would take time and presumes a well-informed voter. In the 2010 Australian federal Senate election, 96 per cent of voters chose to vote above the line.

The ballot in *Figure 10.27* illustrates another feature of STV-PR: the challenge, for each party, of knowing how many candidates to run. This is particularly the case where, as in Ireland, there is no voting "above the line." Each candidate is competing, party alliances notwithstanding, with every other candidate. Suppose that the sample ballot in *Figure 10.28* is for a four-seat Irish constituency. By running three candidates, the Conservatives are indicating their confidence that they will win at least two of the four seats, and are hoping they can get one more. At the same time, they risk splitting their vote among the three candidates, and depending on how other parties fare, perhaps winning only one. By the same token, the Green and Pirate parties each hope to elect one Member from this district, but are not in a position to capitalize on a sudden surge in support for their party.

It has been suggested that because candidates from the same party are also competing with each other for preferences, STV-PR does an excellent job of keeping Members accountable to their constituents as they scramble to outdo each other in looking after local interests. In fact, it does this so well that some Members will not support a policy that is in the national or regional interest if it affects the local constituency in any negative way. STV-PR also seems to elect a higher proportion of independent (non-party) Members than other systems. Because STV-PR districts tend to be

STV-PR BALLOT
(MODELLED ON THE BALLOT FOR THE IRISH DÁIL)

C	Bourq – Conservative	[face of candidate]	○
SD	Fitzgerald – Social Democrat	[face of candidate]	○
	Hynes – non party	[face of candidate]	○
G	Jones – Green	[face of candidate]	○
	Khan – non party	[no face]	○
C	McNey – Conservative	[face of candidate]	○
SD	O'Malley – Social Democrat	[face of candidate]	○
C	Rawls – Conservative	[face of candidate]	○
	Swift – non party	[face of candidate]	○
P	Zark – Pirate	[face of candidate]	○

Figure 10.28

CANDIDATE	PARTY	COUNT 1	Transfer of surplus from Lenihan COUNT 2	Transfer of votes from Kelly COUNT 3	Transfer of surplus from Hayes COUNT 4	Transfer of surplus from Rabbitte COUNT 5	Transfer of votes from Murphy COUNT 6
Lenihan	FF	8,542	-211 8,331	8,331	8,331	8,331	8,331
Hayes	FG	8,346	8,346	8,346	-16 8,331	8,331	8,331
Rabbitte	LAB	8,325	+17 8,342	8,342	8,342	-11 8,331	8,331
O'Connor	FF	7,813	+172 7,985	+117 8,102	+4 8,106	+3 8,109	+330 8,439
Crowe	SF	5,066	+10 5,076	+107 5,183	+2 5,185	+4 5,189	+577 5,766
Davidson	G	1,546	+4 1,552	+103 1,655	+7 1,662	+4 1,666	+568 2,234
Murphy	Soc	1,580	+4 1,584	+75 1,659	+2 1,661	1,661	-1,661 eliminated
Kelly	FRR	434	+2 436	-436 eliminated			
Non-transferable papers not effective				+34 34	34	34	+186 220
Total valid		41,652	41,652	41,652	41,652	41,652	41,652

Figure 10.29 (Data source: Elections Ireland)

smaller than districts in other PR systems, its results are sometimes best described as semi-proportional.

The counting of votes under STV is the most complicated of any system in use at the national level, and may take days in Ireland, weeks in the case of the Australian Senate. This is because of the number of candidates and the number of preferences to be taken into consideration. In a multi-member constituency, a *quota* is established—usually the number of valid votes divided by one more than the number of seats to be awarded, plus one. If there are 10,000 votes and four seats, the quota is (10,000 ÷ 5) + 1 = 2,001. This is the smallest number of votes that four parties could win, but not five.

Figure 10.29 provides one of the least complicated counts from the 2007 election, a district in which there were only eight candidates seeking four seats. With 41,652 valid votes, the quota for this district was 8,331 votes. Two candidates exceeded the quota with first-preference votes and were accordingly elected. The 211 surplus votes for the first place candidate (Lenihan) were then transferred on the basis of the next preference to the remaining candidates. This put the third-place finisher (Rabbitte) over the quota, filling the third seat. Under Irish counting rules, the lowest total (Kelly) was then eliminated and his ballots transferred. On the sixth count, the fourth seat was filled as O'Connor's total exceeded the quota. This series of transfers of

STV

distribution proportional	distribution proportionate	distribution unidirectional	majority manufact'd	stable coalition	party sys. two/multi	legal threshold	ease of voting	voter choices	system transparency
semi	no	no	no	yes	multi	no	diff	high	D-y/sys-med

Figure 10.30

surplus votes and the votes of eliminated candidates happens in each district until all seats have been filled.

The 2007 Dublin South West count is also straight-forward in that the four candidates who finished first were also the four candidates who ended up winning the four seats. That is often not the case. In the same election, Dublin North East's three seats ultimately went in order to the candidates who initially finished third, fifth, and first, and in Dublin Central the fourth seat went to the candidate who initially finished ninth with 2.71 per cent of the first-preference ballots.

Party List PR

Party List PR employs multi-member constituencies in which voters choose between each party's list of candidates. As *Figure 10.4* indicates, List PR is the most commonly used electoral system in the developed-world democracies. List PR has the largest electoral districts, both in absolute terms and on average, of all electoral systems. The principal difference between List systems concerns the ballot. The easiest to explain is the closed list; each party presents a list of its candidates for the electoral district to the electors, who vote by placing one of the lists in the ballot box. Whatever seats a party wins are filled by the names on its list, in the order that the party has determined. The closed list is a categorical multi-candidate ballot.

The open list allows the voter to express some degree of preference among the candidates. This may vary from the Swedish system, where voters may place a mark beside one (and only one) candidate on the list in an attempt to move that candidate higher on the list, to the Finnish and Brazilian systems, where the determination of which candidates will fill a party's seats is based entirely on the preference votes they received. Finally, the free list, used in Switzerland, allows voters to do any or all of the following:

1. re-order the list of candidates supplied by the party;
2. vote for any candidate twice by using a blank line or crossing out another candidate's name and replacing it with the voter's preferred candidate;
3. cross out candidates' names and substitute the name(s) of a candidate or candidates from *other* parties' lists; and
4. use a blank list to assemble the names of candidates from several parties' lists (an activity called *panachage*).

The number of seats each party gets is determined by its share of the party votes in the district. In (1) and (2) the voter is casting a ballot for one party and indicating preferences for certain of the party's candidates. In (3) the voter is casting a ballot for one party but expressing can vote for the party I prefer, change the order of its candidates and/or double the weight given to one or more of its candidates, *and* influence which candidates win the seats awarded to the other parties. In (4), the voter can vote for as many candidates from different parties as there are spaces on the ballot without casting a party vote for any of the parties.

The vote counting in a List PR system consists of two stages. The share of ballots each party receives in a district determines the *number* of seats it wins. This is usually done through a **highest averages** or **largest remainders** calculation. The second stage is to determine which of the party's candidates will fill the seats. In a closed list system whatever number of seats (N) the party has won is filled by the top N candidates on the party's list. In the open and free list versions of List PR, the preferences expressed for individual candidates on the ballots are counted and applied to the determination of which candidates are the top N, and therefore winners of seats.

More than any other system, with the possible exception of some MMP systems, List PR is concerned with generating proportional results. Unlike MMP, it accomplishes this solely with multi-member districts. This means that the unique identification of a member with a geographical constituency is missing, and though citizens may have several representatives to whom they

preferences for that party's candidates *and* for a candidate or candidates from other parties. These votes for candidates from other parties will not count towards their parties, but contribute towards the ranking of the other party's (or parties') candidates. In other words, I

PARTY LIST

distribution proportional	distribution proportionate	distribution unidirectional	majority manufact'd	stable coalition	party sys. two/multi	legal threshold	ease of voting	voter choices	system transparency
yes	yes	yes	no	yes	multi	often	easy	low med-high	D-y/sys-y

Figure 10.31

can bring their concerns, any accountability of individual members to their constituents is weakened. In many respects, members are more accountable to their party than to their constituents. On the one hand, this requires that the *party* be accountable to the electorate, which is the case in PR systems more than in any other type. On the other hand, systems that allow voters to express preferences for candidates on the party lists and thereby influence, if not determine, which candidates will fill a party's seats, restore some measure of accountability. Party List PR systems are second only to STV-PR in the complexity of their counting systems, which reduces their transparency with respect to the election of the constituency members. The high degree of proportionality, however, means that voters know the parties' seat shares will reflect their votes, regardless of how these results are calculated.

ELECTORAL ADMINISTRATION

The reason some regimes are pseudo-democracies is not the absence of an electoral system, but the absence of an impartial electoral administration (or corrupt electoral administration officials).

Ensuring fair elections take place under any system requires as a bare minimum:

· an impartial, non-partisan body at arm's length from the government, charged with permanent responsibility for administering the regime's electoral legislation;
· built-in processes of transparency and accountability to limit the possibility of corruption;
· the ability to challenge election results where a corrupt practice or misadministration has occurred; and

· openness to observation by officials from international organizations.

There are many possible elements to the administrative machinery for holding a fair and impartial election, and these are independent of the actual electoral system. Among them are the following:

PROFESSIONAL STAFF

From the chief electoral officer, down to the poll workers, the ideal system will be staffed by impartial, well-trained election professionals. Given the periodic nature of elections and the number of voting transactions to be processed in a short period of time, in many cases it is inevitable that a large number of election workers will be contracted for a short period of employment. Procedures for hiring, training, and paying election officials, as well as safeguards against possible corruption, are critical.

NON-PARTISAN REDISTRIBUTION OF ELECTORAL BOUNDARIES

To ensure that each citizen's vote carries the same weight in the electoral process, it is necessary to adjust electoral-district boundaries periodically to reflect demographic changes or, in the case of multi-member districts that reflect local administrative units or municipal boundaries, to revisit the number of members elected from each district. There should be no ability for one political party or an alliance of parties to control this process in order to maximize its own electoral prospects. Manipulation of electoral boundaries for partisan advantage is called **gerrymandering**, an activity to which plurality systems are much more susceptible than proportional ones. To avoid gerrymandering, legislation may establish a process that is placed in the hands of an impartial, non-political panel answering to the legislature. It may also be one of the ongoing responsibilities of the regime's independent election administration officials.

ELECTOR REGISTRATION

It is imperative on election day that every person who is entitled to vote is able to vote *and* that the phrase "vote early, vote often" remains just a joke (not to be shared with election officials). Among the principal preoccupations of election administration officials are establishing methods of registering the electorate, keeping an accurate list of electors' addresses, and allowing for registration of new electors or electors who have moved or changed their names. In many regimes, in recent years, removing the barriers to voting by persons with disabilities has become a priority. As important as providing access to all who are eligible to vote is ensuring that no-one votes *more* than once. This is accomplished by rules about how electors identify themselves at the polling place and proper recording

ELECTORS AND VOTERS

A technical but useful distinction is between *electors,* those entitled to cast a vote in an election, and *voters,* those who actually cast a vote. When people talk about **voter turnout**, they are comparing the number of voters with the number of electors—in other words, what percentage of those who are eligible to vote voted? The value of that number depends, in turn, on the adequacy of the registration/enumeration process. A high turnout is less impressive if the system failed to register significant portions of the population, as might happen in places where literacy is low or some groups are systematically discouraged from registering.

by electoral officials of each person who votes, without compromising the confidentiality of their ballot.

Until quite recently, enumeration of voters was not uncommon: during the election period, individuals hired by the election office would canvass all residences to compile a voters' list for each district. In most jurisdictions today, a permanent voter's list is maintained, pooling all the various government databases where individuals' names and addresses are collected. In fact, in most regimes, and in most of the democracies in the data set, voter registration is compulsory.

ACCESSIBLE, INCORRUPTIBLE VOTING PROCESS

One of the biggest challenges for electoral administrators is the mechanics of the voting process. The guiding principles are twofold: to maximize the ability of anyone who wishes to vote (or, in some regimes, of everyone who is required to vote), and to maintain the integrity of every ballot. How many polling places are there, how many people are expected to vote at each polling place, and how many electors is each election official expected to process? How many hours are provided for the people to vote, and are there provisions to ensure that everyone has enough time outside of work hours to visit the polling place and vote? Are there voting opportunities (advance polls or special ballots) for those who will unavoidably be away from their electoral district on polling day? How are the ballots printed, distributed to polling stations, kept track of, and accounted for after the polling is done? What processes are in place to ensure that no one votes more than once, that the number of ballots in the ballot box corresponds to the number of persons who are recorded as having voted, and that the votes are secure until the counting? What processes are in place to ensure that the count is accurate, that it can, if necessary, be replicated, and that it may be witnessed by observers (scrutineers)?

Although these seem like very minor elements or technical issues, inadequacy with respect to any one of them could call into question the fairness and hence the validity of the election. When international observers report about election irregularities in countries where the electoral machinery has yet to be fully developed, or there are people attempting to cheat the process, it is often very practical matters like those noted above that are compromised. Equally, it is the challenge of meeting some of these very elementary requirements (such as the ability to recount, and the ability to witness the elector's interaction with the ballot—paper or mechanical—without compromising the secrecy of the vote) that has so far inhibited the growth of electronic voting.

CANDIDATE REGISTRATION

Full adult suffrage, a minimum requirement of democracy today, includes not only the right to vote, but the right to run for office—to be a candidate. Even in countries with full adult suffrage, rules govern the right to be a candidate (such as valid citizenship status and, in a provincial or state legislature, residency requirements) and the conditions that must be satisfied, or the process to be followed, for the valid nomination of a candidate. Here, as above, the more onerous the conditions or cumbersome the process, the less open the system. Many jurisdictions require the payment of a fee to accompany the nomination papers (which may or may not be refundable for candidates receiving a prescribed percentage of the vote). While such a condition does not aim to exclude any particular person, being designed rather to discourage frivolous nominations, it may nonetheless exclude certain portions of the population from seeking office.

A related issue is how the candidates' names are presented on the ballot (depending on the type of ballot used). Should they be listed "First (name), Last (name)"; "First, LAST"; "LAST, FIRST"; or "LAST, First"? Should they be presented in alphabetical order by name or by party affiliation (if this is included), or should ballots be printed to present a random order that differs ballot by ballot? The latter is an important consideration where voters may (or are required to) rank the candidates in order. If there is only one order of the names, it takes only a small percentage of "donkey votes" (ranking the names in the order they are presented) to skew the results.

PARTY REGISTRATION

In most systems, most candidates contest the election as members of an officially recognized political party. The electoral administration body is usually responsible for the registration of political parties and for administering laws that apply to their organization and finances. Only officially registered parties will have their name appear on the ballot, a status they may lose if certain conditions, such as continuing to contest elections, are not satisfied. In 2003, a notable decision by the Supreme Court of Canada in *Figueroa vs. the Attorney General (Canada)* struck down provisions in the election law that provided for deregistration of any party failing to nominate 50 candidates in a federal election. The provision would also have turned the net assets of the de-registered party over to the federal government. Under the current law, a party need endorse only one candidate in an election to maintain its status (it must also submit annually a list of the names and addresses of 250 members, and affirm annually that one of its fundamental purposes is to endorse and support the candidacy of one or more of its members).

PARTY AND ELECTION FINANCES

Political parties must raise funds to finance their election campaigns, which have become increasingly expensive as they become more technologically sophisticated. On the other hand, democracy requires that no individual, group, class, or partial set of interests should be able to buy (or unduly influence) an election. Where party finances and campaign donations are most loosely regulated, the less equal the playing field is for all parties. Regulation of this field includes rules about who can donate (individuals? corporations? trade unions? foreign interests? anonymous donors?); how much and how often they can contribute (annual limits, campaign-period limits); public disclosure and/or reporting of donations and party finances to the electoral authority; limits on election expenses (by the party, by the candidate, by "third parties"—an association or organization); and about reporting deadlines and requirements.

Balancing the restrictions and limits that may be placed on the support of political parties by the elements of civil society are the supports that the state may provide to parties, recognizing and thereby confirming their institutionalization as essential components of democracy. These supports can range from tax credits for donations to political parties, to reimbursement of party and/or candidate election expenses (either as a percentage of the expenses or an amount per vote received, usually conditional on the party or candidate receiving a prescribed level of support), to direct subsidies of political parties (again on a per-vote basis).

ADVERTISING AND OPINION POLLS

Some of the largest expenses incurred by political parties are for advertising and public-opinion polling. Both of these activities may also be subject to regulation. In many European regimes political parties may not *purchase* advertising time on television, but in some cases receive an allocation of free time for political broadcasts (Gallagher, Laver, and Mair, 259).

In Canada, political parties can purchase advertising time, but they are limited to the share allocated to each registered party from the six-and-a-half hours of prime time that each broadcaster is required to make available during the campaign. The allocation is made on the basis of a number of factors, including the support received by each party in the previous election, and is worked out between the parties by a broadcast arbitrator appointed under the election legislation. Parties also receive an amount of free broadcast time allocated in the same proportions. Bans in Canada on "third party" advertising were struck down as unconstitutional and have now been replaced by regulation of the same. Similarly, regulations that prohibited the publication of a poll or commissioned survey in the last three days of a federal election campaign were ruled unconstitutional by the Supreme Court of Canada. Currently, the election legislation prohibits the publication or transmission of any new election opinion surveys or public-opinion polls on voting day. Restrictions on the publication of polls are not uncommon in other democracies, where the period covered by the "gag law" may be as long as a week.

ENFORCEMENT

Finally, none of the laws governing the conduct of elections will matter if the electoral authority lacks the means to enforce them, including penalties that serve as a sufficient deterrent to anyone tempted to gain an advantage by subverting the provisions that make for a fair election. In most developed democracies, electoral legislation has been a work in progress, with provisions constantly under review for their

(see explanatory notes below for more information on each numbered column)

	(1)	(6)	(8)	(13)	(10)	(14)	(15)
ALL REGIMES (45)		**ELECTORAL SYSTEM**	**LAST ELECTION**	**PARTY SYSTEM (ENEP)**	**PARTY SYSTEM (ENLP)**	**ELECTORAL SYSTEM FILTERING (13) – (10)**	**GALLAGHER INDEX**
PARLIAMENTARY (36)							
PROPORTIONAL (27)							
Denmark		List PR(C)	2011	5.72	5.61	0.11	0.46
Netherlands		List PR(C)	2010	6.98	6.74	0.23	0.67
Sweden		List PR(O)	2010	4.79	4.53	0.26	1.13
Serbia		List PR(C)	2008	3.73	3.48	0.26	1.37
Israel		List PR(C)	2009	7.39	6.77	0.62	1.40
New Zealand		MMP(FPP)	2011	3.16	2.98	0.18	1.42
Iceland		List PR(C)	2009	4.57	4.18	0.39	2.00
Norway		List PR(O)	2009	4.55	4.07	0.48	2.83
Germany		MMP(FPP)	2009	5.60	4.83	0.77	2.84
Finland		List PR(O)	2011	6.46	5.83	0.63	2.90
Austria		List PR(C)	2008	4.83	4.27	0.56	2.94
Latvia		List PR(O)	2011	5.20	4.52	0.68	2.96
Belgium		List PR(O)	2010	10.13	8.43	1.70	3.41
Slovenia		List PR(O)	2011	5.56	4.52	1.04	3.43
Switzerland		List PR(F)	2011	6.37	5.57	0.80	3.51
Romania		List PR(C)	2008	3.94	3.23	0.71	4.73
Portugal		List PR(C)	2011	3.67	2.93	0.74	5.54
Italy		List PR(C)[4]	2008	3.79	3.05	0.74	5.65
Poland		List PR(O)	2011	3.75	3.00	0.75	5.67
Estonia		List PR(O)	2011	4.74	3.84	0.90	5.78
Spain		List PR(C)	2011	3.34	2.60	0.74	6.87
Bulgaria		Parallel[1]	2009	4.41	3.34	1.07	6.98
Greece		List PR(O)[4]	2009	3.16	2.59	0.57	7.27
Slovakia		List PR(O)	2010	5.54	4.01	1.53	7.32
Czech Republic		List PR(O)	2010	6.76	4.51	2.25	8.67
Hungary		MMP(TRS)	2010	2.86	2.00	0.86	12.05
Croatia		List PR(C)	2011	4.42	2.35	2.07	13.62
SEMI-PROPORTIONAL (3)							
Ireland		STV	2011	4.45	3.46	1.00	8.54
Lithuania		Parallel[2]	2008	8.95	5.79	3.16	10.95
Japan		Parallel[3]	2009	2.99	2.10	0.89	14.66
MAJORITARIAN (6)							
Trinidad and Tobago		FPP/SMP	2010	1.95	1.71	0.24	10.58
Australia		AV	2010	3.83	2.95	0.88	11.16
Canada		FPP/SMP	2011	3.43	2.40	1.03	12.59
France		TRS	2007	4.37	2.49	1.88	13.05
United Kingdom		FPP/SMP	2010	3.73	2.58	1.15	14.81
Mauritius		Block Vote	2010	2.36	1.91	0.45	14.84

[1] FPP/SMP= 31/List PR(C)= 209   [2] TRS=71/List(C)=70   [3] FPP/SMP=300/List(C)=180   [4] R Reinforced PR system (see Chapter 10)

ALL REGIMES (45) (1)	ELECTORAL SYSTEM (6)	LAST ELECTION (8)	PARTY SYSTEM (ENEP) (13)	PARTY SYSTEM (ENLP) (10)	ELECTORAL SYSTEM FILTERING (13) – (10) (14)	GALLAGHER INDEX (15)
NON-PARLIAMENTARY (9)						
PROPORTIONAL (5)						
Brazil	List PR(O)	2010	11.26	10.44	0.82	2.47
Uruguay	List PR(C)	2009	2.98	2.65	0.33	2.51
Costa Rica	List PR(C)	2010	4.81	4.04	0.77	4.51
Argentina	List PR(C)	2009	8.94	7.39	1.55	4.91
Chile	List PR(C)	2009	7.41	5.64	1.77	6.31
SEMI-PROPORTIONAL (3)						
Panama	Parallel[1]	2009	4.18	3.65	0.53	7.08
South Korea	Parallel[2]	2008	3.98	2.93	1.05	8.44
Taiwan	Parallel[3]	2008	2.49	1.75	0.74	17.55
MAJORITARIAN (1)						
United States	FPP/SMP	2010	2.15	1.97	0.18	3.01

[1] FPP/SMP=26/List(O)=45   [2] FPP/SMP=254/List(C)=45   [3] FPP/SMP=73/List=40

EXPLANATORY NOTES

(1) **ALL REGIMES:** regimes from table in Figure 4.2 averaging 1, 1.5, or 2 on the 2011 Freedom House scores; with population >1,000,000, plus Iceland (>100,000 km^2); scoring Very High or High on 2011 UN Human Development Index, sorted by Gallagher index (see 15).

(6) **ELECTORAL SYSTEM:** electoral system used to elect the legislature, or, in bicameral systems, the lower house of the legislature.

(8) **LAST ELECTION:** date of last legislative election, mid-term in Argentina and United States.

(13) **PARTY SYSTEM: ENEP**=effective number of **ELECTORAL** parties, based on results in last election.

(10) **PARTY SYSTEM: ENLP**=effective number of **LEGISLATIVE** parties, based on results in last election.

(14) **ELECTORAL SYSTEM FILTERING:** Measures the difference between the **ENEP** and the **ENLP**.

(15) **GALLAGHER INDEX:** Measures the degree of disproportionality in electoral systems. Each subsection has been sorted on this variable, from lowest to highest.

effectiveness in meeting complementary but different goals, from ensuring fairness, to increasing transparency and public knowledge about the electoral process, to improving voter turnout. The one matter that any electoral authority should be least concerned about is *who* wins the election.

REFERENCES

Duverger, Maurice. *Political Parties.* New York: Wiley, 1963.

Gallagher, Michael, Michael Laver, and Peter Mair. *Representative Government in Modern Europe.* New York: McGraw-Hill, 1995.

Laakso, Markku, and Rein Taagepera. "The 'Effective' Number of Parties: A Measure with Application to West Europe." *Comparative Political Studies* 12.1 (April 1979): 2–27.

FURTHER READINGS

Colomer, Josep. "The Strategy and History of Electoral System Choice." *The Handbook of Electoral System Choice* Ed. Josep Colomer. London: Palgrave Macmillan, 2004. 3–78.

———. "It's Parties that Choose Electoral Systems (or Duverger's Laws Upside Down)." *Political Studies* 53.1 (March 2005): 1–21.

Curtice, John. "So What Went Wrong with the Electoral System? The 2010 Election Result and the Debate about Electoral Reform." *Parliamentary Affairs* 63.4 (October 2010): 623–638.

Hix, Simon, Ron Johnston, and Iain McLean. *Choosing an Electoral System.* London: The British Academy, 2010. [Publication may be downloaded from the Academy's website.]

Kelly, Richard. "It's Only Made Things Worse: A Critique of Electoral Reform in Britain." *The Political Quarterly* 79.2 (April–June 2008): 260–268.

Leduc, Larry. "The Failure of Electoral Reform Proposals in Canada." *Political Science* 63.2 (December 2009): 21–40.

Lijphart, Arend. "Unequal Participation: Democracy's Unresolved Dilemma." *American Political Science Review* 91.1 (March 1997): 1–14.

Lundberg, Thomas Carl. "Electoral System Reviews in New Zealand, Britain and Canada: A Critical Comparison." *Government and Opposition* 42.4 (Autumn 2007): 471–490.

Orozco-Henríquez, Jesús. *Electoral Justice: The International IDEA Handbook.* Stockholm: International IDEA, 2010. [Publication may be downloaded from the Institute's website.]

CHAPTER 11

Who Is Heard? Varieties of Representation

...WHICH PROVIDES THE READER WITH

- a contrast between political parties and interest groups as organized vehicles of representation
- a contrast between parties that primarily serve their leaders and those that primarily serve the electorate
- a discussion of how parties function collectively within a regime's political process and legislature (party systems)
- consideration of how parties campaign and if this can be compared between or within regimes
- a contrast between organized interests with an institutionalized role in the policy process (corporatism) and those competing for policy influence (pluralism)
- the contrast to both political parties and organized interests provided by (new) social movements

Democracy in the age of mass society is necessarily representative. The individual can accomplish little in today's political world. Behind each successful individual stands an organization or network providing expertise, financial backing, communications support, transportation, and so on. Because of this, voters choose not just a candidate, but the whole organization of staff, supporters, and volunteers whose passion, wit, and labour have sustained this candidacy. Ironically, this is increasingly true even as the predominance of the modern media campaign obscures to us anything except the images of the candidate.

Electing representatives is just one part of the political process, but in the other avenues where the public is able to provide input, it is the group, the organization, the association, the individual who speaks on behalf of other individuals rather than for him- or herself who has a chance, perhaps, of being heard.

Finally, there are times in history when significant portions of the public become disillusioned with the existing institutional structures and the ability of traditional vehicles, such as the political party or the interest group, to provide effective delivery of their concerns and aspirations. This is when the mass movement forms to raise its voice, express its discontent, demand change, and sometimes move from peaceful protest to civil disobedience to something more violent. How far the latter road is travelled depends on many factors, including the desperation of the protesters, the responses of those in authority, the co-optation of the movement by organized interests, and the type of regime in which the movement occurs. Having a process by which citizens may express their policy preferences directly, through referenda and/or initiatives, is an institutional outlet through which to channel popular discontent. This edition is written at a time when dissatisfaction with the existing structures of political and economic authority is being expressed in public squares and city centres in both democratic and non-democratic regimes around the word, assisted by the digital revolution and the tools of social networking. What all this protest (particularly the "Arab Spring") will ultimately produce is still anyone's guess.

POLITICAL PARTIES

The central role of political parties within the democratic state has been demonstrated in the preceding chapters. The observation that political parties have been *institutionalized* in modern democratic systems is another way of saying the same thing, by pointing to their incorporation in electoral law and parliamentary rules. Parties have become so indispensable because they perform a variety of functions central to the political process— some that are performed consciously and some that are by-products of the activities parties deliberately engage in. For example, parties organize the electorate by recruiting candidates, organizing campaigns, assisting voters with registration, and arranging for child care or providing transportation on polling day. Parties can help stimulate policy development through conventions, workshops, and debates. In the effort to construct broad bases of public support, parties may build bridges between disparate communities within society and help balance competing interests. By engaging citizens within the political process and organizing opportunities for activity, debate, and dissent, parties may increase citizens' feelings of efficacy and enhance the legitimacy of the political system. In a similar way, parties can be **agents of socialization** for the broader population and for organizations that recruit and groom future political leaders. Parties are said to simplify to a manageable level the range of

PARTIES ARE ...

... structured, articulated and hierarchical groups adapted to the struggle for power.
(Duverger 1963, 104)
... agencies for the acquisition of power.
(Lawson, 23)
... organizations designed to secure the power of the state for their leaders.
(Jackson and Jackson, 373)
... publicly organized groups of people who are motivated by some common set of political ideas and whose goal is to have their particular members win public office so that those ideas can be put into practice.
(Malcolmson and Myers, 183)

issues and options presented to the public—something some observers would argue they do *too* well.

PARTY FUNCTIONS

Political parties serve at least three masters: their leaders, their members, and the broader public. Consider the definitions in *Parties are...* (p. 254); the overwhelming theme is that parties are means of securing scarce positions of authority and power. This puts the emphasis on what parties do for their leaders, on their **mobilization function**. While this is an important part of the picture, we should not expect leaders to be the only beneficiaries of party politics. Powell describes what parties can do for the political system at large and for citizens generally:

> Political parties are the institutions that link the voting choices of individual citizens with aggregate electoral outcomes in the competitive democracies. The parties set the alternatives offered to the citizens in elections and their organized activities can encourage both registration and election-day turnout. The relationships between party systems and national cleavage structures should play a major role in shaping voting participation levels. (115)

In other words, in rounding up support for leaders (the mobilization function), parties also perform an electoral administration function for the political process and the electorate at large. In between the party leaders and the broad public at large, however, stand the party members and supporters: those who join a party and/or sustain it with their labour, time, and money. Two components are present in the definition of political parties offered by Malcolmson and Myers that go missing in most other definitions: the relationship of the party to its members, and the suggestion that members might be linked by something more than ambition—namely, a common set of ideas. If anything is missing here, it is reference to the party's relationship with those in the public who form attachments to it without actually becoming members, persons who are supporters or *partisans*. Few parties succeed solely on the strength of their membership. The definition offered here, intended to focus on the party's **representation function** is this: parties are *voluntary organizations that seek to further the interests and principles of their members and supporters by gaining elected office.*

The political party (however much it may fall out of favour in public opinion) has a relatively unique status as a bridge between civil society, where it is formed and sustained, and the state, where it is a fundamental institution in the electoral system (*and* in most legislatures). This is reflected in its three functions: mobilization for its leaders and candidates, representation for its members and supporters, and administration for the political process.

It is possible to approach any of the issues relevant to the discussion of political parties in terms of these three functions, whether it is the process by which party leaders are selected, the rules of party finance, or the internal organization of the party. It may be useful, for example, to consider the possible, if not inevitable, tension between the mobilization function and the representation function. To put the matter another way, parties can operate primarily as **electoral vehicles**, focused on electing candidates or generating support for their leaders, *or* they can operate primarily as **agents of representation**, focused on furthering the interest of their members and supporters. Obviously this is an analytic distinction; parties can (and must) be both electoral vehicles *and* agents of representation. While this is true, the question is, to use an antique turn of phrase, which horse is pulling the cart? Does widespread disillusionment with political parties reflect the tendency of parties to refine and perfect their technique as electoral vehicles at the expense of performing their representative function?

In the best of all possible worlds, parties will elect their candidates *because* they are good agents of representation, but in the real world, it is quite possible that electoral success may depend on practices or strategies that are contrary to good representation. The discussion below about the use of technology in the modern campaign indicates some of the ways that parties' presentations to the electorate are technologically sophisticated but superficial with respect to their issue content. These include the emphasis on images of leadership and the politics of "character," the preference for 15-second sound bites over the explanation of policy positions. It is hard to see how media-driven strategies enhance the parties' abilities to represent supporters' concerns or interests. Similarly, parties cultivate members to provide organizational resources and financial support, but turn to pollsters and public relations firms to pitch their campaigns to the larger, less-active public: in-depth policy positions articulated by party members could, in this context, be a nuisance.

By the same token, parties that cannot elect members to official positions will not be very effective in representing their members' concerns. This can be a matter of degree; in minority or coalition government, parties may very well be able to influence public policy without controlling, or even participating in, the government.

THE POLITICS OF BROKERAGE PARTIES

In the passage quoted above, Powell noted the relationship of parties to societal cleavages. Parties can reflect the structure of cleavages in the regime, or they can attempt to bridge these divisions. The challenge in democracy is to mobilize the support of a majority of citizens for public policy, and within pluralistic societies this requires building a coalition out of diverse interests and identities. This majority-building can take place between parties (as in coalition-government formation) or within parties.

Where parties closely correspond to the cleavage structure of a society (i.e., their basis of support corresponds to class identities, or ethnic solidarities, or religious affiliations), it may be necessary and

BELGIAN PARTIES

One example where the political parties reflect the cleavage structure most closely, and with detrimental effect, is in Belgium. In the June 2010 federal election, 12 parties won seats: two social democratic parties, two Christian democratic parties, two liberal parties, two Green parties, two conservative liberal parties, each pair consisting of a Walloon (French-speaking) party and a Flemish (Dutch-speaking) party; plus two Flemish separatist parties. Each party fields candidates in its own linguistic community and in the bilingual community (Brussels); there are no longer any effective national parties. Eighteen months after the election and 541 days after the collapse of the previous administration, a new government was finally sworn in: a six-party coalition of the two social democratic, two Christian democratic, and two liberal parties. This excluded the largest Flemish separatist party (New Flemish Alliance), which finished first among all of the parties.

appropriate for majorities to be built through negotiation and bargaining between the elected representatives of the various communities represented by political parties. In such cases, it would appear that the representation function of parties is primary, and the mobilization function is limited by the constraints of the government formation process. The role of the electoral system will also be a key ingredient here, as is explained later.

A party may, conversely, attempt to transcend or bridge the societal cleavages by accommodating a broad coalition of supporters (members and partisans). Such parties have been called "catch-all" (after Kirchheimer) parties or, more typically in Canada, **brokerage parties**. As both terms indicate, these parties seek to build support from very diverse sources within society, appealing to many constituencies at the same time. Such a party will be quite flexible about its ideology or long-term policy commitments. The authors of *Absent Mandate* (Clarke et al., 16), a study of Canadian electoral politics, argue that Canada's brokerage parties

- re-create coalitions at each election (i.e., a collection of supporting groups and interests, not always the same, is assembled every election);
- constantly compete for the same policy space and the same votes (i.e., the parties do not differ much in their policy directions nor do they attempt to make specific groups of voters their own);
- present voters with appeals to narrow interests, and proposals that tinker with existing arrangements, rather than a clear choice between worldviews and the political projects that follow from them;

- practice inconsistency as they search for electorally successful formulae (i.e., they do not worry about whether their proposals contradict each other or what was presented in the last campaign); and
- organize around leaders rather than around political principles and ideologies (i.e., the election becomes a popularity contest between the leaders).

This sketch highlights the elements that have led many observers to conclude that brokerage parties function poorly as agents of representation. To the extent that they *do* articulate policies, these will stand on no clearly principled foundation but appeal to the diversity of interests whose support the party is seeking. The brokerage party courts everyone, and if it does so with policy, this means promising something to each interest it hopes to represent (increasing the likelihood that its promises are not consistent). Delivering on such promises once elected is almost impossible: policy-making will require choices that please some interests and disappoint others. This is why the brokerage party must "re-create" its coalition at each election and explains its unwillingness to be pinned down by ideology or other principles.

The implication is that brokerage parties succeed electorally but fail at providing good representation to citizens; both of these observations need qualification. First, brokerage parties can perform an important function within the polity, namely that of knitting together diverse communities that are otherwise in tension or have conflicting interests. The brokerage party builds bridges across the societal cleavages that otherwise fracture the political community. Historically, parties that wished to govern Canada had to play a brokerage

PARTISAN INSTABILITY

One measure of the performance of political parties is how well they retain their support over time, despite the changing intangibles such as leadership, the economy, and the campaign. Partisan stability, all else being equal, should reflect well on the parties involved. Fortunately, partisan stability (or its opposite, partisan volatility) is relatively easy to calculate, as in the following application to the 2011 Canadian general election.

	2011 %V	2008 %V	+/-
CON	39.62	37.65	1.97
NDP	30.63	18.18	12.45
LIB	18.91	26.26	7.35
BQ	6.04	9.98	3.94
GRN	3.91	6.78	2.87
		Total:	28.58
		÷ 2 =	14.29
		Avg (÷ 5) =	2.87

To put these results in context, the following graph shows the average partisan instability scores for a number of regimes based on their elections between 2000 and 2011. In each case, the country had at least three general elections during this period, and scores have been calculated for the three most recent elections. In every case but two (Norway and Sweden), the partisan instability scores are higher after the third election than they were after the first, indicating a general upward trend in partisan instability.

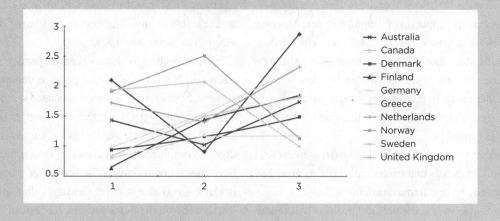

role, bridging the divide between English- and French-speaking Canada. It was once almost impossible to secure a majority government without a strong measure of support in Quebec. More recently, it seems two out of the three consisting of Quebec, Ontario, and the West can provide the basis for a winning formula.

In 1956, Neumann (47–48) distinguished between the party of *individual representation* ("characteristic of a society with a restricted political domain and only a limited degree of participation. . . . membership activity is ... limited to balloting, and the party organization—if existent at all—is dormant between elections periods"), and the party of *integration* (which "demands not only permanent dues-paying membership ... but, above all, an increasing influence over all spheres of the individual's daily life. . . . The party can count on its adherents; it has taken over a good part of their social existence."). This distinction was most applicable in the developed European democracies, where the parties of integration were also often associated with class alignments and informed by ideology.

Ten years later, Kirchheimer suggested that the parties of integration were turning into catch-all parties: "turning more fully to the electoral scene, trying to exchange effectiveness in depth for a wider audience and more immediate electoral success" (52). These parties found that close attachments to a class-based membership were "counter-productive since they deter segments of a potential nationwide clientele" (52). Besides, as Kirchheimer observed, describing the effects of the affluent society that emerged in the two decades after World War II, "there is enough community of interest between wage-and-salary earning urban or suburban white- and blue-collar workers and civil servants to designate them all as strategic objects of simultaneous appeals. . . . If the party cannot hope to catch all categories of voters, it may have a reasonable expectation of catching more voters in all those categories whose interests do not adamantly conflict" (53).

It appears that in North America, parties went from being parties of individual representation to becoming catch-all parties. In other words, the party of integration (or mass integration) seems not to have developed on this side of the Atlantic. In fact, on closer examination it seems that North American brokerage parties displayed the organization characteristics of the party of individual representation and the strategic approach to the electorate adopted by the catch-all party.

THE PROFESSIONALIZATION OF PARTY POLITICS

Beginning in the 1960s, just as Kirchheimer was observing a shift in some European parties towards becoming catch-all parties, brokerage politics in North America began to change with the emergence of another important factor: television. Campaigning and marketing via this medium required new skills and talents, and led to leaders being assessed, critiqued, and eventually chosen by their parties on the basis of a whole new set of criteria. The party leader as the pre-eminent member of a team of strong regional players gave way to the leader on whose performance the party's fortunes would depend. Carty has characterized Canadian party politics since 1963 as the age of **electronic politics**, which includes not just television but also the use of public-opinion polling as a tool for agenda-building and shaping campaign strategy. Similarly, Thorburn: "Most important is the capacity to build a sophisticated political machine that, using the modern electronic technologies of polling, communication and constant monitoring, can mobilize a national constituency" (138). It is not difficult to see how a politics based on constructing images of political leadership and a platform of issues based on the results of public-opinion polling reinforce many of the features identified above as central to brokerage politics, including the need for flexibility on issues and the focus on the broad public. In the electronic age this becomes true of every party, while paradoxically, the ability of parties actually to perform the integrating function once associated with brokerage politics seems weakened. The modern North American party seems to fit well Panebianco's reformulation of the catch-all party as the *electoral-professional* party— which Wolinetz describes as something "characterized by the centrality of professionals, its electoral orientation and weak vertical ties to its membership, the prominent role of elected representatives, financing through organized interests or government subsidies, and stress on issues rather than ideology" (146–147).

The refusal of parties to distinguish themselves in terms of ideology or long-term policy commitments forces the attention of both strategists and voters elsewhere, and in an era of electronic politics, this has meant a focus on leaders. Insofar as parties are only as popular as their leaders (or as popular as the images associated with their leaders), and because parties change leaders, or their leaders' public image changes, their popularity is inevitably volatile.

The surprising finish of the New Democratic Party in the 2011 Canadian election illustrates many of these points, from the volatility in the electorate to the effectiveness of the late NDP leader Jack Layton in matching his personality with a message that inspired great support but had less to do with policy ideas or ideology, and more with intangibles such as hope and a desire for something other than politics as usual, combined with a disillusionment in Quebec with the Bloc Québécois and, to a lesser degree, the Liberals.

PARTIES IN CONTEXT: THE ELECTORAL SYSTEM

The observation that brokerage parties succeed electorally also needs to be qualified; they do so only in part, and to some degree because of the electoral system. In an FPP/SMP electoral system, the brokerage party has needed to attract around 40 to 44 per cent of the vote to secure a majority government. By successfully identifying segments of the electorate and concentrating resources on winnable districts, a majority may be possible with less than 40 per cent. Under a PR system, a majority of seats requires having won a majority of the vote, which is difficult at the best of times in *any* system.

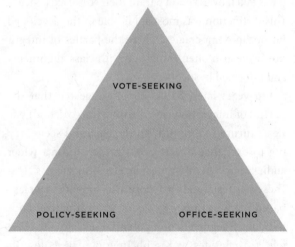

Figure 11.1

The electoral system makes a difference in the viability of smaller, more narrowly focused parties, dedicated to representing a particular segment of society or a particular set of causes. Such parties, by definition, have their sights set on attracting a limited portion of the electorate and, in an FPP/SMP setting, cannot expect to win very many seats, if any, and certainly have no hope of ever forming a government. In a PR setting, where such parties can expect a share of the legislature that corresponds to their share of supporters, the possibility of participating in a government is much more realistic. Potential supporters realize this and know that the party is not trying to represent a number of other interests as well.

Wolinetz has proposed classifying parties on the basis of three dimensions—policy-seeking, vote-seeking, and office-seeking—that incorporate some of the distinctions discussed above but are also sensitive to the electoral and institutional contexts in which parties might operate. Although the dimensions are "neither mutually exclusive nor entirely independent of each other, . . . parties giving higher priority to one orientation will typically be lower on at least one of the other two" (150). Parties could be placed within the triangle (see *Figure 11.1*) depending on the emphasis they give to each of the dimensions (see *Figure 11.2*).

PARTY SYSTEMS

Political parties operate within a number of contexts; one of the most important is the nature of the party system. The earlier discussion of electoral systems provided an introduction to this idea by noting that majoritarian electoral systems, and in particular FPP/SMP, tend to be associated with two-party systems, and PR electoral systems with multi-party systems. The previous discussion also noted the difference between the effective number of electoral parties and the effective

	POLICY-SEEKING PARTY	VOTE-SEEKING PARTY	OFFICE-SEEKING PARTY
PARTY CHARACTERISTICS	issue-oriented, priority on its policies, seeks to re-define the political agenda to bring about change in a variety of areas; includes parties with well-defined programs or ideologies as well as single-issue and protest parties	emphasis on winning elections; policies and positions are manipulated in order to maximize support; likely to rely on private or government funds for capital-intensive campaigns run by campaign professionals and marketing agencies	priority is securing government office, even if at the expense of policy goals or maximizing votes; should avoid policy positions that make it less attractive as a coalition partner and election strategies that attack possible partners too fiercely
EXAMPLES OF PARTIES DISPLAYING FEATURES	most northern European social democratic parties, many liberal and some Christian democratic parties, as well as green, left-libertarian, and new-right parties	the intermittently active Canadian parties whose policy commitments can vary depending on the leader, American parties, leader-centred parties in France, classical catch-all parties like the German CDU	parties participating in coalitions in consociational systems or in one-party dominant systems; the mainstream Belgian parties, all more concerned with being in office than with particular policies

Figure 11.2 (adapted from Wolinetz, 150–153)

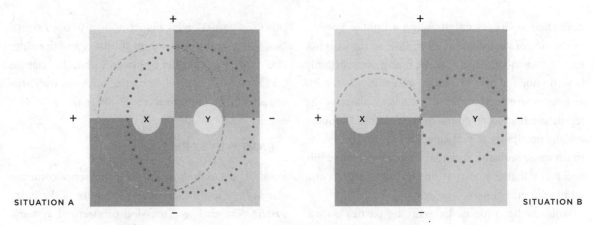

SITUATION A

SITUATION B

Figure 11.3

number of legislative parties. The interest in party systems in this chapter is for their tendency to promote or inhibit political parties in the various functions they might perform, such as vote-seeking, office-seeking, or policy-seeking.

A party system is a "set of political parties operating within a nation [regime] in an organized pattern, described by a number of party-system properties" (Lane and Ersson, 175). This system, most observers agree, is something larger than the sum of its parts, as the behaviour and characteristics of individual parties are shaped by the systems within which they operate and, more specifically, by the properties of those systems. In addition to the size of the system, discussed earlier, and with data provided in Chapter 5, two other party-system properties are worth a closer look: its ideological polarization and its capacity to express distinct issue dimensions.

POLARIZATION

More significant than the *number* of parties in a system is the *degree of choice* presented to the electorate. It hardly matters if there are two or 12 parties if the policy choices that they present to the voters are more or less indistinguishable. Conceptually, determining the degree of **polarization** entails plotting the policy positions of parties on an issue-dimension scale and observing the patterns that result. Consider two very different situations within a two-party system (*Figure 11.3*).

Situation A is very unpolarized, with parties X and Y approaching the middle on both ideological dimensions and appealing to a large group of common voters clustered around the middle. Situation B presents a polarized scenario where the immediate appeal of each party is to a distinct set of voters. Over the years it was common to refer to the US party system (Democrats and Republicans) as an example of A and the UK system (Tories and Labour) as an example of B (ignoring the nagging presence of a small party positioned between the Tories and Labour and winning seats). More recently, it seems that the US party system has become more polarized, and the British much less so. Situation B offers a much clearer choice to voters than A, but a single-party government in a polarized system will be extremely distasteful to its non-supporters, and changes in government will also involve significant

Far Left Parties   Socialist/Social Democrats   Green Parties   Liberal Parties   Conservatives/Christian Democrats   Far Right Parties

Figure 11.4

changes in policy. In the case where dominant parties "crowd the middle," a change in government may not make much difference in policy directions.

Most multi-party systems also appear to have a bipolar dimension, in which there is a family of parties on the right and another on the left. The lead party in a coalition is usually the largest party on the right or the largest party on the left. Centre parties, as a rule, tend to be smaller, but can often provide a link between parties from the two families. For most of the past 60 years, the German Liberal Democrats, holding about 10 per cent of the vote in the centre, have been potential partners for the two main parties, the Christian Democrats on the right and the Social Democrats on the left. With the emergence of the Green Party and another party on the left as a result of the reunification of Germany, the system has become more complicated. The French and Italian elections are both contested by an alliance of parties on the right and another on the left. Within each alliance, the range of positions covered by the member parties can sometimes be quite broad.

ISSUE DIMENSIONS

Figure 11.4 shows the range covered by parties winning seats in some of the most differentiated systems produced under PR systems (reflecting the most recent election in each regime, as of late 2011). In many of these systems, the simple left-right classification of parties is inadequate, quite apart from the fact that placing *any* party on *any* scale is a matter of judgment, not an exact science. Most right-left scales are largely concerned with party positions on socio-economic policy—issues that pertain mostly to class cleavages (see Chapter 9). Lijphart has argued that at least six other issue dimensions play a role in the stable democracies under consideration: the religious,

cultural-ethnic, urban-rural, regime support, foreign policy, and post-materialist dimensions. Parties with very similar positions on social and economic policy may disagree completely on matters of foreign policy, or, in the European context, be opposed on the benefits of membership in the European Community.

The presence of different issue dimensions poses intriguing challenges for government formation and explains many of the sources of internal division between coalition partners. Lijphart found a fairly strong correlation between the number of issue dimensions present and the number of effective parties. The higher the number of effective parties, the more issue dimensions a party system seems able to accommodate. This implies that multi-party systems will be better able to accommodate multiple issue dimensions (and thus, conceivably, accommodate social cleavages) than two-party (duopolistic) systems.

ELECTION CAMPAIGNS

Election campaigns are complicated affairs, with formal elements that are subject to laws and regulations, and informal elements that involve strategic decisions, professional judgment, and personalities. With respect to some of these elements, election campaigns can be compared across regimes, but other elements ensure that every campaign is a unique event. *Figure 11.5* suggests some of the variables that are relevant to the explanation of any particular election campaign.

SYSTEM VARIABLES

Electoral System

The electoral system can play a major role in the strategic decisions of parties with regard to the expenditure

SYSTEM VARIABLES	TECHNIQUE AND TECHNOLOGY	INEVITABLE INTANGIBLES
electoral system	messaging and marketing	personalities
type of government	polling, fundraising, and mobilizing	electoral history
campaign rules	use of the manifesto	state of the economy

Figure 11.5

of their campaign resources, a role not necessarily obvious to those within the system. For example, in majoritarian systems, particularly FPP, but to a lesser degree AV and TRS also, the emphasis is on winning seats by finishing first in as many districts as possible. However, those districts where voting for one's preferred candidate is virtually guaranteed to be a wasted vote are also, for the political parties of those candidates, lost districts. When electoral history, current polling results, and word on the street confirm that a party has no chance of finishing first, there is little point in diverting resources to this district from others where the party is in a close race and has a better chance of winning. In the modern SMP/FPP campaign, political parties prioritize the districts that they will focus on, where the leader will spend time, where the central party will provide support, where volunteers will be brought in for campaign blitzes, and where resources will generally be concentrated. Loyal candidates and their supporters in marginal districts will be left to their own devices.

By contrast, in a fully proportional system, *every* vote counts towards the final distribution of seats among the parties, whether it is cast in a district in which the party finishes first, or one in which it finishes last. It is in each party's interest to try to hold on to every supporter it has while trying to attract new electors to its position. The focus of the campaign will be less on trying to win particular districts and more on trying to increase the party's vote share by identifying and making a pitch to electors without party attachments or whose support for another party is soft.

Type of Government

In regimes where a single-party government is the norm, parties will campaign on the basis that they are going to win and form the government. The volatility of majoritarian electoral systems usually makes this at least a possibility for two or more of the parties. Even a party that has no hope of forming a government on its own is expected to campaign as if it could form the next government—to admit otherwise is almost to say "there's no reason to vote for us."

The pretence that *any* party might win an FPP/SMP election is aided by the fact that knowing how the political parties are polling is no sure guide to what their actual seat share will turn out to be. In a PR system, polling numbers give a much more probable picture of the final result. (This comparison assumes in each case—the SMP/FPP election and the PR election—that polling numbers are an accurate reflection of the voting intentions of those who will actually vote.) Most often, in a regime with a PR system, there will be no basis for *any* party to pretend it will win enough seats to govern alone. Most parties will campaign on the prospect of winning enough seats to be part of a post-election coalition, and the campaign will address what possible partnerships might be made and what compromises might be made to achieve those partnerships.

Campaign Rules

The electoral law will set out campaign rules, from setting the length of the campaign, to campaign finance regulations, to restrictions on advertising and polling. The more unregulated the campaign environment, the more likely it is that "anything goes," moral and cultural constraints not being likely to trump the chance of gaining a strategic advantage wherever possible. Almost everyone says that they hate attack ads and negative campaigns, yet these tactics persist because the evidence appears to show that they work.

TECHNIQUE AND TECHNOLOGY

Campaigning has always been about candidates presenting a message to the electors in an attempt to attract their votes. Four basic questions can be asked in this respect:

- What is the nature of the message?
- How is it delivered?
- Who delivers it?
- Who gets the message?

Three types of message tend to dominate: the presentation of a policy agenda (platform, manifesto) that appeals to voters' interests or ideological predispositions; an emphasis on the personality of the party leader, stressing values and affect ("best leader," "most trustworthy," "speaks for the people," "will make (name of jurisdiction) great/ prosperous/ a place to raise your family again"); or a focus on the deficiencies of the other party and/or its leader.

While these variations have always been the staples of electioneering, many observers believe that for various reasons, the first type of message (the appeal to the rational voter on the basis of a coherent set of policy commitments) has declined in favour of the latter two (which are really two halves of the same coin—emphasis on the personal qualities or deficiencies of the leaders). One factor is the emergence of television in the latter decades of the twentieth century as the dominant medium through which the campaign came to be conducted. In the twenty-first century, the emergence of new digital media and social networking has the potential to transform campaigning yet again.

Prior to the emergence of mass media, only a small percentage of the electorate would see or hear the party leaders, relying more on the local candidates and on the platform of ideas and proposals that all candidates of a particular party would be using to identify their party to the voter. With radio and then television, the leader could appear in every elector's living room every night. TV, as we have all learned, does not favour the detailed discussion of policy positions, but rather the delivery of short, carefully crafted messages that contain an effective **sound bite**. Each day on the campaign trail is designed around "the event," a carefully selected encounter with "real" people that is intended to provide favourable images of the leader/candidate and today's version of the message to be picked up by the media as something new and wonderful.

In majoritarian elections, one of the variables measured afterwards is the efficiency of each party's vote: how many votes did it take to elect each member? *Figure 11.6* shows the results for the 2011 Canadian election, in which vote efficiency ranged from 35,000 per seat for the Conservatives to 572,000 per seat for the Greens. (In some respects this is the issue of wasted votes looked at from the other side. In a PR system, of course, the efficiency of each party's votes should be about the same.) It is in any party's interest to increase the efficiency of its vote, and this is reflected in the campaign in several ways.

PARTY	SEATS	VOTES/SEAT
CON	166	35,152
NDP	103	43,810
LIB	34	81,855
BQ	4	222,856
GRN	1	572,095

Figure 11.6

There is no point, for example, in spending resources on committed supporters (preaching to the converted) except to extract their resources (money, time, or expertise) for the campaign. Similarly, targeting the committed supporters of other parties may be even more of a waste. The goal is to identify the soft supporters, the undecided, or the **flexible partisans** whose minds are not yet made up *and* are likely to vote. This portion of the electorate is likely to be larger in a regime with a majoritarian system than one with PR. Secondly, as noted above, a party in a majoritarian system would be foolish to treat all electoral districts equally; resources should be maximized where polling, historical voting patterns, and other types of intelligence indicate there is a realistic chance of making a gain (if not a win, it should at least be in a district where an improved showing might lay the groundwork for a future victory).

This kind of strategizing leads to a difference between the larger or "macro" campaign and all the targeted "micro" campaigns. The former, conducted through the national media by the leaders and the party's advertising and marketing consultants, is aimed at public opinion generally, attempting to build momentum or reverse any downward movement in the polls. The latter, conducted a few decades ago on a district-by-district basis, is now conducted on a polling area-by-polling area or demographic-by-demographic basis. The micro-campaign is all about identifying segments of the electorate and the messages to which they might be receptive in order to sell the party to them. Whether the message delivered to one section of the electorate is consistent with the message pitched to another (or to the general theme of the macro-campaign) is not necessarily a prime consideration.

The preceding describes perhaps too simplistically the way that modern communications technology and sophisticated marketing and polling techniques are used to spin the party and its candidates to a number of different audiences. Nonetheless, the professionalization of the business of winning elections and the reliance on special expertise, often grounded in the social sciences, should not be underestimated. Whether it is consistent with democracy is another matter entirely. Technology and technique are important in other ways, too, such as fundraising and mobilization of volunteers and supporters. At the time of writing this, it is only seven years since US Democratic presidential candidate Howard Dean revolutionized fundraising with his use of the Internet to solicit small donations from many contributors.

While the use of social media appears to be making serious inroads in both North American and European election campaigns, there are still large differences between the strategies that dominate in the former (with majoritarian systems) and the latter (with PR). It has been noted here more than once that in a PR system every vote (subject to legal thresholds) makes a difference—there are no wasted votes. All votes are worth pursuing, as much in a district in which the party is likely to finish fourth or fifth as in a district where it last finished a close second. Whereas the majoritarian instinct might be to target the latter, in a PR system where all votes count, it might make greater sense to target districts where the party has the most room for growth. European campaigns seem to be conducted much more on the macro level and are much more about communicating the contents of the parties' manifestos. The following characterization of the 2009 German election campaign, while admittedly one blogger's perception, has a ring of truth to it and describes a situation that one suspects could be applied to many other European jurisdictions:

> Though there are gradual differences among the parties of the German Bundestag, all five parties have organized their campaign in a top down manner. They all share the general principle that a party organization defines positions and politicians communicate these positions to the voter. They largely lack the aspect of interaction and self-organization, activation and participation on the side of the voters. Rather it seems like politicians and a few experts exchange their views and the voter finds himself in the position of a viewer. (http://sozlog.wordpress.com/2009/09/06/german-election-campaign-merkels-game/ [sozlog is the personal page of Dr. Tina Guenther, a sociologist teaching at the universities of Bamberg and Würzburg])

Similarly, a working paper by two Danish academics (Green-Pederson and Mortensen) reinforces this perception that European election campaigns are much more seriously focused on ideas than are North American contests: "To understand electoral outcomes we need to understand the dynamics that structure the issue emphases of political parties including the question about why political parties at election times focus on certain issues rather than others. Nevertheless, it is striking how little is actually known about the answers to this question in the literature on party competition."

One reason for the European campaign focus on policy ideas may be the limits on political advertising:

> ... political advertising is statutorily forbidden in the vast majority of Western European countries (e.g., Germany, France, Ireland, Sweden, UK, Malta, Norway, Denmark etc.). The traditional justification for this prohibition is that rich or well-established parties would be able to afford significantly more advertising time than new or minority parties. In this context, paid political advertising is considered as a discriminatory practice.

> However, parties are usually granted free airtime, often but not exclusively on public service broadcasters to present their programmes ... (EPRA, 2002)

In Sweden, the 2010 election was the first in which political parties were able to purchase television advertising time.

The ideas or programs being debated are found in the party manifesto, which, in the context of a PR system, is not simply a campaign document (as it is in North America) but the starting point for any post-election negotiations on coalition formation. One is tempted to conclude that this gives European parties an incentive to be much more serious about the ideas they put forward in their manifestos. A platform cannot consist simply of vague promises unsupported by program details or accurate estimates of the cost of their implementation. In a coalition context, the manifesto is the document brought to the table for negotiation of the policy agenda that will follow the election. In a majoritarian context, the manifesto is an election document that a winning party may decide has largely served its purpose and is not going to set the agenda going forward.

INEVITABLE INTANGIBLES

The three elements under this heading are, perhaps, rather self-explanatory. In *any* setting where human actors are involved, personality remains an unpredictable intangible. Many an election has turned on a momentary lapse in judgment or an inspired remark in the heat of debate. When the style of campaign depends so much on the party leader, it is inevitable that personalities will play a large role, and for this reason constitute an element in election campaigns that cannot be compared between regimes, or even between campaigns in the same regime. The same is surely also true of the role of electoral history. Past elections and past campaigns influence how current contests are structured and how electors come to the polls (or stay away) guided by their own experience of past elections, and the media are rarely content to let the past stay in the past. Finally, every election takes place not only at a certain point in the life of a parliament (i.e., the state) but also at a certain moment in the life of civil society. Many social factors can influence a campaign, but most prominent among them, in most cases, is the state of the economy. None of these intangibles is predictable, and it is for that reason that every election campaign is its own story.

ORGANIZED INTERESTS

However important political parties—and therefore membership in and support for them—may be, far more of us are likely to belong to an alternative vehicle of representation: the **interest group**, or **organized interest**. Like political parties, organized interests are usually presented as voluntary organizations that exist to further the interests of their members; unlike parties, they hope to accomplish this by influencing policymakers rather than by seeking political office. They are content to operate from within civil society.

While the work of most political parties is governed by the election cycle, which means that the extra-parliamentary party (in the constituencies) virtually disappears for a time in between elections, organized interests are engaged in a more continual calendar of activity. They may mobilize most intensely at any point in the political cycle, being driven primarily to political activity by policy considerations.

Most citizens are likely to belong to only one political party (if any) and at election time must choose between parties. By contrast, there is no limitation to membership in or support for organized interests. Multiple membership may sometimes mean that a citizen belongs to or supports groups that correspond to his or her interests, but whose purposes are not always complementary. On this basis, the claim of any group to represent a particular segment of society needs to be considered for what it really means—often, a very partial representation.

Not all organized groups are alike. The applicability of generalizations to these groups will vary according to the type of group being discussed. Many schemes for characterizing groups have been advanced, but at the risk of over-simplification, the remainder of this discussion will distinguish between **stakeholder groups**

	STAKEHOLDER GROUPS	ACTIVIST GROUPS
PURPOSE	economic interest	social or public concern
MEMBERSHIP BASE	occupational/class position	voluntary
SIZE OF MEMBERSHIP	fixed	unlimited
FINANCES	dues/fees	donations
ACCOUNTABLE TO MEMBERS?	more so	less so
ABLE TO MOBILIZE MEMBERS?	stronger	weaker
PARTNER WITH STATE?	more likely	less likely

Figure 11.7

and **activist groups**. The former emerge from the structure of the economy (and the state) and represent those with a common occupation, profession, or place in the employer/employee relationship (sometimes called capital and labour groups). The term "stakeholders" indicates that the purpose of these organizations is the very way of life of their members. By contrast, activist groups organize around issues, from the rights of political prisoners to ending homelessness to fighting climate change, and are supported by people from all walks of life, people whose interests on any number of other questions might be at odds. Also falling into this category are *public interest* groups such as Greenpeace, the Campaign for Nuclear Disarmament, and (in their own view, at least) the US National Rifle Association.

The relationship with its members is likely to be more direct with the stakeholder group; many of a group's activities can involve service to members, from education and training courses, to group health and insurance plans, to negotiating collective agreements, to certification and credentialing. In and of themselves, these activities are not very political, but they create a relationship between the association and its members that has political potential in at least two ways. One is the ability to mobilize the members on matters that affect their common interest. The other is to increase the value of the stakeholder group as a partner for the state.

A prime example is the professional association, which now commonly performs many tasks on behalf of the state. Self-regulating professions control membership by setting standards, examining qualifications, providing further training opportunities, and performing quality-control functions such as handling complaints and disciplining members. (In some cases, members of a profession may be doubly represented: by a regulatory college, to which all members belong in respect of their professional capacity, and by an association, which represents them in their capacity as employees and is concerned with their socio-economic interests.) The stakeholder group can assist government in the implementation of policy by ensuring that all group members are informed and understand the policy's implications, including any requirements for action on their part. Perhaps most importantly, stakeholder groups can provide valuable feedback on proposed legislation or regulatory changes. In other words, the resources that groups command and employ to influence public policy can be tapped into by policy-makers looking for alternative sources of expertise.

Activist groups are less about improving the lives of their supporters and more about using their supporters' resources to further a cause they believe in. Because the activist organization does not provide the same level of services for its supporters that the stakeholder group does for its members, the activist group's hold on its supporters and its level of interaction may be less strong and its ability to mobilize them politically more doubtful. On the other hand, the supporters of an activist group may far outnumber the members of the stakeholder group.

Consider the contrast between, for example, an association of conservation officers (stakeholder group) with its few hundred members and the Sierra Club (activist group), with its thousands of members. When budget cuts threaten the protection of wildlife habitat, which group will mobilize more effectively to oppose the policy? The activists will be less likely to mobilize on behalf of issues that directly affect conservation officers most, such as a change to their certification or re-certification requirements, but more likely to take an interest in a broader range of environmental issues than this particular stakeholder group. (The artificiality of this distinction between stakeholder and activist is demonstrated by asking to which category the Association of Anglers and Hunters should be assigned.)

The types of group also differ in their approaches concerning the matter of most concern here: their ability to influence public policy and thereby their effectiveness as vehicles of representation. This ability is a product of the strategies available to groups and the nature of the policy process in the regime in which they operate. *Figure 11.8* presents a range of strategies available to groups seeking to change or block a proposed policy measure or seeking change in existing policy. Some strategies, such as non-cooperation in the implementation of policy are most likely to be used by stakeholder groups; others, such as promising or withholding support to policy-makers or influencing public opinion (in order to influence policy-makers) may be the most effective approaches for activist groups.

The other major variable here is the policy process that exists in the regime. To anticipate the next few chapters, the policy process always involves a number of stages, and in liberal democracies under the rule of law, the authority for any policy can be identified (a) in a particular statute passed by the legislature or (b) in the discretion an existing statute gives to the executive to make a regulation, issue a directive, or prescribe guidelines (see *Figure 11.9*).

In the former case—legislative policy-making— the process can be simplified into three phases:

STAKEHOLDER GROUP	STRATEGY	ACTIVIST GROUP
●●●	PERSUASION(I): present reasons for policy-makers to re-think position	●
●●●	PERSUASION(II): present amendments to mitigate impacts of policy	●
●●	WITHHOLD SUPPORT: deny future funds, volunteers, votes to government party/parties	●●●
●●	SUPPORT: opposition party/parties with funds, volunteers, votes	●●●
●●●	BE NON-COOPERATIVE in the implementation of policy	○
●●●	BE DISRUPTIVE: work to rule, go on strike	○
●	CHALLENGE IN COURT: seek a judicial solution	●
●	INFLUENCE PUBLIC OPINION FOR OR AGAINST: marketing, demonstrating, civil disobedience	●●●●

FIGURE 11.8

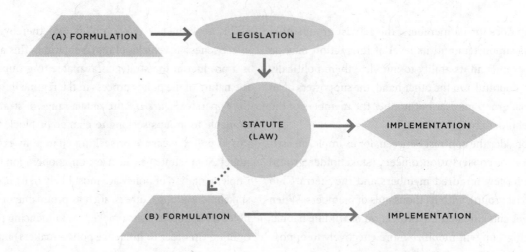

Figure 11.9

formulation, legislation, and implementation; in the latter case—administrative policy-making—it consists of two phases: formulation (on the basis of existing law) and implementation. The opportunities for organized interests to influence policy-makers will be found within these phases and will depend on the institutional structure of the process as well as the degree of openness with which the government follows that process.

The most open phase is the legislative phase, which takes place within an institutional setting that requires open debate and decision making. The formulation and implementation phases are in most cases much more secretive, although in many jurisdictions there are requirements for a period of notice to allow feedback on proposed administrative policy-making activities such as posting a new regulation. As a rough generalization, the stakeholder group is more likely than activist groups to have access to policy-makers during the formulation and implementation phases, particularly if the stakeholder group has an existing partnership with the state in some capacity.

On the other hand, the type of government will also make a difference. At one extreme is the single-party majority government in a parliamentary system. The policy formulation stage here is entirely outside the legislature; and a policy often does not become publicly known until it is first introduced to the legislature, or new regulations are posted. With its majority, the government will have little difficulty proceeding with its policy intentions; there will be no amendments or changes that it does not agree to accept. The influence of groups in this setting is often limited to whatever feedback the government decides to solicit during either the formation or the implementation phase. The executive dominance referred to in Chapter 6 is particularly at play with respect to the policy process, and a major challenge for interest groups is to be able to gain access to the executive at the right stages in the development of a policy.

At the other extreme are the separated powers of the Madisonian presidential model, in which the executive has no role in the legislature. Policy formation is much more public (and therefore accessible to influence) for two reasons. First and foremost, the development of policy takes place primarily in the legislature where, because the executive has no control, two developments are typical: any matter that attracts a legislative solution will attract many competing bills, to be compared, consolidated, or rejected by the legislators, and, for that reason, any bill that is passed has likely been amended a number of times since it was introduced. Second, when the executive (i.e., the White House) wishes to make a policy change that requires legislative action, it will need to make that known to legislators, and sometimes, like an interest group, it will need to influence public opinion to get legislators to co-operate. Because legislators are not subject to the party discipline that exists in a government/opposition setting, their votes on any matter are potentially subject to influence. Lobbying, the activities by which interests attempt to influence the votes of policy-makers, is much more prevalent in the US system because there are so many more policy-makers and so much more potential for those policy-makers to be able to block or change policy.

Falling in between the extremes of parliamentary executive dominance, on the one hand, and the legislative free-for-all of a separated-powers model is the policy process of European coalitional governments. Noteworthy here are (a) the degree to which policy formation takes place during first, the election process and second, the government-formation process that creates a coalition agreement on a policy agenda; (b) the closer relationships between organized interests and political parties in the European setting;

and (c) the higher degrees of **corporatism** in many of these regimes.

The concerted effort of organized interests to influence the policy agenda raises questions about their accountability and whether their activity is complementary or detrimental to the larger democratic process. How democratic are these organizations? How well do they represent their constituents? Some may indeed demonstrate a leadership clearly representative of and accountable to the membership, but others may simply solicit members' money and support without inviting or allowing any input over decisions about the issues that supposedly unite them. Stakeholder groups may score better on internal democracy than activist groups, in part because the governance structure—particularly in the case of those that partner with government—may be prescribed by law or regulation.

Some observers question the legitimacy of interest-group activity in the political process, usually on grounds of fairness, noting inequities in the resources that groups are able to draw on. Similar concerns about the way money talks in the political process attend the development of lobbying firms, who sell their ability (whether through personal acquaintance or expertise) to connect clients with policy-makers. The greater the apparent influence of lobbyists, the greater the calls for public registration of lobbyists and full disclosure of their clients and the issue positions they have been hired to promote.

CORPORATISM

The model whereby groups compete in civil society and the political process to influence policy-makers is known as **pluralism**. In this model the participation of

Sandstone carving, Ontario Legislative Building. Toronto, Ontario.

groups in policy discussions is informal and ad hoc, dependent in part on the strategies and styles of the political party or parties in power.

From the pluralist perspective, so long as there is fairness in the competition of interests, no one interest or set of interests will be able to dominate, and policy outputs generally, over time, represent a compromise between the favoured positions of different interests. In the minds of some, this is as close to the "will of the majority" or the "common good" as any other mechanism is likely to produce in today's complex societies. Pluralism has been championed most strongly in the United States, where its roots are traced back to the early Federalists, in particular to James Madison. Critics argue, of course, that the playing field of organized interests is *not* level, that interest-group activities—whether lobbying or mobilizing public opinion—are expensive, and that the advantage rests with those who have the most resources.

In corporatism, the place of organized interests is not left to haphazard competition but is institutionalized.

Corporatism is the regular, official participation of organized interests in the formation of public policy. Typically, corporatism is described as trilateral (or tripartite) negotiation and consensus between representatives of the state, the business community, and organized labour on matters of economic policy. It is also possible for other actors such as farmers or consumers to be involved, depending on the policy under consideration; a relevant example is the government, which funds education expenditures, sitting down with representatives of school boards (the formal employers) and teachers' unions (the employees) to negotiate salary, benefits, and working conditions across the jurisdiction. Another would be representatives of the auto manufacturers, the CAW (Canadian Auto Workers union), and the government negotiating an industrial strategy for the auto industry.

Ideally, the non-state actors are agents of **peak associations** (or **umbrella organizations**), which are granted a representational monopoly. This means that interest groups are organized hierarchically on the basis of functional (class) interests (like labour or business or agriculture) and the umbrella organization for each functional group is recognized by the state as speaking for all the bodies and their members falling under that umbrella (see *Figure 11.10*). This often means that there is an extra-parliamentary institution or forum (a council or chamber, etc.) where these interests meet, negotiate, and come to decisions. The aim of corporatism clearly is to ensure that all major interests are involved in the formation of a social consensus on policy—which should increase the likelihood that policy will be acceptable to the public at large. However, those interests that fall outside the functional or institutionally recognized categories—such as consumer groups or environmental groups—and whose interests may well be affected by the decisions made will not be included here.

Gallagher, Laver, and Mair emphasize that corporatist interaction is not simply about making policy decisions: "The stress ... on policy *implementation* is what sets corporatism fundamentally apart from other systems for involving interest groups in political decision making" (240, emphasis added). This, in turn, means that the peak associations must truly represent the particular sector of society for which they stand and "be able to police their membership" (241). Of course, if these conditions were not the case, the state would have no incentive to engage in corporatist arrangements.

Obviously, the degree of corporatism can vary, depending on the degree to which interest-group participation in policy formation is formalized, *and* depending on the definition of corporatism that is used. Siaroff has defined corporatism as "the

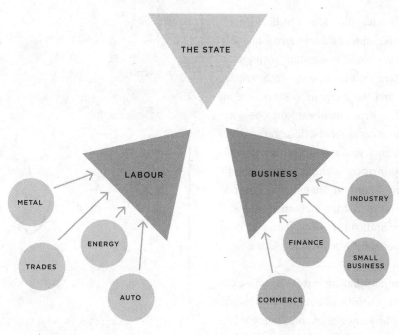

Figure 11.10

co-ordinated, co-operative, and systematic management of the national economy by the state, centralized unions, and employers (these latter two co-operating directly in industry), presumably to the relative benefit of all three actors" (177). Within the context of "an advanced industrial society and democratic polity" corporatism represents a model of *integrated* management of the economy. Analyzing ratings of advanced industrial economies in almost two dozen separate studies, Siaroff has produced a frequently cited ranking of corporatism scores for these regimes, as well as "integration scores" for four separate decades in the late twentieth century. His corporatism scores for the countries in the data set of this book are presented in *Figure 11.11*. They confirm what many have suggested, that corporatism is strongest in Western Europe and weakest in North America and Mediterranean European regimes.

Moreover, Siaroff's integration scores indicate that it is possible for some regimes to achieve a considerable measure of political economic integration without displaying the centralized features of corporatist tripartism. Siaroff argues that the integration scores are an improvement on the corporatism rankings because they are focused "on roles and behaviour rather than the broader supposedly favourable structures and contexts" (199). This is consistent with the observation by Gallagher, Laver, and Mair that "an effective corporatist system involves far more than mere institutions. It rests upon a history and culture of collective accommodation that cannot simply be invented as the need arises" (246).

In countries where corporatism is weak or non-existent, the term has a bad reputation, being linked sometimes to fascism or to authoritative one-party states. This is state corporatism and should be distinguished

	corporatism scores	integration scores (mid-1990s)
AUSTRIA	5.000	4.625
NORWAY	4.864	4.625
SWEDEN	4.674	4.625
NETHERLANDS	4.000	4.000
DENMARK	3.545	4.250
GERMANY (WEST)	3.543	4.125
SWITZERLAND	3.375	4.125
FINLAND	3.295	4.375
ICELAND	3.000	2.875
ISRAEL	3.000	3.500
JAPAN	2.912	3.625
BELGIUM	2.841	3.750
IRELAND	2.000	2.625
NEW ZEALAND	1.955	2.375
AUSTRALIA	1.680	3.000
FRANCE	1.674	2.250
UNITED KINGDOM	1.652	2.000
PORTUGAL	1.500	2.375
ITALY	1.477	3.000
SPAIN	1.250	2.000
CANADA	1.150	1.875
UNITED STATES	1.150	2.125
GREECE	1.000	2.000

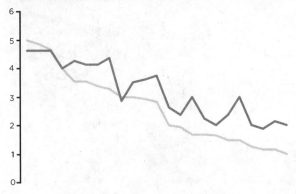

Source: Siaroff, Table 5, p. 198.

Figure 11.11

from the societal corporatism of Western Europe, which is entirely compatible with political pluralism. Also, and not surprisingly, in countries where organized labour is weak and business interests are strong, like the United States, corporatism is not seen to be an attractive option.

What distinguishes pluralism and corporatism is the nature of the interaction among competing non-state elites, and the nature of the interaction between non-state and state actors. Both are essentially about the role of elites in the policy process. Regardless of their concerns with consensus, or a fair representation of social diversity, or balanced competition, neither is fundamentally democratic in the sense of inviting or requiring participation by non-elites. If democracy is not possible in the longer term in our changing world, or if the degree of democracy possible will always be constrained by other factors, then pluralism or corporatism (or something in between?) may be an important alternative. In either case, the organized group provides an alternative mode of representation to that provided by the political party.

SOCIAL MOVEMENTS

Informing political parties and organized interests and often providing linkages between them are the much more loosely structured bodies known as **social movements**, or more commonly *new social movements* (NSMs). NSMs unite and mobilize sections of society in a cross-cutting fashion, appealing often to members of different socio-economic classes, and tend to be less formally organized than stakeholder and activist groups. Some NSMs, such as the anti-globalization movement, may include a coalition of diverse political parties, trade unions, and occupational groups among

their supporters. Some NSMs are about creating awareness of the challenges facing a specific population, such as persons with disabilities, or recognizing and breaking down stereotypes concerning a segment of society, such as the **LGBT** (lesbian, gay, bisexual, and transgender) community, and (in either case) working to enhance rights and promote an acceptance of differences that is reflected in enlightened policy-making. Two of the social movements that have generated the greatest attention over the last fifty years are feminism and environmentalism.

FEMINISM

Some might prefer to treat feminism as an ideology because it has a vision, a perspective, and a program. On the other hand, there are many feminisms, and in some cases these are variations on the ideologies discussed above: liberal feminism, Marxist feminism, and anarcho-feminism, to name a few. Still other currents, particularly radical and postmodern feminism, appear to reject any accommodation with ideologies from the past. The approach here is to highlight what all these feminisms share to the degree that they have a common perspective.

Patriarchy

Feminists see traditional and most contemporary social relations as expressions of patriarchy, a structure of domination of women by men. The primary goal is to dismantle patriarchy and create gender equality. Okin defines gender as "social institutionalizations of sexual difference" and notes that much of this sexual difference is not immutably biological but "socially constructed"(67). Feminists work to overturn these constructions of sexual difference that have been institutionalized at women's expense, seeking to create a structural equality in which women, as women, have full autonomy. In this, they often make common cause with members of the LGBT community who face similar challenges with the social constructs of sexual difference (as opposed to sexual preference). Achieving feminist goals requires action on a variety of policy issues such as pay (and promotion) equity, reproductive choice, and child care.

The Personal Is (The) Political

One distinguishing mark of feminism has been its examination of the dynamics of power within what "mainstream" political science usually treats as the private sphere—that is, families, marriages, and sexual relations. This focus is captured in the phrase "the personal is (the) political," which rejects the more orthodox dichotomy of private/public. "Feminists of all stripes insisted that what goes on in private, personal, 'emotional' life is as deeply political as what happens in the 'rational' public sphere of economic production and formal government. Thanks in part to their research and activism, we better comprehend how they all intertwine—with one another, and with unequal, gendered divisions of labour and power" (Rossi, 6).

Feminism's adherents differ in the intensity of their involvement (in this case, the degree to which their perspective is wholly feminist). First-wave feminism sought to increase opportunities for women within the existing structures and processes of capitalist liberal (patriarchal) society without challenging their legitimacy. Important strides were made in terms of gaining for women rights that were previously lacking or inadequately enforced, but many felt this was insufficient. Second-wave feminists challenged the very structures

by which gender inequality has been reinforced and perpetuated. For its more radical adherents, second-wave feminism is a revolutionary perspective that calls for a fundamentally different kind of society and social relations.

German Green Party Poster: "Every second representative is a woman."

Women in Politics

One effect of feminism on the narrowly defined political realm has been an increase in the number of women in politics. In some respects, this has been even more noticeable in the number holding high political office. Nonetheless, progress is slow and women remain seriously under-represented in politics, even in the most "advanced" democracies (see the InterParliamentary Union [IPU], *Women in National Parliaments* [www.ipu.org/wmn-e/world.html]. In addition, there have been few signs of a "feminization" of the political process, a shift to a less confrontational, adversarial, and partisan politics that was predicted would accompany the rise of women to positions of power.

ENVIRONMENTALISM

Many date the beginning of the environmental movement to the public awareness created by *Silent Spring*, Rachel Carson's 1962 book documenting the effect on the environment of pesticides, herbicides, and other man-made chemicals. *Ecology* (the science) supplies the perspective, a way of seeing the world that informs *environmentalism* (the political movement).

Lives in Balance

The ecological perspective stresses interdependence, insisting that the relationship between humanity and nature be considered with the same systems approach that examines how species and their environments move in and out of balance with each other. Ecologists observe how human activity in the world upsets the balance between creatures and their environment by destroying habitats, polluting the environment, using up non-renewable resources, transforming the climate, crowding out other species by overpopulating the planet, and so forth. As humanity progressively makes the world a less hospitable place for *all* life forms, the diversity of which is steadily declining, the quality of life lived by humans is diminished, the survival of humanity threatened. Ultimately, as the ecological perspective reminds us, there is a finite limit on the ability of the planet to sustain life. The human population and its consumption of resources cannot grow ad infinitum. In the past two decades, an increasing emphasis has been placed on global warming and the impacts of climate change, which threaten to transform the entire planet.

The Challenges of Development

The concern of environmentalism, informed by this ecological perspective, is to slow down and eventually reverse the trend of an ever-increasing human consumption of resources and human domination and degradation of "the environment." This issue is not confined to the economically developed "post-industrial" economies, but also intersects with the question of uneven economic development and efforts by many of the world's nations to "catch up" to the standard of living of advanced industrial societies. Accelerating growth in the developing world economies means a tremendous increase in the consumption of resources and the production of associated wastes. Much attention has focused on the notion of "sustainable development," a term implying a modernization and enrichment of life that is neutral in its effects on the environment, or, as defined by the United Nations' Report of the World Commission on Environment and Development: "development that integrates production with resource conservation and enhancement, and that links both to the provision for all of an adequate livelihood base and equitable access to resources" (chapter 1, para. 47).

As this indicates, environmentalism challenges the very economic and political-economic assumptions that have been central to the ideologies of the modern world. Conservatism, liberalism, and socialism alike have accepted the desirability of economic growth and development without limits. According to dominant schools of economic thought and most economic policy-makers, an economy is only "healthy" when it is growing. Environmentalism is a post-industrialist and post-materialist ideology; a popular slogan among Greens has been "neither right nor left nor in the centre," indicating their distinction from all established parties.

Environmentalist Strategies

The program of environmentalism is diverse, comprehensive, and still very much contested. There is consensus on the need to reduce, if not eliminate, the production and eventual release of toxic substances into the environment, but how this should be done is a question of competing strategies: While some look for non-toxic alternatives, others stress eliminating the need for such substances in the first place. While some emphasize the use of regulatory mechanisms, others promote the use of market mechanisms to motivate producers to become more "green." Some debate whether it is more appropriate to develop new ecologically sound technologies, such as alternative energy sources, or work to change human consumption habits. All environmentalists challenge new development that is harmful to the environment; all would eliminate those activities currently harming the environment. Is this enough? Does saving the planet require more drastic changes in lifestyle? Must humans eventually consider a process of deindustrialization?

CONCLUSION

Just as governments are several (i.e., the state exists at several levels), so too in modern society are there many vehicles of representation to serve citizens. Although they may sometimes compete among themselves, these vehicles ultimately serve the public in different ways, in different contexts. It is not necessary to choose between political parties, organized interests, or social movements; ideally, citizens can turn to each as the context and issues seem to require. None will serve perfectly; the point, perhaps, is to recognize how the ways in which they do serve us might be improved, and generate the will to make such improvements.

It should also be clear that in contemporary society political activity is organized activity. Whether it is political parties, stakeholder groups, activist groups, or the campaign organizations that support one side or the other of a referendum question, organization is critical to the marshalling and employment of the resources that are necessary to communicate with a mass public. This is the inevitable consequence of the size and complexity of the communities in which we live today. The challenge is to ensure that the representative organizations remain responsive and accountable to those they claim to represent.

REFERENCES

Carty, R. K. *Canadian Political Party Systems*. Peterborough, ON: Broadview Press, 1988.

Clarke, Harold D., et al. *Absent Mandate*. 3rd ed. Toronto: Gage, 1996.

Duverger, Maurice. *Political Parties*. New York: Wiley, 1963.

EPRA (European Platform of Regulatory Agencies). *Working Group 2: Political Advertising*. Working Paper EPRA/2002/09 (October 2002). Web.

Gallagher, Michael, Michael Laver, and Peter Mair. *Representative Government in Modern Europe*. New York: McGraw-Hill, 1995.

Green-Pedersen, Christoffer, and Peter B. Mortensen. "Issue Competition and Election Campaign Avoidance *and* Engagement." Aarhus University. Aarhus, Denmark. N.P. (December 2010): 39 pp.

Jackson, Robert J. and Doreen Jackson. *Politics in Canada: Culture, Institutions, Behaviour and Public Policy*. 4th ed. Scarborough, ON: Prentice Hall, 1997.

Kirchheimer, Otto. "The Catch-All Party." *The West European Party System*. Ed. Peter Mair. Oxford: Oxford University Press, 1990. 50–60.

Lane, Jan-Erik, and Svante O. Ersson. *Politics and Society in Western Europe*. London: Sage, 1991.

Lawson, Kay. *Political Parties and Linkage: A Comparative Perspective*. New Haven, CT: Yale University Press, 1980.

Lijphart, Arend. *Electoral Systems and Party Systems: A Study of Twenty-Seven Democracies, 1945–1990*. Oxford: Oxford University Press, 1994.

Malcolmson, Patrick, and Richard Myers. *The Canadian Regime*. Peterborough, ON: Broadview Press, 1996.

Neumann, Sigmund. "The Party of Integration." *The West European Party System*. Ed. Peter Mair. Oxford: Oxford University Press, 1990. 46–49.

Okin, Susan Moller. "Gender, the Public and the Private." *Political Theory Today*. Ed. David Held. Stanford, CA: Stanford University Press, 1991. 67–90.

Powell, G. Bingham. *Contemporary Democracies*. Cambridge, MA: Harvard University Press, 1982.

Rossi, Michèle L. "Democracy and Care Unbound: On Feminism's Abiding Political Value." *Democratic Left* (Spring 2003): 4–10.

Siaroff, Alan. "Varieties of Parliamentarianism in the Advanced Industrial Democracies." *International Political Science Review*. 24.4 (October 2003): 445–464.

Thorburn, H. G. *Party Politics in Canada*. 6th ed. Scarborough, ON: Prentice Hall, 1991.

United Nations. *Our Common Future*. Report of the World Commission on Environment and Development. 1987. Web [www.un-documents.net/wced-ocf.htm] accessed November 5, 2011.

Wolinetz, Stephen B. "Beyond the Catch-all Party: Approaches to the Study of Parties and Party Organization in Contemporary Democracies." *The Future of Political Parties*. Ed. Juan Linz, Jose Ramon Montero, and Richard Gunther. Oxford: Oxford University Press, 2002. 136–165.

FURTHER READINGS

Debus, Marc. "Party Competition and Government Formation in Multi-level Settings: Evidence from Germany." *Government and Opposition* 43.4 (October 2008): 505–538.

Dunn, Kris. "Legislative Diversity and Social Tolerance: How Multiparty Systems Lead to Tolerant Citizens." *Journal of Elections, Public Opinion and Parties* 19.3 (August 2009): 283–312.

Dür, Andreas, and Dirk de Bièvre. "The Question of Interest Group Influence." *Journal of Public Policy* 27.1 (May 2007): 1–12.

Gauja, Anika. "State Regulation and the Internal Organisation of Political Parties: The Impact of Party Law in Australia, Canada, New Zealand and the United Kingdom." *Commonwealth and Comparative Politics* 46.2 (April 2008): 244–261.

Kenig, Ofer. "Classifying Party Leaders' Selection Methods in Parliamentary Democracies." *Journal of Elections, Public Opinion and Parties* 19.4 (November 2009): 433–447.

Leuprecht, Christian, and James McHugh. "Fixed Election Cycles: A Genuine Alternative to Responsible and Responsive Government?" *Commonwealth and Comparative Politics* 46.4 (November 2008): 415–441.

Taagepera, Rein. "The Tailor of Marrakesh: Western Electoral Systems Advice to Emerging Democracies." Center for the Study of Democracy, University of California, Irvine.

White, Jonathan, and Lea Ypi. "Rethinking the Modern Prince: Partisanship and the Democratic Ethos." *Political Studies* 58.4 (October 2010): 809–828.

CHAPTER 12

The Official Response: Public Policy and Administration

...WHICH PROVIDES THE READER WITH

- opening considerations about the degree of control or chaos in the making of public policy
- a look at who does what in the various stages of a "policy cycle"
- discussion of different approaches to vertical and horizontal policy-making
- examination of the role of bureaucracy and a professional public service

People look to the state to solve problems or to take action on pressing issues, and one way to think of the state is as a collection of resources organized for solving public problems. The two preceding chapters were concerned with the opportunities that citizens have to bring their concerns, their ambitions, and their talents from civil society into the state/government. Whatever the personal motivations for this political participation, the larger purpose is to generate outcomes in response to situations that require the exercise of public authority for their resolution. There is always debate about what kinds of demands should be made of the state, or what tasks the state should be set to do (and elections are often an important part of this debate). This dialogue is a sign of regime health in that it suggests the public has not lost interest in the state, nor has the state made such a discussion irrelevant.

As noted previously, the state's scope of activity greatly expanded in the latter two-thirds of the twentieth century. Appropriately, then, there has been much interest in the past few decades in the problem-solving activity of the state, its organization for doing so, its efficacy and efficiency, and its coordination and rationales. This interest is the study of **public policy**.

Pal has defined policy as "a course of action or inaction chosen by public authorities to address a given problem or set of problems" (2). Note the important point that policy can sometimes be a decision *not* to act; policy-makers may consider some problems but find themselves unwilling or unable to attempt a solution to them. Recognizing the difference between deliberate inaction and neglect is not always easy, nor conducive to study, so most policy analysis focuses on the actions rather than the inactions of the state. Pal's definition also refers to a "course of action," which implies a relatively coherent or coordinated set of discrete interventions.

Policy is made in response to problems in the environment of the policy actors, and it involves decisions at various levels. The commitment to become involved will also require an agreement about the goal or purpose to be achieved (e.g., reducing health-care costs, increasing consumer safety, maintaining levels of service to low-income seniors). When committing to a goal or specific set of outcomes, the means with which to achieve these purposes must be identifed and selected. The means that governments employ to achieve their purposes are usually several, ideally coordinated into a coherent strategy of action. Whether it involves providing services, transferring resources, facilitating private actions, or delivering public goods, much of what governments do is captured by the term *programs*. Student loans, legal aid, labour-market retraining, social assistance, and assistance to small and medium-sized enterprises are examples of government programs. Policy decisions may be about whether to create or end a program, but they are more often about making changes to existing programs. Programs are the means or instruments through which governments implement policy, and are the ongoing legacy of policy decisions past.

Part of the study of public policy is observing how and by what means specific policies come to be chosen, implemented, and administered. Of particular interest is the **policy process**, the stages linking the behaviour of various political actors within a regime's institutional structures to deliver policies that are designed to produce an identifiable outcome. Obviously, within any state, such a process depends on the institutional structure, the political culture, the experience of political actors, the resources available, and other relevant factors.

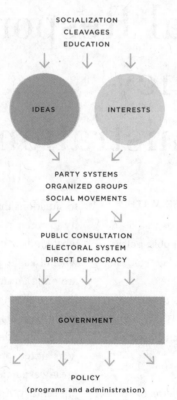

SOCIALIZATION
CLEAVAGES
EDUCATION

IDEAS   INTERESTS

PARTY SYSTEMS
ORGANIZED GROUPS
SOCIAL MOVEMENTS

PUBLIC CONSULTATION
ELECTORAL SYSTEM
DIRECT DEMOCRACY

GOVERNMENT

POLICY
(programs and administration)

Figure 12.1

TWO THEORIES ABOUT PUBLIC POLICY

The definition of public policy, the idea of a policy process (especially when this is conceptualized as a **policy cycle**), and much of the study and literature on public policy rest on the idea that governmental outputs are deliberately chosen, that someone is "in charge," and that there is control over what emerges. Simply put, this is less certain than it appears, depending on circumstances, and the degree of control implied by the discussion of public policy is more or less so, rather than absolutely so. Public policy is a field where analytic distinctions abound.

One theory of public policy, then, employs an ideal-type model of the process, in which policy is designed, implemented, administered, and evaluated, and then, with an appropriate revision or redesign of policy, the process begins again. This theory views the policy process as a policy cycle. Even the briefest search of public-policy literature reveals the diversity in models of the policy cycle, differing in terms of both the number of stages and the conceptualization of what those stages are. This diversity is a clue to the artificiality of any presentation of a policy cycle. Nonetheless, to provide a basis for discussion, *Figure 12.2* presents yet another policy cycle:

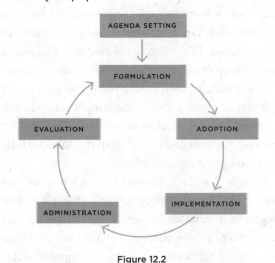

Figure 12.2

Any diagrammatic presentation of a policy cycle obscures the following:

- every stage includes a number of steps, each representing a decision point or an action that may alter the policy;
- the transition from one stage (or step) to another often involves a transfer of

responsibility from one institution to another, or from one set of actors to another *within* an institution;
- within many of these stages, there is a potential role for non-state actors (the process does not necessarily remain within the control of the government at all times); and
- depending on the constitutional system (parliamentary, Madisonian separation of powers, Latin American semi-presidentialism) or type of government (single-party majority, minority, coalition), the typical route or path through the steps and stages may differ considerably.

In other words, when one looks more closely inside each of these boxes labelled "formulation" or "implementation" or "administration," it becomes tempting to argue that sometimes policy *just happens,* that there is no overall coordination or control from beginning to end. The truth, arguably, lies somewhere between the view of the policy cycle as a coherent process of design and execution and the view that it is a chaotic ensemble of uncoordinated transactions involving state and non-state actors.

POLICY COMMUNITIES AND POLICY NETWORKS

As noted, the scope of the activities contained in the policy cycle is not confined to the state/government, but also involves non-state actors, such as stakeholder and activist groups, think tanks, non-governmental organizations, academic institutes and academics, and other levels of state/government. Two useful concepts for thinking about the broader range of possible activity in the public-policy process are the **policy** community and the **policy network**. A policy community is all those actors, governmental and private, who "have a continuing stake in, and knowledge about, any given policy field or issue" (Doern and Phidd, 76–77). In other words, for any **policy sector**, such as health care, or education, or national defence, a cluster of institutions, associations, and individuals has an ongoing interest in whatever policy is made in this sector. The policy community is often further divided into the **sub-government** and the **attentive public** (Pross, 120). This is largely equivalent to a distinction between those who make policy and those who attempt to influence policy-makers.

The sub-government is a relatively small group that includes the minister of the relevant department, senior departmental bureaucrats, officials from central coordinating agencies or departments, and, sometimes, key parliamentarians or representatives from partnering stakeholders. These individuals are linked by their responsibility (in one way or another) for policy.

The attentive public is a much larger collection of individuals and organizations with interests that are affected by policy decisions in a particular sector. The most important segment of the attentive public is usually the organized interests directly concerned, such as activist groups, professional associations, and corporate interests. Academics, private-institution scholars, and journalists provide other key components. Officials of other governments, domestic or foreign, opposition politicians, and interested individuals with no institutional affiliation may round out the policy community. What they all share, in addition to their interest in the policy sector, is their willingness to influence policy outcomes. Importantly, many of them will be seeking different and sometimes incompatible solutions to their problems.

As might be guessed, the term policy network is used to describe relationships that form between the actors in the policy community. In the Canadian literature, it has been applied to the interactions that develop between the sub-government and actors in the attentive public, particularly organized interests. Pross suggests that networks bring together people with common ideas and approaches to policy: "Just as a village divides into camps over divisive issues, so policy communities divide into networks" (120). Atkinson and Coleman developed an influential classification of networks, focusing on the structural characteristics of the relationship between the state (sub-government) and organizational interests (groups). This typology, later employed by Coleman and Skogstad in a collection of case studies, focused on the number of "actors" in the sub-government and in the attentive public of any particular policy community, and where there are multiple actors in any segment, the degree of co-operation or competition between them. *Figure 12.3*, adapted from Pal (112), displays some of these networks.

Outside Canada, as Skogstad notes, it is more common to distinguish "policy networks in terms of their degree of integration, membership, and distribution of resources among members. At one end of this continuum are policy communities, as integrated, stable and exclusive policy networks; at the other end are issue networks of loosely connected, multiple, and often conflict-ridden members" (208). Because these networks are determined only in part by the institutional structure of the state, they will vary from policy community to policy community, depending a great deal on the makeup of the particular attentive publics involved. Ultimately, mapping these networks is useful in explaining, in part, how some segments within

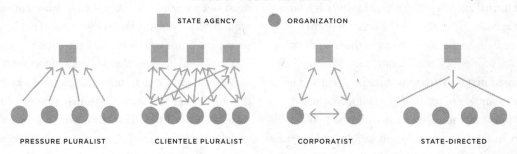

TYPES OF POLICY NETWORKS

■ STATE AGENCY ● ORGANIZATION

PRESSURE PLURALIST   CLIENTELE PLURALIST   CORPORATIST   STATE-DIRECTED

Figure 12.3

society succeed in exerting influence on the formation of public policy, and, perhaps, why some are not so successful.

WHO DOES WHAT: EXAMINING THE POLICY CYCLE

All of the considerations above point to one conclusion: there is not *one* policy process but many. Nonetheless, whether the policy process is structured or unstructured, coherent or chaotic, and irrespective of the makeup of the particular policy communities and networks, there are six stages that deserve closer consideration.

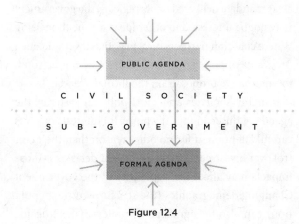

Figure 12.4

AGENDA FORMATION

If it is appropriate to view the state as a problem-solving mechanism, and policies as deliberate responses to societal problems, it is important to consider *whose* problems catch the attention of policy-makers and how they do so. This stage of the policy process is often identified as the business of **agenda formation**. If the public policy agenda is conceived of as a list of possible problems looking for state solutions, with those items most likely to receive a response at the top of the list, it matters who controls that list, how items make it onto the list, how items move to the top of the list, and even more nuanced considerations such as whose view of the problem makes it to the list.

In *Figure 12.2*, agenda setting is placed outside the policy cycle proper. This is to permit the distinction between the **public agenda**, the list of highly visible problems in which the public is interested, and the **formal agenda**, the list of problems that policy-makers have noticed and prioritized for consideration (see *Figure 12.4*). Clearly, **policy-making** requires that an issue reach the formal agenda, and it may or may not do so by first becoming an important item on the public agenda (see Cobb, Keith-Ross, and Ross). An issue may become high on the public agenda and yet never make it onto the formal agenda. Some problems arrive on the formal agenda without ever having been on the public agenda. This is where the concept of the policy community is useful, since many of the issues that are candidates for policy consideration are identified and articulated first by a group within the attentive public or from somewhere within the sub-government.

It is important to realize that while the policy community in any sector is united in its interest in getting "policy attention," different groups within the community may be working to achieve very different solutions. Patent-drug manufacturers and generic-drug manufacturers share some common policy goals, but also, on key issues, have strongly opposing interests. So too, the various types of childcare providers (non-profit or commercial), different classes of nurses (registered, practical, or extended), or various financial institutions (banks, trust companies, and credit unions) have a common general policy interest, but they favour specific solutions that are in their own interest when it comes to the details on narrower matters. The nature of the policy network(s) within a community may determine who succeeds in placing their issue on the formal agenda.

Some groups succeed at influencing policy-makers by influencing the broader public first and mobilizing public demand for policy action. Some may wish to influence policy-makers without arousing the attention of other interested parties in the public. There are numerous strategies for moving issues from the public to the formal agenda, or onto the formal agenda while bypassing the public agenda. Some issues will originate with state actors, who may be able to use their privileged access to the sub-government to place their concerns on the formal agenda.

When policy proposals arrive on the formal agenda having bypassed the public agenda, policy-makers must decide whether the policies being considered require public support for their successful resolution. If so, the challenge will be to move the issue from the formal to the public agenda and build support for it there.

The factors that determine which issues arrive on the formal agenda vary. Obviously, the ideology of those in government and those who advise them is an important factor. So, too, is where the government stands with respect to the electoral cycle: the prudent course being to take painful measures early in the cycle, to start delivering new programs, providing tax cuts, and making infrastructure investments as the election approaches. The ability to manage popular and potentially unpopular but necessary policy decisions in a strategic manner may be supported or undermined by the state of the economy. Unfortunate indeed is the government that takes office just as the economy sputters, having no responsibility for the state of affairs, but in danger of being associated with the downturn, or unable to deliver on the policies it promised because of the changed economic circumstances.

It may be that a government comes into power with its formal agenda more or less set. Where there has been a detailed election manifesto presented and a clear mandate delivered on its policies, the government may not be interested in other ideas for the time being. Where coalition partners have negotiated very detailed programs of policy positions, there may not be room for alternative proposals on the formal agenda.

In many societies and most political systems, the agenda of the economically powerful interests receives careful attention, if for no other reason than their control over investment and employment decisions whose impacts may affect the popularity of the government. Changing demographics (the structure of the population) can also be significant if policy-makers decide to concentrate on policies that are going to appeal to those most likely to vote (here is an example where compulsory voting can mean more than just a high turnout on election day), or, where policy decisions will affect different generations in an unequal manner, choose the option favouring the generation with the most votes.

Finally, moving an item onto the formal agenda is no guarantee (a) that the government will take action, or (b) that in taking action, it will implement the solutions preferred by those originally seeking the response. Entrance onto the broader public agenda or the formal agenda may be the precise moment when the group responsible for initiating and specifying an issue loses control of it.

FORMULATION

By definition, placing an issue on the formal or official agenda means that a decision will be made, even if it is a decision to take no action. Just as the earlier discussion of the policy process suggested two theories: coherent design and control versus uncoordinated chaos, two very different models of policy formulation have been contrasted by many educators.

On the one hand, the **rationalist model** proposes an orderly process of identifying goals, evaluating means, and matching ends according to specified criteria such as effectiveness, efficiency, consistency with other known goals, and so on. In this model, the process undertaken by policy-makers is expected to identify the best possible solution to the problem at hand before proceeding to decision and implementation.

By contrast, the **incrementalist** or **pluralist exchange model** describes a competition among interested parties out of which policy emerges as a result of concessions, bargains, and trade-offs. What results here is a compromise between competing ideas of what is best, or indeed, between the opposing positions of self-interested actors; rather than the "best" policy, this model generates what is the most practical or feasible given the circumstances that constrain policy-makers.

It has been suggested that the contrast between these models is one of the ideal versus reality: one describes how policy should be made, the other describes how it *is* made. However, supporters of the incrementalist model argue that it is not only a more accurate portrait but a superior approach to the rationalist model, which rests on assumptions about information, knowledge, and resources that are unlikely to be met in the real world. For example, rationalist decision making implies a degree of control that is incompatible with most policy environments—consider the complexity and potential fragmentation of not only the policy community but also the sub-government. If rationalist decision making were possible, it would certainly create the possibility of very radical change, governed only by the desire to implement the "best" solution. The very constrained nature of actual policy-making, the incrementalists argue, could also be its advantage. Since the success or failure of policies cannot be predicted with any great accuracy, radical changes are disruptive and potentially destabilizing. Policy-making that proceeds in small ("incremental") steps from existing practices is more prudent and likely to produce long-term success. The incrementalist model has a clearly "conservative" character, while the rationalist model has the potential to be radical.

The incrementalist model has been closely associated with the work of US political scientist Charles Lindblom, and this model may be particularly apt for describing policy-making in the United States, given the fragmentation and dispersion of power within its

RATIONALIST	INCREMENTALIST
orderly, rule-governed process	unpredictable bargains and trade-offs
produces ideal solution to problem	results in most practical solution to problem
has capacity for radical change	moves in small steps (increments) from status quo
how policy should be (and sometimes is) made	how policy is (and should be) made

Figure 12.5

system of government. Whether it is always the best approach, in the United States or elsewhere, is an open question. In other institutional environments where policy-making is more focused, some degree of rationalist decision making may be feasible. Certainly, radical and deliberate shifts in policy *do* occur in regimes, most often in majoritarian parliamentary systems (no surprise here), and Margaret Thatcher's so-called revolution in public policy in the 1980s in Britain is a good example.

Finding the dichotomy between rationalist and incrementalist models somewhat artificial, some observers have proposed models that fall somewhere between these extremes or that employ rational cost-benefit analysis for some decisions while bargaining with competing interests for an acceptable compromise for others. Etzioni's theory of mixed scanning, for example, proposes that long-term or more fundamental decisions are made in an essentially rationalist fashion, while detailed decisions about means or implementation are more incrementally achieved. There is something intuitively attractive about this: the decision to launch a new social program, for example, must surely be made deliberately, and not simply emerge as a by-product of pluralist exchange among political actors; the details about how to realize the objectives of this program may, however, be concluded through just such a process.

Similarly, in a proportional system, and particularly in a consensual context where coalition is the norm, each of the parties will have arrived at a set of policies for almost all of the issues currently on the public agenda as they approach the election. As noted, these policies will be designed with at least part of one eye looking to the coalition partnerships that the election may make possible. In this regard, policy proposals will be deliberately designed, evaluated, and selected on the basis of several criteria—a very rational calculating process—but, at the same time, they will be unlikely to strike out in radical new directions or require massive overhauls of what has been in place; to do so would in all likelihood diminish the chances of finding willing coalition partners. Once the election has occurred and determined which parties have a chance at becoming partners, the negotiations will begin. When a government is announced it will be because there was enough compatibility in the parties' policy positions to reach an agreement, *and* that agreement will involve numerous instances where parties compromised, made trade-offs, basically settled for what was not their ideal position, but something close enough or better than nothing. This sound very incremental, too, but in a more controlled way than the pluralist tangle of a US-style legislative free-for-all.

Policy formulation involves many different types of decision, which may be arranged in a hierarchy or be connected in an algorithm best presented by a flow chart. These will range from the simple decision to seek a policy solution to a problem, to the articulation of policy goals, to the consideration of different possible approaches, to decisions about funding, and the timelines for approvals and implementation. One example of the types of decisions to be made is the matter of which policy instrument(s) to use.

Instrument Choice

Given the goals that policy-makers establish, there is almost always a variety of possible means or instruments for achieving them. Most simply, instruments are the different ways governments exercise authority, from laws and regulations, to penalties such as imprisonment or fines, to taxation, to the provision of public goods such as education, or services such as postal delivery. Different factors may determine the choice of instruments, including ideology, which is usually disposed to some instruments and wary of others. Cost or difficulty of implementation may be prime considerations: the rationalist view of decision making would emphasize efficiency, that is, the instrument or combination of instruments that will most closely achieve the desired objectives while incurring the least cost. It is possible, though, to distinguish between **technical efficiency** and **political efficiency.**

Technical efficiency is the ability of an instrument to achieve objectives without an undue or unreasonable expenditure of resources. If the goal of childcare policy is to increase the number of available spaces, then the technical efficiency of promoting commercial versus not-for-profit establishments will simply come down to which strategy creates more new spaces per public dollar of expenditure. If, in addition, the policy goal is

to improve the quality of care provided, then the tendency of profit or non-profit care to deliver high staff-to-child ratios or to employ staff trained as early childhood educators must also be measured. Considering the short-, medium-, or long-term efficiency of instruments is also important. In recent years, many US states have realized that some "tough on crime" measures, such as tighter sentencing laws and more prisons to accommodate the increased number of incarcerated persons, are economically inefficient *and* less effective in reducing crime than spending money on rehabilitation and community programs.

Political efficiency, by contrast, has to do with the benefits or costs of the policy instrument for the policy-makers: will the use of an instrument create goodwill among a particular constituency that will come in handy later, or will it cost the governing party key votes in the next election? A tough-on-crime agenda, for example, may win more votes in the short term, whatever the longer-term consequences. The example of the reversal of the Harmonized Sales Tax (HST) by a referendum vote in British Columbia in 2011 (see Chapter 13), is a classic case in which technical and political efficiency clashed. Economic experts and the business class were almost unanimous in their support of the HST as a technically efficient instrument for enhancing the province's competitiveness and prosperity. The only problem was that its political inefficiency (unpopularity) motivated the government to deny during the election campaign that it intended to proceed with the tax, only to do so almost immediately following the election. The public backlash led to the resignation of the premier; in the words of one commentator, "an entire decade of political capital was swiftly consumed by the HST debate" (Roy, 54). In almost any policy environment, the political efficiency of instruments will be as much a part of the calculation as their technical efficiency, if not more so.

There are almost as many catalogues of the kinds of instruments available to policy-makers as there are writers on the topic, but typical categories include *exhortation* (advertised guidelines), *taxation* (the HST), *expenditure* (government money for subway construction), *regulation* (anti-noise bylaw), *subsidy* (free prescriptions for seniors), *grant* (arts funding), *self-regulation* (delegation to professional associations), *enterprise* (government-owned casinos and lotteries), and *direct provision* (national parks). These instruments differ in the way they employ resources; some—like regulation—tend to be less expensive than others—like expenditure. They also vary in terms of the amount of coercion or force involved; exhortation is low in its coercive content, taxation and regulation are potentially high. These are the ingredients in designing programs to fulfill the policy objectives identified, and a policy often involves choosing a mix of instruments. Reducing the public-health costs associated with smoking can be tackled by public education campaigns, higher tobacco taxes, stricter enforcement of restrictions on selling to minors, requirements for graphic warnings on packaging, and subsidies for tobacco farmers to produce alternative crops. Policy-making may not be about choosing between these but rather the relative weight of each in a coordinated strategy.

FROM DECISION TO APPROVAL

The policy cycle modelled here includes a stage between formulation and implementation called approval. Separating approval from the decisions that conclude the formulation or design stage reflects the parliamentary context that prevails in established democracies, and the very different role of the legislature in most parliamentary systems from that played in systems based on a separation of powers. The discussion in the previous chapter of three stages—formulation, legislation, and implementation—was a partial look at the full policy cycle, and more accurately applies to a parliamentary situation where policy formulation and the passage of legislation are quite distinct, particularly in a majoritarian situation.

In a parliamentary context, policy formation largely takes place in those portions of the sub-government (e.g., central agencies, senior bureaucrats, party advisors) that have access to the cabinet, where both the initial commitment to formulating a policy and the final decision to bring it forward for approval are made. If the policy is made under the authority of existing legislation, the approval is made at cabinet, the appropriate regulatory instrument is drawn up and published, and implementation proceeds. If new legislative authority is required, either through changes to existing laws or the passage of a new law, the necessary bill (legislative proposal) that is required will be introduced to the legislature by the government. Bringing the legislation through the legislative stages is the responsibility of the government. In the context of a majority government (single party or coalition), the only reason the bill would not pass is a lack of determination on the part of the government, and the only amendments that will pass will be those to which the government agrees. In a minority government situation, the defeat of a bill is quite possible, as is amendment against the will of the government, and deal-making with another party or parties in order to bring about the intended policy may result in its modification. In a coalition government, the compromises and bargaining take place between the governing partners prior to the introduction of the bill. The major difference between the majoritarian and the coalition government is that the sub-government involved in the formulation of policy may be larger in the latter case.

In a regime like the United States, a situation such as that in the bottom half of *Figure 12.6* is possible, in which the executive branch has the capacity, on the basis of existing legislation, to make a policy decision and move to its implementation. On the other hand, if the executive has a policy ambition that requires legislative approval, it must find a sympathetic member of Congress (either House) to introduce legislation. Once a bill is introduced to a US legislature, anything is possible, from its defeat, to its complete overhaul and revision, to swift passage unchanged. It is entirely up to the legislators how proposals from the executive are received; at the same time, almost every elected member of either House is working to promote their own legislative projects, looking for allies, bargaining for support in various committees or sub-committees, and making trade-offs or compromises to keep a bill alive. In the two years that constituted the 111th US Congress (2009–2010), over 6,500 bills were introduced in the House of Representatives, and in the Senate more than 4,000.

In other words, policy formulation takes place *within* the legislature—much of it happening in committee—and it is only when a bill has received its final vote that the policy design is complete (if then). And because this system is one of checks and balances, any bill that emerges from Congress must go to the president for approval. The president can veto a bill, sign it into law, or do nothing and it will become law after 10 days. Congress can overrule the presidential veto of a bill with a two-thirds majority in each house, but if a president ignores a bill within the last 10 days of a session, it is a veto that Congress cannot overturn (the so-called **pocket veto**).

In short, the approval stage is not likely to have much impact on the content of a policy in the parliamentary model, except in minority situations, where a government bill might be defeated. In a congressional system, which has been called "a legislator's legislature," the approval stage has tremendous impact, with the defeat of most policy proposals that come before it, and the consolidation, amendment, or reconsideration of most of the remainder that eventually become law.

IMPLEMENTATION

With policy approved, the legislature or executive has reached its Jean-Luc Picard moment: "Make it so!" Decision making and the design now give way to delivery and *implementation* of the policy. At this stage policy is turned over from its designers and architects to the public servants who administer and coordinate programs in their exercise of bureaucratic authority. That authority either derives from the legislation that is approving and authorizing the policy, or it derives from broader provisions in existing legislation. This

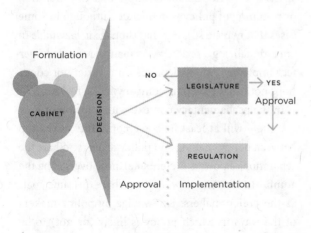

Figure 12.6

exercise of power falls under a hierarchy of super-vision that stops at the Minister or Cabinet Secretary who—in parliamentary systems—is accountable to the legislature.

The activity required to implement a policy can range from simply revising computer software so that a change in the amount of a benefit or tax is put into effect, to bringing into being a program or agency where there was none before, such as the creation of a public automobile-insurance program or the reorganization of health care service delivery. At the minimal end, revising rules and procedures or printing a revised manual may be all that is needed. At the other, decisions about funding, staffing and training; possible infrastructure requirements (both a physical plant and IT); coordination with other departments, stakeholders, and the public; and timelines for becoming operational will collectively represent a considerable grant of delegated authority. (In addition, at this point, the evaluation stage will have begun, as public servants begin to recognize where the holes are in the design or where additional legislative or regulatory authority or clearer direction is required to make the program truly effective.)

In this exercise of authority that constitutes its implementation, the policy is further transformed. As a general rule, one might suggest, whenever the responsibility for policy shifts from one set of actors to another, the policy itself will be affected by this shift, in ways that those handing off the policy might not anticipate. The distinction between policy-making and policy administration is an artificial one, not simply because policy administrators are frequently involved in the design and decision stages but because policy is also effectively made by administrators in the decisions they take when implementing the program entrusted to them. The term "slippage" has been used to describe

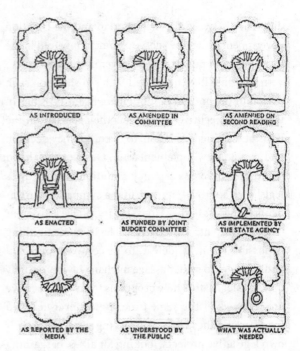

AS INTRODUCED   AS AMENDED IN COMMITTEE   AS AMENDED ON SECOND READING

AS ENACTED   AS FUNDED BY JOINT BUDGET COMMITTEE   AS IMPLEMENTED BY THE STATE AGENCY

AS REPORTED BY THE MEDIA   AS UNDERSTOOD BY THE PUBLIC   WHAT WAS ACTUALLY NEEDED

Policy Stages. *Unknown source.*

the difference between the intentions of policy-makers and the actual results brought about by policy managers. This is not meant to imply that the alteration or re-tuning of policy is deliberate (although in some cases that may be so), but that slippage is *inevitable* in operationalizing a program. As many have noted, "perfect implementation" depends on a variety of conditions not usually keeping company in the real world.

In the parliamentary context, with a fusion of powers, there will at least be some continuity at the top between policy-making and policy delivery. Where the separation of powers is complete, those overseeing the administration of policy may not share the same goals as the policy-makers. Knowledge by policy-makers of the ways in which policy is likely (or not) to be changed in the process of implementation may in turn influence their choice of policy instrument(s) or other design considerations.

ADMINISTRATION

This is perhaps the most important stage in the policy cycle, because it is here that the policy is in operation, following implementation, a stage that may go indefinitely—in some cases long after those who initiated, designed, approved, or even implemented it have left the scene. The original context and the rationale for the policy being the way it is may no longer be obvious, or may have become the source of conflicting narratives. This may be unproblematic if the program continues to serve a public purpose in a more or less efficient manner. It is more likely that over time the program could come to require improvements, or outlive its purpose, or turn out to perform less well than an approach developed in another jurisdiction or another context. An important part of administration, therefore, is monitoring the success or failure of a policy, and measuring it against criteria such as efficiency, effectiveness, and fairness. With this, the transition is made to the final stage in the cycle.

EVALUATION

The stage of *policy evaluation* is not without controversy. On the one hand, there are debates concerning the methods of evaluation: What are the criteria by which policies should be assessed? What quantitative or qualitative methods are most useful?

A second question concerns who the evaluators are. Is evaluation best done by experts or by the general public? In fact, as noted above, evaluation begins with the implementation process and continues thereafter by one interested party or another, from those whose job it is to deliver the program, to the "clients" it serves,

to the academic community studying it, to those who are critics on principle (not believing that this type of program—charter schools, say, or fire-arms registries—should exist), to the affected stakeholders or activists, to the wider public. These ongoing judgments about public policy are different from, say, a program review exercise undertaken periodically on an ad hoc basis to eliminate waste in government, or the very focused evaluation of an auditor general who performs value-for-money audits on specific programs on a regular basis.

Thirdly, what is the evaluation worth, formal or otherwise? Does it lead to revision or improvement? Do policy-makers pay attention to the results of the evaluation? Skepticism about evaluation is closely associated with the incrementalist view of policy as the product of pluralist exchange. On the other hand, for the rationalist paradigm of policy-making, evaluation is essential. If policy-making is a form of problem solving, then evaluation provides information about the problem-solving capacity of specific policies, data that might help policy-makers make informed decisions in other, similar situations. As in many areas, there is in policy, too, a powerful disincentive for evaluation: It is not necessarily in the best interest of managers and administrators to have attention drawn to failures, mistakes, or miscalculations that may have less to do with the policy than with its management. On the other hand, the feedback that is received in the stages of the policy cycle is often a factor in determining what gets to the formal agenda, starting the cycle over again.

It should be clear that policy is *not* a simple five-step process; rather, this discussion has concerned elements or dimensions of the policy cycle that are present in one fashion or another in most policy environments. The specific "process" will vary by country, by policy sector, and even by specific policy cases—no two instances of policy are alike. This is one reason why many analyses of public policy focus on case studies.

TYPES OF POLICY

Figure 12.7 lists the ministries and ministers of the Swedish government (November 2011). In this case, ministries are organized around broad policy sectors and each contains from one to four ministers with specific areas of responsibility within that sector. The minister listed first under each ministry is designated as the lead for that ministry. Eleven is not a large number of ministries, especially considering that Sweden is a unitary state, nor is 24 ministers a large cabinet. The Canadian government, at the same point in time, contained 39 ministers, with a much more differentiated list of policy responsibilities, including ministers for Fisheries and Oceans, Natural Resources, Aboriginal Affairs and Northern Development, National Revenue, Veterans Affairs, and Citizenship, Immigration and Multiculturalism. The Canadian counterparts to many of the Swedish ministries, such as Education and Health and Social Affairs, are found at the provincial level.

The view taken here is that almost all ministries or ministerial portfolios can or could be placed in one of seven policy boxes presented in *Figure 12.8*. The placement of specific ministries in such categories is not always going to be identical. For example, in some regimes, Research and Innovation is aligned with Education. In others, it may be placed with Economic Development. In each case, the placement may influence the emphases that will inform research and innovation policies, education perhaps being more conducive to "pure" research, economic development more inclined to stress applied research and the "marketization" of ideas. Placement can make a significant difference for departments responsible for natural resource development, such as forestry, mining, and agribusiness, where there is a potential for tension between policies focused on jobs and revenue for the state and policies emphasizing conservation and sustainable resource management.

THE SWEDISH CABINET: MINISTRIES AND MINISTERS

PRIME MINISTER'S OFFICE
Prime Minister
Minister for EU Affairs

MINISTRY OF CULTURE
Minister for Culture and Sports

MINISTRY OF DEFENCE
Minister for Defence

MINISTRY OF EDUCATION AND RESEARCH
Minister for Education
Minister for Gender Equality

MINISTRY OF EMPLOYMENT
Minister for Employment
Minister for Integration

MINISTRY OF ENTERPRISE, ENERGY, AND COMMUNICATIONS
Minister for Enterprise
Minister for Energy and IT
Minister for Infrastructure

MINISTRY OF THE ENVIRONMENT
Minister for the Environment

MINISTRY OF FINANCE
Minister for Finance
Minister for Financial Markets

MINISTRY FOR FOREIGN AFFAIRS
Minister for Foreign Affairs
Minister for Trade
Minister for International Development Cooperation

MINISTRY OF HEALTH AND SOCIAL AFFAIRS
Minister for Health and Social Affairs
Minister for Children and the Elderly
Minister for Public Administration and Housing
Minister for Social Security

MINISTRY OF JUSTICE
Minister for Justice
Minister for Migration and Asylum Policy

MINISTRY FOR RURAL AFFAIRS
Minister of Rural Affairs

OFFICE OF ADMINISTRATIVE AFFAIRS

Figure 12.7

CULTURAL
Culture, Citizenship, Immigration, Sport, Multiculturalism

DEFENCE & FOREIGN AFFAIRS
Defence, Foreign Affairs, International Trade, Veterans Affairs

ECONOMIC
Finance, Revenue, Commerce, Labour, Economic Development, Tourism, Transportation, Infrastructure

ENVIRONMENTAL
Agriculture, Natural Resources, Energy, Environment, Forestry, Science, Oceans

GOVERNMENT SERVICES
Aboriginal Affairs, Intergovernmental Relations, Government Services, Municipal Affairs

JUSTICE
Attorney General, Policing, Corrections, Human Rights, Consumer Protection

SOCIAL
Education, Health, Long-Term Care, Child and Family, Social Services, Seniors

Figure 12.8

Policy developed within ministries or departments, such as those in *Figures 12.7* and *12.8*, is often called **vertical policy-making**, because in each case, the focus is on the problems and programs internal to that department. The greater challenge all governments face is effective **horizontal policy-making**, decision making that cuts across ministerial or departmental borders. One goal is to coordinate the activities of different ministries that may impact common stakeholders. For example, in some Canadian provinces that have public auto insurance, the public insurer (an institution under the finance ministry) is also responsible for issuing drivers' licenses (transportation) and collecting payments of fines for driving violations (justice). Specific departments of Government

CENTRAL AGENCIES

Central coordinating agencies are offices that play a key role in the operation of government, but often do so out of the public view. A primary example in Westminster-style parliaments is the Cabinet Office (in Canada, the Privy Council Office, or PCO). The Cabinet Office is a secretariat of public servants providing support in the form of research, advice, communications, policy development, and any number of other services to the government of the day. The Cabinet Office is staffed by members of the public service, many of whom are on secondment (temporary assignment) from their department for a fixed period of time. It is generally believed that the most able and promising public servants are recruited for Cabinet Office; although their tenure is temporary, it is a chance to shine at the centre and show that they are future leadership material (at the deputy minister or assistant deputy minister level). The head of Cabinet Office is often the Secretary of Cabinet and, in practice, is the prime minister's deputy minister.

The role of Cabinet Office officials is to provide impartial but "politically sensitive" advice, a description that applies to all senior bureaucrats. This body, however, is a primary resource for the government in any efforts to engage in horizontal policy-making, coordinating policy efforts in various ministries with each other and with the Ministry of Finance (responsible for preparing the budget and expenditure estimates). Central coordinating agencies bring knowledge about matters (such as legislative drafting, timetabling, and implementation) that elected officials, coming to the legislature from a non-parliamentary background, could not be expected to have acquired.

Whitney Block, home to the Ontario Government's Cabinet Office, Toronto, Ontario.

Services (in *Figure 12.7*, the Office of Administrative Affairs) are commonly designed to implement directives and coordinate policies common to all ministries or departments, and to manage the interaction of all departments with the public.

Many issues are best addressed by a coordinated strategy involving two or more departments. Apprenticeship training may require the attention of ministries of education, training, labour, and industry; effective settlement of immigrants is likely to involve programs from various social and economic ministries

in addition to the department responsible for immigration. The Swedish grouping of ministers with distinct but related portfolios under one ministry is one way to increase coordination or minimize the instances of needless duplication of services or programs working at cross-purposes. Another approach is the creation of committees within cabinet that correspond to some of the policy boxes noted above. The circulation of policy plans and draft policies through both policy and coordinating committees helps ensure that policies are not made in isolation from one another.

THE BUREAUCRACY

Almost everyone comes into regular, if not daily, contact with the state with regard to one of the many programs or services it provides or one of the taxes it collects. The human dimension of that contact (assuming we *do* interact with a human rather than transact our business online, at a self-serve electronic kiosk, or by automated voice mail) is our interaction with public servants, the employees of the state. The interchangeable terms *bureaucracy, civil service,* and *public service* refer to the (diminishing) army of full- and part-time employees of the state who staff its various departments, agencies, and enterprises. The term "bureaucracy" is rarely used with warmth and affection, implying instead needless layers of personnel and rules and regulations that get in the way of action—what is known as "red tape."

Nonetheless, **bureaucracy** is the underlying structure of authority for all manner of medium and large-scale organizations, including corporations and universities, a structure designed to provide accountability, rationality, and impartiality to the conduct of operations. Max Weber (referenced in Chapter 1) was one of the first to study bureaucracy and identify many of its key components. These include

- hierarchical organization
- clear job descriptions and lines of command
- officials trained in areas of expertise
- action taken according to rules, applied impartially
- written documentation of actions taken
- promotion on the basis of merit

Some of the aspects of bureaucracy that are most despised—its impersonality, its fidelity to rules and processes, its treatment of cases as files (being assigned a number)—are, in fact, some of its strengths, embodying in ordinary organizational functioning the depersonalization of authority that characterizes the modern state. Otherwise, cases (will always) get decided on the basis of who has influence, or money, or good looks, or is related to the official deciding the matter (rather than just occasionally). Everyone believes that their case is unique, or deserving of special attention, but if *that* were the basis for considering matters, someone would need to judge which of these cases needing preferential treatment should move to the top of the line. Whose claim is the *most* special? And with this, what is the difference from the medieval court where those lucky enough to get (or buy) an audience before a feudal aristocrat could plead their case and be subject to his or her personal whims?

THE PROFESSIONAL PUBLIC SERVICE

The professionalization of the public service accompanied the emergence of the modern state. Once upon a time, most government jobs were **patronage** appointments, which is to say that one of the great benefits of winning elections and forming governments was the ability to give employment to one's supporters, friends, and family. A change in governing party often meant a wholesale change in the public service from supporters and friends of one party to the supporters and friends of the newly triumphant party. With the growth of government, and with the increasing complexity and specialization of the tasks of government, there was an increasing need—increasingly recognized—for permanence, the development of expertise, and promotion on the basis of merit: in short, for a *professional* public service.

All advanced democracies today employ a professional public service, where "professional" indicates several elements. First of all, entrance to the public

THE PLUM BOOK

The spectacle following each US presidential election of ambitious partisans descending on Capitol Hill in search of an appointment by the executive branch is routinely commented upon in the press. Immediately after the election, the *United States Government Policy and Supporting Positions* (commonly known as "the Plum Book") is published. The Foreword to the 2008 edition describes its contents as follows:

> This publication contains data (as of September 1, 2008) on over 7,000 Federal civil service leadership and support positions in the legislative and executive branches of the Federal Government that may be subject to noncompetitive appointment (e.g., positions such as agency heads and their immediate subordinates, policy executives and advisors, and aides who report to these officials). The duties of many such positions may involve advocacy of Administration policies and programs and the incumbents usually have a close and confidential working relationship with the agency head or other key officials.

Included in this total are 1,455 positions classified as subject to Presidential Appointment (1,141 with Senate confirmation, 314 without Senate confirmation).
www.gpoaccess.gov/plumbook/2008/index.html

service and promotion within its ranks are based on merit, that is, demonstrated ability, aptitude, and accomplishment, not personal connections or political ties. The degree and the means by which this is enforced vary from country to country. Usually, entrance to the public service is gained on the basis of competitive, public examinations. In some countries (e.g., France, Italy, and Germany) the examinations favour those with specialized knowledge, often those with particular legal training; in other countries (e.g., Britain and Canada) generalists are more commonly sought. The merit principle was established by law in Canada in 1918. However, many senior administrative posts are still filled by appointment by the prime minister and cabinet, including deputy ministers and members of agencies, boards, and commissions.

A second principle is that the public service should be non-partisan or politically neutral. This is based, in part, on the notion that a clear distinction can be made between decisions of policy (which are political and should be left to elected, publicly accountable officials) and their implementation (which is non-political and should be carried out in a disinterested, efficient manner by professionals). In practice, this has often meant clear rules or even laws restricting public servants from engaging in partisan political activity, but variations exist. In Canada, restrictions on the partisan activity of public servants were challenged successfully on the basis of the *Canadian Charter of Rights and Freedoms,* except for senior bureaucrats, whom the Court ruled should continue to be seen to have no partisan attachments. Arguably, it is precisely at the senior levels of the bureaucracy where politicization of the bureaucracy matters most, and politicization may mean other things than partisan attachment. As a consequence, top-ranking public servants (deputy ministers) are often replaced by an incoming government that suspects these deputies may be too closely aligned with the previous government or its policies.

A third principle is security of tenure. If public servants adequately perform their duties in an impartial, disinterested manner, they should be secure in their employment, not subject to the whims of political superiors. A professional public servant is a career public servant, and just as in other walks of life, the loyal, competent performance of duties should be rewarded with secure employment. On the other hand, in a society where, increasingly, all employment is tenuous, the security of public-sector employment is sometimes a cause of resentment.

The model of a professional public service is, of course, an ideal that is realized in different settings and under different governments to a greater or lesser degree. Each country has its own traditions and expectations about public-sector management and performance. In any country, the model probably works less well when the state itself is the object of public policy because public servants have a real, abiding interest in the state, an interest they cannot be expected to set aside easily, if at all.

NEW PUBLIC MANAGEMENT

In the last quarter of the twentieth century, a range of reforms importing practices and organizational techniques from the private sector began to be implemented in the public service with varying degree of fervour. Called New Public Management (NPM), this approach was adopted for at least two reasons: to achieve greater efficiency and fiscal accountability; and to improve "customer service," addressing the traditional criticisms of the impersonal aspects of bureaucratic functioning with a client-focused ethic. Indeed, one of the most profound shifts was to regard those receiving government services as "clients." Business planning models were imported, competitive bidding for service delivery by non-state entities was adopted, and in some cases restructuring delegated

PUBLIC SECTOR EMPLOYMENT 2008 GENERAL GOVERNMENT AND PUBLIC ENTERPRISES		
	% of labour force	change since 2001
NORWAY	34.5	-1.01
DENMARK	31.5	-1.61
FRANCE	24.3	-0.69
FINLAND	22.9	0.70
SLOVENIA	22.7	-1.50
ESTONIA	22.4	-1.04
POLAND	21.5	-3.47
NETHERLANDS	21.4	1.08
GREECE	20.7	1.44
HUNGARY	19.5	-0.83
CZECH REPUBLIC	19.4	-1.71
SLOVAKIA	19.3	-6.02
CANADA	18.8	1.10
UNITED KINGDOM	18.6	0.54
IRELAND	16.7	-1.45
ISRAEL	16.5	-0.89
AUSTRALIA	15.6	0.48
UNITED STATES	14.6	-0.18
SWITZERLAND	14.5	-0.25
ITALY	14.3	-1.06
GERMANY	13.6	-2.89
SPAIN	12.9	-0.61
NEW ZEALAND	11.7	0.30
CHILE	9.1	-0.57
JAPAN	7.9	0.11

Source: OECD *Government at a Glance 2011*

Figure 12.9

particular responsibilities of a ministry or department to an autonomous or semi-autonomous, self-financing agency. While this latter approach was most popular in the United Kingdom, Australia, and New Zealand, Canada was not immune. The devolution of responsibility for Canada's largest airports to local authorities starting in 1992, and the commercialization of the

PUBLIC-SECTOR EMPLOYMENT—SEASONALLY ADJUSTED (2011)			
	2nd quarter	3rd quarter	change (2nd to 3rd Q)
	thousands		% change
PUBLIC SECTOR	3,643	3,632	-0.3
GENERAL GOVERNMENT	1,412	1,393	-1.3
Federal	446	430	-3.6
Provincial and territorial	357	358	0.3
Local	610	606	-0.6
EDUCATIONAL INSTITUTIONS[1]	1,062	1,061	-0.1
Universities and colleges	385	383	-0.4
School boards	677	678	0.1
HEALTH AND SOCIAL SERVICE INSTITUTIONS	857	861	0.4
GOVERNMENT BUSINESS ENTERPRISES	318	319	0.3

[1] Includes vocational and trade institutions. Note: Numbers may not add to totals because of rounding
Source: Statistics Canada, The Daily, August 29, 2011 (re-formatted)
http://www.statcan.gc.ca/daily-quotidien/110829/t110829a1-eng.htm

Figure 12.10

management of Canada's largest ports as self-financing Canada Port Authorities starting in 1998, provide prominent examples.

NPM is not without its critics, and in countries that adopted its principles with the greatest zeal, there has been some back-pedaling, or pause for a re-think. In many cases, the rhetoric of NPM was used to cover the downsizing of bureaucracies or their outright privatization, always under the guise of improving customer service. In fact, it now seems that all organizational change is accompanied by the phrase "to serve you better!"—even when the change is to make services less accessible, if not remove them altogether.

THE SIZE OF THE PUBLIC SERVICE

Although NPM has been associated with the privatization of government services, contracting out, and other downsizing measures, evidence that the result has been a decline in the size of the public sector is mixed, for several reasons.

First, NPM became popular in many regimes after the recession of the early 1990s, a period during which many governments were forced, by the size of their deficits and debt, to limit growth in public expenditures, if not try to reverse them. Once economic recovery was underway, the natural tendency of government and bureaucracy to grow (not unlike business enterprises and most other institutions) reasserted itself in most places. To some degree, the size of the public sector seems more dependent on the health of the national economy than anything else. *Figure 12.9* shows the size of the public sector in 25 regimes in 2008, with the amount of change since 2001: employment is measured as a percentage of the labour force.

Second, good and consistent data about the public service are hard to come by. Not all government employees or those whose paycheque is ultimately financed by the taxpayer are public servants in the respects identified above (career employees secure in their positions on performance of their duties with impartial expertise). Members of the military are not public servants, nor in most cases are employees of government enterprises—agencies that offer a commercial product to consumers in the marketplace. Neither are most employees of the broader public sector, sometimes called the MUSH (municipalities, universities and colleges, schools and hospitals) sector. Doctors are not public servants in Canada, even though most of their income comes from public health insurance; they are public servants if employed by a national health service, as in the United Kingdom. In short, how regimes define public-service membership varies considerably. Comparing national government public-service composition will not be adequate in the case of federal countries where many services and the

public service to deliver them are employed at the sub-national level. Getting timely and accurate information about sub-national or municipal public servants complicates comparison even further. *Figure 12.10* provides a typical breakdown of public-sector employment, as measured by Statistics Canada.

Third, with public-sector reforms, many apparent shifts in the size of the public service simply reflect re-classification of positions, so that the change is only apparent, the real number of public employees having not changed.

While there is no consistent pattern to the trends shown in *Figure 12.9*, OECD data collected in 2010 indicates most countries will be decreasing the size of their public service in the coming decade (*Government at a Glance 2011*). In part this is a reaction to the increase in public expenditures that was undertaken by most regimes in response to the 2008–09 financial crisis, and in part to the slow pace of recovery since.

REFERENCES

Atkinson, Michael, and William Coleman, "Strong States and Weak States: Sectoral Policy Networks in Advanced Capitalist Societies." *British Journal of Politics* 19.1 (1989): 47–67.

Cobb, Roger, Jennie Keith-Ross, and Marc Howard Ross. "Agenda-Building as a Comparative Political Process." *American Political Science Review* 70.1 (March 1976): 126–138.

Coleman, William, and Grace Skogstad. *Policy Communities and Public Policy in Canada: A Structural Approach.* Mississauga, ON: Copp Clark Pitman. 1990.

Doern, G. Bruce, and Richard W. Phidd. *Canadian Public Policy: Ideas, Structure, Process.* 2nd ed. Toronto: Nelson, 1992.

Etzioni, Amitai. "Mixed Scanning: A 'Third' Approach to Decision Making." *Public Administration Review.* 27.5 (December 1967): 385–392.

Lindblom, Charles, "The Science of 'Muddling Through.'" *Public Administration Review* 19.2 (Spring, 1959): 79–88.

_____, "Still Muddling, Not Yet Through." *Public Administration Review* 39.6 (Nov.–Dec., 1979): 517–526.

OECD *Government at a Glance.* Directorate for Public Governance and Territorial Development (2011). Web.

Pal, Leslie A. *Public Policy Analysis: An Introduction.* 2nd ed. Toronto: Nelson. 1992.

Pross, A. Paul. *Group Politics and Public Policy*. 2nd ed. Toronto: Oxford University Press. 1992.

Roy, Jeffrey. "Politicians and the Public: Bridging the Great Divide." *Policy Options* 32.9 (October 2011): 53–57.

Skogstad, Grace. "Policy Networks and Policy Communities: Conceptual Evolution and Governing Realities." *The Comparative Turn in Canadian Political Science.* Ed. Linda A. White, Richard Simeon, Rob Vipond, and Jennifer Waller. Vancouver: University of British Columbia Press, 2008. 205–220.

FURTHER READINGS

Beetham, David. *Bureaucracy*. 2nd ed. Minneapolis: University of Minnesota Press. 1996.

Gains, Francesca, and Gerry Stoker. "Delivering 'Public Value': Implications for Accountability and Legitimacy." *Parliamentary Affairs* 62.3 (July 2009): 438–455.

Hallsworth, Michael, Simon Parker, and Jill Rutter. *Policy-making in the Real World: Evidence and Analysis*. London: Institute for Government, 2011. [Publication may be downloaded from the Institute's website.]

Kirchner, Stephen. "Why Does Government Grow?" Center for Independent Studies Policy Monograph. No. 117 (2011): 25 pp. [Publication may be downloaded from the Center's website.]

McConnell, Allan. "Policy Success, Policy Failure and Grey Areas In-Between." *Journal of Public Policy* 30.3 (December 2010): 345–362.

Rimington, John. "Public Management and Administration: A Need for Evolution." *The Political Quarterly* 80.4 (December 2009): 562–568.

CHAPTER 13

The Rule of Law in Practice: The Justice System

...WHICH PROVIDES THE READER WITH DISCUSSIONS ABOUT

- the nature of law, where it may be found, and the text of a small act
- how public law is made
- the instruments and use of direct democracy
- the difference between common law and civil law traditions (private law)
- administrative law
- court systems
- rights
- judicial review

The suggestion was made in Chapter 1 that politics is an alternative to settling matters by the use of force, an alternative to "might is right." The depersonalization of authority in the modern era has been another driving theme of this book, something found embodied in bureaucracy, in doctrines of accountability, in checks and balances, in constitutionalism. Underlying all of this is the principle of the rule of law, rooted in the Enlightenment's confidence in human rationality and presupposing a fundamental equality of all individuals despite all evidence to the contrary. The rule of law is so basic to the structure of modern liberal democracies that it is rarely discussed at length, often taken for granted, and sometimes blatantly ignored. Examples of the latter often involve officials exercising or attempting an exercise of power that is not rightfully theirs.

THE NATURE OF LAW

In modern developed democracies, practically every exercise of power can be traced to a law that provides the authority for it. The discussion of the policy cycle in the previous chapter noted the passage of a law as the formal approval of a policy *and* the ability of policy-makers to formulate policy on the basis of

THE RULE OF LAW

The "rule of law" is the principle that *obliges everyone, including those in power, to obey formal, public, neutral rules of behaviour.* In theory, the rule of law requires that citizens be governed by consistent, publicly known, impartial rules *and* that those who exercise authority do so by publicly known, impartial, and consistent rules. In practice, the rule of law requires the exercise of public authority to meet five requirements (R) and satisfy four institutional conditions (IC).

R—LEGAL CULPABILITY

Punishment is only for breaking a law—for what one has done or failed to do—and is subject to uniform, known sanctions. Displeasing or annoying those in authority is not grounds for action.

R—PUBLIC LAW

To remove the excuse of ignorance, all law must be published or otherwise capable of being known.

R—VALIDITY

Hobbes argued that there must be a sign indicating that the law is the Sovereign's will, a real enough concern in bygone days. Today, the law is not counterfeit when it is made according to known and accepted procedures, such as the various stages in the legislative process.

R—UNIVERSALITY

The law must be enforceable against everyone, without exceptions for those in authority or who exercise power.

R—IMPARTIALITY

All individuals stand equal before the law, and only relevant criteria, such as the facts of the case, are applied. Neither the biases of those judging nor the personal attributes of those before the court should play any role; this is the sense in which justice must be "blind."

IC—CONSTITUTIONALISM

Respect for the body of fundamental laws concerning the exercise of authority and the relation between the state and the people is necessary, particularly for the requirement of universality.

IC—INDEPENDENT JUDICIARY

Judges must be able to decide cases without concern for the interests of third parties, including the government. Neither should the state nor its officials be able to influence proceedings to which they are a party, either as the accused or defendant.

IC—PUBLIC LEGISLATURE

Law-making must occur in public; only in this way can citizens have any certainty that good and correct procedures have been followed.

IC—CIVILIAN CONTROL OF THE POLICE AND MILITARY

Two cases where the rule of law is violated are captured by the terms "police state" and "military dictatorship." In these situations the necessary distinction between lawmakers and law enforcers has collapsed.

provisions that are present in laws made previously. It is important to recognize—and even lawmakers sometimes ignore this fact—that a law made today remains in effect until some other law is passed to replace or **repeal** it (or unless it expressly provides for its own demise). Constitutions that are made with an impossibly rigid amending formula (see Chapter 8) provide examples of how the enduring nature of law limits the scope of future legislators or policy-makers.

To the degree that laws, once made, are there until revised, replaced, or revoked, it is accurate to speak of "the law," which is a **consolidation** or a **codification** of the laws in force at a particular point in time. The legislative function of a parliament or legislature is about adding to, changing, or subtracting from this body of law. Proposals are introduced to the legislature in the form of bills, which, when passed, become Acts or Laws. In Canada, every bill contains the word "Act" in its title, but does not become an Act until it has been passed (see below), and does not become law until it comes into force. A bill may amend an existing Act (or Acts), be a new Act, repeal an existing Act, or do any combination of all three.

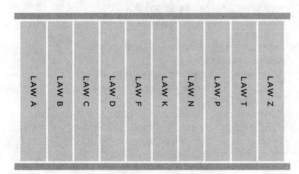

Figure 13.1

Primary legislation (or statutes), passed by the legislature, often includes provisions allowing the

executive to make secondary laws, known as **regulations**. Regulations often deal with the technical aspects of implementing programs or the specific rules for achieving the goals identified in the primary legislation and are often drafted by or with the assistance of the branch of the public service responsible for the Act. Regimes vary in terms of the degree to which public input may be solicited or permitted with respect to draft regulations, but all have rules about the publication of regulations, which is necessary for them to take effect. Ideally, there is also a legislative committee or body charged with making sure regulations are consistent with the regulation-making power in the legislation.

CONSOLIDATION OR CODIFICATION

It is more or less standard knowledge that "ignorance of the law is no excuse," despite the increasing unlikelihood that a person could ever be acquainted with the entire content of the law. Nonetheless, the principle, necessary for practical reasons, presupposes that *it is possible to become acquainted* with any part of the law. Where is the law kept? How does one determine what the law is at any given moment? And how, given the fact that disputes and trials may not be resolved until years after the critical event, does one know what the law was at any point in time? These are not idle questions, and failure to be able to answer them adequately can have serious consequences.

The challenges of keeping track of changes to the law, and keeping the publicly available publications of law current, are considerable and are met in different ways, depending on how the law is organized. Canada, like most regimes in the English common-law tradition, maintains a consolidation of its legislation, both statutes and regulations. Statutes are listed alphabetically

U.S. CODE (TABLE OF CONTENTS)

Title 1 General Provisions
Title 2 The Congress
Title 3 The President
Title 4 Flag and Seal, Seat of Government, and the States
Title 5 Government Organization and Employees
Title 6 Domestic Security
Title 7 Agriculture
Title 8 Aliens and Nationality
Title 9 Arbitration
Title 10 Armed Forces
Title 11 Bankruptcy
Title 12 Banks and Banking
Title 13 Census
Title 14 Coast Guard
Title 15 Commerce and Trade
Title 16 Conservation
Title 17 Copyrights
Title 18 Crimes and Criminal Procedure
Title 19 Customs Duties
Title 20 Education
Title 21 Food and Drugs
Title 22 Foreign Relations and Intercourse
Title 23 Highways
Title 24 Hospitals and Asylums
Title 25 Indians
Title 26 Internal Revenue Code
Title 27 Intoxicating Liquors
Title 28 Judiciary and Judicial Procedure
Title 29 Labor
Title 30 Mineral Lands and Mining
Title 31 Money and Finance
Title 32 National Guard
Title 33 Navigation and Navigable Waters
Title 34 Navy (repealed)
Title 35 Patents
Title 36 Patriotic Societies and Observances
Title 37 Pay and Allowances of the Uniformed Services
Title 38 Veterans' Benefits
Title 39 Postal Service
Title 40 Public Buildings, Property, and Works
Title 41 Public Contracts
Title 42 The Public Health and Welfare
Title 43 Public Lands
Title 44 Public Printing and Documents
Title 45 Railroads
Title 46 Shipping
Title 47 Telegraphs, Telephones, and Radiotelegraphs
Title 48 Territories and Insular Possessions
Title 49 Transportation
Title 50 War and National Defense
Title 51 National and Commercial Space Programs

Figure 13.2

Title 20—Education

Chapter 1—Office Of Education (§§ 1,_2—6)
Chapter 2—Teaching Of Agricultural, Trade, Home Economics, And Industrial Subjects (§§ 11_To_14—35_To_35n)
Chapter 3—Smithsonian Institution, National Museums And Art Galleries (§§ 41—80s3)
. . . .
Chapter 28—Higher Education Resources And Student Assistance (§§ 1001—1161aa1)
. . . .
Chapter 31—General Provisions Concerning Education (§§ 1221—1235_To_1235g)
Chapter 32—Vocational Education (§§ 1241_To_1244—1247_To_1393f)
Chapter 33—Education Of Individuals With Disabilities (§§ 1400—1482)
. . . .
Chapter 48—Department Of Education (§§ 3401—3510)
Chapter 50—National Center For The Study Of Afro-American History And Culture (§§ 3701—3703)
Chapter 51—Elementary And Secondary Education Block Grant (§§ 3801_To_3808—3871_To_3876)
. . . .
Chapter 65—National Environmental Education (§§ 5501—5510)
. . . .
Chapter 69—School-To-Work Opportunities (§§ 6101_To_6104—6251)
. . . .
Chapter 75—Early Learning Opportunities (§§ 9401—9413)
Chapter 76—Education Research, Statistics, Evaluation, Information, And Dissemination (§§ 9501—9631)
Chapter 77—Financial Literacy And Education Improvement (§§ 9701—9709)
Chapter 78—Science, Technology, Engineering, Mathematics, And Critical Foreign Language Education (§§ 9801—9882)

Figure 13.3

Chapter 28—Higher Education Resources And Student Assistance

Subchapter i—General Provisions (§§ 1001—1019d)
Subchapter ii—Teacher Quality Enhancement (§§ 1021—1041)
Subchapter iii—Institutional Aid (§§ 1051—1068h)
Subchapter iv—Student Assistance (§§ 1070—1099e)
Subchapter v—Developing Institutions (§§ 1101—1103g)
Subchapter vi—International Education Programs (§§ 1121—11327)
Subchapter vii—Graduate And Postsecondary Improvement Programs (§§ 1133—1141)
Subchapter viii—Miscellaneous (§§ 1151—1155)
Subchapter ix—Additional Programs (§§ 1161a—1161aa1)

Figure 13.4

Note: the U.S. Code can be found in its entirety at the website of the U.S. Government Printing Office (GPO) at http://www.gpo.gov/fdsys/browse/collectionUScode.action?collectionCode=USCODE

by title, and regulations are listed according to the statute under which they were made. It was once practice to publish a set of volumes of the revised statutes, up-to-date at that point and incorporating in each statute any of the changes made by various Acts passed since the last revision. Reference to the *Schools Act,* R.S.X. 1990, for example, would indicate the *Schools Act* as it appeared in the Revised Statutes of (jurisdiction) X as of 1990, incorporating all the changes made to the Act since the Revised Statutes of X 1980. In between revisions, there would have been an annual publication of the statutes passed each year, every statute being given a chapter number as it was passed. The *Schools Amendment Act,* S.X. 1983, c.2, would indicate an Act amending the *Schools Act,* passed by the legislature of jurisdiction X in 1983, c.2 meaning "chapter 2", indicating that the Act is the second passed by the legislature in 1983. Until 1990, the changes made by the *Schools Amendment Act, 1983,* would only have been available in the annual statutes volume; afterwards they would have been incorporated in the revised statute. Anyone wishing to consult the statutes (and/or regulations) would have needed access to a library with a good government documents collection, or to a lawyer.

With the Internet, many (if not most) jurisdictions no longer publish a periodic printed revision of the consolidated statutes and regulations—the last Revised Statutes of Canada was in 1985—but maintain an electronic consolidation that revises each statute and law as soon as a change comes into force. These legal sites usually contain a number of lists, including the current consolidated laws, the annual Acts as passed by the legislature, and even "point in time" law, which allows the researcher to determine what the content of any law was at any particular point in time (since the statutes went online). Nonetheless, it is still not easy for the lay person to know where to look for the various Acts that pertain to a specific area of government responsibility; fortunately, government websites usually have a link to the legislation for which they are responsible.

In the United States (and each of its states), the law is codified, and each jurisdiction has its own Code. In a codification, all the laws pertaining to a subject, such as education or transportation, are brought together and organized systematically under headings and subheadings. Each legislature also publishes an annual collection of Acts, in the order in which they are passed—this is known as sessional law (and at the federal level as "Statutes at Large"). Whenever a new Act is passed, its provisions are inserted into the Code at the relevant place. In the figure above, *Figure 13.2* lists the Titles of the US Code, *Figure 13.3* lists some of the Chapters within Title 20: Education, and *Figure 13.4* presents the subchapters under Chapter 28—Higher Education Resources and Student Assistance.

A SHORT LOOK AT A SMALL ACT

Curiously, it is probably a safe observation that most citizens have never looked very closely, if at all, at an actual piece of legislation. Perhaps they believe that they will need a law degree to make sense of it. While this isn't necessarily or usually the case, legislation does have its own vocabulary and its own way of presenting material. This section provides a brief examination of the Province of Ontario's *Ticket Speculation Act.*

Act title

Act was included in 1990 revised consolidation

This version has been the up-to-date version since December 21, 2010 to the "e-Laws currency date," which is usually within three business days of the date accessed

Ticket Speculation Act

R.S.O. 1990, CHAPTER T.7

Head note (not part of the Act itself, but an assist to the reader)

Consolidation Period: From December 21, 2010 to the e-Laws currency date.

Last amendment: 2010, c. 27.

Indicates Act was last changed in 2010, the amending legislation being Chapter 27 in the 2010 source law

DEFINITION

Section Number

1. In this Act,

Most Acts begin by defining some of the key terms

"primary seller" means a person, other than a secondary seller, who is engaged in the business of making tickets available for sale, and includes the owner of the place to which a ticket provides admission, the promoter of the event occurring at that place and any agent or broker of those persons; ("vendeur principal")

"secondary seller" means a person who is engaged in the business of making available for sale tickets that have been acquired in any manner and by any person from or through a primary seller; ("vendeur secondaire")

"ticket" means a card, pass or other document upon presentation of which the holder is entitled to admission to any theatre, opera house, public hall, show, game, grandstand, race meeting, exhibition or amusement of any kind. ("billet de spectacle") R.S.O. 1990, c. T.7, s. 1; 2010, c. 27, s. 1.

Indicates that this section contains the version published in the Revised Statutes in 1990, as amended in 2010

OFFENCES:

Section 2 makes it an offence to engage in the activity commonly known as "scalping" —selling a ticket for a price higher than that paid for it

2. Every person who,

selling

(a) being the holder of a ticket, sells or disposes of the ticket at a higher price than that at which it was first issued, or endeavours or offers so to do; or

purchasing as a speculation or at a higher price than advertised

(b) purchases or attempts to purchase tickets with the intention of reselling them at a profit, or purchases or offers to purchase tickets at a higher price than that at which they are advertised or announced to be for sale by the owner or proprietor of any place mentioned in section 1,

is guilty of an offence and on conviction is liable to a fine of not more than $5,000. R.S.O. 1990, c. T.7, s. 2.

Indicates that this section has not been revised since it was published in the Revised Statutes in 1990

A fine of $5,000 (maximum) is set

PROHIBITION, PRIMARY SELLER

2.1 (1) No primary seller shall make a ticket available for sale for admission to an event in Ontario if a ticket for admission to the same event is or has been made available for sale by a secondary seller who is related to the primary seller. 2010, c. 27, s. 2.

PROHIBITION, SECONDARY SELLER

(2) No secondary seller shall make a ticket available for sale for admission to an event in Ontario if a ticket for admission to the same event is or has been made available for sale by a primary seller who is related to the secondary seller. 2010, c. 27, s. 2.

Related

(3) For the purposes of subsections (1) and (2), a primary seller and a secondary seller are related if a relationship between them, whether corporate, contractual or other, results, directly or indirectly, in an incentive for the primary seller to withhold tickets for sale by the primary seller so that they can be sold by, through or with the assistance of the secondary seller instead. 2010, c. 27, s. 2.

OFFENCE

(4) A person who contravenes subsection (1) or (2) is guilty of an offence and on conviction is liable to,

(a) if the person is an individual, a fine of not more than $5,000; and

(b) if the person is a corporation, a fine of not more than $50,000. 2010, c. 27, s. 2.

EXCEPTION AS TO SALE ON COMMISSION AT HOTEL STANDS AND STORES

3. This Act does not apply to the sale of tickets by the proprietor of a shop or hotel stand or a servant of the proprietor when such proprietor is an agent of a theatre, opera house, public hall, or grandstand, or of the owner or promoter of a show, game, race meeting, exhibition, or amusement of any kind for the sale of tickets, and where the commission charged upon the sale of each ticket does not exceed the maximum prescribed in the Schedule to this Act. R.S.O. 1990, c. T.7, s. 3.

REGULATIONS

4. The Attorney General may make regulations exempting any person or class of persons from this Act and prescribing conditions attaching to an exemption. 2010, c. 27, s. 3.

SCHEDULE

Price of Ticket	Maximum Commission
Up to $1.99	.25
$2.00 to $2.99	.35
$3.00 to $3.99	.45
$4.00 and up	.50

R.S.O. 1990, c. T.7, Sched.

Section 2.1 creates two new offences in response to a situation that developed whereby a ticket vendor redirected customers to its resale site on which tickets were available at a higher price

Added to the act in 2010

Section 3 provides for exemptions to the Act

A fine of $5,000 (maximum) for an individual, $50,000 for a corporation

This section was added to the Act in 2010

Indicates an addendum to the Act where specific maximum commissions are prescribed

Not revised since publication in Revised Statutes of 1990

This section added in 2010

Section 4 gives the Attorney General the power to make regulations...

...and indicates the subject matter for those regulations

Schedule unchanged since Revised Statutes of 1990.

THE LEGISLATIVE PROCESS

In modern democracies, the making of law occurs in the legislature and its committees. Whether that legislative activity involves an active engagement in policy-making depends on the constitutional system. In the majority of legislatures, which are parliamentary, most policy that requires legislative approval is introduced by the government in what it intends will be its final formulation. This is not to rule out the possibility of amendment, but this will be a matter of more or less, determined to some degree by the willingness of the government to accept "improvements" to its legislative proposals. In a majoritarian context, amendments will often be limited to the government's second thoughts

WHAT LEGISLATURES DO (BESIDES LEGISLATE)

Legislatures, by definition, make law, but that is only part of their business. One of the most important tasks of a legislature is to approve the government's planned expenditures and give approval to the revenue measures with which it will pay for them.

In both the parliamentary and separated-powers models, the legislature has an important role in holding the executive accountable. In parliamentary legislatures, there are a number of proceedings that allow **private members** (those who are not ministers) to question, respond to, and debate with ministers concerning the administration of their departments and the policies for which they are responsible. Some of this, such as Question Period, or responses to ministerial statements, takes place on the floor of the legislature. Other exercises of this function take place in legislative committees, where smaller groups of legislators meet to perform particular parliamentary functions. This is particularly true of **oversight committees**, which exist for the very purpose of holding the executive accountable. Typical examples are committees on expenditure estimates, which require ministers to answer for the planned expenditures that the legislature will later be asked to approve, and committees on public accounts, that may require senior bureaucrats to answer for the management of programs on the basis of value-for-money auditing principles. Other oversight committees may examine government agencies or review regulations.

In the separated-powers systems, where the executive has no place in the legislature, much of the oversight is also done through committees, which may compel officials to appear before them and give an account of their activities. The US Congress is a legislature that performs much of its work in its committees and subcommittees, many of which have built up a considerable body of expertise in their particular fields of responsibility.

At least two conditions are necessary for committees to be effective in whatever they do: sufficient powers, including some ability to determine their own agenda, rather than simply deal with matters referred to them, and a willingness and ability for committee members to work together across party lines to accomplish the committee's purposes. This has been more true, perhaps, in the US Congress, where party discipline is weaker and a tradition of bipartisanship still survives.

Legislators also have a function of presenting their constituents' opinions to the debate and commentary that occurs in the legislative chambers. They are, after all, there to represent their constituents, not simply to speak as their party or their own perspective dictates. Again, the daily calendar of proceedings provides opportunities for constituents' viewpoints to be presented, in addition to the opportunities afforded in legislative debate, or in questioning ministers.

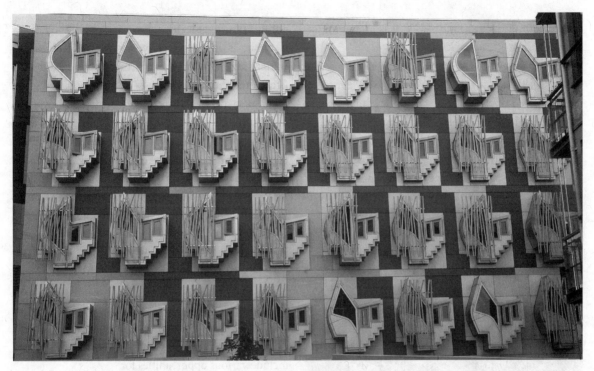

Offices of the Members of the Scottish Parliament. Edinburgh, United Kingdom.

about the matter, perhaps having received advice from stakeholders about difficulties or inconsistencies in the legislation that their experience led them to recognize more readily than those drafting the provisions. A minority government, by contrast, may be forced to accept amendments in order ensure passage of its bill and avoid defeat on the matter, or worse (a loss of confidence). In a coalition government, the susceptibility of legislation to amendment in the legislature may fall somewhere between majority and minority contexts. Bills that represent a consensus or common position of coalition partners are unlikely to receive more than merely technical amendments; those that represent a compromise between differing views may be more malleable as the trade-offs originally made are revisited in the legislature or in committee and readjusted.

THE IMPACT OF LEGISLATIVE ACTIVITY

What matters in each of these situations is the control of the executive over its legislators. In the majority situation this borders on being absolute. In a minority, it may be equally strong, but it is only a minority, so support of some other members not under the control of the executive must be sought. In a coalition, the agreements that coalition partners reach in the executive may not sit as well with the parties' caucuses, who may demand revisions. In a separated-powers legislature, such as the US Congress, policy very often *is* made on the floor of the legislature (as well as its committee rooms, hallways, and backrooms).

It may be useful to think of legislatures in the democratic world as being *active* or *reactive*—Mezy, who made this distinction about the policy influence of assemblies, had two more categories: *marginal* and *minimal*, which applied to assemblies in non-democratic regimes. The US Congress is cited as the epitome of active legislatures; it has been noted earlier more than once that policy is made by the legislature, independently of the executive. Westminster-style parliaments are regarded as being *reactive*, on the basis that they are limited to trying to influence the policy that is presented by the executive. Hague, Harrop,

and Breslin suggest that the parliament of the French Republic is another reactive assembly: "It does not initiate legislation, is not the main channel for ministerial recruitment, and does not function well as an arena of national debate. However, it does examine, improve and legitimize legislation" (301). These authors also suggest that Italy's and Sweden's parliaments have been more active: the former for negative reasons associated with its notorious instability; the latter for more positive reasons, including a history of collaboration and compromise involving stakeholders.

COMMON FEATURES OF THE LEGISLATIVE PROCESS

Once introduced, a bill will go through a variety of stages that differ from one legislature to another but nonetheless contain certain common elements. These include various opportunities for

- · careful examination of the contents of legislation;
- · discussion and debate over its merits or weaknesses;
- · change to its contents through amendment; and
- · decision over its fate by votes.

These stages are governed by strict procedural rules and take place in public so that formal law-making can be witnessed by the people. Dedicated parliamentary channels that broadcast proceedings have made this more true than ever before (although, ironically, this takes place at a time when the news outlets generally pay less and less attention to the substance of legislative debate than ever before). A brief discussion of the more common stages of the legislative process follows.

Legislative Library, British Columbia Legislative Assembly.

Presentation

Before anything can happen, a legislative proposal must be put before the members of the legislature. In the British parliamentary tradition this has meant three "readings"—a bill is brought before the legislature on three distinct occasions, at which time various things may happen (debate, a vote, a referral to committee) depending on the local rules. Most legislative processes involve some variation on this three-reading model. First reading is often a formality, necessary to put the bill before the House and distribute it to the legislators. One of the principal distinctions between legislative processes is what happens after the introduction or initial reading. In the United States, for example, the bill is immediately referred to the appropriate committee. This is possible but less likely in parliamentary processes.

Debate

An essential part of rational decision making is the chance for legislators to speak for or against a proposal. In this way the strengths and weaknesses of the proposal have the best chance of being uncovered and perhaps lead to a better proposal. The debate by legislators over the relative merits and demerits of a bill also provides the public the opportunity to learn about the bill, hear from its supporters and critics, and provide feedback to them.

Scrutiny and Testimony

For the same set of reasons that debate is important, so is the opportunity for *scrutiny* and *testimony*: scrutiny being the close examination of the bill in all its details, and testimony being the opportunity for legislators to hear the views of others with an interest in the bill, such as those who would be affected by it, or those who would administer it, or experts in the subject area the bill concerns. This stage of the consideration of a bill is done in legislative committee, not on the floor of the legislature. The committee is better situated than the whole legislature to perform detailed examination of the contents of the bill, and committee hearings provide an opportunity for non-parliamentarians to speak about a proposal.

Amendment

Out of debate and scrutiny may well come ideas about improvement, or second thoughts by the sponsors about what will achieve their purposes; for these or other reasons, there may be a desire to change the proposal. Providing an opportunity for amendment suggests that the legislature is really engaged in taking a proposal and making law from it. The decision by a government not to accept certain amendments to a bill may be one of the factors on which its performance is judged by those who are familiar with the legislation.

Decision

Eventually, there will be a time of decision and a determination of whether the bill lives or dies. In fact, there are usually several stages of decision in the legislative process, which enhances the legitimacy of the bill by demonstrating that its passage was truly the will of the legislature. In a legislature like the US Congress, where so many bills are introduced, it is necessary that proposals be rejected (or amalgamated with similar bills) sooner rather than later, so that the limited time of the legislature may be used most effectively. In some systems there is an "approval in principle," which indicates consent to the idea behind the bill but, as yet, no agreement on its specifics. In practice, if a bill is a

PARLIAMENTARY SYSTEM (AUSTRALIA, CANADA)   PRESIDENTIAL SYSTEM (UNITED STATES)

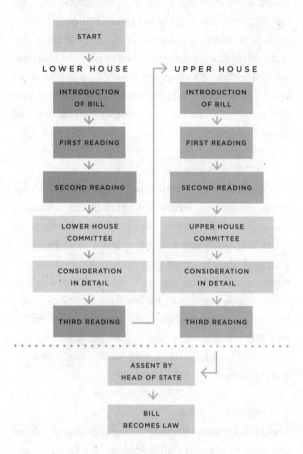

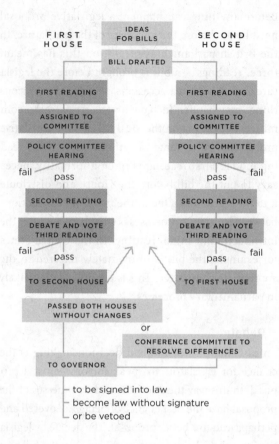

Figure 13.5

government bill, it is likely to pass, since the government has determined that it is a good idea.

Procedure

In addition to the above elements of a legislative process, there are some common procedural devices or issues involved. One is the use of committees to perform one or more of the stages in the legislative process, in particular that of scrutiny and testimony. Such committees are drawn from the legislature and meet separately; their composition usually reflects the balance of parties within the legislature as a whole. A second point concerns the passage of legislation in bicameral legislatures and whether or not a bill goes through both chambers concurrently (at the same time), as is common in the United States, or consecutively, as in most parliamentary systems (Canada included).

Most legislative systems make special rules or provisions for bills that commit the state to the expenditure of money or impose a tax. It is common in bicameral systems to limit the introduction of such "money bills," as these proposals are known, to the lower or first chamber (the House of Commons or House of Representatives). In most bicameral legislatures the approval of both chambers is necessary for a bill's passage, and a process may be in place to reconcile any differences in the versions passed by each chamber. This often involves a special committee drawn from both chambers.

Once a bill has passed through all the stages of approval by the legislature, it may require the consent of the head of state. In a parliamentary system, **executive assent** is more or less an automatic formality. In presidential or semi-presidential systems, the president commonly has the ability to veto legislation, which may or may not be overridden by the legislature voting for the legislation one more time, usually by a higher margin—commonly a two-thirds vote.

Systemic Differences

Because of strong party discipline and the majority position of the government, most bills introduced into the legislature in a parliamentary system become law. In addition, it is unusual (if not contrary to procedural rules) for more than one bill on the same subject to be introduced at any one time, and bills in bicameral systems tend to go through the two houses in sequence, proceeding from the lower to the upper chamber.

The picture is very different in the US system, which may be thought of as an obstacle course: of the many bills introduced into Congress, a small fraction succeed in surmounting all the hurdles. The legislative process is characterized by a series of veto points that filter out or select which bills proceed to the next stage.

DIRECT DEMOCRACY

On October 31, 2011, Greece's prime minister George Papandreou surprised the world when he announced a referendum would be held on the proposed bailout by the European Union and the International Monetary Fund of his country's debt crisis. The announcement came only days after the bailout had been finalized by the EU-IMF partners, following weeks of difficult negotiations. Because one condition of the bailout was that Greece continue to implement unpopular austerity measures, many observers felt that the referendum threatened to undo the whole deal, and with it, the stability of the Eurozone. A "no" vote in the referendum could mean the default of Greece's debt, and the partners who had agreed to the bailout package indicated that the referendum was also a vote on Greece's continued participation in the Eurozone. When he first revealed plans for a nationwide vote on the bailout, Papandreou was under fire from the public, the parliamentary opposition, and even members of his own party. Four days later, having secured the public support of the opposition for the bailout, he announced there would be no referendum. On November 11, 2011, Papandreou resigned to make way for a government of national unity (i.e., a grand coalition) to carry out Greece's economic restructuring.

This synopsis of the referendum-that-wasn't illustrates several features of direct democracy:

· how it can be used to decide politically unpopular or potentially divisive issues;
· how it may allow the political executive to bypass the legislature by appealing directly to the public; and
· how the decision whether or not to call a referendum often rests with the government.

There are only a few western democracies that have not held a national referendum, the United States being one of them. (This is ironic, because direct democracy at the sub-national level in the United States is probably rivalled or surpassed only by its use in the Swiss cantons.) On the other hand, few countries use referenda regularly, and only a handful (including France, Denmark, Australia, and Switzerland) have held more than ten. Direct democracy, then, is common but infrequent. Direct democracy includes all instruments that involve direct citizen participation or input on questions of policy or that challenge the mandate of an elected representative. The device of direct democracy most commonly employed is the referendum, but some important distinctions are collapsed by applying this term indiscriminately to all instances of popular voting on questions rather than for candidates.

The first distinction is whether the result of a vote is binding upon the state, or only consultative (advisory). Those that require a government response, or by a negative vote veto a government action, are properly referenda. Votes that have no legally binding force (one way or the other) are best described as plebiscites. For example, all three national votes in Canada—including the most recent, the 1992 vote on the constitutional package called the Charlottetown Accord—were plebiscites, the government not being bound by the results. However, in democratic states, proceeding contrary to the result of a plebiscite may not be politically prudent. To proceed with a measure despite a negative vote or to refuse to go forward with a proposal that the public has endorsed is to invite a popular backlash, which might influence the next election. To a large degree, then, a plebiscite carries almost as much force as a referendum in countries with a democratic tradition. A second difference, though, is that while the decision to hold a plebiscite is almost always (since it is consultative) at the discretion of the government, referenda are mandatory in a number of contexts:

·   to ratify constitutional change (Australia, Ireland, and Switzerland, to name but three);
·   to surrender sovereignty to a supra-national body (the first referendum ever in the Netherlands, in 2005, was held on the European Constitution);
·   to become an independent regime (Slovenia in 1990, Croatia in 1991); or
·   to ratify an international treaty (Costa Rica's first referendum, held in 2007, on the Dominican Republic–Central America Free Trade Agreement (DR-CAFTA).

Third, there is a difference between votes in which the question originates with the state, as is the case in most referenda or plebiscites, and those where the

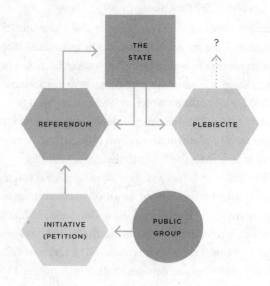

Figure 13.6

question originates somewhere in the electorate—usually in what is known as an initiative. An initiative is a process by which a segment of the public is able to force the state to put a question before the wider population. It normally requires the collection of a specified number or proportion of signatures within a limited time period (150,000 signatures in 90 days, for example, or signatures representing 10 per cent of the total votes cast in the previous election in 45 days). In addition, there are usually procedures to ensure that the question put before the public is constitutional, and in some jurisdictions (Switzerland) the government may present the public with a counter proposal. There are several purposes to which an initiative may be employed:

- to propose a new law;
- to propose a revision of the constitution;
- to defeat or veto a bill passed by the legislature (**abrogative referendum**); and
- to challenge the mandate of an elected representative (recall).

While initiatives are popular in many American states, Switzerland is the only country that employs them with any frequency on a national level, where they are limited to proposals for revision of the constitution. Popular initiatives have placed matters on the national ballot in Austria and Italy, among other jurisdictions.

The abrogative referendum (or popular veto) puts an act passed by the legislature before the electorate for ratification (or defeat) in a referendum. Usually this must take place within a prescribed time period after the passage of legislation and will be initiated by opponents of the law in question. In Denmark, such a vote may be requested by one-third of the members of the legislature, except for laws concerning finance and international law. The very existence of this device might well cause governments to think twice about passing legislation it knows is unpopular.

There are many reasons why regimes allow and citizens choose to bypass representation and employ direct-democracy instruments, although it should be emphasized that in all cases direct democracy is supplementary or complementary to the processes of representative government and has never replaced them. Most commonly, referenda seem to meet one of two needs. The first is to give legitimacy to a decision, the scope or status of which is too large or too important to be decided by representatives on the people's behalf. Hence the common use of referenda to ratify constitutional changes, declare independence, or ratify treaties. Similarly, entry into the European Union has required a successful referendum on the question in each potential member country; in the round of expansion occurring in 1995, which saw the admission of Austria, Finland, and Sweden, the people of Norway in a referendum rejected membership.

A second basis for direct democracy is to locate responsibility for deciding questions of a politically sensitive or potentially divisive nature squarely with the public; in this way, parties can avoid internal division over an issue, or being forever identified with a decision that might be unacceptable to a significant segment of the population. Questions that deal with moral issues have often been decided directly; in Italy and Ireland, abortion and divorce have been addressed by referendum. In the first half of the twentieth century, questions about the prohibition (or ending the prohibition) of the sale of alcohol were commonly addressed in popular ballots. Of Canada's three national plebiscites, one addressed constitutional questions (1992), one concerned conscription of soldiers (1942), and one was about prohibition of alcohol (1898). There have also been 36 provincial plebiscites or referenda on the sale or prohibition of alcohol.

Switzerland's unique political and constitutional arrangements (see Chapter 7), in particular the seeming permanence of a grand coalition and the inability of the legislature to defeat the executive, provide a compelling basis for direct democracy. It is no accident that this country leads the world in the variety and frequency of its use of direct instruments. With no effective parliamentary opposition to the government, the referendum and initiative allow Swiss citizens to assume the oppositional role of providing a check on the government.

It is also possible that the Swiss have just come to believe in the value of direct democracy, and principle is another reason for advocating non-representative decision making. In Canada in the 1990s, the official platform of the Reform Party called for referenda, initiatives, and a recall process. It is no accident that Canada's loudest voice for direct democracy came from a populist conservative party; it has long been noted that the general tenor of direct democracy is conservative. Public opinion is generally wary of change, slow to embrace new causes, and always resistant to new taxes. For those wishing to limit or reduce the size of the state, direct questions on tax cuts and other fiscal measures seem a promising strategy. Hence the emergence over the few decades of so-called "taxpayer protection" legislation, which requires governments to put any tax increases or new taxes that were not part of an election platform or manifesto before the public for approval in a referendum.

Depending on one's perspective, then, the conservative character of direct democracy can be seen as a virtue or a defect. Clearly, there are practical limits to the type of issue that can be addressed by referendum; only some matters are capable of being addressed by a question that permits only "yes" or "no" responses. In forcing categorical responses, the referendum also forces decisions and thereby may exclude the possibility of compromise or consensus. As in all situations where the majority has clear control of the outcome, minorities may feel threatened by direct democracy. In the 1942 Canadian plebiscite on conscription, for example, the national Yes vote (affirming the possibility of conscription) was 63.7 per cent, but in Quebec it was 29 per cent, reflecting very different attitudes towards Canada's war participation by English-speaking and French-speaking Canadians.

Another issue is the expertise or competence of the general public; how well-informed are the referendum voters on the issue(s) being decided? The onus of educating the citizens on the positions for or against the referendum or initiative question usually falls to the groups campaigning on either side of the issue. This means that the rules governing direct-democracy campaigns are also important: do they provide a level playing field or provide advantages to some interests and not others?

In the absence of rules, the referendum campaign becomes a free-for-all in which those with the most influence have the advantage: in all likelihood, those with the most resources to spend on advertising, polling, and the other tools of mass communication. In many jurisdictions, referendum legislation requires the establishment and registration of umbrella organizations for both sides of the question, and these organizations in turn are subject to regulations concerning financing, expenditures, and advertising. The effectiveness of these rules in creating open, fair, and informative campaigns varies considerably.

NO Freeman shall be taken or imprisoned, or be disseised of his Freehold, or Liberties, or free Customs, or be outlawed, or exiled, or any other wise destroyed; nor will We not pass upon him, nor [condemn him,] but by lawful judgment of his Peers, or by the Law of the Land. We will sell to no man, we will not deny or defer to any man either Justice or Right.

Figure 13.7

In short, in addition to the principled belief that "the people should decide," there are many practical reasons why referenda or initiatives may provide important enhancements to the processes of representative government. At the same time, the clear limitations to the feasibility of such mass instruments means they are always likely to be supplementary rather than form the basis of modern democracy. The ability of such instruments to provide citizens with "good government" will ultimately depend on the citizens themselves and their preparation for sound decision making. Here, no less than in voting for representatives, what matters is the quality of information on which citizens depend, the activity of the mass media, the distribution of resources among competing actors, and the susceptibility or immunity of the public to manipulation.

PRIVATE LAW

The law made by legislatures is **public law**, which Duhaime's Legal Dictionary defines as "Those laws which regulate the structure and administration of the government, the conduct of the government in its relations with its citizens, the responsibilities of government employees and the relationships with foreign governments." In addition, there is a large body of **private law** that applies to the relations between individuals. Where this law is found, how it is made, and where it is adjudicated is determined by whether a regime falls within the common law or **civil law** tradition.

COMMON LAW

Regimes that were once part of the British Empire have inherited the English common-law system for most matters of private law. This has its origins in the development of the jury system in England in the twelfth century, under which certain disputes between individuals would be heard by a jury; the right to a jury trial was included in the Magna Carta and is one of the three clauses still in effect today (see *Figure 13.7*). In this system, private law consists of the body of decisions reached in specific cases, articulated by judges ruling on the basis of the precedents (the doctrine of *stare decisis*—to stand by decided matters). The guiding principle is that cases with similar circumstances should be decided in a similar fashion. Common law is sometimes called "judge-made" law. In regimes within the common-law tradition, much of the fundamental law concerning contracts, property, and torts (wrongs) is contained only in the common law. Hearing a case involves the legal representatives of the parties presenting arguments as to the facts of the matter and the appropriate decisions that should be considered as providing a precedent to be followed. In a case where circumstances are unique, the judge (or judges) will be

COMMON LAW	CIVIL LAW
emphasis on precedent, prior rulings of the court	emphasis on first principles, application of systematic legal science
judges proceed on the basis of previous cases	judges proceed from provisions of the code
reasoning is inductive, deriving judgements from series of specific decisions	reasoning is deductive, moving from stated general principles to specific solution
integrated court systems with courts of general jurisdiction	specialized court system to deal with separate areas of law
a trial is a single-event (continuous) proceeding	a trial is an extended series of hearings and consultations
judge manages the trial and referees the adversarial conflict between the prosecuting and defending attorneys	judge is principal interrogator of witnesses in an inquisitorial process designed to uncover the truth

(based on Apple and Deyling, 34–37)

Figure 13.8

required to make a ruling not based on those that have gone before, which will now stand as a precedent for similar cases to come.

CIVIL LAW

The civil-law tradition is much older than the common-law system, being traced back to Roman law, but its most famous modern version was the Napoleonic Code, which was exported to the lands Napoleon conquered in the early nineteenth century and is now known as the Code Civil. Apple and Deyling also note the importance of other Codes, such as the German, the Chilean, and the Brazilian. In North America, private law in Quebec and Louisiana, as former French colonies, follows the civil-law tradition. The "Code" is an attempt to draft a comprehensive set of laws, deduced from first principles, to apply to the various areas of private law, including family law, contract law, property, and inheritance. The authors of law are not judges but legal scholars, also known as "jurists." The civil law prevails in Europe (outside of Britain and Ireland), Central and South America, and much of Africa and Asia (37 of the 45 regimes in the data set). In many common-law countries, criminal law is codified, but the Criminal Code remains heavily influenced by judicial precedents that have been incorporated into the Code by legislatures. In civil-law countries there may be separate civil, criminal, commercial, and constitutional codes.

The basic differences between common law and civil law are far reaching, affecting the structure of courts, the nature of trials, the roles of judges, and other related matters. *Figure 13.8* presents some of these contrasts, drawing upon Part III of Apple and Deyling (34–37). The authors also suggest that some of the differences between these traditions are becoming blurred.

ADMINISTRATIVE LAW

The discussion of the policy process in Chapter 12 drew attention to the fact that a great deal of authority is delegated to the bureaucracy for the purpose of administering the laws passed by the legislature, in particular the ongoing programs by which governments provide services, benefits, regulation, inspection, and numerous other public functions. It would be ideal, but quite remarkable, if every exercise of bureaucratic authority was correct, fair, and timely. In the real world, disputes arise over administrative decisions, and regimes provide differently for their resolution.

In common-law countries such as Australia, Canada, New Zealand, and the United Kingdom, the venue for disputes about administrative decisions is often an administrative (or adjudicative) **tribunal**, a quasi-judicial body with the power to hear appeals of administrative decisions. It is *quasi*-judicial because it is not chaired by a judge, and its members may not be legally trained but bring expertise of a different sort. The degree to which a decision by a tribunal can be appealed to the courts for judicial review also varies. In many cases, the decision of a tribunal is final, except where an error in law has been made. Tribunals have the ability, which is not commonly true of a court, to engage in alternative dispute resolution (ADR) methods, such as mediation or arbitration, and avoid an actual hearing. Although tribunals are designed to provide quicker decisions than would be delivered by the

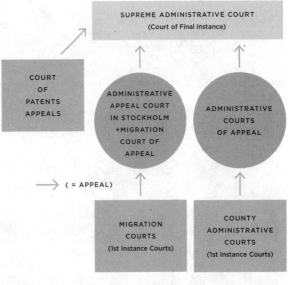

Figure 13.9

ACKNOWLEDGEMENT

Information on the court systems presented in this chapter draws upon resources on the website of the Association of the Councils of State and Supreme Administrative Jurisdictions of the European Union (www.juradmin.eu), including Newsletter 18 (2007) detailing the legal structures of the member states.

courts, and provide them much more cheaply, inadequate resources can sometimes create considerable case backlogs. In Canada, most positions on tribunals are government appointments, which may raise concerns about the impartiality and quality of the appointees. In some cases, appointments may be reviewable by the legislature (usually one of its committees).

In civil-law regimes, the tradition of specialized courts extends to special administrative courts that exist for the purpose of hearing appeals against decisions taken by the state and its officials. A long tradition of such courts means that a significant body of administrative law exists within these regimes. These include not only courts of *first instance* (where the initial trial is heard) but one or two levels of **appellate** courts (where appeals are heard). *Figure 13.9* provides a diagram of the Swedish system of administrative courts. This system is entirely separate from Sweden's system of ordinary courts.

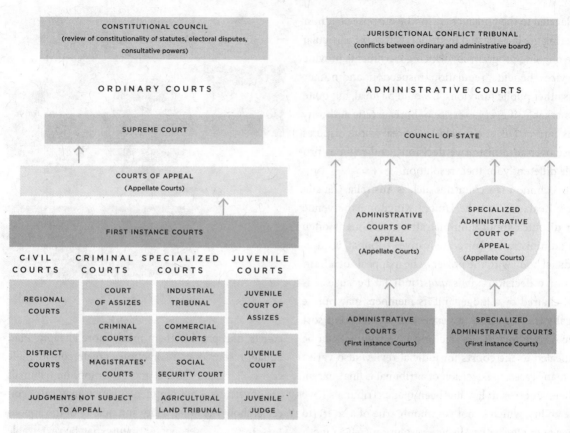

COURT SYSTEM OF THE FRENCH REPUBLIC

CONSTITUTIONAL COUNCIL
(review of constitutionality of statutes, electoral disputes, consultative powers)

JURISDICTIONAL CONFLICT TRIBUNAL
(conflicts between ordinary and administrative board)

ORDINARY COURTS

ADMINISTRATIVE COURTS

SUPREME COURT

COUNCIL OF STATE

COURTS OF APPEAL
(Appellate Courts)

FIRST INSTANCE COURTS

CIVIL COURTS	CRIMINAL COURTS	SPECIALIZED COURTS	JUVENILE COURTS
REGIONAL COURTS	COURT OF ASSIZES	INDUSTRIAL TRIBUNAL	JUVENILE COURT OF ASSIZES
DISTRICT COURTS	CRIMINAL COURTS	COMMERCIAL COURTS	JUVENILE COURT
	MAGISTRATES' COURTS	SOCIAL SECURITY COURT	
JUDGMENTS NOT SUBJECT TO APPEAL		AGRICULTURAL LAND TRIBUNAL	JUVENILE JUDGE

ADMINISTRATIVE COURTS OF APPEAL
(Appellate Courts)

SPECIALIZED ADMINISTRATIVE COURT OF APPEAL
(Appellate Courts)

ADMINISTRATIVE COURTS
(First instance Courts)

SPECIALIZED ADMINISTRATIVE COURTS
(First instance Courts)

Figure 13.10

COURT SYSTEMS

Like Sweden, most civil-law countries have a parallel court system of ordinary courts and administrative courts. *Figure 13.10* provides the architecture of the court system of the French Republic, which culminates in a Supreme Court (the court of final instance for ordinary courts), a Council of State (the court of final instance for administrative courts), a Jurisdictional Conflict Tribunal (to settle conflicts between ordinary and administrative courts), and a Constitutional Council (which reviews the constitutionality of legislation).

By contrast, courts in common-law systems tend to have a more pyramidal structure, in which a Supreme Court sits at the apex, charged with being the final court of instance for all matters: civil, criminal, administrative, and constitutional. *Figure 13.11* shows the structure of the Canadian court system, which reflects the federal division of powers that has given provinces the responsibility for the administration of justice.

Canada's Supreme Court is the final court of appeal for all criminal, civil, military, and constitutional cases. Just under one-half of the countries in the dataset (21 of 45) have a constitutional court separate from the High or Supreme Court that is the final authority on other appeals. Not all of the regimes in the civil-law tradition have a separate constitutional court, but each regime with such a court has a civil-law system. In some other cases, in which the Supreme Court has separate panels to hear different types of cases, one panel is dedicated to constitutional questions.

RIGHTS

The rule of law is a *procedural* rather than a *substantive* principle. That is to say, it deals with *how* the law is made rather than with *what* the law concerns. The rule of law is concerned with the grading practices of a course rather than its curriculum, with the rules of the road but not the journey. For the most part, the rule of law is silent concerning the *content* of the law. Does the law ban all abortions or permit all abortions? Does it forbid religious practice or allow the private ownership of semi-automatic weapons? Does it permit pollution of the environment or limit public nudity? None of these questions, or an infinite number of others, can be answered on the basis of the principle of the rule of law.

Rights, on the other hand, are very much about the content of the law. As *entitlements that citizens can expect to be enforced against others and the state*, rights confine the content of the law within established limits. They attempt to reduce the possibility that the government will make unjust laws or exercise power

OUTLINE OF CANADA'S COURT SYSTEM

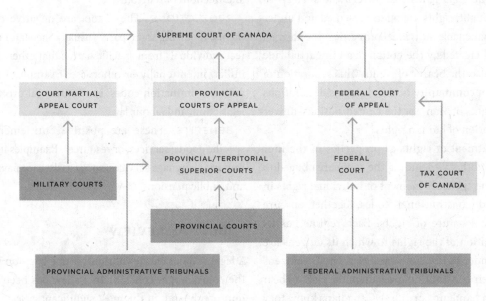

Figure 13.11

unjustly. Rights state that there are certain subjects about which the government may not legislate, certain freedoms that the government may not abridge, or certain actions that the state may not take. If nothing else, the story of justice in the twentieth century narrates the triumph of rights. Almost every issue that receives attention is presented by at least one of the interested parties as a question of rights. We live in an age in which people not only speak seriously about rights for animals, but in which governments have legislated such rights. The discourse on rights has become so ingrained that a list of the entitlements that people believe are theirs would be unimaginably long.

Rights are claims that you or I make and that some other party, such as the state or another individual, is required to respect *because these rights have been embedded in law*. Regardless of the different moral beliefs citizens may have, their rights are recognized through the legal rules that govern the society. In liberal thought, rights are often presented and understood as inalienable individual properties. The abstract individual created by the notion of an impartial rule of law is also the bearer of rights. This separation of rights from community is what informs declarations of the "Rights of Man," or the United Nations' universal declaration of human rights.

The treatment of rights as properties of the individual that others (including the state) are obliged to respect, and the enshrinement of individual rights in entrenched (constitutional) codes, together, obscure the political nature of rights. Each regime has its own definition of the rights to which its citizens are entitled under its law. For example, many US citizens believe their constitution gives them the right to bear arms (own handguns or rifles); Canadians know they have no such entitlement (or rather, that any claim they might make to such an entitlement is not recognized by Canadian law). The rights actually enjoyed are defined by law, and law is itself a political act, the result of humans legislating. As such, rights exist only so long as the legislation that defines them remains in force, and even constitutionally entrenched rights can be changed through subsequent political actions. In this respect, an individual enjoys rights not as a result of being an individual but in his or her capacity as a member of a political community. The status of the rights enjoyed depends upon the political decisions made within the regime, and upon the distribution of the power to make such decisions.

The objects of rights are of basically three kinds:

FREEDOMS. These are negative entitlements, which require others to refrain from interference with an individual's specific actions or behaviours. Examples include freedom of expression, freedom of association, and freedom of religion.

PROTECTIONS. These, too, are negative entitlements, requiring some party (usually the state) to protect individuals from specific harms that others might inflict, intentionally or otherwise. Examples include anti-discrimination codes, environmental protection legislation, and labour laws.

BENEFITS. These are positive entitlements to specific goods, services, or resources. Examples include minority language services, social assistance payments, and public pensions.

JUDICIAL REVIEW

A legal code or charter of rights is one basis on which the courts might conclude that a law has been made improperly and, in the most significant cases, unconstitutionally. The process by which the courts evaluate legislation proposed or passed by the legislature and are able to confirm or reject it is known as judicial review. It is one of the most serious elements of the system of checks and balances in the Madisonian model, but it also plays an important role in most parliamentary system and in all federal regimes. Judicial review involves two elements: a written constitution, and a court of final instance (a court from which there is no appeal) empowered to reject legislation that it judges to be contrary to the constitution. In this system the court acts as a check on the legislature, protecting the rights of citizens as defined within the constitutional document and ensuring that legislation is consistent with other constitutional provisions, such as the division of powers.

Where there is judicial review (and to the extent that judicial review is possible), parliamentary supremacy has been eliminated; the courts have the ability to second-guess policy-makers by subjecting their acts to scrutiny on the basis of the written constitution. Judicial review means a replacement of parliamentary sovereignty with constitutional sovereignty. In theory the final word (in a democracy) remains with the people; if the constitution becomes a roadblock to popular or necessary legislation, it is always possible to amend the constitution. In practice, though, this is often difficult, and this is precisely why rights that are defined by the written constitution are said to be *entrenched*.

THE SCOPE OF JUDICIAL REVIEW

The ability of a court to judge an action of the state/government (including its legislation) to be unconstitutional rests, in almost all cases, on the conclusion that the body taking the action did not have the authority to do so. This, in turn, implies one of three circumstances: the body taking the action (the executive, for example) was exercising the authority belonging properly to *another* part of the state (the legislature); one level of state (national) was exercising authority in a field of jurisdiction belonging to another level of government (sub-national); or the government/state was infringing a constitutionally entrenched right. In the first two cases, *what* is being done is not the issue so much as *who* is doing it. To strike down an executive order because it was something that should have been done by the legislature, or to reject an act of one level of state because it is a power belonging to the other level of state, means that if the legislature had acted in the first case, or the proper level of state in the second case, there would have been no constitutional bone to pick. In the third case, the problem is not with which body is taking the action so much as that *any* body is taking the action. This applies only with respect to constitutional rights.

The entrenchment of rights and the provision of judicial review allow an independent institution (the courts) to protect minorities against the actions of a legislative majority. It is not a guarantee of such protection, nor does it ensure that the minorities that receive the protection afforded by judicial review are those that actually need it. Just as securing rights through the political process requires having the resources on which political success rests, successfully challenging the constitutionality of a law requires legal resources, namely legal expertise and the ability to fund a sustained legal challenge. A constitutional challenge may involve three separate trials (court of first instance, court of appeal, court of final instance) and favours those with resources: either wealthy individuals or corporations, or organized groups that pool the more meagre resources of their members.

One concern with judicial review is the unaccountability of the judges who ultimately rule on the constitutionality of legislation. To a certain degree, this unaccountability is the necessary flip-side of the principle of judicial independence (which requires that courts be free from political influence). Nonetheless, the length of tenure for judges means that political opinions consistent with public values at the time of appointment may increasingly fall out of step over time; appointment to the Court for life may bless (or burden) subsequent generations with the political values of a preceding era.

None of this would matter if the decisions that the Court makes were simply (as many citizens seem to regard them) findings of fact and as legal questions, merely "objective" matters for which nothing else is relevant but legal expertise and judicial experience. However, as many have noted, in performing judicial review the courts are making political decisions. They may be hearing legal arguments and rendering legal decisions on the basis of legal precedents, but the content of what is being decided is very political. One simple reason for this is that the phrases contained in any constitutional code are generally vague enough so as to require considerable interpretation by the courts before they can be applied to particular cases. Judges individually, and courts collectively, gain a reputation for the styles of interpretation that they favour. One common distinction is between **judicial activism** and **restraint**. There are two different ways this distinction has been presented: one focusing on outcomes, the other on the style of interpretation. Russell, Knopf, and Morton argue that the distinction refers either to the willingness or reluctance of a court to set aside legislative or executive acts: "Activism refers to judicial vigour in enforcing constitutional limitations on the other branches of government and a readiness to veto the policies of those branches of government on constitutional grounds.

Self-restraint connotes a judicial predisposition to find room within the constitution for the policies of democratically accountable decision-makers."(19)

	ACTIVISM	RESTRAINT
readiness to veto government action	willing	reluctant
style of interpretation	broad and creative	narrow and literal

Figure 13.12

A different application of these terms is made by Landes, who sees restraint when "the courts take a very narrow view of their own powers of interpretation ... the judges seek to divine the literal and intended meaning of the initial constitution," while activism "reflects a willingness on the part of judges to use their powers vigorously, if necessary, to take a broad view of any powers delineated in the constitution" (255). It is not clear that these two competing applications of judicial activism and judicial restraint can be reconciled. In some circumstances, a narrow (restrained) interpretation could lead to support for governmental actions (e.g., ruling that "freedom of peaceful assembly" does not entail the picketing by public servants of courthouses), while in other circumstances it could lead to judicial review of legislation (e.g., the "right to the enjoyment of property" is improperly infringed by environmental regulations). Similarly, a broad, "between the lines" interpretation could, depending on circumstances, enlarge the legislative competence of the state or limit it on behalf of individuals. At any rate, what either set of distinctions makes clear is that there is no neutral, objective middle ground that the courts are in a position to articulate simply because they contain judges, not elected representatives.

AUTOMATIC JUSTICE?

Common to the rule of law and rights is the depersonalization of authority that accompanied the transformation from feudalism to liberal modernity in Western Europe. There is a tendency in liberal notions of justice to look for a procedure, a formula, or a process that by being followed or invoked will ensure that justice ensues. This reflects the concern with the bias, discrimination, or prejudice that can result when too much discretion is given to those in positions of authority. However, there are times when it is worth recalling Aristotle's view that justice is never wholly a matter of applying the rules, but sometimes requires wisdom and judgment to be applied to the particularities or circumstances of a matter. This may be more feasible in the more informal setting of adjudicative tribunals, where many decisions are taken concerning non-constitutional rights such as the protections and benefits contained in ordinary statutes.

Perhaps because of the broad degree of public consensus (or lack of dispute) over their utility, the rule of law and rights have largely departed from the political realm, almost entirely with the former, and increasingly with rights as they become further judicialized. As noted above, political decisions continue to be made, particularly when it comes to rights, even though the forum for decision making (i.e., the courts) is not generally seen to be political.

In addition, there remain important rights questions that are *not* constitutionalized, but are left to legislatures to determine and define and, thus, are still understood to be legitimate political questions. For example, however much the Charter has transformed justice and politics in Canada since 1982, it applies only to the activities of the institutions of state. The rights of Canadians with respect to each other,

VEIL OF IGNORANCE

One liberal thinker who contributed greatly to modern debates concerning social justice was John Rawls (*A Theory of Justice*). Like many of his predecessors, Rawls asks his readers to imagine social arrangements as the result of a contract that they enter into with other individuals. However, in Rawls's scenario people determine the nature of this contract behind a "veil of ignorance" concerning where they will be situated in that society.

Most of the time, people are well aware of their social position or standing and can imagine social arrangements by which it would be improved. Rawls's question is: What set of arrangements would we construct if we didn't know where we might end up, or if it was entirely up to chance which position we came to occupy? Rawls concludes that our self-interest would lead us to establish arrangements consistent with equality. In other words, if equality is the principle of justice governing our social arrangements, it does not matter which social position we occupy; we are left no better or worse off than others. This argument further allows that any inequality must tend to the benefit of those who are least advantaged. In other words, for Rawls, justice consists of initial conditions of equality and action to correct or compensate for any inequalities that arise.

of employees with respect to employers, of consumers with respect to corporations—all these are rights (insofar as they are rights) defined in ordinary legislation. Entrenched rights codes such as the Charter put limits on the power of the state, but not the significant sources of private power in our world. One legitimate concern with constitutionally entrenched rights is their potential to limit the state from making policies that shift the balance of private power in society—yet another reason why some are very pleased to constitutionalize rights. Early in the twenty-first century, the role of the state in society and the relationship of public power to private power remain important questions still seeking a consensus.

REFERENCES

Apple, James G., and Robert P. Deyling. *A Primer on the Civil-Law System.* Federal Judicial Center (April 1995): 68 pp. Web.

Hague, Rod, Martin Harrop, and Shaun Breslin. *Comparative Government and Politics.* 3rd ed. London: Macmillan, 1992.

Landes, Ronald. *The Canadian Polity.* 4th ed. Scarborough, ON: Prentice Hall, 1995.

Mezy, M. *Comparative Legislatures.* Durham, NC: Duke University Press, 1979.

Rawls, John. *A Theory of Justice.* Cambridge, MA: Harvard University Press, 1971.

Russell, Peter, R. Knopff, and F. L. Morton. *Federalism and the Charter: Leading Constitutional Decisions.* Ottawa: Carleton University Press, 1989.

FURTHER READINGS

Arter, David. "Comparing the Legislative Performance of Legislatures." *Journal of Legislative Studies* 12.3–4 (September–December 2006): 245–257.

Huneeus, Carlos, Fabiola Berrios, and Rodrigo Cordero. "Legislatures in Presidential Systems: The Latin American Experience." *Journal of Legislative Studies* 12.3–4 (September–December 2006): 404–425.

Ingram, James D. "What is a 'Right to Have Rights?' Three Images of the Politics of Human Rights." *American Political Science Review* 102.4 (November 2008): 401–416.

Kerrouche, Eric. "The French Assemblée nationale: The Case of a Weak Legislature?" *Journal of Legislative Studies* 12.3–4 (September–December 2006): 336–365.

Lundberg, Thomas Carl. "Competition between Members of the Scottish Parliament and the Welsh Assembly: Problem or Virtue?" *The Political Quarterly* 77.1 (January 2006): 107–116.

McGann, Anthony. "Social Choice and Comparing Legislatures: Constitutional versus Institutional Constraints." *Journal of Legislative Studies* 12.3–4 (September–December 2006): 443–461.

Newell, James. "Characterizing the Italian Parliament: Legislative Change in Longitudinal Perspective." *Journal of Legislative Studies* 12.3–4 (September–December 2006): 386–403.

Nijink, Lia, Shaheen Mozaffar, and Elisabete Azevedo. "Parliaments and the Enhancement of Democracy on the African Continent: An Analysis of Institutional Capacity and Public Perceptions." *Journal of Legislative Studies* 12.3–4 (September–December 2006): 311–335.

Owens, John, and Burdett Loomis. "Qualified Exceptionalism: The US Congress in Comparative Perspective." *Journal of Legislative Studies* 12.3–4 (September–December 2006): 258–290.

Stemplowska, Zofia. "Making Justice Sensitive to Responsibility." *Political Studies* 57.2. (June 2009): 237–259.

CHAPTER 14

Governing in an Age of Decline? Social and Economic Policy

Among the characteristics of modern liberal democracies that contemporary readers are likely to take for granted are three: (1) the private ownership of property, (2) the reliance on "free" markets to allocate resources, and (3) the responsibility of the state for the functioning of an economy based on (1) and (2). This is a somewhat paradoxical reliance on a set of economic arrangements that call for minimal state intervention but hold the state accountable for (and/or expect its quick response to) any economic crises that arise, even when the crises are created by poor business or financial decisions. Similarly, while mainstream ideologies long ago reached a consensus that the capitalist market economy is here to stay, the role of the state in its management is a central dimension on which ideologies differentiate themselves. There may be widespread disagreement about what the state should do about "the economy," but everyone expects it to do something.

Arguably, economic policy-making has always been one of the principal responsibilities of the state, but in the democratic era the expectation is that political authority will be exercised on behalf of all, not simply the dominant economic class. (One does not need to be a Marxist to recognize that under *any* system of economic organization there will be a group or class that is most favoured by these arrangements. In feudal times, for example, this was the nobility.) The capitalist market economy created, over time, a sizeable educated "middle" class, which may not be the dominant economic class but, under the political arrangements of representative democracy, can be a dominating political class. One of the challenges facing liberal democracies today is the continuing decline of the middle class, a decline that began in the 1970s and has become more noticeable since 2000.

The state's economic policy-making and the state of the economy determine the state's capacity for policy-making in other fields, particularly social policy. The role of the state in providing (and/or funding the provision of) education, health care, social assistance, arts funding, parks and recreation funding, and basic infrastructure such as water, sewers, energy, roads, and bridges, was either invented or expanded during the time since the property requirements for voting were eliminated. Periods of sustained prosperity permitted the growth of the modern welfare state. Sustained uncertainty and looming changes in the global economy early in the twenty-first century raise questions about the long-term viability of the programs associated with the welfare state. If they are not economically feasible are they nonetheless politically necessary? Without them, can the capitalist market economy be justified to a majority of the electorate?

THE NATURE OF CAPITALIST MARKET SOCIETY

There are two fundamental components to the capitalist market economy. One is the private ownership of property; the other is the use of market transactions to allocate inputs and outputs. Private property *and*

markets long pre-date the emergence of capitalism. What changed was the emergence of new modes of production: manufacturing (making goods in quantity, although often still by hand) in the seventeenth and eighteenth centuries, and industry (using technology to manufacture things) in the nineteenth. Combined with urbanization and improved means of transportation, the significance of both private property and markets was transformed.

Prior to manufacturing and industry, the dominant mode of production was agricultural, and the dominant economic class comprised wealthy landowners and nobility with their large estates. Wealth was produced through *rent,* paid in money or in product. The role of markets (or "the market") was minimal. With manufacturing and industry, a new class—the capitalist—emerged. Wealth was used to invest in raw materials, a production process, and human labour to produce goods. The market was involved in the purchase of the inputs and in the sale of the outputs. Depending on the availability of money, investment capital might also be obtained in the financial market. The private property that mattered at the outset of market society, then, was the ownership of the means of production. Most individuals were unlikely to own anything except a few personal possessions. At the outset of market society there was no middle class to speak of; there were landlords and tenants on the one hand, and owners and workers on the other. It would take time for the emergence of a middle class, characterized, at least today, by home ownership and disposable income. Personal property, which had little to do with the growth of capitalism in the nineteenth century, has had a large role in the health of the economy in recent decades. In part, this reflects the transformation of advanced capitalist societies from technologically intensive industry to a

Shopping in Shanghai, China.

post-industrial stage relying on an expanding service sector and the explosion of information technology.

In a fully developed market society, all production is for "the market," which is simply the aggregate of individual transactions, the purchase and sale by individuals of goods, services, or labour. The principal alternative to the market in modern times is the authoritative transfer of resources by the state, which accounts for a significant share of the modern economy. In a completely "free" or unregulated market, resource allocation occurs by non-authoritative means, that is to say, private, voluntary exchanges subject only to the "natural" forces of the market (the so-called "laws" of supply and demand).

The modern market economy servicing a consumer society and organizing the largest part of socially productive labour is the result of several centuries of development, of the emergence and development of technology, of the organization and employment of labour by capital, and of many processes and techniques that have had to be invented, learned, used, and perfected. Moreover, all this was not spontaneous but, rather, required countless laws, policies, and programs to be implemented by governments and secured after much struggle among competing interests over the shape of these policies.

The market economy that emerged out of feudalism required two developments: (1) that individuals be removed from the traditional structures of medieval society in order to be "free" to be active in the market (mainly as sellers of their labour, but later as consumers, too); and (2) that political authority be exercised in ways consistent with the needs of the market-based classes (entrepreneurs, industrialists, merchants, financiers). These correspond with the two ideological themes stressed by believers in the efficiency of markets: (1) that governments *respect the autonomy of the market,* and (2) that governments *provide the structure of law, services, and incentives* deemed optimal for market activity, that is, provide *support.*

Market autonomy is idea that the laws and regulations made by the state should interfere as little as possible with the operation of market forces in the determination of matters such as prices and profits. *Market support* is the demand that the state provide the conditions and infrastructure necessary for individuals to produce, buy and sell, employ, and be employed in the market. These conditions include a stable currency, enforcement of contracts, freedom from theft or extortion, and limitation of the number of holidays (which, as holy days exempting peasants from their labours, were quite numerous in the medieval period). While the exchanges that characterize market economies are private, voluntary transactions, these rely in turn on a public system of involuntary laws that enforce contracts, protect property from theft, and settle disputes over title. The state's role in establishing the framework of law in which market activity can occur is indispensable. It is never a question of *whether* the state should make policies that affect the market, but rather *how* the state's policies should affect the market. On this there is no consensus, not least because of differing assessments of the market and of who benefits from it most.

CLASSIC LIBERALISM AND LAISSEZ-FAIRE

Liberalism, as the original ideology of market society, promoted the conditions of rational government and economic (social) liberty conducive to the development of market forces, and supported policies meeting the needs of the market's dominant producers. As the market became more securely established, liberal thinkers turned their emphasis to the need for market autonomy.

Near the end of the eighteenth century, these policies were summed up in Adam Smith's landmark treatise *The Wealth of Nations*; the doctrine of economic liberalism represented by this work came to be known as laissez-faire (meaning "let do," or "leave it alone"). As this term suggests, its theme was minimizing state interference in order to maximize competition among producers, consumers, and labourers. This competition would result in the most efficient and productive use of resources, an economy by which the interests of all would best be served.

According to the model, markets are not only efficient but also progressive: competition improves the standard of living of all by lowering prices that consumers pay for goods, improving the quality of products, encouraging research that produces beneficial goods and by-products, employing society's resources productively, and increasing workers' wages. These socially beneficial results are the unintended consequence of rational self-interested activity in the marketplace, as if produced, Smith says, by "an invisible hand."

Smith argued that any attempt by the state to regulate market activity or artificially determine its outcomes will undermine the beneficial social effects of market activity. Faith in the ability of the unfettered market to produce socially optimal outcomes informs support for the **minimal state** (a state that interferes least with the "free" operation of markets). What explains the efficiency (and the socially beneficial outcomes) of laissez-faire, according to its supporters, is the incentives or penalties imposed by competition between producers and buyers and sellers. Anything that inhibits this competition is likely to produce unwelcome results.

While the laissez-faire doctrine calls for a minimal state, it nonetheless relies on this state to perform some important roles and to perform them in ways that benefit entrepreneurs or producers. For Adam Smith, these functions were the administration of justice, the provision of defence, the provision of public works (necessary to facilitate economic activity), and the reform of "various institutional and legal impediments to the system of natural liberty" (Skinner, 79).

By the nineteenth century, laissez-faire had become the dominant economic theory of liberalism and the economic approach of the British government, managing what was then the world's most advanced market economy. Laissez-faire was the doctrine of successful industrial capitalism; it is, arguably, not the optimal policy for less developed industrial economies, or for other segments of the economy, that is, merchants, financiers, landlords, farmers, or (especially) workers. Thus, while laissez-faire became the economic theory of classical liberalism, it should be no surprise that other ideologies were critical of this policy and its effects.

MODELS VERSUS REALITY

Much of modern economics is involved with testing and revising models of economic behaviour. The very strength of a model—that it allows the researcher to control the factors involved and remove whatever he or she decides is extraneous—is also, from a practical perspective, its weakness. If the model requires us to make highly implausible assumptions or set aside certain inevitable facets of reality, its use to us becomes less certain.

ECONOMIC MODELS AND ECONOMIC REALITY

Economic models like laissez-faire often rely on assumptions that are never going to be approximated in real life. For example, models involving human behaviour must necessarily make assumptions about how people make decisions, and these often presume a consistent way of reasoning and equal access to information, neither of which is likely to prevail in real life. All exchanges in the market model are supposedly "voluntary," when in fact there are many decisions about acquiring the necessities of life that are not completely unforced, many exchanges in which one party is much more able to walk away from a proposed transaction than the other.

Joseph Stiglitz, the 2001 Nobel laureate in Economics and a former Chief Economist at the World Bank, has observed that the reason the "invisible hand" is invisible is because most of the time it isn't there. The assumption that unfettered markets will produce socially optimal results is undermined by the pervasiveness of **externalities**, instances where information that would contribute to the determination of a socially optimal result is missing from the transaction. Positive externalities are hidden benefits, such as positive outcomes for society, for which the party providing them will not be compensated (the homeowner converting to solar-heated water does not get a discount for the social benefit of reducing electricity consumption); negative externalities are hidden costs (such as health care costs of those living downwind from buyers of wood-burning furnaces). As Stiglitz has noted:

> Whenever there are "externalities"—where the actions of an individual have impacts on others for which they do not pay or for which they are not compensated—markets will not work well. But recent research has shown that these externalities are pervasive, whenever there is imperfect information or imperfect risk markets—*that is always*. The real debate today is about finding the right balance between the market and government. Both are needed. They can each complement each other. This balance will differ from time to time and place to place. (quoted in Altman; emphasis added)

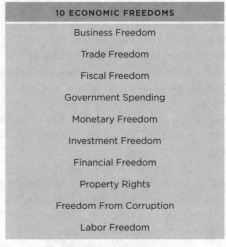

10 ECONOMIC FREEDOMS

Business Freedom

Trade Freedom

Fiscal Freedom

Government Spending

Monetary Freedom

Investment Freedom

Financial Freedom

Property Rights

Freedom From Corruption

Labor Freedom

(from the *Economic Freedom Index*)

Figure 14.1

ECONOMIC MODELS AND POLITICAL REALITY

Even if it were possible to realize the laissez-faire dream of a totally unfettered market, it is not obvious that this would be regarded as the best of all possible outcomes by all of the market's participants. There would still be classes, and there is no reason to suspect that the working and middle classes would be entirely satisfied by their position in market society. What might be the most efficient outcome from an economist's perspective is not necessarily the ideal political outcome. In addition, experience indicates that two tendencies occur when markets are left to their own devices (or regulations are loosened): an accumulation of wealth in the hands of those owning the means of production, and a consolidation

MARX'S CRITIQUE OF CAPITALISM

In contrast to the classical liberal approach that treats the market economy as the system of voluntary transactions between individuals, Marx analyzed it in terms of class relations. Marx felt that industrial capitalism had created a two-class society divided between the owners of the means of production (the **bourgeoisie**) and the workers who sell their labour (the **proletariat**). Whatever middle class existed in this society was obviously small enough for Marx to ignore. In time, he believed, all other classes in society would disappear, and social life would be dominated by the class conflict between the two primary classes of industrial capitalism.

Marx belonged to the tradition of political economy that included Adam Smith, David Ricardo, and others, which argues that the source of value added in production is the human labour involved. On this theory, the worker is paid less than full value for his or her labour, and this surplus extracted from the worker is the source of profits and capital. At various points, Marx also suggested that the capitalist organization of labour activity in factory production is dehumanizing, alienating individuals from the full expression of their humanity in creative, self-directed activity.

Once the proletariat became sufficiently conscious of itself as an oppressed class, Marx believed, this would lead to a revolution—perhaps even by democratic means with the election of a proletarian party—that would replace class-divided society with a classless community in which the economic machinery created by capitalism would be organized on socialist principles.

The chief impediment to socialism was the existence of the state operating as an instrument of the bourgeoisie. Marx believed that the government in capitalist societies not only creates the conditions necessary for capitalism to flourish, but supports and promotes the ideas and ideology that support the economic system. This helps prevent workers from gaining revolutionary class consciousness as they accept, instead, the legitimacy of the system that exploits them.

Nonetheless, Marx concluded that capitalism would eventually self-destruct because of its own internal contradictions; the product of this would be a socialist revolution led by a class-conscious proletariat. These contradictions would be connected with the business cycle (the cyclical pattern of growth and decline that, in Marx's day, regularly brought market economies into prolonged periods of economic stagnation). This revolution, he felt, was most likely to occur in the more developed industrial societies, such as Germany or Britain.

Despite the strengths of Marx's analysis of mature industrial capitalism—and they were many—his prognosis of its future was flawed in two respects. First, Marx overestimated the revolutionary potential of the working class, which, as Lenin recognized, is more concerned with improving its conditions within the existing state than with embarking on a grand experiment. Second, Marx failed to foresee that capitalism could be reformed without abandoning its basic commitment to private property or to the market as the principal means of allocating resources and values. Most specifically, he did not anticipate the rise of a significant middle class, which would become, with representative democracy, a politically dominating class.

of capital that reduces the number of owners of the means of production and thereby reduces the competitiveness of the market.

The rise of industrial capitalism in the nineteenth century, operating under a minimal state, brought into being a class of industrial workers dependent on the market for their existence. Real wages after the Industrial Revolution were *lower* than before, working conditions were generally abominable, and at one time it was normal in the mill towns for every man, woman, and child over the age of four or five to work 12 to 14 hours a day for a subsistence wage, the minimum necessary to feed, clothe, and house the workers. It was in this context that Karl Marx wrote his critique of capitalism, and given these realities it is not surprising that a number of socialist movements were formed in the nineteenth century.

The nineteenth century socialists, Marx chief among them, offered no detailed economic program to replace market relations, beyond the replacement of private ownership of the means of production with collective ownership by (or in the name of) the people. Marx seemed to believe that after playing a transitional role in managing the transformation from capitalism to socialism, the state would "wither away." The main promise of socialism was that it would inherit the productive forces created by market capitalism, but organize labour in a way so as to eliminate class division and the effects of class exploitation. However vague the economic details of socialism may have been, in the context of the late nineteenth century it was politically appealing to many in the working and lower-middle classes.

(The economic systems developed in the former Soviet Union and its Eastern European satellites replaced private ownership of production with centralized state ownership, where the state was monopolized by the Communist Party. These **command economies** collapsed at the end of the Cold War period, and have been transforming into market economies since.)

THE REFORM OF MARKET CAPITALISM

The reform of market capitalism from nineteenth century laissez-faire and the minimal state to twentieth-century regulated capitalism and the activist/welfare state can be attributed to several circumstances and developments.

THE THREAT OF SOCIALISM

As indicated, from the mid-1800s on, capitalism had a rival ideology that claimed to be able to organize the productive powers of capitalist technology in ways that would eliminate the exploitation of the worker. After 1890, a significant portion of the socialist movement was committed to achieving its goals by democratic, reformist means. Organizing the working classes for political action became a primary focus of socialist organizations, along with the creation of like-minded political parties to contest elections in the representative democracies.

SOCIAL REFORMERS

Appalled by the conditions endured by much of the labour force under nineteenth-century industrial capitalism, social activists worked for legislative reforms such as limiting the length of the working day, eliminating child labour, improving the conditions workers were forced to endure (occupational health and safety), and others—none of which, however socially beneficial, would have occurred under laissez-faire.

In addition, reformers pushed for compulsory education for all children, improvements in sanitation and the supply of drinking water, better health care, and (along with trade unions) for the provision of a "living wage"—a wage that would permit one parent (a mother) to remain at home with the children.

THE RISE OF TRADE UNIONS

Contrary to the efforts of employers and (in some cases) the state, trade unions began to form. Collective action, including strikes by workers and eventually collective bargaining, modifies the relationship between workers and employers dramatically, with negotiations securing improvements in wages, in working conditions, and even benefits such as health insurance and pensions. Unions argue that the gains they are able to make for their own members lead to gains for non-unionized workers in similar jobs. The ability to organize and act collectively did not come easily, and legislation permitting or protecting the ability of unions to strike, to picket, to speak for the entire body of employees in an enterprise (there will always be some workers who would prefer to make their own arrangements with the employer) was not always quickly forthcoming.

A union aggregates the minimal power of individual workers so that they can sell their labour on more equitable terms. Unions do not threaten or change the basic wage-labour relationship at the heart of capitalist production; if anything, they legitimize it and strengthen the system by providing a route for resolving grievances *within* the structure of market society. As Lenin recognized, trade union activity is not revolutionary and the conservatism of many trade unions is well documented.

In the capitalist economy, the state is required both to regulate labour relations in general and referee particular labour disputes. Many of the particulars of labour legislation, such as certification or decertification rules, banning or allowing replacement workers, the use of mediation and arbitration, or banning strikes in the case of "essential services," continue to be the subject of dedicated lobbying by representatives of business or labour, attempting to shift policy in their favour.

Free-market advocates, not surprisingly, fail to see unions as a progressive development. The Heritage Foundation's senior policy analyst in labour economics, James Sherk, describes them as follows:

[W]hile unions can sometimes achieve benefits for their members, they harm the overall economy. Unions function as labor cartels. A labor cartel restricts the number of workers in a company or industry to drive up the remaining workers' wages, just as the Organization of Petroleum Exporting Countries (OPEC) attempts to cut the supply of oil to raise its price. Companies pass on those higher wages to consumers through higher prices, and often they also earn lower profits. Economic research finds that unions benefit their members but hurt consumers generally, and especially workers who are denied job opportunities. (1)

POLITICAL POWER OF THE WORKING-CLASS VOTE

Nineteenth-century advocates of laissez-faire were suspicious of democracy—and thus reluctant to remove the property requirement for voting—knowing it would give significant political influence to those least advantaged by unfettered markets. The divergence between how markets operate in theory and how they work in practice is either a cost that falls on those least able to bear it, or a benefit that accrues to those least in need of it (and often it is both of these together).

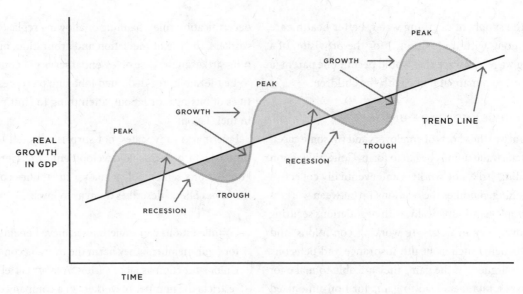

REAL GROWTH IN GDP

PEAK

GROWTH →

PEAK

GROWTH →

PEAK

RECESSION

TROUGH

RECESSION

TROUGH

TREND LINE

PEAK

TIME

Figure 14.2

Once the vote was granted to all classes, regardless of their property, all interests had to be considered by the political players. A political party supporting laissez-faire must convince a sufficient portion of the working and middle classes that the minimal state is in their best interest. In the latter half of the nineteenth century and the first part of the twentieth, many workers had experiences that convinced them to the contrary. Extending the vote to all adults made it possible for there to be political parties targeting working- and middle-class voters, and made it more likely that all parties would begin to support regulation of the market economy.

THE BUSINESS CYCLE

When Marx indicated that capitalism's contradictions would bring about its demise, he was thinking, at least in part, about the business cycle, often depicted as in *Figure 14.2*. The economic growth that is considered to indicate a healthy economy is not a steady upward progression but moves through successive periods of advance and decline. Some of these periods of decline can last for many years. The business cycle challenges the arguments for laissez-faire in several ways.

For example, the inequality that accompanies a capitalist market economy is rationalized on two grounds. One is the claim that a market economy will generate prosperity for all and that it is better to be unequal and secure than to be equal and poor (this is the "a rising tide lifts all boats" argument). The second is that the "invisible hand" of the unregulated market improves the position of the least advantaged by bringing about full employment, which increases the price of labour. In this way, inequality is diminished over time. Both these arguments are undermined by the persistence of the business cycle.

Full employment and an increasing price for labour are conditions that laissez-faire meets only

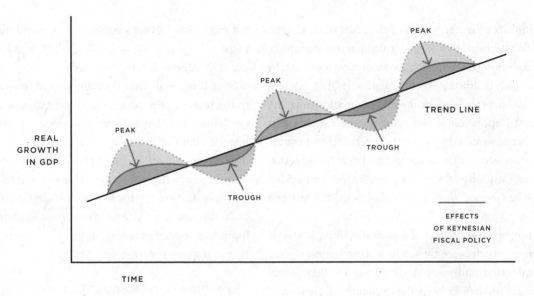

REAL
GROWTH
IN GDP

PEAK

PEAK

PEAK

TROUGH

TROUGH

TREND LINE

EFFECTS
OF KEYNESIAN
FISCAL POLICY

TIME

Figure 14.3

occasionally; instead, considerable unemployment and periods of low or diminishing wages exist. The claim that policies increasing or sustaining market autonomy benefit everyone needs to be examined critically in light of the possibility that only some interests will benefit or will benefit disproportionately (*and* that others will be worse off). These are considerations to which liberalism is particularly vulnerable, since it claims not to discriminate between individuals but to give all equal regard. If liberalism is indifferent to the treatment by the market of the poor and working classes, then it risks confirming Marx's critique that liberalism is the ideology of the propertied classes passing itself off as something more universal.

The supposed benefits that accrue from the efficiency a market system promotes are accompanied by the costs of weeding out inefficient or outmoded production: competition produces losers as well as winners. It might be that all will eventually benefit from

the elimination of inefficient producers, but who pays this cost of restructuring? The owners of the firms that close or are put into receivership lose their investment, but they also have the ability to retreat from their investments before their own survival is threatened. The employee is likely to have no surplus: the wage is all that stands between him or her and the unemployment line or the food bank. The greater economic cost may well be borne by the employer or owner, but the more immediate and human cost falls upon the worker. Increasing efficiency (the epitome of market rationality) almost always means fewer jobs, and there is no reason to expect that improved efficiency will lead to job creation that sustains those displaced by the rationalization.

The Keynesian State

Arguably, the kind of market society that is politically justifiable in a democracy should be one that minimizes the imposition of the costs of its restructurings, downturns, or modernizations on the middle and working classes. Such a system requires action by the state. Following World War II, and in an attempt to avoid periods of prolonged stagnation like the Great Depression of the 1930s (or the earlier Great Depression of 1873 to 1896), governments in most market economies adopted the **fiscal policy** that economist John Maynard Keynes had recommended in *The General Theory of Employment, Interest and Money* (1936).

Keynes argued that the periodic slumps capitalism experiences are caused by a combination of overproduction and insufficient demand—there is not enough money to keep the exchange of goods and labour in equilibrium. To compensate, he proposed a system of **demand management** whereby governments stimulate consumer demand in slow times and put a brake on its acceleration in good times, thereby moderating the ups and downs of the cycle (see *Figure 14.3*). Governments could accomplish this by adjusting their spending and taxation. Conventional wisdom was that governments should plan for balanced budgets (government expenditures=government revenues), apart from exigencies such as wartime. Keynes suggested that the government spend more money than it collects when the economy is contracting, and collect more than it spends when the economy is expanding.

Deficit budgeting during periods of decline would mean accumulating debt, but this would be erased by surplus budgeting in periods of growth. In effect, Keynes was proposing a "government cycle" that would offset the business cycle; government finances would not be in balance in any given year but would even out over time. To varying degrees, Western industrial nations made Keynes's strategy of demand management the new orthodoxy, although they often found it easier to achieve deficits than surpluses.

Something more than the minimal state may not be in the interest of producers, entrepreneurs, or investors (although many arguments suggest it *is* in their interest), but that is *their* economic interest; politically, they are not the only portion of the electorate seeking specific policy outcomes. In a democracy, those who are more likely to pay the human costs of the business cycle also have a valid claim to policy space, and their input may compel governments that care about re-election to respond accordingly.

THE RISE OF BUREAUCRACY AND WHITE-COLLAR JOBS

Several factors contributed to an expansion in the bureaucratic organization of labour—the emergence of the modern corporation, of a public education system, of modern medicine and a health care infrastructure; the expansion of government in regulating new spheres of economic activity created by scientific discoveries and technological breakthroughs; and the funding of infrastructure that markets, left to their own devices, could or would not have produced—in both public *and* private sectors. This meant the emergence of white-collar jobs, an increase in the size of the skilled workforce, and the creation of a middle class working for a salary rather than a wage. This class has its own interests, which sometimes coincide with the workers', sometimes with the employer-owners', but are unlikely to be satisfied by the minimal state.

CREATION OF A CONSUMER CLASS

The twentieth century brought about a fundamental shift in the nature of capitalist production, from

Cranes in Dublin, Ireland, in 2005.

heavy industry focused on capital goods (machinery, railroads and rolling stock, shipbuilding, bridges), to the production of consumer goods (automobiles, furniture, pianos, appliances, clothing, household goods). This shift was interrupted by two World Wars and the Great Depression, but proceeded very quickly in the latter half of the century, aided by some of the circumstances and developments noted above. The point to note is that a consumer economy requires a consumer class. Workers paid a minimum or minimal wage cannot participate in a consumer economy. It is in the interest of a consumer-driven economy that as many of its participants as possible have a disposable income that permits them to be consumers.

THE WELFARE STATE

The distance travelled in the transition from laissez-faire capitalism to the twentieth-century welfare state was considerable, but it did not challenge the *primary* reliance on the market to allocate resources. Neither did it challenge the private ownership of productive property or the dependence of the majority of individuals on a payment (wage or salary) that they receive for their labour. A strong argument has been made by its supporters (and by some of its critics) that the welfare state did much to preserve and strengthen the market economy, undermining the appeal of collectivist alternatives that would have required more fundamental revision of the political-economy system.

The welfare state is an **activist state**, intentionally involved in the economic life of the nation, performing economic-management functions with specific social and political goals in mind. Ringen emphasizes the *redistributive* character of the welfare state: its attempt to eliminate poverty and create equality through a system of taxes and transfers. This depiction is more accurate of the welfare state in the Scandinavian regimes (with which Ringen was most familiar) than in states such as Canada and the United States). By contrast, Mishra identifies the welfare state as a "three-pronged attack on want and dependency" (18), involving three elements:

(a) government commitment to *full employment;*
(b) delivery of universal *social programs,* such as health care and education; and
(c) provision of a "safety net" of assistance (such as *income maintenance*) for those in need.

While some have characterized the welfare state as the result of a post-war (World War II) consensus among the interests of business, labour, and government, others argue that business interests have always resisted implementation of the elements of the welfare state. The truth is probably somewhere in between; a balance of political forces in the post-war period, coupled with a prolonged period of sustained economic growth, made the welfare state "affordable." In addition, the welfare state was the result of numerous policy decisions, sometimes only loosely connected or coordinated. The welfare state came in many varieties, ranging from small welfare states in the United States and Switzerland to large welfare states in France and Sweden. (The "size" of welfare states is simply the share of a nation's economy accounted for by government spending).

The growth of the state with regard to the economy takes many forms, from public-works programs (building highways, bridges, hydroelectric dams, etc.) to assuming ownership of companies. The increase in the size of the state has its own impact by increasing the number of employees, the scale of government purchases in the economy, and so on. A central element of the welfare state is transfers to citizens, either directly in the form of income payments (pensions, unemployment insurance, student aid, income maintenance, childcare subsidies, workplace injury insurance) or indirectly in the form of social programs such as health care, education, and long-term care. Such transfers allow government to achieve particular public policy goals, including relief for those who fall victim to the market economy's contractions and compensating for some of the market's systemic inequality.

Whether or not the welfare state reflected an agreement by business, labour, and the state, it did represent a compromise or even consensus among ideologies. Reform liberals, social democrats, and even market Tories (including European Christian Democrats) could agree on the continued justification of the welfare state, even when they might disagree on its optimal size or shape (the particular programs it should encompass). Standing outside this consensus were those economic liberals (fiscal conservatives) advocating a return to the minimal state, and those radical socialists (communists) convinced that a private-property market economy should be overthrown. While such radical socialists remain mostly at the margins, economic liberalism has made a significant enough comeback that the question that seemed more or less settled a few decades ago—the proper role of the state in the economy—has once again become central to political and policy debates.

THE AGE OF DEFICIT AND DEBT

For a considerable period after World War II, the Keynesian welfare state seemed to be working; market economies were able to achieve relatively stable economic growth in conditions of relatively full employment and low inflation. At the same time, government services and transfers continued to be introduced and enriched. During a period of economic turmoil in the 1970s (characterized by high inflation *and* unemployment), the Keynesian strategy and all that was associated with it fell out of favour. An oil crisis triggered by a deliberate reduction in output by the OPEC nations, the movement of the world currency system to floating exchange rates, and the shift of industrial production from developed to developing world labour markets led to a prolonged period of government deficits.

Keynesian policies were officially replaced with **monetarism**, a policy seeking to influence the rate of economic growth by control of the money supply (hence "supply-side economics") and the use of interest-rate policies. This meant the end of the commitment to full-employment economies in favour of policies focused on fighting inflation.

Governments continued to spend more than they were raising in revenue. There was considerable debate about why deficits seemed so irreversible. Governments had found it difficult to budget for surpluses in the best of times (when, according to Keynes, that is exactly what they should have been doing), the dampening effect of a surplus on the economy being unlikely to win many votes; in a period of economic stagnation, moving to eliminate deficits was even more difficult. The end of a full-employment economy meant that more people required or were eligible for income maintenance, either through unemployment insurance or general social assistance. At the same time, in economically depressed times, it is difficult to raise sufficient revenue to match spending commitments. In the age of globalization (transnational corporations and free trade), it is relatively easy for wealthy individuals and corporations to move investments away from jurisdictions that impose higher taxes. The middle class came to bear an increasingly higher proportion of the tax burden, which laid the groundwork for the strategy of economic stimulus (and political gain) through tax cuts later down the road.

While it was once possible to distinguish adherents of ideologies by their attitude towards deficits, fiscal conservatives (economic liberals) condemning them and reform liberals and social democrats dismissing them as short-term expedients that could be paid down at some future date when the economy turned around, the seriousness of the accumulating debt load came to be recognized by right and left alike. The practical problem is that governments must at least meet the interest payments on their accumulated debt, even if they are not in a position to reduce the overall amount. As interest payments on debt constitute an ever-increasing proportion of government expenditures, the ability of government to pay for the programs to which they are committed is inhibited. More and more revenue is transferred to the investors from whom the government has borrowed, and proportionately less is spent on services or transfers to the public. The internal logic of this situation caused even reform liberals and social democrats to raise concern about fiscal imbalances.

While increasing taxes might seem one answer to this question, the political difficulty of (and potential political price for) doing so made most governments look instead to reducing government spending. This meant reducing the size of the public sector by cutting back or eliminating government programs, or reducing government transfers. The fiscal crisis that many states experienced placed the continued shape (if not the existence) of the welfare state in question. In the debate about how to downsize government, and about the impact of this exercise on the welfare state, competing ideologies collided.

The mounting debt of governments provided ammunition for fiscal conservatives who argued for dismantling much of the welfare state. On the other hand, conservative administrations in the 1980s, such as the Thatcher government in the United Kingdom and the Reagan presidency in the United States, had mixed records on reducing the size of the state. Increased military outlays during the Reagan years (which contributed to the end of the Cold War by forcing the Soviet Union to devote more to military purposes than it could afford) brought US debt to unprecedented levels. Many elements of the Gingrich Republicans' "Contract with America" (mid-1990s) involved a rolling back of the public sector (despite the reality that among developed nations, the United States has always had one of the smallest public sectors). Liberals who once participated in the design and expansion of the welfare state began to discuss the need for its reform, to redesign programs, to "do more with less." Two of the most notable achievements of the Clinton Administration (1992–2000) were a significant reform of federal welfare law, reducing entitlements and adding workforce requirements for recipients of federal assistance, and bringing the US budget into surplus. (The US budget has since recorded a deficit every year from 2002 to the present [2011].) The Canadian federal government budget was brought into surplus by a Liberal government in 1997, achieved in part by reducing the real level of fiscal transfers to the provinces, transfers designed to pay for the social programs that fall under provincial jurisdiction. (The Canadian budget remained in surplus numbers until 2009.)

At one point, the only defence of the post-war welfare state came from the left, from democratic socialists or social democrats. A generation earlier, these groups would have argued that the welfare state did not go far enough in redressing inequalities created by a market economy. Most recently, even socialists, when in power, have found themselves holding the line or cutting back on government expenditures. The so-called Third Way of Tony Blair (Labour Party prime minister of the United Kingdom, 1997 to 2007) and other contemporary social democrats involved a serious rethinking of the assumptions behind the welfare state.

THE POST-WELFARE STATE

Just as advanced democracies are now said to have post-industrial economies, with the shift of much manufacturing and heavy industry to the developing world and the emergence of large service and information technology sectors, most of these regimes can now also be described as post-welfare states. As the twenty-first century dawned, the political climate favoured those who sought to roll back the welfare state, often able to capitalize on *tax fatigue* and resentment by the working middle classes of the non-working poor, or by the non-working poor of immigrants and newer citizens. Looking again at the three components of the welfare state identified above—full employment, universal social programs, and income maintenance for the poorest—the first has been more or less abandoned, and the last has remained stagnant or been restructured on a meaner basis. Only the universal provision of education and health care (where applicable) seems to be immune from downsizing in terms of overall expenditure levels. In these sectors, though, the pressures to achieve greater efficiencies and the contracting out of some services to the private sector have led to service cuts. In some jurisdictions, maintaining or expanding expenditure levels for health care and education has only been possible by cutting programs in other government departments, such as agriculture, the environment, natural resources, and consumer protection.

The notion that the welfare state serves a redistributive function has been demonstrated to be mostly false. It is true that some notable improvements were made (in some regimes) with respect to poverty levels. The most accurate generalization would be that the welfare state held in check the upward redistribution of wealth to those at the top of the social pyramid that is the natural tendency of unregulated market activity. There is no natural mechanism within the market to halt this upward accumulation of wealth. The justification is that the wealthy will use this capital to invest in new production and employment (what is known as "trickle down" economics), a view that can be sustained only by ignoring a wealth of evidence to the contrary. In all of the countries that reformed income-maintenance programs, abandoned the commitment to policies favouring full employment, and implemented significant corporate and personal income tax cuts, the effect has been greater economic inequality.

Data on inequality, the size of the public sector, and taxation rates found in the Economic Appendix at the end of this chapter support an observation that the welfare state has been smaller *and* more vulnerable in the Anglo-American democracies (Australia, Canada, New Zealand, the United Kingdom, the United States) than in the European democracies that have a history of coalition. The welfare state in Europe was often a product of agreement between social democratic and Christian democratic parties. Even when parties of the right have had clear control of government in countries such as France and Germany, there has been no significant effort to reduce the size of the state.

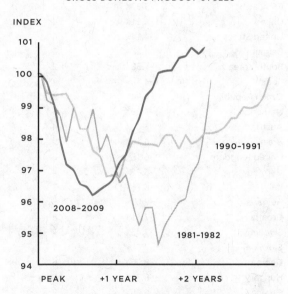

GROSS DOMESTIC PRODUCT CYCLES

Source: Statistics Canada, *The Daily*, January 23, 2011, Comparing Recessions

Figure 14.4

A society that becomes more unequal also becomes more fragmented and, in the long term, less stable politically; crime becomes a more common response to social and economic despair. It is tempting to think that political equality (i.e., democracy) provides a

LENGTH AND SEVERITY OF THE RECESSION		
	TOTAL GDP LOSS	LENGTH (NO. OF QUARTERS)
Poland	-0.40%	1
Australia	-1.00%	1
Israel	-1.21%	2
Argentina	-1.69%	2
South Africa	-2.65%	3
Switzerland	-3.25%	4
Canada	-3.36%	6
Norway	-3.44%	11
New Zealand	-3.45%	5
Portugal	-3.68%	4
France	-3.87%	4
Chile	-4.11%	4
United States	-4.14%	6
Belgium	-4.23%	3
South Korea	-4.58%	2
Spain	-4.89%	7
Czech Republic	-4.94%	3
Netherlands	-5.29%	5
Austria	-5.44%	4
Brazil	-6.14%	2
United Kingdom	-6.15%	6
Germany	-6.62%	4
Italy	-6.76%	7
Bulgaria	-7.05%	5
Croatia	-7.41%	8
Sweden	-7.43%	7
Slovakia	-7.62%	1
Denmark	-8.06%	6
Hungary	-8.32%	6
Greece	-8.95%	9
Slovenia	-9.71%	3
Finland	-9.96%	4
Romania	-10.00%	9
Ireland	-12.24%	13
Iceland	-15.07%	11
Lithuania	-16.95%	6
Estonia	-20.33%	7
Latvia	-25.14%	8

Source: OECD, *Quarterly National Accounts*

Figure 14.5

natural feedback mechanism; that is, that those who are threatened by increasing inequality will use their votes to pressure political parties for policies that will heal division, address inequities, and meet basic needs universally. There are two flaws with this. One, as we have seen throughout much of this text, is the incomplete character of the democracy that citizens inhabit, particularly in those countries without proportional representation and in those countries where corporate interests have an undue influence over the political process, or where the political process lacks the ability (or the will) to provide citizens with the kinds of serious information they need to make informed, meaningful choices. The second flaw is to imagine that political equality can persist (to the degree that it ever exists) in the face of economic inequality. Modern politics does not come cheaply, and those with resources can be expected to manage much better than those without in shaping (if not controlling) the political agenda.

2008 AND AFTER

In 2008, most advanced market economies followed the US economy into a steep economic decline, technically a recession (two or more successive quarters of negative economic growth), and, depending on the measure and the economy, one of the more serious recessions in the post-war period. *Figure 14.4* compares the 2008–2009 recession in Canada with previous recessions in 1990–1991 (known for its "jobless" recovery) and 1981–1982 (with one of the quickest and sharpest recoveries on record). *Figure 14.5* compares GDP loss and the length of the 2008–2009 recession in the OECD countries in the dataset.

The response of almost all regimes was not simply to let the market find its own recovery but to inject massive amounts of stimulus spending into their respective economies. (Suddenly, Keynes was back in favour.) *Figure 14.6* provides preliminary data on the total amount of fiscal stimulus provided by OECD countries between 2008 and 2010. Much of that stimulus was provided through tax cuts and much through direct government expenditures. As a result, government deficits grew further, adding to the accumulated debt in these regimes, and increasing the level of debt payments owed to lenders, domestic and foreign.

ABSOLUTE SIZE OF FISCAL PACKAGES ($US MILLIONS)	
United States	804,070
Germany	107,789
Japan	99,992
Canada	61,551
Spain	56,754
Australia	45,673
Korea	42,667
United Kingdom	38,003
France	18,568
Netherlands	13,367
Sweden	13,109
Denmark	8,668
Finland	8,575
Belgium	8,016
Czech Republic	6,500
New Zealand	5,404
Poland	5,145
Austria	4,600
Switzerland	2,486
Portugal	1,963
Slovakia	35

Source: OECD (*Divided We Stand*: 19)

Figure 14.6

GOING FORWARD

This final section considers some of the challenges facing policy-makers in the short and the long term, given the commitment of democratic regimes to a private-property market economy.

INTERNAL ISSUES

At some point in the last 30 or 40 years, the primary emphasis of the modern capitalist corporation shifted from producing a good or service at a sustainable level of profitability to maximizing shareholder value. Profitability *per se* was no longer a sufficient justification for the operation of a business. If more money could be gained by closing the plant and moving it to a more tax-friendly regime (or a regime with lower labour costs), or by closing it to sell off its physical assets, or by selling it to a competitor whose plans might include closing the plant, then the jobs and production at any particular facility might be deemed expendable. Greater shareholder value became the motive behind countless rounds of layoffs and rationalizations to improve *productivity* (rather than boost productivity by investing in new technology or innovation). There is a limit to how far this strategy can be taken.

Also at some point during the same period, it became sound economics to make consumer credit more readily available, to allow minimal down payments to fund housing purchases with very large mortgages in inflated real-estate markets, and for governments to continue to finance their accumulated debt with foreign lenders. According to OECD statistics (Central Government Debt Statistical Yearbook 2000–2009), the US marketable central government debt in 2000 was just over $3 trillion, with one-third of that debt held by non-resident investors. In 2009,

US marketable central government debt had climbed to $7 trillion, one-half of it held by non-resident investors. Percentages for some other OECD member countries (data was not available for all) are provided in *Figure 14.7* (note that Canada has the lowest proportion of foreign-held debt). *Figure 14.8* presents data on total sovereign debt for selected regimes published in July 2011. Increasing indebtedness is a trend that cannot continue indefinitely.

In two major reports, *Growing Unequal?* (2008) and *Divided We Stand: Why Inequality Keeps Rising* (2011), the OECD has examined the growth in inequality in almost all its member countries during the two decades prior to the global financial crisis and recession of 2008. There are two common statistical approaches to measuring inequality: one is to compare the average income of the richest 10 per cent of the population with the average income of the poorest 10 per cent. According to the OECD, in late 2011, the ratio of the top 10 per cent to the bottom 10 per cent was 9:1 across advanced economies, lower in many European countries, and approaching 14:1 in the United States and Israel (*Divided*, 22). In the United States, between 1979 and 2007, the after-tax share of the top 1 per cent of the population doubled

MARKETABLE CENTRAL GOVERNMENT DEBT (2009)			
	Total ($US billions)	Investor type	
		resident	non-resident
United States	6,998	50.0%	50.0%
Italy (2008)	1,887	51.3%	48.7%
France	1,633	32.7%	67.3%
United Kingdom	1,202	71.7%	28.3%
Spain	683	53.4%	46.6%
Canada	509	85.7%	14.3%
Austria	233	21.9%	78.1%
Poland	206	64.6%	35.4%
Sweden	157	59.9%	40.1%
Denmark	121	56.6%	43.4%
Finland	86	0.0%	100.0%
Norway	86	55.6%	44.4%
Hungary	74	53.4%	46.6%
Czech Rep.	61	74.3%	25.7%
Slovakia	29	66.3%	33.7%
New Zealand	28	56.0%	44.0%
Iceland	8	38.4%	61.6%

Source: OECD, Central Government Debt Statistical Yearbook, 2000–2009

Figure 14.7

to 17 per cent of household income, while the share of the bottom 20 per cent fell from 7 per cent to 5 per cent (17). (See *Figure 14.9*.)

The second common indicator of inequality is the Gini coefficient, a value between 0 (complete equality of income) and 1 (one person receives all the income). According to the OECD, the average Gini coefficient for OECD countries increased by 10 per cent from the mid-1980s to the late 2000s. This was during a time when average disposable incomes rose by 1.7 per cent per year in these countries (22). (See Economic Appendix below for Gini co-efficients for selected regimes in the data set.)

In an editorial that opens *Divided We Stand*, OECD Secretary-General Angel Gurría suggests why the trend of increasing inequality cannot continue indefinitely:

The economic crisis has added urgency to deal with the policy issues related to inequality. The social compact is starting to unravel in many countries. Young people who see no future for themselves feel increasingly disenfranchised. They have now been joined by protesters who believe that they are bearing the brunt of a crisis for which they have no responsibility, while people on high incomes appear to have been spared. From Spain to Israel, from Wall Street to Syntagma Square, popular discontent is spreading rapidly. (17)

The policy implications that the OECD report identifies involve reforming tax and benefit policies with an eye to more effective redistribution, as well as growing employment in jobs that offer career prospects, and investing in human-capital policies that offer better training for the low-skilled worker and *equal* access to tertiary education for all individuals. Collectively, this implies an agenda that moves in a different direction from the policies that prevailed in the decade before the 2008 financial crisis: "from the mid-1990s to 2005, the reduced redistributive capacity of tax-benefit systems was sometimes the main source of widening household-income gaps" (264).

INFRASTRUCTURE AND DEMOGRAPHICS

A 2010 World Economic Forum report estimated there to be a worldwide infrastructure deficit that would

TOTAL SOVEREIGN DEBT, 2011 (GOVERNMENT, HOUSEHOLD, FINANCIAL AND NON-FINANCIAL DEBT)	
	% OF GDP
United Kingdom	495
Japan	492
Spain	370
France	347
Italy	316
Switzerland	314
South Korea	306
United States	288
Germany	282
Canada	261
China	158
Brazil	142
India	129
Russia	71

Source: *The Economist*, Web (July 2011)

Figure 14.8

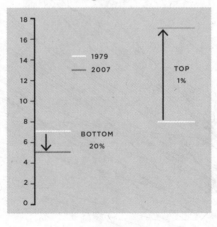

Figure 14.9

require the expenditure of $2 trillion per year for 20 years (5). Estimates of Canada's infrastructure deficit vary widely, but all are in the $100 billion plus range; the US infrastructure deficit could be more than $2 trillion. In most cases, this deficit refers to the cost of repairs and upgrades to the existing systems of roads, highways, bridges, municipal water delivery and sewers, telecommunications and public utilities, much of this infrastructure having been constructed in the 1950s and 1960s. The cost of infrastructure that has yet to be put in place, whether it is smart grids, energy-efficient urban transit systems, or high-speed rail networks, represents another large commitment yet to be made. Even assuming that these projects will involve innovative types of public-private partnerships, meeting infrastructure needs will be a huge challenge for states operating under the fiscal constraints identified above.

To make it even more interesting, the most developed capitalist economies face the challenge of sustaining economic growth with an aging population and a declining workforce (barring significant increases in immigration, a problematic issue in many of these countries). *Figure 14.10* shows Canada's population pyramid, which has a fairly typical shape, with values for 2000 and projected values for 2050. In addition,

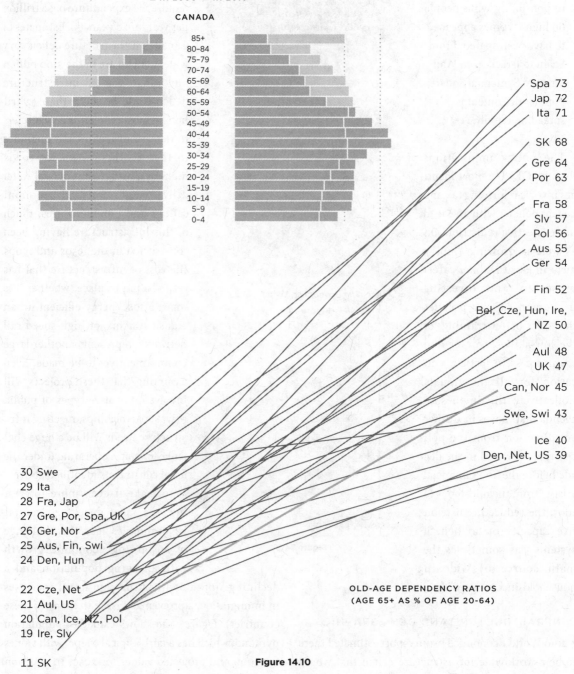

OLD-AGE DEPENDENCY RATIOS
(AGE 65+ AS % OF AGE 20-64)

Figure 14.10

Figure 14.10 shows the projected change in old-age dependency ratios from 2000 to 2050 throughout the OECD (OECD, 2007).

During this time frame, the aging post-industrial democracies will compete with the emerging economies, currently led by China, India, Brazil, and Russia, which are expected to increase their share of the world's economy, given their large internal markets.

CLIMATE CHANGE, PEAK OIL, AND OTHER IMPENDING DOOMS

Nature, it seems, is quite comfortable in a state of equilibrium. Shifted out of that state by an event or changing circumstance, it seeks to re-establish the previous or settle into a new state of equilibrium. Capitalist market society does not seek equilibrium, at least at the macro-economic level; a "healthy" economy is a growing economy. Even in the context of the business cycle, the long-term trajectory is always presented, as in *Figures 14.2* and *14.3*, as upward, ever upward. The difficult reality faced by an economy structured on growth is the finite capacity of the planet to provide the resources that such an economy consumes, and capitalism consumes resources like no other economic system humans have employed.

A large number of people have considered the possibility of a "no-growth" economy, or "steady-state" economics, particularly since the publication of *Limits to Growth* by the Club of Rome in 1972. However, apart from contributing concepts such as "sustainable development" to everyday discourse and political rhetoric, the ideas of those who have thought carefully about how to move to such an alternative economy have not made their way to any regime's formal political agenda. This is not surprising, when one realizes just how thoroughly a no-growth economy challenges the ways of life that are fundamental to advanced economies (and to which emerging economies aspire), not just economically but politically also. Tim Jackson, Economics Commissioner with the (UK) Sustainable Development Commission, has observed that

> For better or worse, government also "co-creates" the culture of consumption, shaping the structure and signals that influence people's behaviour. At the same time, of course, government has an essential role to play in protecting the "commitment devices" that prevent myopic choice and support long-term social goals.
>
> ...
>
> Government ... has a role in "securing the future"—protecting long-term social and ecological goods; on the other it holds a key responsibility for macro-economic stability. For as long as macro-economic stability depends on economic growth, government will have an incentive to support social structures that undermine commitment and reinforce materialistic, novelty-seeking individualism. (11)

Although the private ownership of property and the use of markets may still have a place in a no-growth economy, it is clear that a no-growth economy is not compatible with capitalism as we know it. Too many people have too much invested in the existing economic and political order to simply embrace such wholesale changes in what and how and why we produce and consume. Nonetheless, if the logic of the Club of Rome, the Sustainable Environment Commission, and countless others is true, sooner or later change will not be a matter of choice, but something forced upon all of us.

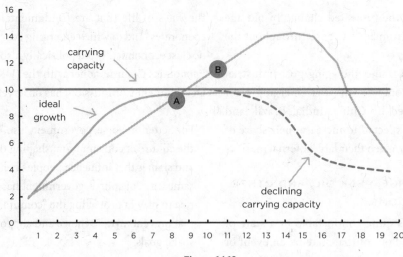

Figure 14.12

Although Canada has one of the largest proportions of climate-change skeptics, this author is not among them. The elementary science of global warming, the rates of economic growth in the emerging economies, particularly China and India, and the failure of the advanced democracies to limit their own greenhouse-gas–producing industries all suggest that serious climate change is a matter of when, not if—if it has not already begun. Although some regions may believe their economic opportunities will be enhanced by the effects of climate change, these benefits may be immediate and short-lived, or take a considerable period of time to materialize. There is far more certainty about the damaging consequences of melting ice caps, rising sea levels, and the expansion of tropical zones. The capacity of governments to respond to these changing circumstances, even in the best-case scenarios, may fall short.

The flip side to the global warming caused (in part) by the prodigious consumption of fossil fuels is the certainty that at some point in time, oil and/or natural gas will become too expensive to be used as fuel (rather than as the basis for valuable synthetic compounds). Rubin has argued that when the cost of oil escalates beyond a certain level, it becomes uneconomical to transport certain commodities or manufactured goods around the world. The ability of an emerging market country such as China to transport inputs from around the world to its factories, and then transport its outputs to markets worldwide, depends on affordable oil prices. Suggesting that higher oil prices may put the brakes on (if not reverse) globalization, Rubin recommends that "in order to insulate ourselves from even greater oil price shocks in the future, we must move from the hugely energy-intensive model of a global economy to the far more sustainable model of a local economy. And that means we must re-engineer our lives to adapt to the contours of a much smaller world" (Author's blog at www.jeffrubinssmallerworld.com/about-the-book, accessed December 15, 2011).

From China's near monopoly on the current world supply of rare-earth metals (whose critical role in the modern economy came as news to many), to predictions of shortages of natural rubber as automobile sales increase significantly in the emerging markets, to worldwide increases in food prices, the material pressures of a planet with too many people consuming too much are beginning to make their presence felt regularly. In this respect, a relevant concept is the *carrying capacity* of an environment: What, for example, is the population that the planet could sustain indefinitely? The world's population reached the seven billion mark, according to the United Nations, in October 2011. It is projected to reach somewhere near 10.5 billion by 2050. Most of those reading this paragraph will, presumably, still be alive, this book long forgotten. What kind of world will it be?

Although estimates of the Earth's carrying capacity vary widely, depending on assumptions about resources and technology and climate change, many believe it falls much below the current population, let alone the projected levels to come. In addition, the carrying capacity depends on the degree to which this generation and the ones to come consume the Earth's resources. In *Figure 14.12*, the ideal growth curve approaches, but does not exceed, the carrying capacity, which remains constant. In the "overshoot" scenario, the population grows too quickly and exceeds the carrying capacity. As a result, two things happen: a drastic decline in the population and, depending on how much beyond the carrying capacity the overshoot goes (and for how long), a decline in the carrying capacity of the environment. These are scenarios that are commonly observed with populations of various species in different environments. What no one knows is where the earth's current population sits vis-à-vis the planet's carrying capacity. Are we at point A or at point B in *Figure 14.12*? Quite clearly it makes a difference, and if the answer were known, appropriate policy responses could be considered, debated, and acted upon.

Do apparent shortages in commodities that are critical to the current standard of living suggest that we are approaching or have exceeded the carrying capacity for this level of global consumption of resources? Will the future course of history be driven by market forces, the invisible hand pushing humanity to the brink and then over? Or, as it has done previously, can liberal democratic capitalism reform itself in time, and if so, in which direction will it move?

At the end of the Cold War, the triumph of liberal democracy seemed complete to some; the big questions seemed to have been answered. Issues such as those raised above suggest that some of the biggest questions have not yet been answered, are not even being considered by most in the broader public or in the state. (In contrast, the seriousness with which the probability of an impact event—an asteroid or meteorite collision—is taken is quite striking.) The time for answering these questions may fall within the next fifty years. The advantage of democracy is that it can widen the range of voices contributing to the policy solutions—it may even include you.

(see EXPLANATORY NOTES below for more information on each numbered column)

	UN HUMAN DEVELOPMENT INDEX (HDI) DATA, 2011										HERITAGE FOUNDATION DATA 2011				
	(1)		(2)		(3)		(4)		(5)		(6)	(7)		(8)	(9)
	TOTAL HDI		NON-INCOME HDI		INEQUALITY-ADJUSTED HDI		TOP-TO-BOTTOM QUINTILE		PER CAPITA GNI		P/CAP GDP	EFI (ECONOMIC FREDOM INDEX)		TAX AS % OF GDP	GOV'T EXPEN. AS % OF GDP
	score	rank	score	rank	score	rank	ratio	rank	$US (ppp)	rank	rank	index	rank	rank	rank
Norway	.943	1	.975	3	.890	1	3.9	5	47,557	1	1	30	21	38	21
Australia	.929	2	.979	1	.856	2	7	31	34,431	9	6	3	1	19	11
The Netherlands	.910	3	.944	6	.846	4	5.1	17	36,402	4	4	15	11	34	33
United States	.910	4	.931	14	.771	22	8.5	36	43,017	2	2	9	7	11	18
New Zealand	.908	5	.978	2	n.a.	n.a.	6.8	30	23,737	24	25	4	2	26	24
Canada	.908	6	.944	7	.829	12	5.5	20	35,166	7	8	6	4	20	19
Ireland	.908	7	.959	4	.843	6	5.7	23	29,322	17	5	7	5	18	26
Germany	.905	9	.940	9	.842	8	4.3	10	34,854	8	14	23	17	37	30
Sweden	.904	10	.936	12	.851	3	4	7	35,837	5	10	22	16	44	43
Switzerland	.903	11	.926	15	.840	9	5.4	19	39,924	3	3	5	3	16	10
Japan	.901	12	.940	10	n.a.	n.a.	3.4	1	32,295	14	17	20	14	12	13
Iceland	.898	14	.943	8	.845	5	n.a.	n.a.	29,354	16	9	44	28	35	45
South Korea	.897	15	.945	5	.749	26	4.7	12	28,230	18	23	35	25	10	9
Denmark	.895	16	.926	16	.842	7	4.3	9	34,347	10	11	8	6	45	42
Israel	.888	17	.939	11	.779	20	7.9	33	25,849	21	22	43	27	23	28
Belgium	.886	18	.914	20	.819	15	4.9	16	33,357	11	12	31	22	43	41
Austria	.885	19	.908	23	.820	14	4.4	11	35,719	6	7	21	15	39	38
France	.884	20	.919	18	.804	16	5.6	21	30,462	15	15	64	36	42	44
Slovenia	.884	21	.935	13	.837	10	4.8	14	24,914	22	24	66	37	31	32
Finland	.882	22	.911	22	.833	11	3.8	4	32,438	13	16	17	13	41	40
Spain	.878	23	.920	17	.799	17	6	24	26,508	19	20	32	23	24	25
Italy	.874	24	.914	21	.779	21	6.5	28	26,484	20	21	88	42	40	37

	UN HUMAN DEVELOPMENT INDEX (HDI) DATA, 2011									HERITAGE FOUNDATION DATA 2011				
	(1)		(2)		(3)		(4)		(5)		(6)	(7)		(8)	(9)
	TOTAL HDI		NON-INCOME HDI		INEQUALITY-ADJUSTED HDI		TOP-TO-BOTTOM QUINTILE		PER CAPITA GNI		P/CAP GDP	EFI (ECONOMIC FREDOM INDEX)		TAX AS % OF GDP	GOV'T EXPEN. AS % OF GDP
	score	rank	score	rank	score	rank	ratio	rank	$US (ppp)	rank	rank	index	rank	rank	rank
Czech Republic	.865	27	.917	19	.821	13	3.5	2	21,405	26	26	28	20	29	27
United Kingdom	.863	28	.879	26	.791	18	7.2	32	33,296	12	13	16	12	33	36
Greece	.861	29	.902	24	.756	25	6.2	25	23,747	23	19	87	41	28	35
Estonia	.835	34	.890	25	.769	23	6.3	26	16,799	30	32	14	10	21	20
Slovakia	.834	35	.875	27	.787	19	4	6	19,998	28	28	37	26	15	12
Hungary	.816	38	.862	28	.759	24	4.8	13	16,581	31	30	51	30	36	39
Poland	.813	39	.853	31	.734	27	5.6	22	17,451	29	31	68	38	27	29
Lithuania	.810	40	.853	32	.730	28	6.7	29	16,234	32	34	24	18	17	15
Portugal	.809	41	.833	36	.726	29	7.9	34	20,753	27	27	69	39	32	34
Latvia	.805	43	.857	30	.717	30	6.3	27	14,293	35	37	56	32	14	17
Chile	.805	44	.862	29	.652	36	3.6	3	13,329	36	36	11	8	5	4
Argentina	.797	45	.843	33	.641	38	12.3	39	14,527	34	35	138	45	9	5
Croatia	.796	46	.834	35	.675	34	5.2	18	15,729	33	33	82	40	8	22
Uruguay	.783	48	.828	37	.654	35	8.7	37	13,242	37	38	33	24	4	7
Romania	.781	50	.841	34	.683	32	4.9	15	11,046	41	40	63	35	13	16
Bulgaria	.771	55	.822	39	.683	33	10.2	38	11,412	40	41	60	34	22	14
Panama	.768	58	.811	40	.579	41	15.8	41	12,335	39	42	59	33	1	2
Serbia	.766	59	.824	38	.694	31	4.1	8	10,236	43	43	101	43	30	31
Trinidad and Tobago	.760	62	.750	42	.644	37	8.3	35	23,429	25	29	52	31	7	8
Costa Rica	.744	69	.785	41	.591	40	13.2	40	10,497	42	44	49	29	3	3
Mauritius	.728	77	.745	44	.631	39	n.a.	n.a.	12,918	38	39	12	9	6	6
Brazil	.718	84	.748	43	.519	42	17.6	42	10,162	44	45	113	44	25	23
Taiwan	(replaced by the People's Republic of China at the UN in 1971)										18	25	19	2	1

(1) total HDI: Annually since 1990, the UN Development Programme has produced a Human Development Report ranking member countries on its Human Development Index (HDI), which measures health, education and living standards according to a standardized methodology relying on a number of indicators. The UN measures human development for 187 regimes. The top 47 countries are regarded as having "very high" human development, the second 47 as having "high" human development. This column shows the HDI values and rankings (out of 187) for the 45 data set regimes.

(2) non-income HDI: In this column the impact of national income on the HDI has been removed. Note how much the position of the United States changes when income is removed from the index, especially when compared with regimes such as Norway and Canada. By contrast, South Korea moves up considerably on the basis of this index, indicating strong health and education indicators. Data set regimes are ranked relative to each other.

(3) Inequality-adjusted HDI: Beginning in 2010, the Report introduced an inequality-adjusted HDI or IHDI, which is described as "the actual level of human development (taking into account inequality)." Note how the United States falls from ranking fourth to 22nd once inequality is factored in, while Denmark and Iceland move up into the top ten.

(4) top-to-bottom quintile: One of the inequality indicators is the ratio of the income of the top 20% (fifth or quintile) to the income of the bottom 20%. (Recently, the ratio of the top 10% to the bottom 10% has also been used.) Ranking 36th on this measure is one reason why the United States is only 22nd on the IHDI; and being 4th on this measure helps explain Finland's rise from 22nd on HDI to 11th on IHDI. On the other hand Slovenia also gains 11 places on the IHDI, but was 14th in the rankings for this indicator.

(5) per-capita GNI: For HDI purposes, income is measured in per capita GNI (gross national income). The OECD defines GNI as "GDP less primary incomes payable to non-resident units plus primary incomes receivable from non-resident units," while GDP is defined as "an aggregate measure of production equal to the sum of the gross values added of all resident institutional units engaged in production (plus any taxes, and minus any subsidies, on products not included in the value of their outputs)." In short, GNI and GDP are two slightly different ways of measuring a national economy's total output. These values are usually expressed, as here, in purchasing power parity (PPP) terms in $US. Again, according to the OECD, PPPs "equalise the purchasing power of different currencies by eliminating the differences in price levels between countries."[1]

(6) per capita GDP: This column provides the rankings of the data set regimes (relative to each other) on the Heritage Foundation per capita GDP data. Significant differences between numbers in this column and numbers in column (5) may reflect differences in the time lag between the data compilation and its publication.

(7) EFI (economic freedom index): The EFI is generated by the Heritage Foundation according to its measure of the 10 economic freedoms described in Figure 14.1. The column contains the actual EFI rankings for the data set countries as well as their rankings on these scores relative to each other. Note the significant difference that often exists between a regime's HDI and its EFI.

(8) tax as % of GDP: This column provides the rankings of the data set regimes (relative to each other) on Heritage Foundation data on tax as a percentage of GDP.

(9) government expenditure as % of GDP: This column provides the rankings of the data set regimes (relative to each other) on Heritage Foundation data on government expenditure as a percentage of GDP.

1 OECD, Glossary of Statistical Terms, Web [http://stats.oecd.org/glossary/index.htm].

REFERENCES

Altman, Daniel. "Managing Globalization: Q & A with Joseph Stiglitz." *The International Herald Tribune* (2006–10–11): n.p. Web.

Heritage Foundation. *Index of Economic Freedom 2011*. January 2011: 460 pp. Web.

Jackson, Tim. *Prosperity without Growth? The Transition to a Sustainable Economy.* The Sustainable Development Commission (2009): 134 pp. Web.

Mishra, Ramesh. *The Welfare State in Capitalist Society.* Toronto: University of Toronto Press, 1990.

OECD. *Divided We Stand: Why Inequality Keeps Rising.* December 2011: 400 pp. Web.

_____. *Growing Unequal? Income Distribution and Poverty in OECD Countries.* October 2008: 310 pp. Web.

_____. *OECD Population Pyramids in 2000 and 2050* (2007). Statistics Portal. Web.

Ringen, Stein. *The Possibility of Politics.* Oxford: Clarendon Press, 1987.

Sherk, James. "What Unions Do: How Labor Unions Affect Jobs and the Economy." *Backgrounder.* The Heritage Foundation. Web. (May 21, 2009): 17 pp.

Skinner, Andrew. "Introduction." *The Wealth of Nations.* Ed. A. Skinner. By Adam Smith. Harmondsworth: Pelican, 1970.

World Economic Forum. *Positive Infrastructure: A Framework for Revitalizing the World Economy.* 2010: 59 pp. Web.

FURTHER READINGS

Antonio, Robert J., and Robert J. Brulle. "The Unbearable Lightness of Politics: Climate Change Denial and Political Polarization." *The Sociological Quarterly* 52.2 (Spring 2011): 195–202.

Bigelow, Gordon. "Let There Be Markets." *Harper's Magazine* (May 2005): 33–38.

Courchene, Thomas J. "Rekindling the American Dream: A Northern Perspective." Institute for Research on Public Policy 2011 Policy Horizons Essay (2011). [This publication can be downloaded from the Institute's website.]

Dorey, Peter. "A Poverty of Imagination: Blaming the Poor for Inequality." *The Political Quarterly* 81.3 (July–September 2010): 333–343.

Dunleavy, Patrick. "The Backlash against the State." *Political Insight* 2.1 (April 2011): 4–6.

Einhorn, Eric S., and John Logue. "Can Welfare States Be Sustained in a Global Economy? Lessons from Scandinavia." *Political Science Quarterly* 125.1 (Spring 2010): 1–29.

Fraile, Lydia. "Lessons from Latin America's Neo-liberal Experiment: An Overview of Labour and Social Policies since the 1980s." *International Labour Review* 148.3 (September 2009): 215–233.

Jacobs, Alan. *Governing for the Long Term: Democracy and the Politics of Investment.* Cambridge: Cambridge University Press, 2011.

Stiglitz, Joseph. "The Global Crisis, Social Protection and Jobs." *International Labour Review* 148.1–2 (June 2009): 1–13.

Glossary

abrogative referendum: a popular vote to negate a bill or act of the legislature

activist (or issue) group: group organized to influence policy on behalf of a cause

activist state: manages the market economy for political and social purposes—created the welfare state

adjustment seats: compensate for initially disproportional election results

adversarial justice system: derives from the relationship between prosecution/defence or plaintiff/defendant in common-law regimes

agenda formation: stage of the *policy process* determining which issues receive attention

agents of representation: bodies acting on behalf of sections of the electorate—political parties, stakeholders, activist groups

agents of socialization: individuals or institutions involved in the transmission of political attitudes and beliefs—parents, peers, teachers, the mass media

amending formula: rules for changing a constitution, particularly in a federal regime

anti-clerical: pertains to promotion of a secular state in a mainly Roman Catholic regime

appellate: describes a level of court hearing appeals from other courts

ascriptive: describes traits that are inherited or acquired at an early age

asymmetrical federalism: a system in which the sub-national units have different powers

atomism: a theory (such as liberalism) focusing on the competition of the fundamental units

attentive public: the part of a *policy community* falling within *civil society*

authoritarian: a regime with no political process for renewing the executive

authority: the recognized ability to direct or command

AV (alternative vote): an electoral system with single member districts and an *ordinal ballot*

band: the most basic form of pre-political community, usually in a hunter-gatherer economy

behaviouralism: social-scientific approach that studies what people do and say

bicameral: literally "two chambers," describes a legislature with two houses

Bill of Rights: constitutional document in the United Kingdom and the United States describing limits on the state/government

bipartisan brokerage: occurs when members of two competing parties (in the United States, especially) make a deal to support or oppose a bill or measure

block funding: a transfer of monies from one level of state to another

bourgeoisie: the class of persons owning the economic means of production

brokerage party: political party seeking broad support across *class* and *social cleavage* lines

bureaucracy: the offices and agencies that carry out, administer, or deliver government policies and programs

cabinet solidarity: a *convention* requiring all cabinet members to support all cabinet decisions

canton: sub-national unit of state in Switzerland

capitalism: see *market economy.*

caretaker government: a cabinet in place to administer existing programs until a new government is formed; it has no mandate to implement new initiatives

categorical: describes a ballot that permits only one selection from the available options

caucus: the elected members of a political party (or a meeting of the same)

censure: a vote reprimanding (or expressing non–confidence in) the government

checks and balances: rules allowing separate branches of state to control each other

chiefdom: a pre-political society with hierarchy and centralized leadership, but lacking means of coercion to enforce commands

citizens: the legally recognized members of a regime, but particularly of a republic and/or democracy

civic republicanism: the idea that a state is comprised of citizens who owe it their loyalty and participate in its affairs

civil law: describes a legal system with codified private law applied by magistrates

civil liberty: a freedom fundamental to a democratic society, such as freedom of speech, of expression, of association, of religion, and of the press

civil society: that portion of social life where the state is inactive

class: stratification or rank in society created by wealth, ownership, occupation, education, and/or status

classical antiquity: historical period spanning ancient Greece and the (western) Roman empire

coalition government: a government in which two or more parties share the executive (cabinet)

coalitional presidentialism: in Latin America, directly elected presidents work with coalition cabinets assembled from the parties in proportionally elected legislatures

codification: when public laws are integrated into a coherent body based on their subject matter

coercion: the use or threatened use of force

cohabitation: occurs in semi-presidential regimes when the president and prime minister are from opposing political parties

Cold War era: political, economic, and military rivalry between the United States and its allies and the former Soviet Union and its allies

collective responsibility: the convention in a parliamentary regime that every member of cabinet is responsible for every cabinet decision

command economy: exists where resources are allocated and production decisions are determined by the state

community: a social whole characterized by a high degree of cohesion and homogeneity

compulsory voting: where the law requires an eligible voter to attend a poll and cast (or formally decline) a ballot

confederal: a constitution in which the sub-national units control the national state

confederate: the act of creating a federal (or confederal) state from autonomous units

confidence: support of a majority of the legislators—conventions vary as to what type(s) of defeat in the legislature constitute a loss of confidence

confidence chamber: in a bicameral system, the legislative house in which the government must maintain the support of a majority

connected coalition: a coalition in which the partners are "adjacent" if compared on the dominant ideological dimension

consensual: a style of decision making seeking to maximize the number of parties in agreement

consent: the willing agreement to follow a direction or command

consociational: describes a policy-making arrangement intended to accommodate both sides of a major social cleavage

consolidation: when public laws are integrated into a coherent whole on the basis of their titles

constitution: a body of special law that defines the institutions of state, their powers, and their relationships to each other and to the people

convention: an unwritten rule which, by common agreement, is considered binding

corporatism: policy-making by institutionalized participation of the state and peak interest associations

corrupt regime: when the authority of the state is regularly used for personal gain

cross-cutting cleavage: when some of the people who are on opposite sides of one cleavage are united on one side of a second cleavage

deference: a willingness to please or comply with those considered to be superior

delegation (of power): a revocable transfer of authority from one body of state/government to another

demagogue: someone who takes power by inflaming the passions and prejudices of the people

demand management: an economic strategy to regulate the business cycle by stimulating or dampening spending by means of budgetary policy

demissionary phase: the period when a government remains in power after its defeat and prior to its replacement by a successor government

democracy: a system of government by the people (*demos*, Greek), usually indirect, electing representatives

dependent variable: in an experiment, the variable that is being measured for its response to the researcher's manipulation of a second (*independent*) variable

depersonalization: the process of separating the exercise of authority from the individual exercising it—see *offices*

devolution: the creation of a sub-national government and the delegation of powers to it, in some parts but not all of the regime

direct democracy: when citizens vote in a *plebiscite* or *referendum* on a matter, or participate in an *initiative* to force such a vote

dissolution: the formal termination of the legislature by the head of state in order to call for an election

divine right of kings: the medieval idea that royal authority is derived from God

division of labour: the allocation of different economic tasks to members of a community or society

division of powers: the allocation of authority to make and enforce laws between independent levels of state—see *federal*

dogmatic: describes an attitude held regardless of the evidence for or against it

dual executive: exists in parliamentary systems where there is a head of state and a head of government

DWEMs: dead, white, European males

ecclesiastical: describes church-related matters

eclecticism: an approach influenced by a diversity of sources

effective number of parties: statistical measure of the number of political parties in a system, taking into account their relative sizes, either according to the vote shares received (electoral) or the seat shares awarded (legislative)

egalitarian: pertaining to equality

electoral coalition: a partnership of parties designed to maximize the electoral chances of each, usually involving arrangements to support each other's candidates in prescribed situations

electoral college: a device under the US Constitution that facilitates the indirect election of the president and vice-president

electoral democracy: a regime with regular elections but lacking the political freedoms necessary to be a liberal democracy

electoral justice: describes fairness in electoral results, ideally as close a correspondence as possible between voters' inputs and the system's outputs

electoral system: a set of rules and procedures for filling elected offices

electoral vehicle: describes a political party that exists for the purpose of electing its candidates

electoral vs. legislative parties: the (effective) number of parties receiving votes versus the (effective) number of parties winning seats

electronic politics: the era in political campaigning that began in the 1960s with the use of television

elite: those occupying the top positions in any social system

elite accommodation: governing a group or population by making concessions to its leaders

elite dominance: when authority and power rest in the hands of a few

empirical: concerned with what can be measured or demonstrated in experience

empiricism: a theory of knowledge focusing on the observable and measurable

endogeneity: when a result that is supposed to be external to the process of measurement is influenced by that measurement

(the) Enlightenment: period of intellectual revolution based on the primacy of reason and experience rather than tradition and revelation

equalization: a fiscal transfer from the national state to allow sub-national units to provide equivalent levels of services to citizens

excommunication: an act of punishment by a religious community of one of its members by withholding participation in the essential rituals or "sacraments" of that religion

(the) executive: that part of the state primarily responsible for the *executive function*

executive assent: the approval by the head of state of a bill passed by the legislature—often a formality in parliamentary systems

executive coalition: see *coalition government*

executive function: the role of the state in carrying out, overseeing, and/or enforcing policy decisions

externalities: real-world conditions that the economic models of market theory cannot explain

federal: describes a regime in which the state exists at (at least) two levels—national and sub-national—each of which is constitutionally independent of the other

federate: when autonomous territories create a common regime with a national state, surrendering some, but not all, of their own authority to it

feudalism: the medieval socio-economic system based on land-owning nobility and peasant (farm) labour

fiscal policy: a state's strategic decisions about public expenditure and revenue levels

flexible partisans: electors who identify with a party but whose support is not absolute

formal agenda: the policy issues that are considered by policy-makers

formateur/informateur: person asked by a head of state to lead a government/to negotiate with parties in order to find a workable coalition

FPP: First Past the Post electoral systems (sometimes FPTP), called such because the winner is the candidate finishing first—see *SMP*

free vote: a vote to which normal expectations of party discipline do not apply

full adult suffrage: all adult citizens have the right to vote (and to seek office)

fusion of powers: describes the aspect of responsible government whereby the executive is accountable to (and often drawn from) the membership of the legislature

general will: Rousseau's idea of the collective sovereignty of all the citizens (and never less than all the citizens)

gerrymandering: drawing electoral boundaries to maximize the benefit to one's own party

government: 1. the collective executive in a parliamentary system, consisting of the prime minister and cabinet; 2. the offices and agencies (and their employees) who carry out, administer, or deliver the policies and programs of the state—also known as the *bureaucracy*

grand coalition: all (or the greatest part) of the legislative parties are partners in the coalition

greatest good of the greatest number: utilitarian ethical or political principle

head of government: chief political executive in a parliamentary system, the leader of the cabinet: premier, prime minister, chancellor

head of state: chief constitutional executive: the president in a republic, the monarch in a monarchy

hereditary monarchy: the office of monarch is filled according to rules of succession based on definitions of next of kin

highest averages: a means of allocating seats in a PR electoral system using divisors

hinterland: see *metropole/hinterland*

home rule: when a specific region in the regime has its own legislature—see *devolution*

horizontal equity: the condition in federal systems whereby all sub-national governments have the same fiscal capacity to provide services to their citizens

horizontal imbalance: in federal systems, where horizontal equity is absent

horizontal policy-making: see *vertical policy making*

House of Commons: popularly elected legislative chamber in the United Kingdom and Canadian parliaments

House of Lords: chamber in the United Kingdom parliament consisting of hereditary or appointed peers (persons holding an aristocratic title)

hypothesis: a provisional statement, to be tested, about the relationship between variables

ideology: a systematic set of political beliefs organized for action

imperialism: the ideology of empire—having and ruling territories (colonies) external to the regime

incongruence: the failure of election results to reflect voter inputs

incrementalist (pluralist exchange) model: a theory that policy-making involves moving in small stages away from the status quo

independent variable: that which is being tested (age, education, gender) for its effect on something else (voter turnout)—the *dependent variable*

informal ballot: see *spoiled ballot*

initiative: instrument of direct democracy by which a portion of the public can require a referendum to be held on a specific matter

inquisitorial justice system: describes the trial dynamics of civil-law systems, where the judge takes an active role in examining witnesses

institution: a structure of routines, rules, and roles that organizes behaviour for a generally understood social or collective purpose or set of purposes

instrumentalism: the modern notion that reason can serve any purpose, in contrast to the classical identification of reason with the good

instruments: types of authoritative decision making at the disposal of government, including penalties, rewards, impositions, and benefits

interest group/organized interest: organizations designed to represent a membership, based on their members' economic or social interests or issue attachments, by influencing policy-makers

intergovernmental relations: state-to-state or government-to-government relations within a regime, usually in a federal context

intervening variable: an extraneous (unmeasured) variable that may be responsible for the apparent influence of Y on X

investiture vote: in some parliamentary systems, a vote that a proposed government must pass in order to take office

issue group: see *activist group*

judicial activism (vs. restraint): 1. the degree of willingness of the courts to overturn legislation or executive acts; 2. broad versus narrow interpretations of the law by the courts

judicial function: ruling on disputes over the application, enforcement, or interpretation of law

judicial independence: conditions required to ensure courts are free from political influence

judicial review: the ability of the courts to evaluate (possibly overturn) acts of the legislature or executive on the view that they contradict the constitution

(the) judiciary: that part of the state primarily responsible for the *judicial function*

junta: a government of military officers

jurisprudence: decisions about the law that inform the activity of the courts

just regime: one in which the authority of the state is exercised on behalf of its citizens

kinship: familial (blood) relations

Land/Länder: the sub-national unit(s) of state in Austria and Germany

landed gentry: the layer of society below the aristocracy, consisting of those able to live off the rental income from their tenants

largest remainders: a means of allocating seats in a PR district using quotas

law: a published rule, backed by the authority of the state, that binds everyone

law-like generalization: something that social-scientific research seeks to establish—reliable non-trivial statements about the relationship between two variables

legal threshold: a level of support in a PR electoral system that a party must obtain to be guaranteed a proportional share of seats

legislative coalition: when parties have an arrangement to vote together in the legislature

legislative function: the responsibility for making authoritative decisions in the form of law

legislative parties: see *electoral vs. legislative parties*

legislative process: the procedures a legislature follows in making law

(the) legislature: that part of the state primarily responsible for the *legislative function*

legitimacy: the quality possessed by or attributed to a regime that has the consent of its citizens

LBGT: lesbian, gay, bisexual, and transgendered persons

liberal: an ideology focusing on the rights and freedoms of the individual

libertarian: an ideology favouring minimal state activity in all spheres: economic, social, and political

limited state: the public norm that the authority of the state should be exercised within publicly accepted and defined limits

loss of confidence: occurs when a parliamentary cabinet loses the support of a majority of the legislature—usually requires the resignation of the government and the formation of a new administration, after an election if necessary

Madisonian model: US system of separated legislative, executive, and judicial powers linked by *checks and balances*

majoritarian system: electoral system that tends (or is designed) to produce a majority—AV, FPP/SMP, TRS

majority: more than all the rest (50% plus 1)

majority government: control of a majority of the legislators by a single-party cabinet

manifesto: detailed document of a political party's policy positions and proposals for governing

market economy (capitalism): a system in which most goods and services are obtained in (and produced for) exchanges between buyers and sellers

materialism: a philosophy that matter is the most fundamental reality (opposing idealism)

median legislator: hypothetically, the legislator in the exact middle when all legislators are arranged from one ideological extreme to the other

medieval age: feudal period in Western Europe from roughly 500 to 1500

metropole/hinterland: a social cleavage dividing those at the centre of the regime from those in outlying regions

minimal state: the political counterpart of the economic doctrine of laissez-faire—a state that intervenes the least in economic life

minimal winning coalition: any coalition that controls a majority in the legislature but would cease to do so if any of its partners were to leave the coalition

minimum winning coalition: in any parliament, the smallest possible minimal winning coalition

ministerial responsibility: the convention that a minister is accountable to the legislature for the administration of the departments for which he or she is the minister

(the) Ministry: in Westminster-style regimes, refers to all ministers appointed by a prime minister during his or her continuous time in office

minority government: a cabinet composed of one party or a coalition of parties controlling less than a majority of the legislators

mixed government: the eighteenth-century idea of combining the monarchic, aristocratic, and democratic elements—said to be reflected in the institutions of the US Constitution

MMP (mixed member proportional): an electoral system in which voters choose a constituency candidate and select a national party; the latter determines the overall number of seats and a second tier of seats is used to adjust for the constituency wins

mobilization function: performed by political parties when they engage the electorate, organize its political activity, and seek its votes

modernity: the last three or four centuries (minus the years that are part of "post-modernity")

monetarism: an economic theory stressing control of the money supply and using interest-rate policy as a means to accomplish this

multivariate analysis: statistical techniques that permit measurement of the influence of several independent variables

nation-state: alternate term for country, combining a social–territorial component (the nation) with a political component (the state)

natural law: medieval concept that principles of right apply to the human world in the way that the laws of nature govern the physical world

normative: describes principles, theories, philosophies about what "ought" to be

obligation: the duty to obey that citizens owe to a legitimate regime

offices: the attachment of duties, powers, and responsibilities to institutional positions or roles regardless of who holds them

oppositional: describes politics of division within legislatures—usually in majoritarian systems

ordinal: describes a ballot on which choices are ranked in order of preference

organic hierarchy: a stratified social system in which reciprocal duties and responsibilities link the different classes or ranks—characteristic of feudal society

organized interest: see *interest group*

outcome: the product of a process, also known in systems theory as an output—in political theory, the relationship of outputs to inputs is one way to evaluate a process or system

overdetermined: describes when a particular social phenomenon is acted upon by so many factors that determining the degree of influence of any one of them is impossible

overhang seats: extra seats temporarily added to a parliament elected under an MMP system when parties win more constituency seats than the total number of seats that their vote entitles them to

oversight committee: legislative committee with a primary responsibility of scrutinizing the government's exercise of the executive function; often has a financial focus

pariah party: a legislative party that no other party will partner with, usually because its values fall outside a consensus shared by the other parties—for example, a separatist party

participatory democracy: type of direct decision making where citizens meet to discuss, debate, and vote on matters

party discipline: the degree of conformity of legislators to a common party position, as well as the mechanisms used to promote or enforce such conformity

party system: the parties in an election or legislature considered as a whole and in their relationships to each other within that whole

patriarchy: a social structure reinforcing the dominant authority of the male gender

patronage: the non-competitive appointment of individuals to public positions or offices

peak association/umbrella organization: a body uniting all organized interests of a similar kind or basis (often economic)

plebiscite: a non-binding vote on a question put to the public by the government

pluralism: a view that society is composed (and the political process is best understood by studying the activity) of groups

pluralist exchange model: see *incrementalist model*

plurality: having more than any other (having the most)

pocket veto: refers to the US president's ability to veto a bill during the last 10 days of a Congress by simply not signing it

polarization: applied to party systems to describe degree(s) of difference in party positions

policy: the deliberate response of a government with respect to a state of events falling within its jurisdiction, including the decision to take no action at all

policy community: the totality of those interested in a particular policy space

policy cycle: the stages by which policy is considered, formulated, approved, implemented, evaluated, and revised

policy instruments: see *instruments*

policy-making: taking an authoritative response to a particular situation or problem

policy network: describes a relationship between different members of the policy community, usually between state actors (the sub-government) and citizens (the attentive public)

policy process: how public policy is made—see *policy cycle*

policy sector: subject area for consideration by policy-makers—education policy, health policy, economic policy, foreign policy

polis: name for ancient Greek city states meaning "body of citizens"

political centralization: the degree to which power is exercised at the regime's capital

political culture: the dominant political beliefs, attitudes, and values within a regime

political efficiency: see *technical efficiency*

political process: activities and mechanisms by which policy preferences and individuals to fill political offices are brought from civil society to the state

political system: describes the total set of interactions between society and the state

popular sovereignty: 1. the view that the ultimate source of the state's authority derives from the consent (expressed or tacit) of its citizens; 2. when the authority of the state is exercised by its citizens

portfolio: the area(s) of government for which a minister (member of the executive) is responsible

power: the ability to secure obedience from those who do not consent

precedents: rulings by a body (usually a court) that are applied by other bodies ruling in similar circumstances

preferential voting: ranking candidates and/or parties in order of the voter's preferences—see AV and STV

prerogative: an exclusive right or privilege, often referring to power(s) the executive may exercise without the approval of the legislature

presidentialism: theory of state favouring a politically active, elected head of state

private law: see *public vs. private law*

private member: in parliamentary legislatures, a legislator who is not part of the executive

process: a transformation, change, or exchange of a resource (information, commodities, money) into something else (knowledge, goods, services)

proletariat: the class of those who receive a wage for their labour

propaganda: the selective presentation of information for partisan purposes

proportional systems: electoral systems designed to maximize the correspondence between parties' vote shares and their seat shares

proportionality: the degree to which the distribution of one value matches the distribution of another, related value

propositions: conditional statements about the relationships between variables

prorogation: the formal ending of a parliamentary session

province: 1. a sub-national unit of state in a federal system; 2. an administrative division in a unitary state

pseudo-democracies: regimes that hold uncompetitive elections or lack the civil liberties and standard of living necessary to make competitive elections possible

public agenda: the informal list of policy issues that have the most public salience or traction

public choice theory: (also "rational choice") an approach to political science using techniques from economics and game theory to develop models that reveal the responses "rational" actors would make in specific political or social situations

public policy: a deliberate course of action (or a decision not to act) in response to a specific set of circumstances

public vs. private law: public law is made by legislatures; private law is set down in codes (civil law) or is made by the courts (common law)

ratification: a vote of approval, usually used for a multi-lateral agreement or treaty

rationalism: a belief in the power of human reason to find solutions to problems—scientific, ethical, or political

rationalist model: an ideal type of policy-making designed to weigh costs and benefits of various possible responses in order to identify the best possible solution for a policy issue

recall: a process by which constituents may force a vote on the continued tenure in office of their elected representative

referendum: a binding vote on a question put to the public by the government, sometimes required under a law or the constitution

regulations: laws made by the executive (usually) under authority delegated by a statute

(the) Reformation: a split in the Christian Church beginning in the sixteenth century with the emergence of Protestant sects not recognizing the authority of the pope at Rome

reinforcing cleavage: when two or more social cleavages (A/B; X/Y) overlap so that they divide a population the same way (every A is an X; every B is a Y)

repatriate: the process by which the Parliament of the United Kingdom passed legislation giving control over the amendment of the Canadian constitution to Canada's legislatures

repeal: when one Act of the legislature extinguishes a previous Act, in whole or in part

representation function: the role of parties in communicating to the legislature and government the views, concerns, and preferences of voters who support them

representative democracy: citizens vote for representatives to act on their behalf in the legislature and executive

reservation and disallowance: constitutional provisions allowing the Canadian government to override provincial legislation, modelled on similar provisions (no longer in effect) that allowed the UK Parliament at Westminster to overrule Canadian legislation—provisions regarded by many as "spent" (no longer usable)

residual clause: part of a constitution identifying who wields any powers not expressly assigned by the constitution to the state (or levels of state)

responsible government: a constitutional system in which the executive must retain the support of a majority in the legislature

revenue capacity: the ability of a government to raise funds for its programs

run-off: an additional round of voting held when no candidate receives a majority (or other set level of support) in the current round, the least successful candidate or candidates being taken off the ballot

second tier: seats in a PR or parallel system awarded proportionally or in such a way as to create overall proportionality

semi-presidentialism: a hybrid constitutional system combining parliamentary government with a politically active, elected head of state

separation of powers: constitutional system where the branches of government are independent from each other; most specifically, the executive has no legislative power

single transferable ballot: an ordinal ballot used in a multi-member district: ballots may be moved (transferred) to another candidate's count when the first candidate has been elected with a surplus (more than the quota) or is being eliminated (as the candidate with the least number of ballots); technically, AV also uses a single transferable ballot

slippage: term used to describe the degree to which, in its implementation, a policy is diverted from its original design or intent

SMP (single member plurality): electoral system using single-member districts and electing the candidate with the most votes—see also *FPP*

social cleavages: the identities that form a basis for political action

social contract: a hypothetical construct in early liberal thought describing the origin of government in an agreement of individuals to create and obey a sovereign power

social mobility: the degree (often overestimated) to which it is possible for any individual to change his or her social position (class) within a given socio-economic system

social movements: broad, loosely organized sections of society uniting around a common identity and issues associated with that identity—often cutting across cleavages, parties, and organized interests

social whole: the collective entity within which human life is experienced

society: a social whole characterized by heterogeneity (diversity) in significant variables such as class, ethnicity, religion, and occupation, and by the presence of low degrees of cohesion or connection between its members

sound bite: a quote or phrase in a speech or address designed to attract media attention and promote subsequent coverage

sovereignty: the authoritative control exercised by the state over a territory and its peoples

sovereignty-association: a bilateral arrangement proposed as a form of economic union between Canada and a sovereign Quebec

spoiled ballot: (also informal ballot) a ballot marked contrary to the rules—it cannot be counted for any candidate or party

stakeholder group: organized interest based on occupation, profession, or other factor associated with a person's livelihood

state: 1. a social whole with social hierarchy and centralized leadership that possesses means of coercion to enforce its commands; 2. the permanent structure of authority/power by which the people of a specific territory are governed; 3. those areas of public life that are actively governed, in contrast to *civil society*, where the state is absent; 4. a sub-national structure of authority/power in a federal regime

state of nature: an imagined or hypothetical condition of humanity in the absence of laws, prior to the social contract

status: the esteem or honour that attaches to a particular rank or occupation within society

STV: the electoral system employing an ordinal ballot in multi-member constituencies—see *single transferable ballot*

sub-government: part of a specific policy community or network consisting of relevant state/government actors in that policy sector

subjects: those who are governed by a monarch or a dictator

sub-national state: in a federal constitution, the junior level of autonomous government

subsistence agriculture: farming for immediate consumption, rather than producing for sale

surplus majority coalition: a coalition government controlling a majority of the legislative seats and containing at least one more party than is necessary to achieve that control

suspensive veto: the ability to delay but not reject a measure

symmetry: in the context of federalism, refers to a identical division of powers between the national state and each of the sub-national states

tacit consent: the idea that silence on particular matters may signal agreement with or acceptance of them—arguably, this requires the opportunity to freely dissent

technical (vs. political) efficiency: the economic cost of a policy achieving its goals versus the political costs

telos: Aristotelian notion of the end or purpose to which an object or essence is directed

theocracy: a state run by religious leaders or according to religious principles

theory: an organized body of concepts intended to provide an explanation

third wave (of democratization): a period, after 1974, of significant increase in the number of electoral democracies

totalitarian: a state that, in theory, controls every aspect of life (there is no civil society)

transitional regimes: regimes with the potential to become liberal democracies or to lapse into authoritarianism

tribe: a social whole consisting of integrated bands inhabiting a region

tribunal: a body with quasi-judicial status constituted to hear appeals from adjudicative decisions

TRS (two round system): electoral system employing a *run–off*; most frequent type of presidential election

type of government: used here to describe the various forms of cabinet government within a parliamentary system

tyranny of the majority: when a group with the majority share of the government and/or population uses its political strength to disadvantage the minority on a regular basis

umbrella organization: see *peak association*

unicameral: indicates a legislature with only one house

unitary state/regime: regime in which there is only one autonomous level of state

utilitarianism: a variety of liberalism stressing the maximization of pleasure by seeking the greatest good of the greatest number

vertical imbalance: in federalism, when one level of government does not have revenue resources adequate to meet its responsibilities

vertical (vs. horizontal) policy-making: policy-making by ministries within their assigned legislative responsibilities versus policy-making that coordinates ministries or crosses ministry lines

veto: a decision by one body that negates a decision made by another body

vote splitting: voting for a candidate from more than one party, where the ballot permits

wasted votes: ballots that do not contribute to the election of a candidate or party

Westminster: popular name for the Parliament of the United Kingdom

Whig: English political faction from seventeenth to nineteenth century, generally favouring responsible government and liberalism

Index

monarchy, 19

political parties, 256

reinforcing cleavages, 197

Belgium election (2010), 138

benefits (rights), 326

benevolent organizations, 28

Bentham, Jeremy, 89

Bernstein, Eduard, *Evolutionary Socialism,* 212

bicameralism, 109–10, 175, 317

bilingualism, 198

Bill 101, 199

Bill of Rights (1688), 80, 109

bipartisan brokerage politics, 112

bipartisan voting, 149

black markets, 26

Blair, Tony, 348

Bloc Québécois, 122, 200, 260

block funding, 171

block voting, 228–29, 240

Boleyn, Anne, 16

bourgeoisie, 206, 339

Brazil, 151, 176, 355

compulsory voting, 91

election (2010), 214

equal representation in second chamber, 177

federalism, 110

Party List PR, 243

president, 152

bribery, 24

Britain. *See* UK

British Columbia, 231

British North America Act (1867), 183

brokerage parties, 112, 257, 259

changed by television, 259

public-opinion polling and, 260

budget officer, 24

Bulgaria, 19, 240

bureaucracy, 18, 20, 299–303, 344

Burke, Edmund, 79, 90, 210

autonomy of representatives, 79, 88

Reflections on the Revolution in France, 79

Bush, George W., 15, 154

Bush doctrine of an imperial United States, 21

business cycle, 342–44

business planning models, 301

cabinet committees, 139–40, 296

cabinet government, 117–18

cabinet implosion, 128

Cabinet Office, 297

cabinet size and structure, 139–40

cabinet solidarity, 118

Cameron, David, 127

Campaign for Nuclear Disarmament, 270

Canada, 4, 18, 26, 110

administrative law, 323

administrative posts filled by appointment, 300

Arctic sovereignty, 164

asymmetrical federalism, 175

cabinet committees, 139–40

coalition government, 123

Confederation, 111, 164, 166

Constitution (1982), 108, 172, 183

Constitution Act (1867), 168–70

constitutional amending formula, 180–82

devolution of power to Quebec's National Assembly, 185

division of power, 166, 169–70, 185

election (1997), (2004) ,(2006) , (2008), 121

election (2011), 121, 200, 226, 260, 266

equalization payments, 172–73

ethno-linguistic division between English and French, 167, 193, 198, 259

federal - provincial - territorial meetings, 174

federalism, 5, 110, 166–67, 174

fiscal transfers, 171, 173

head of state, 124–27 (*See also* Governor General [Canada])

infrastructure deficit, 353

keeping track of changes to the law, 307, 309

minority governments, 121–22

monarchy, 19

multi-party system in a majoritarian (non-proportional) system, 121, 123

New Public Management in, 301

non-majority governance, 43

plebiscites, 319–20

recessions, 350

rivalry between Liberals and Conservatives, 122

Senate (*See* Canadian Senate)

tax systems (federal and provincial) becoming integrated, 174

vertical fiscal imbalance, 171

weak bicameralism, 179

citizens' expectations of the state, 190

city-state, 16, 58–59, 83

civic republicanism, 66

civil freedoms, 99–100

civil justice, 184

civil law, 113, 322–23

civil liberty, 78

civil rights movement in the US, 209

civil society, 25, 100, 103–4, 151, 209, 269

    Hobbes on, 72–73

    institutions of, 26–27

civil society and democracy, 29

civil society and freedom, 28

civil society and modernization, 28

civil unrest, 30

civil wars, 72, 196

civilian control of the police and military, 99, 104, 306

Clarity Act (2000), 200

Clarke, Harold D. ,*Absent Mandate*, 257

class, 11, 45, 47, 61, 64, 191, 193

    bourgeoisie, 206, 339

    lower-middle class, 340 (*See also* middle class)

    Plato's account of, 60

class analysis, 44–45

class cleavages, 195–96, 264

class relations, 205–7, 339

classic liberalism, 42, 91, 202, 211, 336–40

classical antiquity, 57–61

classical economics, 47

cleavages, structure of, 196–98

Clegg, Nick, 127

Clement VII, Pope, 16

climate change, 30–31, 174, 279, 356–57

Clinton, William, 15

Clinton Administration

    brought US budget into surplus, 348

    reform of welfare law, 348

Club of Rome, 355

co-operation, 8–9

co-operation / coordination distinction, 11

co-operative activity, 44

coalition agreements, 135, 138

    manifesto used to negotiate policy agenda, 268–69

Coalition (Australia), 231–32

coalition cabinets, 152

coalition governments, 5, 43, 112, 122, 126, 129–38

    amendments to legislation, 313

    compatibility of partners, 122, 133

    compromise and cooperation, 124, 135

    consensual approach to governing, 124

    form in response to crisis or serious policy challenges, 119, 123

    forming a partnership, 131

    grand coalition, 137, 160

    indecisiveness (criticism), 138

    lengthy government-formation process, 137, 139

    long-term future of democracy and, 124

    minor parties in, 138

    policy approval in, 136, 292–93

    policy formulation in, 136, 290

    political party approach to issues and, 135

    prime minister's control in, 140

    stability of, 136–37

coalition theory, 131

coalitionist presidentialism in Latin America, 151–53, 161

codified laws, 62

coercion, 11–13, 28

coercive power, 48–49

cohabitation, 158

Cold War, 29, 137, 211, 348

collective activity, 44, 192

collective decision making, 21, 139

collective identity, 191

collective or public ownership, 207

collective responsibility of the cabinet, 118

Colomer, Joseph, 123

colonialism and imperialism, legacy of, 193

colonization, 10

Columbia, 151

command, 12

command economies, 340

common culture, 4, 48

common good, 61, 63

common law, 113, 321–23

    precedents, 55

Commonwealth (Hobbes's version of civil society), 72–73

communism, 60, 212

communism / socialism distinction, 212–13

Communist Party, 122, 212, 340

communitarian strain in modern democratic thought, 78
community, 8–10, 13, 31, 35, 47, 51
  conduct regulated by customs, traditions, and religious beliefs, 12
  diminishing strength of, 56
community/society distinction, 10–11
comparative analysis, 16, 30, 37, 43, 131
comparative framework, 103–16
competitiveness of the market, 340
compulsory childhood education, 35, 340
compulsory voting, 91, 289
conclusion of a government
  head of state's role, 128–29
  in parliamentary system of state, 128–30
concurrent jurisdiction (in federal systems), 170
confederal state, 165, 170
confederate (term), 111
confederation, 111
confidence, 76, 118, 128
  loss of legislative confidence, 128
confidence and supply agreements
  in coalition agreements, 138
confidence chamber, 109–10, 180
confidence (motion of censure), 157
Congressional committees, 145
congressional system
  policy approval in a, 293
connected coalition, 132
conscription of soldiers, Canadian plebiscite on, 320

consensual democracy, 160
consensual politics, 112, 135–36
consensus, 48, 184
consent, 12–14, 21, 73, 83–84
conservatism, 203, 280
  organic conservatives, 204
conservatism[1]
  accepted new economic order of liberal market society, 210
  cautious about rights and democracy, 210
conservatism[o]
  acceptance of inequality as natural, 204
  acceptance of market economy, 205
  position on power and authority, 204
  skeptical of the power of human reason, 205
Conservatives (Canada), 122
Conservatives (Ireland), 241
Conservatives (UK), 127
consociational approach to government, 198–99
consolidation or codification of laws, 307
conspiracy theories, 146
constituents per representative, 96–97
constitution, 19, 21
  limiting state with, 15
  written constitution, 108
constitutional amendment, 17, 181–83
  referenda on, 318–19
constitutional conventions, 108–9
constitutional jurisprudence, 55

constitutional monarchies, 19
  head of government in, 19
  head of state in, 19
constitutionalism, 5, 94, 202, 205, 306
constitutions of ancient Greece, 78
consumer class, 344–45
consumer credit, 351
consumer society, 335
cooperation, 124, 135
coordination, 8–9
Copernicus, Nicolaus, 68
corporatism, 273–77
Costa Rica, 151–52, 154
court systems
  in civil-law countries, 324
  in common-law system, 324–25
courts, 13. See also appellate courts; Supreme Court
covenant that establishes civil society, 72
crime, 30, 349
Criminal Code, 322
criminal law, 170, 184, 322
criteria for evaluating electoral systems
  distribution-based, 223–24
  elector-based criteria, 227–29
  government formation-based criteria, 225
  party-system-based criteria, 225–27
Croatia, 318
cross-cutting cleavages, 198
cross-disciplinary insight, 36
Crown's prerogative, 76

electoral democracy, 98–100, 104

electoral districts, 87, 245

electoral formulae, 221–22

electoral justice, 224, 229

electoral parties, 227

electoral parties *vs.* legislative parties, 226

electoral-professional party, 260

electoral reform, 124

electoral systems, 3, 94, 111, 121, 219–45, 260, 264–65

  filtering effect, 226

  stability of government and, 225

"electoralism," fallacy of, 98

elite accommodation, 199

elite dominance, 93

elites, 86, 277

Elizabeth II, Queen, 76

embezzlement, 24

emergence of the state, 49–51

emerging economies, 355–56

empire, 56–59

empirical dimension of political enquiry, 34, 36, 42

empirical theory, 41

empiricism, 68

employment, 175

  full employment, 342, 347

  "jobless" recovery from recessions in 1990-1991, 350

Encyclopaedia Britannica, 89

end justifies the mean (doctrine), 66

endogeneity, 57

energy intensive global economy, 356

Engels, Friedrich, 205, 207

England. *See also* UK

adjustment from feudal to modern, legal-rational polity, 71

ascendance as major capitalist power, 86

class, 64

development of parliament, 86

monarchy retained but weakened, 76

political transformation, 75

seats in the House of Commons, 87

English Civil War, 71, 74

English Constitution, 108

Enlightenment, 16, 22, 64, 68–69, 74, 192, 305

entrenchment of rights, 326–27, 329

entrepreneurs, 335

enumeration of voters, 246

environment, 31, 167

environmental consciousness, 195

environmental protection laws, 31, 194

environmental strategies, 280

environmentalism, 279–80

equal access to tertiary education, 353

equal representation in second chambers (or upper houses), 177

equality, 11, 21, 24, 44, 69, 78

equality rights, 19

equalization payments, 172

established democracies. *See* developed-world democracies

ethics, 16

Ethics (Aristotle), 59

ethno-linguistic cleavages, 193–94

  preserving language, education, and other cultural supports, 193

ethno-linguistic minorities, 56, 177

  safeguarded in federal constitution, 166

  self-government or guaranteed representation, 194

eudaemonia, 61

Europe, 18

  civil law, 322

European Christian Democrats, 346

European culture, 57

European democracies

  class cleavage, 196

  welfare state, 349

European election campaigns (PR)

  conducted on macro level, 268

  focused on ideas, 268

Evolutionary Socialism (Bernstein), 212

excommunication, 62, 68

executive, 19, 105

executive assent for passing legislation, 317

executive coalition, 121

executive dominance, 140–41

  challenge for interest groups, 272

  Latin America, 153

executive power in the monarch, 74

executive that is neither drawn from nor responsible to the legislature, 161

expanding service sector, 335

fairness, 21, 23, 88, 123

faith, 68

"false consciousness," 207

fame, 66

family, 10, 27–28, 30, 209

Faroe Islands, 185

"Fathers of Confederation," 164

fear of death, 71

federal transfers, 171

federalism, 19, 110

    definitions, 166

    division of powers, 110, 164–65

    fiscal federalism, 170–73

    introduction of "money bills"
        limited to lower chamber, 317

    relations between levels, 5

    written constitution, 167

feminism, 201, 277–79

feudal lord / peasant relationship,
    63, 70

feudal period, 22–23, 62–66

feudalism, 56–57

Fifth Republic (France), 155, 158

    constitution, 156

    court system, 324

    reactive assembly, 314

*Figueroa vs. the Attorney General
    (Canada)*, 247

Fiji, 127

financiers, 335

financing of political parties and
    candidates, 94

Finland, 136, 159

    Party List PR, 243

    referenda, 319

    women cabinet members, 161

First Ministers conferences, 179

First Nations, 174

First Past the Post (FPP). *See* SMP/
    FPP

first-wave feminism, 278

fiscal conservatism, 210–11

fiscal federalism, 170–73

fixed-date elections, 220

fixed electoral terms, 127, 129

Flemish and Walloon in Belgium,
    193

Flemish independence party, 138

force, 12–14, 20. *See also* coercion

foreign-held debt, 352

foreign policy, 30, 264

    contrast between North American
        and European perspectives,
        201

formal agenda, 287–89

formateur, 127

Forms (Plato's), 59

Fourier, Charles, 205

Fourth Republic (France)

    unstable coalitions, 155

Fox, Robin, 56

France, 75, 214. *See also* Fifth
    Republic (France); Fourth
    Republic (France)

    change from monarchy to
        republican form of
        government, 76

    direct democracy, 318

    entrance to the public service, 300

    paid political advertising
        forbidden, 268

    party system, 158

    president, 157–58

    prime minister, 157–58

    rules concerning confidence, 128

    semi-presidentialism in, 155–58,
        161

    TRS (Two Round System), 233–34

    welfare state in, 346

Francophone federalists within
    Quebec, 200

Francophones outside Quebec, 198

Free Democratic Party (Germany),
    239

free votes, 88

freedom, 5, 19, 36, 43, 77

    civil society and, 28

    economic freedoms, 337–38

Freedom House, 43, 99–100, 104,
    113, 151

Freedom in the World, 99

freedom of association and
    expression, 98–99

freedoms (rights), 326

French-Canadian nationalism
    (1763–1960)

    emphasis on preserving language,
        culture, and custom, 199

French colonial possessions (former)
    TRS (Two Round System), 234

French Revolution, 77, 79

Freud's theory of psychoanalysis, 37

Friedman, Milton, 211, 337

full employment, 342

"functional inconsistency," 224

fusion of powers, 106

"gag law," 248

Galileo, 68

Gallagher, Michael, 191, 275–76

game theory, 43, 131

Gaulle, Charles de, 156

manufactured majority, 223, 225, 234

manufacturers, 75, 87

Manzer, Ron, 44

Marbury v. Madison, 150

market autonomy, 207, 336

market capitalism
reform of, 340–45

market economy, 27–28, 64, 69–70, 74–75, 86–87, 203, 210, 335
displaced individuals from subsistence agriculture, 70
government support of, 336
as product of civil society and the state, 27
regulation, 209
reliance on to allocate resources, 333–34
requirement for supply of workers, 70
several centuries of development, 335
socialist view of, 206

market (red) Tories, 210–11, 346

marketable central government debt, 351–52

marketing and polling techniques, 267

markets
divergence between theory and practice, 341

marriage, 192–93

Marx, Karl, 45, 52, 77, 205, 207, 212
critique of capitalism, 339
defined class structurally, 195
liberalism is the ideology of the propertied classes, 342–44

state would "wither away," 340
theory of historical materialism, 37

Marxists, 201

Mary, Princess Royal of England and Princess of Orange, 74, 76, 80

Maslow, Abraham, 44

materialism, 68

Mauritius, 163, 229, 240

maximizing shareholder value, 351

Mead, Lawrence, "Scholasticism in Political Science," 46

mechanical effect, 227

media, 99, 253, 269
competitive mass media, 30
lack of attention to substance of legislative debate, 314
simplistic quality of political debate, 23

median legislator, 132–33

mediation, 323

medieval age, 57, 62–66. *See also* feudal period
focus on relationship between the state and the Church, 62
laws in, 63
organic hierarchy, 63

medieval monarchs, 62

Meech Lake Accord, 183, 185, 199

"Mensalão scandal," 153

mercantile capitalism, 56

merchants, 75, 335

Mesopotamia, 51

methodological eclecticism, 47

methods patterned after the natural sciences, 37

metropole and hinterland. *See* centre-periphery

Mexico, 51, 98, 163

"micro" campaign, 267

middle class, 196, 213, 339, 342
continuing decline of, 334
(dis)satisfied with their position in market society, 338
increasingly higher proportion of tax burden, 347
unlikely to be satisfied with the minimal state, 344

middle-class affluence, 100

military, 13, 58
subordination to elected officials, 99, 104, 306

military budgets during Cold War, 29, 348

military conquest, 10

military coup, threat of, 104

military force in achieving American goals, 211

military juntas, 24

Mill, James, 84, 203
"Government," 89

Mill, John Stuart, 84
On Liberty, 89, 208–9
The Subjection of Women, 89

minimal state, 210, 333, 337, 342, 346

minimal winning coalition, 131–32, 138

minimum standards of well-being egalitarian belief in, 28

minimum vote share, 225

ministerial responsibility, doctrine of, 108

Ministry (Canada), 138

politics as dynamic, 3

politics as philosophy, 34–36

politics as relational, 2

politics as social science, 36, 40

politics as the art of the possible, 60

politics of "character," 256

polity, 17

polls. *See* public-opinion polling

popes, 62. *See also* names of individual popes

struggle with monarchs, 16

popular sovereignty, 23, 31, 69, 73–74, 78, 84

erosion of, 95

limit on state authority, 22

popular support, 24

popular tyrants, 86

population growth, 51

populism, 215

Populist or People's Party in the US, 215

"pork barrel" politics, 153

pornography, 192–93

portfolio, 118

Portugal, 159

post-industrial period, 280, 335, 355

post-materialist dimension, 264

post-welfare state, 348–51

postsecondary education, 174

poverty, 100, 192–93, 349

power, 20, 27, 66, 76. *See also* authority

power, desire for, 71

power, lover of, 16

power of monarchy (became mostly formal), 76

power of the Church, 74. *See also* separation of church and state

practical reason, 60, 65

practice of politics, 52

pre-industrial societies, 13, 47–48

pre-political societies, 28

precedents, 321

preferential voting, 222

president

ability to name and dismiss the prime minister, 159

appointment of senior administrative officials, 145

dominance in Latin American system, 152

elected independently from legislative branch, 144

emergency powers, 157

pre-eminence of, 158

in semi-presidential systems, 155, 158

term of office, 157

who serves as head of state, 153–55

presidential elections, 144, 154

France, 157

TRS (Two Round System), 154, 233

US, 154

presidential veto, 145, 160, 293, 317

Congress may overturn, 145

overridden by vote of legislature, 160

presidentialism, 145

presumption of innocence, 24

prime minister

control (or power), 113, 140

diminished control under coalition government, 140

head of government, 155

head of government and chief political executive, 118

head of political party, 119

in parliamentary system, 148

selection of other ministers, 140

in semi-presidential systems, 155

Prince Edward Island

plebiscite on MMP, 236

seats in Senate, 179

The Prince (Machiavelli), 66

priorities and planning (P&P committee), 140

private law, 321–22

private members, 119, 312

private ownership of property, 333–34

private power, concentration of, 151

private property, 73, 77–78, 210

requirement for government sanction, 27

privatization, 211

Privy Council Office (PCO), 297

probability theory, 40

process, 3, 5

professional associations

tasks on behalf of the state, 270

professional public service, 299–301

professionalization of election campaigns, 267

programs, 284

progress and the notion of human perfectibility, 207

prohibition of alcohol

popular ballots, 319–20

proletariat, 206, 339

propaganda, 14

propertied class, 74. *See also* private
   property
proportional representation (PR)
      electoral systems, 111, 121–22, 127,
      152, 160, 184, 235–45. *See also*
      STV-PR (Single Transferable
      Vote PR)
   associated with multi-party
      systems, 261
   correspondence of outputs to
      inputs, 131
   efficiency of each party's vote, 267
   every vote makes a difference, 268
   filtering effect of, 226
   focus on increasing vote share, 265
   majority of seats = majority of
      votes, 260
   MMP (*See* MMP (Mixed Member
      Proportional))
   multi-party system reinforced
      by, 122
   Party List (*See* Party List PR)
   policy formulation in, 290
   polling accuracy, 265
   small, narrowly focused parties
      can work, 261
   wasted votes in, 230
proportionality, 222
propositions, 39
prosperity for all argument, 342
prostitution, 192–93
protection of the vulnerable, 192–93
protections (rights), 326
Protestant faiths, 67
Protestant succession to the throne,
   74
Protestant work ethic, 20

protesters, 352
Proudhon, Pierre-Joseph, 205
provinces, 164
provincial responsibility for the
   administration of justice, 324
pseudo-democracies, 98, 245
psychological effect, 227
   wasted votes and, 230
psychology, 37, 47, 208
"the public," 93, 320. *See also* "the
   people"
public administration/policy, 104
public agenda in policy formation,
   287–88
public auditor, position of, 24
public choice theory, 43
public disenchantment with political
   realm, 96–97, 254
public disillusionment with political
   parties, 256
public education, 44
public employees, 50
public health, 30–31
public health insurance
   difference in support between
      Canada and US, 201
public information delivery (mass
   media), 96
public interest groups, 270
public legislature, 306
public norms, 21, 23–24, 51
public opinion, 5, 133, 209, 267
   formation of, 3
   tendency to cluster at the centre,
      132
public-opinion polling, 26, 240, 248,
   259–60, 265, 267

public policy, 113, 283
   policy cycle as coherent process
      (theory), 285
   view that it is a chaotic
      ensemble of uncoordinated
      transactions, 285
public-policy outcomes, 146
public-policy process, 94
public political debate
   simplistic quality of, 23
public servants, 170, 293–94,
   299–300
public service, 18, 59, 348
   entrance and promotion based on
      merit, 299–300
   non-partisan, 300
   professionalization of, 299
   size, 302–3, 348
public sovereignty/parliamentary
   sovereignty clash, 23
public will, difficulty identifying, 95
Putnam, Robert, 29

quality, 36
quasi-federalism, 166
Quebec, 5, 194, 259–60
   accommodated in *Constitution
      Act* (1867), 168
   Canadian plebiscite on
      conscription, 320
   civil law, 322
   "distinct society," 186
   expansion of the state, 199
   Francophone business and
      entrepreneurial class, 199
   Quiet Revolution, 75
   referendum (1980), 186, 200

referendum (1995), 186, 200
  sovereignty-association goal,
    185–86
Quebec Act (1774), 75, 199
Quebec nationalism, 198
Quebec Pension Plan (QPP), 175
Quebec within Canada (case study),
    198–200
Québécois, 198
Québécois nationalism, 199
Quebec's civil-code legal legal
    system, 175
Quebec's National Assembly, 185
Quebec's traditional demands, 200
Quiet Revolution, 75, 199

radical conservatives (or
    reactionaries), 204
radical socialists (communists),
    346
rational constitutions, 108
rational self-interest, 75, 336
rationalism, 68, 203
Rawls, John, *A Theory of Justice,* 329
Reagan presidency
  debt from military outlays, 348
reason, 68, 71, 74
  instrumental, 66
rebellions of 1837, Upper and Lower
    Canada, 75
recall, 84, 320
recession (2008–2009), 122, 350–52
recessions in 1990–1991, 350
red tories. *See* market (red) tories
redistribution, 49–50, 207, 346,
    353
  electoral districts, 220–21

referenda, 84, 127, 161, 184, 231, 236,
    254. *See also* direct democracy;
    headings for specific referenda
common uses, 318–19
on constitutional amendments,
    182
mandatory in some contexts, 318
minority rights and, 320
referendum legislation, 320
*Reflections on the Revolution in
    France* (Burke), 79
Reform Act (1832), 87–88
reform liberals, 211, 346–47
reform of market capitalism, 340–45
  business cycle and, 342–44
  creation of a consumer class,
    344–45
  political power of the working-
    class vote, 341
  rise of bureaucracy and white-
    collar jobs, 344
  social reformers and, 340
  threat of socialism, 340
  trade unions, 341
Reform Party, 320
reform ("tax and spend") liberals, 211
Reformation, 16, 22, 64, 67–68, 74,
    192
reformed liberalism, 208–10
  abandonment of laissez-faire, 209
  committed to market and private
    property, 210
  expansion of rights claims, 209
  regulation of market economy,
    209
  support for expansion of franchise,
    209

refugees, 31
regime failure, 144
regime support, 264
regimes, 14–15
regional and municipal governments,
    110
regional disparities, 172
regionalism, 194
regionalism in Canada, 198
  size of cabinet and, 139
regulations, 307
reinforcing cleavages, 197–98
religion, 28, 191–93, 210
  significance during medieval
    period, 62
  underground religious
    congregations, 26
religious beliefs, 12–13, 264
religious minorities, 56
Renaissance, 58, 64
replacing government, 22
representation, 253–80
representation by population, 88, 175,
    179, 220–21
representation of ethnic
    communities, 166, 240
representative democracy, 84–85,
    109, 190, 253
representative government, 74, 89,
    109, 189, 203
repression and violence, 24
republic, 66, 76
  head of state in, 19
The Republic (Plato), 16, 59–60
Republican Party, 148, 262
research process, 39
reservation, 166

secularism, 211
secularization of Quebec society, 199
security, 35
self-interest, 72, 93
semi-presidentialism, 141, 160–61
    in France, 155–58
    popular election of president, 158
    premier-presidential version, 155
    presidential-parliamentary
        version, 155
    strong president in addition to a
        prime-minister-led cabinet,
        153
Senate committee system, 150
Senate Judiciary Committee, 151
Seneca, 58
Senegal, 98
separated powers, 73, 106, 145, 149,
        151–52, 161, 203
    legislative process, 312
separation of church and state, 16, 22,
        26, 192
separation of executive and
        legislative powers, 144–45, 161
separation of political authority
        from religious authority. See
        separation of church and state
Serbia, 165
Service, Elman, 47
Sherk, James, 341
Sierra Club, 271
Sil, Rudgra, "Analytical Eclecticism
        in the Study of World Politics,"
        46
Silent Spring (Carson), 279
Singapore, 98
single-member districts, 88

Single Member Plurality. See SMP/
    FPP
single transferable ballot (STV) also
        known as ordinal ballot, 223
skepticism, 69
skills training, 175
slavery, 23, 56, 209
    Aristotle's understanding, 60
    in classical antiquity, 59, 61
"slippage," 294
Slovenia, 318
small government, 95–96, 205. See
        also limited state
    diminishing representation, 97
small political parties, 260
Smith, Adam, 337, 339
    The Wealth of Nations, 336
SMP/FPP campaign
    prioritization of districts to focus
        on, 265
SMP/FPP electoral system, 121, 175,
        225, 228–29
    associated with two-party systems,
        261
    brokerage party and, 260
    coalition governments in, 229
    emphasis on finishing first in as
        many districts as possible,
        265
    filtering effect, 226
    highest number of wasted ballots,
        230
    interest groups may have limited
        effect, 272
    majority with less than 40 per
        cent of the vote, 260
    minority governments in, 229

oppositional legislative politics,
        123
    stable majority government, 229
    tend to produce majority
        governments, 122
    winner take all, 229
social aspect of politics, 4
social assistance, 29, 334
social changes, 49, 56, 64, 74
social class, 64
social cleavages, 190–98, 264
    centre-periphery, 194
    class, 195–96
    ethno-linguistic, 193–94
    political parties and, 256–57
    religion, 192–93
    urban-rural, 194–95
social compact, unravelling, 352
social conservatism, 210
social contract, 73, 78
    The Social Contract (Rousseau), 78
social democracy, 346–47
    cuts across class lines, 214
    progressive tax system, 214
    regulation of capital, 214
Social Democratic Party (Germany),
        239
social inequality, 86
social justice, 94, 192
social liberty, 208
social media, 85
    inroads into election campaigns,
        267
social mobility
    lacking in feudal society, 64
social movements, 113, 277–80
social networking, 254

social norms and attitudes, 209
social processes, 41
social programs, 346
social reformers, 340
social science, 26–27
    interdisciplinary nature of, 47
    law-like generalizations, 37
social stratification, 50–51, 195. *See also* class
social unrest, 67
social welfare, 27. *See also* welfare state
social wholes, 11, 47
socialism
    belief in a strong state, 206
    on class relations, 205–7
    collective or public ownership, 207
    democratic, reformist, and peaceful, 212
    on economic growth without limits, 280
    egalitarian communalism, 205
    the ideology of 19th century, 205
    political appeal to working and lower-middle classes, 340
    redistribution on rational, egalitarian principles, 207
    reform of market capitalism and, 340
    retreat from radical positions, 214, 348
Socialist International, 214
society, 8, 10–11, 47
Society, 56
sociology, 37, 208
Socratic method, 59
soul, 60, 66

sound bite, 266
South Africa, 113
South Korea, 143, 240
Sovereign, 72–74
    Rousseau's meaning, 78
sovereignty, 164
sovereignty-association, 185–86, 199
Soviet Union (former), 24, 234, 348
    centralized state ownership, 340
    republics (absence of adequately developed institutions), 30
Spain, 185
    ethnic diversity, 193
    federalism, 175
    monarchy, 19
    motion of non-confidence, 128
    women cabinet members, 161
Sparta, 58
specialization, age of, 47
Speech from the Throne, 128
spending cuts, 211
spent ballots, 231. *See also* wasted votes
Spinoza, Benedict, 84
spoiled ballot, 222–23
stability, 59, 72, 93, 127, 225
    of coalition governments, 136–37
stakeholder groups, 269, 271–72
    access to policy-makers, 272
    feedback on proposed legislation or regulatory change, 270
    strategies, 271
stare decisis, doctrine of, 321
state, 12, 18, 47, 103–4
    ability to apply physical sanctions, 50

ability to function without a government, 137
activist (*see* activist state)
authority in, 12, 21–22, 49
bad (corrupt) states, 16–17
citizens' expectations of, 190
definitions, 20
depersonalization of authority, 49
emergence of the, 49–51
functions, 105
growth of, 24, 28
holding accountable for economic crisis (or quick response to), 333
interventions in civil society, 26–27
judicial limits on, 19
leadership in, 11–12
liberal state seen as instrument of dominant economic class, 206
limited state, 15, 19
means to coerce, 13
official abstention of the state from specific areas of social interaction, 26
protection of property, 27
reducing the size, 348
regulation of labour relations, 341
revolution in terms of social organization, 51
secular state, 193
support for laissez-faire, 337
state and civil society
    constantly shifting boundary, 26
state as educative (Aristotle's view), 61

unemployment, 343

unequal human natures, 23

unethical activity by rulers, 66

unicameral legislatures, 110

unitary state, 110, 164

United Kingdom. *See* UK

United Nations. *See* UN

United State. *See* US

United States Government Policy and
Supporting Positions, 300

units of analysis, 43

universities, 65

unregulated activity, 26

Upper Canada (Ontario), 199

upper house. *See* second chamber

urban-rural cleavage, 194–95, 264

urban transit, 174

Uruguay, 91, 151

US, 4, 18, 111

    Articles of Confederation and
        Perpetual Union, 165, 170

    bills go through both chambers
        concurrently, 316

    codification of laws, 309

    direct democracy, 318

    economic inequality, 352

    federal legislation ruled
        unconstitutional during
        Depression, 169

    federalism, 110, 166, 170, 175

    infrastructure deficit, 353

    initiatives (state), 319

    judiciary, 109

    marketable central government
        debt, 351–52

    military force in achieving
        American goals, 211

    mission to export its vision of
        liberal democracy, 211

    most bills don't become law, 317

    no equalization grants, 173

    opposition to gun control, 26

    pluralist democracy, 151

    policy-making in, 289–90

    presentation of legislation in, 315

    rust belt, 172

    second chamber (*See* US Senate)

    separation of powers, 144, 161, 170

    strong bicameralism, 179

    weak government, 148, 151

    weak parties, 148–49

    welfare state, 346, 349

US Bill of Rights (1789), 148, 150, 181

US Congress, 312, 314

US Constitution, 23, 108, 143, 151,
    203

    amending, 145, 148, 181

    checks and balances in, 148

    division of powers, 169

US Electoral College, 154

US federal election (2008), 91

US Madisonian presidentialism. *See*
    Madisonian presidentialism

US National Rifle Association, 270

US party system, 262

US presidential election (2000), 154

US Senate, 47, 109, 145

    each state has equal
        representation, 177

    effectiveness, 179

    election of senators, 176

    term of office, 176

US War of Independence, 75

utilitarianism, 68, 89

"utopian" socialists, 205

Vallière, Pierre, *White Niggers of*
    America, 199

"value-free" political science, 41

veil of ignorance, 329

Venezuela, 151

vertical fiscal imbalance, 171, 173

vertical policy-making, 297

veto, 145

    abrogative referendum, 319

    pocket veto, 293

    presidential veto, 145

    suspensive veto, 180

Vietnam, 213

virtue, 61, 66

voluntary (or adoptive)
    identifications, 191

vote "above the line," 241

vote-seeking political parties, 261

vote-splitting, 236

voter registration, 87, 246

voter turnout, 91, 246

voting rights, 80, 88–89

    full adult suffrage, 84, 88, 342

    property requirements, 87–88

    women, 87, 100

wages, 70, 342

    before and after Industrial
        Revolution, 340

    "living wage," 341

    low or diminishing wages, 343

Wall Street Journal, 337

war against the Taliban in
    Afghanistan, 211

war on Iraq, 212